**Caution**

This work is for intellectual interest of ancient Egyptian ideas. It is definitely not intended for practical use. Many spells seem to have been aimed at the alchemist who once had an assortment of curious substances in his laboratory. The hazardous nature of certain ingredients was not well understood in ancient times, and attempting to try ancient spells at home risks the possibility of dangerous and unintended consequences.

*The publisher and editor strongly urge the reader not to try any spells at home. No responsibility will be accepted for any outcomes arising from acting against this advice.*

# ANCIENT EGYPTIAN SPELLS
# not TO TRY AT HOME

INCLUDING

## Egyptian Magic

## The Demotic Magical Papyrus of London and Leiden

# ANCIENT EGYPTIAN SPELLS
# not TO TRY AT HOME

By E. A. Wallis Budge, Francis Llewellyn Griffith, and Herbert Thompson, introduction and new spell index by Aleister Blackwell (ed.)

Plus Ultra Books

A Plus Ultra Book.
http://www.plusultrabooks.com.au
Melbourne, Australia.



*Egyptian Magic* by E. A. Wallis Budge.
First published by Kegan Paul, Trench, Trübner and Co., London, 1899.
Reprinted in facsimile.

*The Demotic Magical Papyrus of London and Leiden* by F. Ll. Griffith and Herbert Thompson. First published by H. Grevel & Co., London, 1904.
Reprinted in facsimile.



This edition first published by Plus Ultra Books, Melbourne, 2015.
3 5 7 9 CS 10 8 6 4 2

**National Library of Australia Cataloguing-in-Publication entry**

**Creator:** Budge, E. A. Wallis (Ernest Alfred Wallis), Sir, 1857-1934, author.
**Title:** Ancient Egyptian spells not to try at home / E. A. Wallis Budge, Francis Llewellyn Griffith, and Herbert Thompson, introduction and new spell index by Aleister Blackwell, editor.
**ISBN:** 9780987420817 (paperback)
**Subjects:** Magic, Egyptian.
**Other Creators/Contributors:**
Griffith, F. Ll. (Francis Llewellyn), 1862-1934, author.
Thompson, Herbert, Sir, bart., 1859-1944, author.
Blackwell, Aleister, writer of introduction, editor.
**Dewey Number:** 133.440962

Typeset in Computer Modern Roman using the LaTeX typesetting system.

# General Contents

# Introduction

WALLIS BUDGE's Egyptian magic is both an excellent and an entertaining book. While reading it for the first time the thought occurred to this editor that it would make an excellent spellbook for religious persons. Neo-pagans or New Agers would find the details very interesting and not necessarily accessible elsewhere. For example, those seeking information on what the Roman Cult of Isis might have been like, as well as others, not necessarily religious, but who want an easy spell reference, might be fascinated.

I thought about how this would help people. It would bridge the gap between what we genuinely know about Egyptian magical spells from an academic perspective, and the 'New Age' neo-pagan perspective which has been emerging in Europe and elsewhere. In Budge we have something of an authoritative work, still read today. Despite improvements in archaeology and knowledge of Egypt, Budge's information comes from texts which have not altered. Only a few definitions and pronunciations have changed since he wrote his famous dictionary, and the reality seems to remain that students of Egyptology remain fans of his books to this day. The one major criticism would be that his dates for certain Egyptian kings can be ignored. They are a thousand years out of date.

Budge's *Egyptian Magic* is so packed with information that if one simply reads it, one tends to loses track of ideas before they have time to germinate in one's mind, into a myriad of possibility. The version of *Egyptian Magic* I read years ago even lacked an index! It needs a much better index to take into consideration a new audience of people who are interested in locating Ancient Egyptian magical spells.

In Budge's day people were interested in Egyptian spells for the sake of curiosity, or of dressing as ancient Egyptians for theme parties. The 1920s and 30s saw a resurgence in imperial stylings and romantic ideas in England, about Cleopatra, with new majestic paintings being produced in every year of that era. Budge's *Egyptian Magic* is now in the public domain, but simply reprinting it would not do. Others have done that. In order to improve this work, I decided to make an index, together with an introduction into Egyptian spell casting ideas which are not fully discussed in Budge's work.

There are lots of criticisms of magic. Sorcery is something which is generally a big no-no, even in so-called magick circles, with all sorts of books that believe in it, also warning strongly against it. However for intellectual reasons, people want to know, historically, how the Egyptians engaged in mysticism.

## 'Voodoo'

It is to be stressed that the Egyptians considered their magic had an unlimited over-reaching power. In the words of the legendary unknown mythogogue, Hermes Trismegistus, in writings discovered after the third century, and partly based upon earlier thinking, we are taught the concept that some great power 'transcends every substance'.

We see that what we interpret as 'voodoo' today was a significant part of Egyptian magic. This may have been introduced to Egypt, or reintroduced, through the Nubian invasions which occurred periodically throughout Egyptian history. Voodoo is a form of sympathetic magic. It follows the ancient idea that once something has touched, it has *always* touched. Therefore to change the toucher is to change the touchee, sending a ripple backward or forward through time and space. Budge himself considered that basically all African tribal magic seems to have had an Egyptian source.

If one can't possess something that a person has touched, one can at least possess his name. As budge explains on page 157, a person's name is part of his soul. This extends to the names of gods. Know the name of a god and one can command him.

Voodoo works by possessing any part of a person or an item that person has touched—'once touched... always touching'. If one does not have anything from the person, one at least has their name. Just write it down on a paper and then manipulate the paper. It might be a matter of quantum mechanics if we were to treat it scientifically rather than mystically. It is as if Ancient Egyptian people believed all things in the universe are linked by a sort of similarity of concept. All things have labels attached. By knowing what these labels are, sympathetic changes can be affected.

## The Mystical Paradigm

Egyptians did not think as we do today. Naturally we live in the backdrop of a materialist world, sculpted by the enlightenment which bathed in skepticism to wash clean the superstition of the past, starting afresh. Budge's *Ancient Egyptian Dictionary* provides us with a fascinating glimpse into another world. In Latin, a mirror is a 'miracle', or 'mirabilis'. It was technology the Romans could not comprehend. Today we have a model for it which states there is a 'sea of electrons' in a metallic surface and electrons have certain properties of conductance, transmittance, absorbance, which lend them certain properties. The Egyptians had no such ideas and no word for, or conception of what an electron might be. The Egyptian word for 'mirror' is delightful: in his *Ancient Egyptian Dictionary*, Budge translates Ankh, normally a word meaning all sorts of connotations of life in its various forms as 'mirror' where the sacred Ankh cross occurs next to a picture of a mirror. In other words the Egyptians saw in the mirror life itself. Presumably water which represented life was a mirror as well. The hieroglyphs are a language of ideas and mystical pictures and seem to have influenced Egyptian thinking. The mirror is one of the keys to Egyptian magic. 'As above... so below'. As rituals are done in this world (the 'below') they utilise concepts like words relating to the thing we are trying to change to affect that change *above.* Ideas seen in a mirror do not merely reflect life. They *are* life itself.

## Making an enchanted Amulet

These days amulets are the stuff of *The Lord of the Rings*, but for Egyptians, and among many in this present day, they were indeed the 'real deal'. There are many amateur jewel-smiths around so if someone is sufficiently skilled, she or he can make a nice amulet. Millions are on sale in Egypt and elsewhere. Whether or not he thinks it has magical powers is up to him. Budge has provided several pictures of what such amulets look like in Chapter 2: *Amulets and Stones of Power.*

Some amulet spells in the Amulets chapter seem to require physical amulets. In regards to general ideas of magic, the more one believes it, the more it works. Quantum mechanical ideas of subtlety are at work here. Therefore often the more work or trouble one has to put into a spell, the better it is supposed to work. If one believes one has followed the correct formula, or has surely done sufficient work, the increased faith of the spell-caster is supposed to assist in facilitating the spell working.

If one lacks the motivation to make an amulet but still wishes to know an appropriate spell, one can simply draw the amulet. It will be as real as any drawing on a temple was to the Egyptians. That is to say it will be fully real in the other world—the parallel afterlife. This other world could correspond, in some ideas, to the Hermetic *above* world... or what I would describe as 'coded' world, which one perhaps needs magic spells to access, which corresponds to to our *below* world, on Earth.

## Egyptians: Inventors of Black Magic?

Egyptians knew the spirits around them, the Djin, as crafty, but weak. They would hide from the light of the Sun, but were perhaps present in the lesser light of the lamp. Due to their weakness they could be bossed and bullied, as could many Egyptian deities. Perhaps relying upon proto-Hermetic ideas of omnipotence, and that humans are god-like, a sorcerer would even dare that if the god refused to accept his wishes, he would knock over the four great pillars upon which the sky was supported. This would bring down the universe. Sometimes a great threat can cause a great effect.

Budge mentions that it seems that the Egyptians came up with this idea of Gods they could command. It could be a very old idea indeed. We see the 'arrogance' of the Egyptian king in the idea that he was possibly stronger than the gods, and their leader. He was portrayed, in a statue of Khafre, as one step in front of the gods, in the arrogant time of the Old Kingdom. I learned back in archaeology class that the kings of the Old Kingdom were often presented in this arrogant way. The building of the pyramids was a colossal idea, an object of pride. After the disastrous Dark Ages which followed, which some have identified with the Biblical plagues, the Middle Kingdom was more circumspect. Humble Montohotep of the Middle kingdom is presented in statue form as in his proper place. He is shown smaller than the Gods, who now obviously with the benefit of hindsight, rule over all.

In Greek mythology we see a dichotomy which could be similar. On the one hand, some heroes are seen as the 'Son of Zeus'. In other words they are themselves heroes on earth because they are semi-God. However we also have the idea that Odysseus was only permitted to return home, after many disasters, by the favour of certain Gods, who themselves had to defy Poseidon, angry at the blinding of his son Prometheus.

The idea that Gods could be commanded seems to have been Egyptian. Perhaps it was the confidence unleashed by the fabulous structures of the Old Kingdom, or earlier times, which set the scene for such a seemingly arrogant perspective. In Budge's words: 'But whereas the magic of every other nation of the ancient East was directed entirely against the powers of darkness, and was invented in order to frustrate their fell designs by invoking a class of benevolent beings to their aid, the Egyptians aimed at being able to command their gods to work for them, and to compel them to appear at their desire.' (*EM* p. 4). Budge goes on to speculate that Moses seems to have been seen to have had such a power.

Lots of Egyptian magic is all about channelling spirits. For example, lots of spells in which one would make enquiries of spirits require that one has a vessel, like a lamp, or a boy who babbles incoherent messages from above. This is one way how, it seems, the later Egyptians listened to the Gods.

## Words of power

Budge tells us on page ten of *Egyptian Magic* that a magician uses 'words of power' or *hekau* in order to formulate a spell, for instance, to find a lost object underneath a lake. He speaks words of power which allow the lake water from one side of the lake to flop over onto the water on the other half. The object is then located. The Bible writers were obviously fascinated by such ideas and we have a similar story of Moses, written over a thousand years later. Moses of course is a name for a pharaoh of Egypt which means 'Son of God': for instance *Ra-Mose* is the son of Ra, the sun god. *Tut-mose* would be son of Thoth, the knowledge god.

As for what the words of power are, these are located on page 116 and directed at the sun god Amen.

## The vowel chants

Budge provides us with a few very fascinating pages, 177-9, on vowel chants. These are also seen on pages 57-8, regarding how to blind a thief from a distance. One can come across similar spells, in the early proto-Christian *Nag Hammadi Library.* These are a set of manuscripts uncovered in Egypt, at Nag Hammadi in 1945. These are supposed to be very early Christian ideas, infused with pre-Christian ideas, and buried near the Nile by a monastery. A certain monk did not want the old ideas destroyed, yet they were too dangerous to keep in the monastic library. Thank goodness he buried them! For we see a fascinating parallel between vowel chants in pre-Christian and Christian times.

One might hazard a speculation that the vowel chants have something to do with the 'speaking in tongues' spoken of by St Paul in the New Testament. This can never be proven. Meanwhile, across in Asia, vowel chants were used by yogis for the purpose of inducing trance. Vowel chants could be relics of deeply ancient and so far unexplained religions.

## Magical Animation or Sympathetic Magic?

We read a delightful story about a jealous man who made a wax crocodile. Every day he witnessed a man bathing, the same man who had had relations with his female friend. He ordered this wax crocodile to be thrown into the water after the man while bathing. What was then presumably supposed to happen, according to the rules of sympathy, was that one day a real crocodile would actually follow after him and eat him!

The story teller was not the magician in question and possibly lost the meaning. For he tells us that after the crocodile was thrown in, it turned into a real crocodile. This either obscures the original meaning that in future when he bathes, a sympathetic pattern will have been set up (encoding the universe) so that a real crocodile will one-day grab him when he bathes in the river. In the story however, the crocodile keeps the man under water many days. Eventually the king summons the crocodile who brings the man with him. The king then judges the case. He orders the crocodile to take what is his.

The crocodile takes the man back into the water. Justice is served. We should consider that the crocodile is also a god. Making gods in effigy was fine. For the Egyptians, the world expressed itself in many ways. The universe's crocodile energy was perhaps expressed as that animal.

## Datings

The reader should bear in mind that Budge's work is much less useful when it comes to historical dates. Whereas today we consider the first dynasty to have begun around 3100 BC, this was different in Budge's day. For him, the first dynasty began at least a thousand years earlier. Early Egyptologists knew the approximate reigns of kings, from various sources, in particular the Ptolemaic-era historian, Manetho. They stacked kings end to end, not considering the possibility of parallel rule in various parts of a fractured Egypt. They considered that Egypt had been united since the days of King Narmer, at the beginning of Egyptian history, hence there was no parallel rule. In fact many kings or monarchs may have ruled in parallel in various provinces.

Stories should be dated from the time they were written down. We need to consider that the mentioned crocodile story was written down in the *Westcar Papyrus*, in about the $18^{th}$ century BC. It claims to tell of events as far back as the third dynasty: (pp. 67-70). The scribe claims the story circulated in royal circles and was told to Khufu by Prince Khafre about a certain King Nebka of the third dynasty. Nowadays we would discount this and simply date the story to when it was written, just to be conservative: that is, about the $18^{th}$ century BC. Yet Budge took the story literally when it dated itself to '3830 BC'. (Now we date Nebka, or Djoser who may be his successor, to about 2670 BC.) Again we can ignore Budge's longer dates.

What we can infer from all this is that at around 1800 BC, and likely much earlier, we have the practice of sympathetic magic, or magical transformation in Egypt, seen as a magical reality. From our perspective the crocodile story is almost as old as the pyramids.

## Speed

Speed is good. When performing the dastardly deed of invoking, it seems to be a phenomenon that the longer it goes, the more adverse and strange results occur. This is also a phenomenon which seems to occur to those reading tarot cards. It occurs especially in Ouija board sessions. The fastest results are the most 'truthful'. On pages 35-7 of the *Magical Papyrus*, we read: '[enchant] the vessel quickly so that the gods enter and tell you [the] answer truthfully'. It is a way of the Egyptians catching their gods off guard, to hear their true thoughts and relations, before they have time to formulate tricky schemes.

## Philosophers' Stone

We know that alchemy comes from Egypt. It seems to mean 'The Egyptian [practice]'. We might then wonder at the definition of 'philosophers' stone'. In his enigmatic book: *The Pyramids, An Enigma Solved*, 1988, Joseph Davidovits and Margie Morris considered that Egyptians cast superior forms of cement which today resemble stones which they refer to as geopolymers. Wise men (philosophers) were required to formulate the mix, hence the name philosophers' stone!

There is an alternative to this particular Philosophers' Stone definition. Philosophers were not simply men of science, but mystics. Without wishing to generalise too much, in ancient times science and mysticism do not seem to have been as separated as they are today. The Biblical Three Wise Men, for instance, were likely men of astrology, which may have encompassed horoscope casting, just as it may have encompassed various mathematical cycles. Everything back then was simply 'wisdom'.

This brings us to the possible substance of the stone. For we come to the subject of precious stones in amulets. The accoutrements of the magician, as elucidated by Budge, were: 'magical stones or amulets, magical figures, magical pictures and formulæ, magical names, magical ceremonies, etc., and such portions of the Book of the Dead as bear upon these subjects generally' (*EM* p. 24). One would suppose that anybody wanting to emulate the Egyptians would therefore possess such items.

## The Wand

A key aspect of the Egyptian magical practice, ceremony and religion was the wand. Manetho, the Ptolemaic historian, claimed Moses was a priest of Heliopolis ('Sun City'). It might then be speculated that his monotheism was sun-based. Manetho claimed he stirred sedition among the diseased and they marched out of Egypt taking various valuables. To solve the paradox of physically ill people dictating terms to pharaoh, one can speculate that Manetho may have been misinterpreting old Hieroglyphic writings. For instance, wouldn't something like 'cursed ones' also mean 'diseased ones'? To the Egyptians the invaders were Hyksos (shepherds), or plain 'Asiatics'. Alternately, this unknown hieroglyphic expression was to the effect of calling the Hyksos (Asiatic) enemy diseased, perhaps a way of transforming fate for them via propaganda. What is written, to the Egyptian, is truth in the universe: 'As above so below'. I don't think we will ever have the definitive answer regarding the diseased nature of the Israelites. Speculating, within reasonable limits, is really all we can do, from a historical perspective, if we wish to begin to have a clue about some rather enduring historical mysteries.

Manetho tells us many things about Moses one will not read in the Bible. He claims Moses led men to a place in the sea where he knew the tide change would have a dramatic effect, hence the parting of the sea. In the Bible, he had a stick or staff which he used to help him perform magic. For example, we read that he turned it into a snake, and then back into a staff. His snake did battle with other staff snakes. It occurs to me that a snake makes patterns upon the ground. I was intrigued to read a report from the early $20^{th}$ century regarding Egypt. It was in the biography of Beryl Markham (1902-86). She was a remarkable woman who did a lot of things that back in her day women generally didn't do. She trained racehorses, and as a pilot made a living assisting with hunting expeditions in very remote areas where one cannot land a plane. She was sponsored to make the attempt of an Atlantic crossing to New York. Almost at her target, she ran out of fuel and had to ditch the plane, but survived. I noticed a passage regarding her Egyptian sojourn: an Egyptian wise man told her fortune by scratching lines in the dirt with a stick, and then getting imagery through them. Apparently the fortune was accurate. Since not many people are aware of this method, appearing to perhaps be a relic of older time, I thought I would add it to this introduction. Could the Bible myths not relate to Moses scratching out the designs of the other priests?

## The Keys of Solomon

There are several books with titles containing the words 'Keys of Solomon'. These purport to be ancient but are medieval at best. However, they seem to be at least inspired by an ever-ancient tradition of spell-casting which is in line with much older Egyptian ideas. Considering the Jews came out of Egypt it makes sense that both cultures should share, for historical reasons, some common magical traditions. The Keys-of-Solomon books share similar ideas to those found in Egyptian spells... including bossing gods around. Their authors, however, are infinitely more vindictive.

## Please Enjoy this book

Budge seems to have intended an enjoyable book for the reader with which one can really get into the mind of the old Egyptians. In the second book that has been included, the *Magical Papyrus*, we see magic combined with medicine. Ailments, as well as pure spells are listed. The idea is that the introduction provided by Budge will help the person understand how to perform the spells listed in the *Magical Papyrus*. There are no fixed rules. Different magicians performed rituals differently. Some require ingredients. Other spells only require words. To the reader, all the best of reading enjoyment!

— Aleister Blackwell, Editor.

# Spell Index

The original *Egyptian Magic* is lacking in any index, so I have attempted to provide one. The index also covers the *The Demotic Magical Papyrus of London and Leiden*, which contains the bulk of the spells. This is a spell index for any topic which might take the reader's interest. The reader can use this index to quickly look up a particular topic.

It is recommended but not required that the reader first read *Egyptian Magic* to get a feel for how Egyptian spells were performed, and in what circumstances. Then he can move onto the content of the spells themselves, found in the *Magical Papyrus*. Whilst the *Magical Papyrus* does come with a scholarly index of sorts, within the contents, the spells are not in alphabetical order of type. Rather it is composed for a non-general reader. That other index is on pages 14-8 of the *Magical Papyrus*. Here is a contents formulated more for accessibility by the general reader, by page number.

Lots of spells are not written like modern recipes. They tell you what is required as you go through them. Assuming the ancient practitioner would already have a ready stock, for instance, of a brazier, a crocodile egg, an ass's dung, the heart of a hyena and a certain stone, a spell lurches into what you must do with them, as on page 37 of *Magical Papyrus*. It appears spells needed to be read in advance and preparations of all ingredients made. Some love spells cannot be taken literally. Spells involving anointing one's phallus with an ointment made from dung should not really be done. Other love spells seem to be more Hermetic! One is supposed to write words or recite them and that's all there is to it. No complicated ingredients required! This is entirely another side to Egyptian lore which has more to do with what is in modern times called 'white magic'.

**NB:** For some of these spells, a reading of the complete passage is required which may be around ten or more pages. Spells here, for instance bringing in the spirit of a living man, on page 37, require a small variation in the ingredients in the spell. The index of course will usually refer to the specific page in which the variation in the spell is contained, but also at times to the complete spell. Sometimes you need a certain stone to accomplish a ritual. Again on page 37 of *Magical Papyrus* we have reference to a *Karab* stone. It is recommended the reader check with an Egyptian dictionary secondly, but firstly with Budge's *Egyptian Magic*, printed here, to see which stone corresponds with which type of magic.

I have taken the liberty of listing spells involving god and a lamp under GENIE. However sometimes the general phrase 'from a vessel' is used so the user may also search under INVOCATION for similar spells.

**NBB:** It appears that the original editors of the *Magical Papyrus* did not actually know what was going on in various spells, or were too academically cautious. The Contents pages they provide simply groups spells by general method, or concept, rather than type, as here, and is not really useful to the non-academic reader. It must be said that in the Spell Index provided in this work for the first time, some guesses have been made regarding what the spell is actually for. It is up to the reader to read the original, which is provided and decide for himself.

## Key

*EM*— page numbers found in *Egyptian Magic*

*MP*— page numbers found in the *Magical Papyrus.*

## Index

AMULETS
— Lapis Lazuli, beneficial as amulet, *EM*, p. 61.
ASK A GOD A QUESTION, see INVOCATION.
BLACK MAGIC, See DEMON POSSESSION, INVOCATION, LAMP, GENIE, etc.
— repel an approaching enemy army in the desert, *EM*, p. 92.
CHANNELING
— gods, *MP*, pp. 35-7.
— sun, *MP*, pp. 167-9.
CRIMINAL, find him, *MP*, p. 189.
DEMON POSSESSION, *EM*, p. 213.
DESTINY *EM* p. 222.
DESTRUCTION, *MP*, pp. 145-7, 149-53.
DREAMS *EM* pp. 213-8.
— dreams, vision, to procure from God Bes, *EM*, pp. 216-7.
— flying bird, *EM*, p. 213.
DROWNING
— to bring in the spirit of a drowned man, p. 37.
GENIE
— backup formulas in case it doesn't work the first time, a more commanding approach *MP*, pp. 63-5
— direct approach *MP*, pp. 65-7, easy spell, p. 203.
— from a lamp, lamp divination for knowledge of the truth. *MP*, pp. 45-51, 51-63, 163-5.
— invoke souls from a vessel, *MP*, pp. 67-75, 99-105.
EYE OF HORUS, *EM*, p. 120.
GOOD and EVIL
— to test if someone is good or bad, *MP*, p. 35.

HEALING
— anti-venom spell, extract poison from heart, (metaphorical?), *MP*, p. 125.
— bite, dog *MP*, pp. 123-5, 127-9.
— catalepsy, *MP*, p. 151, 173.
— ear, watery, MP, p. 175
— eye, ointment, *MP*, p 49.
— fertility test, in a woman, *MP*, p. 177.
— fever, *MP*, pp. 203-5.
— foot, sprains, *MP*, p. 183.
— gout, *MP*, pp. 181-3.
— menstruation?, pp. 177, 201.
— opthalmia, heal, *MP*, p. 193,
— paralysed limb?, *MP*, pp. 132-3.
— poison, *MP*, 125.
— throat, choking?, *MP*, sore? a bone in throat, p. 133.
— salve, spell to accompany, *MP*, p. 131.
— sleeping potion, *MP*, p. 151.
— sting, *MP*, pp. 129-33.
— water in a woman, (dropsy?), MP, pp. 179-81.
— wound, any, *MP*, p. 177.
HOROSCOPE, assistance on how to make, *EM*, pp. 228-30.
INVOCATION, (usually for asking questions)
— cancel invocation, *MP*, p. 37.
— the dead, and according to a certain phase of the moon, *MP*, pp. 75-9.
— general invocations, p. 197, spirit of a living man, *MP*, pp. 37, 39-43.
— gods of the city, *MP*, pp. 119-23.
— gods, *MP*, p. 191, invocation by force, bringing them back quickly again, *MP*, p. 37.
— gods of the vessel, *MP*, p. 199.
— Osiris, *MP*, p. 135.
— rapid invocation for truthfulness, *MP*, pp. 35-7.
— speak, make the spirits, *MP*, p. 37, 43.

— shadow, invoke the, *MP*, pp. 43-5.
— shadow, to see of every god and goddess, and also to inquire of gods with a vessel, *MP*, pp. 195-7.
— Thoth, *MP*, pp. 25-33.
— wine, *MP*, p. 157.
JESUS, (similar ideas), *EM*, p. xiii.
LAMP, *MP*, pp. 51-7. See also GENIE for divination from a lamp.
— channelling lamp spirits? *MP*, pp. 155-7, 109-13, 113-9, 157-63.
— Moon, *MP*, pp. 147-9.
LOVE
— dreams, create and send to a lover and bring a woman to a man's house, *MP*, p. 191.
— love fury, *MP*, p. 185.
— make a woman love a man, *MP*, p. 137, 175, 203, follow him around, pp. 87-93, 139-41, 155-7.
— separate a couple, *MP*, pp. 93-5.
— to inflame a woman with passion, *MP*, pp. 185-7, 95-9, 105-9, 143-4.
— to make a woman fall in love during sex, *MP*, p. 187, 201.
— to make a woman love sex, *MP*, p. 187.
— to summon a woman from a house and make her love a man, *MP*, p. 189.
— to summon a woman from her house and bring her to a man at any time, *MP*, p. 193.
MUMMY, origin of myth, *EM*, pp. 217-18.
MURDER, to bring in a spirit of a murdered man, *MP*, p. 37.
NUMEROLOGY, horoscope, *EM*, p. 230.
PRAISE
— spell to be praised wherever you go, pp. 81-7.
REVENGE, see also THIEF
— love revenge?, *MP*, p. 139.
— to make someone mad, *MP*, p. 201.
SEDUCTION, see LOVE.
SHIPWRECK, prevent, *MP*, p. 189.
SOUL, parts of, *EM*, p. 217.

SPEED
— make a spell faster, *MP*, p. 39, vessel channelling, p. 39.
SPELL, the name of a spell called Great of Five, *MP*, pp. 143-5.
SPIRIT, bring in a spirit (of one's choosing?), *MP*, p. 37.
STONE, precious, amulet.
— Carnelian, *EM*, p. 32.
— Turquoise, (for protection) *EM*, p.189.
STUDY OF MAGICAL BOOKS, *EM*, p. 144.
TALISMAN
— a lucky sign, *EM*, p. 226.
— an unlucky symbol, *EM*, p. 226.
— prism, *EM*, p. 220.
— to guard a city being built, used by Alexander, *EM*, p. 152.
THIEF
— blind a thief, *EM*, p. 58.
— invoke soul of thief, *MP*, p. 39.
VISION, how to obtain a vision/message from any god, *EM*, p. 216.
WORDS OF POWER, (similar to Lords Prayer), *EM*, p. 116.

# Egyptian Magic

# Biographical Note

Ranking among the most famous of Egyptologists, E. A. Wallis Budge, 1857-1934, was quite a remarkable man.

Although Budge's works are rightfully considered 'obsolete', they continue to fill a niche unfilled in the present day. His works possessed a spirit of free expression which perhaps encapsulated something of the old spirit of the Egyptians. His works were accessible to the general reader and continue to be. *Egyptian Magic* is a great work, free of technical language and excessively dry detail. Budge tried to explain the magical paradigms of the Egyptians to the modern reader.

Being noticed for his linguistic talents whilst studying in the glorious confines of St Paul's Cathedral, London, it was an organist, John Stainer, who very kindly arranged the sponsorship of a place for him at Cambridge. It was here he began his study of Semitic languages. In his life, he worked at the British Museum from 1883 onwards, going on to write a multitude of books on the Egyptians.

As a highly educated man, he perhaps had a considerable influence upon popular culture among his contemporaries. For instance, the Rider Haggard novel *Morning Star*, 1910, is dedicated to him. It is known that Budge would travel to the Middle East as an agent for the Museum, trying to save plundered antiquities. There is a character in a brilliant but lesser-known novel by Bram Stoker called *The Jewel of Seven Stars*, 1903. In it a scholar introduces himself as a famous archaeologist, exceptionally qualified and with a multitude of degrees, who has spent his life tracking down particular odd antiquities for his boss' bizarre resurrection rituals.

It was certainly the work of an early Egyptologist to spend his time hunting for antiquities to piece together the puzzle... to assemble an image of what was Ancient Egypt.

# Egyptian Magic

E. A. WALLIS BUDGE

**To**

SIR J. NORMAN LOCKYER, K.C.B., F.R.S.,

ETC., ETC., ETC.,

A TOKEN OF ESTEEM FOR A GREAT ASTRONOMER,

AND

A MARK OF TRUE REGARD FOR

A FRIEND.

# PREFACE.

A STUDY of the remains of the native religious literature of ancient Egypt which have come down to us has revealed the fact that the belief in magic, that is to say, in the power of magical names, and spells, and enchantments, and formulæ, and pictures, and figures, and amulets, and in the performance of ceremonies accompanied by the utterance of words of power, to produce supernatural results, formed a large and important part of the Egyptian religion. And it is certain that, notwithstanding the continuous progress which the Egyptians made in civilization, and the high intellectual development to which they eventually attained, this belief influenced their minds and, from the earliest to the latest period of their history, shaped their views concerning things temporal as well as spiritual in a manner which, at this stage in the history of the world, is very difficult to understand. The scrupulous care with which they performed their innumerable religious ceremonies, and carried out the rules which they had formulated concerning the worship of the divine Power or powers, and their devotion to religious magic, gained for them among the nations with whom they came in contact the reputation of being at once the most religious and the most superstitious of men. That this reputation was, on the whole, well deserved, is the object of this little book to shew.

Egyptian magic dates from the time when the predynastic and prehistoric dwellers in Egypt believed that the earth, and the underworld, and the air, and the sky were peopled with countless beings, visible and invisible, which were held to be friendly or unfriendly to man according as the operations of nature, which they were supposed to direct, were favourable or unfavourable to him. In nature and attributes these beings were thought by primitive man to closely resemble himself and to possess all human passions, and emotions, and weaknesses, and defects; and the chief object of magic was to give man the pre-eminence over such beings. The favour of the beings who were placable and friendly to man might be obtained by means of gifts and offerings, but the cessation of hostilities on the part of those that were implacable and unfriendly could only be obtained by wheedling, and cajolery, and flattery, or by making use of an amulet, or secret name, or magical formula, or figure, or picture which had the effect of bringing to the aid of the mortal who possessed it the power of a being that was mightier than the foe who threatened to do evil to him. The magic of most early nations aimed at causing the transference of power from a supernatural being to man, whereby he was to be enabled to obtain superhuman results and to become for a time as mighty as the original possessor of the power; but the object of Egyptian magic was to endow man with the means of compelling both friendly and hostile powers, nay, at a later time, even God Himself, to do what he wished, whether they were willing or not. The belief in magic, the word being used in its best sense, is older in Egypt than the belief in God, and it is certain that a very large number of the Egyptian religious ceremonies, which were performed in later times as an integral part of a highly spiritual worship, had their origin in superstitious customs which date from a period when God, under any name or in any form, was unconceived in the minds of the Egyptians. Indeed it is probable that even the use of the sign which represents an axe, and which stands as the hieroglyphic character both for God and "god," indicates that this weapon and tool was employed in the performance of some ceremony connected with religious magic in prehistoric, or at any rate in predynastic times, when it in some mysterious way symbolized the presence of a supreme Power. But be this as it may, it is quite certain that magic and religion developed and flourished side by side in Egypt throughout all periods of her history, and that any investigation which we may make of the one necessarily includes an examination of the other.

From the religious books of ancient Egypt we learn that the power possessed by a priest or man who was skilled in the knowledge and working of magic was believed to be almost boundless. By pronouncing certain words or names of power in the proper manner and in the proper tone of voice he could heal the sick, and cast out the evil spirits which caused pain and suffering in those who were diseased, and restore the dead to life, and bestow upon the dead man the power to transform the corruptible into an incorruptible body, wherein the soul might live to all eternity. His words enabled human beings to assume divers forms at will, and to project their souls into animals and other creatures; and in obedience to his commands, inanimate figures and pictures became living beings and things which hastened to perform his behests. The powers of nature acknowledged his might, and wind and rain, storm and tempest, river and sea, and disease and death worked evil and ruin upon his foes, and upon the enemies of those who were provided with the knowledge of the words which he had wrested from the gods of heaven, and earth, and the underworld. Inanimate nature likewise obeyed such words of power, and even the world itself came into existence through the utterance of a word by Thoth; by their means the earth could be rent asunder, and the waters forsaking their nature could be piled up in a heap, and even the sun's course in the heavens could be stayed by a word. No god, or spirit, or devil, or fiend, could resist words of power, and the Egyptians invoked their aid in the smallest as well as in the greatest events of their lives. To him that was versed in the lore contained in the books of the "double house of life" the future was as well known as the past, and neither time nor distance could limit the operations of his power; the mysteries of life and death were laid bare before him, and he could draw aside the veil which hid the secrets of fate and destiny from the knowledge of ordinary mortals.

Now if views such as these concerning the magician's power were held by the educated folk of ancient Egypt there is little to wonder at when we find that beliefs and superstitions of the most degraded character flourished with rank luxuriance among the peasants and working classes of that country, who failed to understand the symbolism of the elaborate ceremonies which were performed in the temples, and who were too ignorant to distinguish the spiritual conceptions which lay at their root. To meet the religious needs of such people the magician, and in later times the priest, found it necessary to provide pageants and ceremonies which appealed chiefly to the senses, and following their example, unscrupulous but clever men took advantage of the ignorance of the general public and pretended to knowledge of the supernatural, and laid claim to the possession of power over gods, and spirits, and demons. Such false knowledge and power they sold for money, and for purposes of gain the so-called magician was ready to further any sordid transaction or wicked scheme which his dupe wished to carry out. This magic degenerated into sorcery, and demonology, and witchcraft, and those who dealt in it were regarded as associates of the Devil, and servants of the powers of darkness, and workers of the "black art." In the "white" and "black" magic of the Egyptians most of the magic known in the other countries of the world may be found; it is impossible yet to say exactly how much the beliefs and religious systems of other nations were influenced by them, but there is no doubt that certain views and religious ideas of many heathen and

Christian sects may be traced directly to them. Many interesting proofs might be adduced in support of this statement, but the limits of this book will not admit of their being given here.

When we consider the lofty spiritual character of the greater part of the Egyptian religion, and remember its great antiquity, it is hard to understand why the Egyptians carefully preserved in their writings and ceremonies so much which savoured of gross and childish superstition, and which must have been the product of their predynastic or prehistoric ancestors, even during the period of their greatest intellectual enlightenment. But the fact remains that they did believe in One God Who was almighty, and eternal, and invisible, Who created the heavens, and the earth, and all beings and things therein; and in the resurrection of the body in a changed and glorified form, which would live to all eternity in the company of the spirits and souls of the righteous in a kingdom ruled by a being who was of divine origin, but who had lived upon the earth, and had suffered a cruel death at the hands of his enemies, and had risen from the dead, and had become the God and king of the world which is beyond the grave; and that, although they believed all these things and proclaimed their belief with almost passionate earnestness, they seem never to have freed themselves from a hankering after amulets and talismans, and magical names, and words of power, and seem to have trusted in these to save their souls and bodies, both living and dead, with something of the same confidence which they placed in the death and resurrection of Osiris. A matter for surprise is that they seem to see nothing incongruous in such a mixture of magic and religion, and the general attitude of the mind of the Egyptian on the point is well illustrated by the following facts. Attached to the service of Rā, the Sun-god, at Thebes were numerous companies of priests whose duties consisted as much in making copies of religious books and in keeping alive the "divine traditions," as in ministering to the god in their appointed seasons. The members of these companies who wrote the copies of the Book of the Dead which were buried with kings and queens and personages of royal or exalted rank declared the power and omnipotence of Almighty God, Whose visible emblem to mankind was the Sun, and His sovereignty over things celestial and things terrestrial with no uncertain voice, and we should expect them to believe what they proclaimed, *i.e.*, that God was sufficiently powerful to protect His emblem in the sky. Yet the priests of Thebes made copies of works which contained texts to be recited at specified hours of the day and night, and gave directions for the performance of magical ceremonies, the avowed object of such being to prevent the mythical monster Āpep from vanquishing the Sun-god. And it is stated in all seriousness that if a piece of papyrus upon which a figure of the monster has been drawn, and a wax figure of him be burnt in a fire made of a certain kind of grass, and the prescribed words be recited over them as they burn, the Sun-god will be delivered from Āpep, and that neither rain, nor cloud, nor mist shall be able to prevent his light from falling upon the earth. Moreover, the rubric describes the performance of the ceremony as a meritorious act!

E. A. WALLIS BUDGE.

LONDON,
*August 28th*, 1899

# CONTENTS.


| CHAPTER | | PAGE |
|---|---|---|
| I. | Antiquity of Magical Practices in Egypt ... | 1 |
| II. | Magical Stones or Amulets ... | 25 |
| III. | Magical Figures ... ... ... ... | 65 |
| IV. | Magical Pictures and Formulæ, Spells, etc. | 104 |
| V. | Magical Names ... ... ... | 157 |
| VI. | Magical Ceremonies ... ... ... | 182 |
| VII. | Demoniacal Possession, Dreams, Ghosts, Lucky and Unlucky Days, Horoscopes, Prognostications, Transformations, and the Worship of Animals ... ... ... | 206 |

# LIST OF ILLUSTRATIONS.


| CHAPTER | | PAGE |
|---|---|---|
| II. | The Destroyer of Hearts ... ... ... | 31 |
| | The Deceased being weighed against his Heart | 35 |
| | The Deceased holding a Necklace with Pectoral | 40 |
| | The Mummy lying in the Funeral Chamber ... | 45 |
| | The Priest with the "ur hekau" Instrument | 60 |
| III. | Ptah-Seker-Ausar Figure ... ... ... | 87 |
| | The Four Children of Horus | 90 |
| IV. | Hathor in the Sycamore Tree ... ... | 105 |
| | The Deceased drinking Water from a Stream | 106 |
| | The Soul visiting the Mummied Body ... | 113 |
| | The Soul and Spirit outside the Tomb ... | 114 |
| | The Shadow and Soul outside the Tomb ... | 115 |
| | Hypocephalus of Shai-enen ... ... ... | 117 |
| | Cippus of Horus ("Metternichstele I.") ... | 149 |
| | Cippus of Horus ("Metternichstele II.") ... | 153 |
| V. | Greek Amulets ... ... ... ... | 178, 179 |
| VI. | The Ceremony of opening the Mouth ... | 199 |
| VII. | The Stele with the Story of the Princess of Bekhten ... ... ... ... ... | 209 |

# EGYPTIAN MAGIC.

## CHAPTER I.

### ANTIQUITY OF MAGICAL PRACTICES IN EGYPT.

In the first volume of this series an attempt was made to set before the reader a statement of the ideas and beliefs which the ancient Egyptians held in respect of God, the "gods," the Judgment, the Resurrection, and Immortality; in short, to sketch in brief outline much of what was beautiful, and noble, and sublime in their religion. The facts of this statement were derived wholly from native religious works, the latest of which is some thousands of years old, and the earliest of which may be said to possess an antiquity of between six and seven thousand years; the extracts quoted in support of the deductions set forth in it were intended to enable the reader to judge for himself as to the general accuracy of the conclusions there given. Many writers on the Egyptian religion have somewhat blinked the fact that it had two sides; on the one it closely resembles in many respects the Christian religion of to-day, and on the other the religion of many of the sects which flourished in the first three or four centuries of our era, and which may be said to have held beliefs which were part Christian and part non-Christian. In its non-Christian aspect it represents a collection of ideas and superstitions which belong to a savage or semi-savage state of existence, and which maintained their hold in a degree upon the minds of the Egyptians long after they had advanced to a high state of civilization. We may think that such ideas and beliefs are both childish and foolish, but there is no possible reason for doubting that they were very real things to those who held them, and whether they are childish or foolish or both they certainly passed into the religion of the people of Egypt, wherein they grew and flourished, and were, at least many of them, adopted by the Egyptian converts to Christianity, or Copts. Reference is made to them in the best classical works of the ancient Egyptians, and it is more than probable that from them they found their way into the literatures of the other great nations of antiquity, and through the Greeks, Romans, Arabs, and others into the countries of Europe. In the following pages an attempt will be made to place in the reader's hands the evidence as to the magical side of the Egyptian religion, which would have been out of place in the former work, the object of which was to describe beliefs of a more spiritual nature. But, as in the book on the Egyptian Ideas of the Future Life, the facts here given are drawn from papyri and other native documents, and the extracts are quoted from compositions which were actually employed by the Egyptians to produce magical effects.

The "magic" of the Egyptians was of two kinds: (1) that which was employed for legitimate purposes and with the idea of benefiting either the living or the dead, and (2) that which was made use of in the furtherance of nefarious plots and schemes and was intended to bring calamities upon those against whom it was directed. In the religious texts and works we see how magic is made to be the handmaiden of religion, and how it appears in certain passages side by side with the most exalted spiritual conceptions; and there can be no doubt that the chief object of magical books and ceremonies was to benefit those who had by some means obtained sufficient knowledge to make use of them. But the Egyptians were unfortunate enough not to be understood by many of the strangers who found their way into their country, and as a result wrong and exaggerated ideas of their religion were circulated among the surrounding nations, and the magical ceremonies which were performed at their funerals were represented by the ignorant either as silly acts of superstition or as tricks of the "black" art. But whereas the magic of every other nation of the ancient East was directed entirely against the powers of darkness, and was invented in order to frustrate their fell designs by invoking a class of benevolent beings to their aid, the Egyptians aimed at being able to command their gods to work for them, and to compel them to appear at their desire. These great results were to be obtained by the use of certain words which, to be efficacious, must be uttered in a proper tone of voice by a duly qualified man; such words might be written upon some substance, papyrus, precious stones, and the like, and worn on the person, when their effect could be transmitted to any distance. As almost every man, woman, and child in Egypt who could afford it wore some such charm or talisman, it is not to be wondered at that the Egyptians were at a very early period regarded as a nation of magicians and sorcerers. Hebrew, and Greek, and Roman writers referred to them as experts in the occult sciences, and as the possessors of powers which could, according to circumstances, be employed to do either good or harm to man.

From the Hebrews we receive, incidentally, it is true, considerable information about the powers of the Egyptian magician. Saint Stephen boasts that the great legislator Moses "was learned in all the wisdom "of the Egyptians," and declares that he "was mighty "in words and in deeds,"[1] and there are numerous features in the life of this remarkable man which shew that he was acquainted with many of the practices of

[1] Acts vii. 22.

Egyptian magic. The phrase "mighty in words" probably means that, like the goddess Isis, he was "strong of tongue" and uttered the words of power which he knew with correct pronunciation, and halted not in his speech, and was perfect both in giving the command and in saying the word. The turning of a serpent into what is apparently an inanimate, wooden stick,[1] and the turning of the stick back into a writhing snake,[2] are feats which have been performed in the East from the most ancient period; and the power to control and direct the movements of such venomous reptiles was one of the things of which the Egyptian was most proud, and in which he was most skilful, already in the time when the pyramids were being built. But this was by no means the only proof which Moses gives that he was versed in the magic of the Egyptians, for, like the sage Āba-aner and king Nectanebus, and all the other magicians of Egypt from time immemorial, he and Aaron possessed a wonderful rod[3] by means of which they worked their wonders. At the word of Moses Aaron lifted up his rod and smote the waters and they became blood; he stretched it out

[1] Exodus vii. 10 ff. Two of Moses' opponents were called "Jannes" and "Jambres" (See 2 Timothy iii. 8).

[2] That Moses' rod or serpent should swallow up the rods or serpents of the Egyptians is, of course, to be expected, just as his magical powers are declared to be superior to those of the Egyptians.

[3] An interesting paper on the use of the rod by the Egyptians and Hebrews was published by Chabas in *Annales du Musée Guimet*, tom. i. pp. 35–48, Paris, 1880.

over the waters, and frogs innumerable appeared; when the dust was smitten by the rod it became lice; and so on. Moses sprinkled ashes "toward heaven," and it became boils and blains upon man and beast; he stretched out his rod, and there was "hail, and fire "mingled with the hail, very grievous," and the "flax "and the barley was smitten;" he stretched out his rod and the locusts came, and after them the darkness. Now Moses did all these things, and brought about the death of the firstborn among the Egyptians by the command of his God, and by means of the words which He told him to speak. But although we are told by the Hebrew writer that the Egyptian magicians could not imitate all the miracles of Moses, it is quite certain that every Egyptian magician believed that he could perform things equally marvellous by merely uttering the name of one of his gods, or through the words of power which he had learned to recite; and there are many instances on record of Egyptian magicians utterly destroying their enemies by the recital of a few words possessed of magical power, and by the performance of some, apparently, simple ceremony.[1] But one great distinction must be made between the magic of Moses and that of the Egyptians among whom he lived; the former was wrought by the command of the God of the Hebrews, but the latter by the gods of Egypt at the command of man.

[1] For details, see Chapter III. (Magical Figures).

Later on in the history of Moses' dealings with the Egyptians we find the account of how "he stretched "out his hand over the sea, and the Lord caused the sea "to go *back* by a strong east wind all that night, and "made the sea dry *land*, and the waters were divided. "And the children of Israel went into the midst of the "sea upon the dry *ground;* and the waters *were* a wall "unto them on their right hand, and on their left." When the Egyptians had come between the two walls of water, by God's command Moses stretched forth his hand over the sea, "and the sea returned to his strength," and the "waters returned, and covered the chariots, "and the horsemen, *and* all the host of Pharaoh that "came into the sea after them." [1] But the command of the waters of the sea or river was claimed by the Egyptian magician long before the time of Moses, as we may see from an interesting story preserved in the Westcar Papyrus.[2] This document was written in the early part of the XVIIIth dynasty, about B.C. 1550, but it is clear that the stories in it date from the Early Empire, and are in fact as old as the Great Pyramid. The story is related to king Khufu (Cheops) by Baiu-f-Rā as an event which happened in the time of the king's father, and as a proof of the wonderful powers of magic which were possessed by the priest[3] called

[1] Exodus xiv. 21–28.

[2] See Erman, *Die Märchen des Papyrus Westcar*, Berlin, 1890.

[3] He was the chief *kher ḥeb*, *i.e.*, the head of the priests who officiated in funeral ceremonies, and read the service from a book.

Tchatcha-em-ānkh. It seems that on a certain day king Seneferu was in low spirits, and he applied to the nobles of his royal household expecting that they would find some means whereby his heart might be made glad; but as they could do nothing to cheer up the king, he gave orders that the priest and writer of books, Tchatcha-em-ānkh, should be brought into his presence immediately, and in accordance with the royal command he was at once brought. When he had arrived, Seneferu said to him, "My brother, I turned "to the nobles of my royal household seeking for some "means whereby I might cheer my heart, but they have "found nothing for me." Then the priest made answer and advised the king to betake himself to the lake near the palace, and to go for a sail on it in a boat which had been comfortably furnished with things from the royal house. "For," said he, "the heart of thy Majesty "will rejoice and be glad when thou sailest about hither "and thither, and dost see the beautiful thickets which "are on the lake, and when thou seest the pretty banks "thereof and the beautiful fields then shall thy heart "feel happiness." He next begged that the king would allow him to organize the journey, and asked his permission to let him bring twenty ebony paddles inlaid with gold, and also twenty young virgins having beautiful heads of hair and lovely forms and shapely limbs, and twenty nets wherein these virgins may array themselves instead of in their own ordinary garments. The virgins were to row and sing to his Majesty. To these proposals the king assented, and when all was ready he took his place in the boat; while the young women were rowing him about hither and thither the king watched them, and his heart became released from care. Now as one of the young women was rowing, she entangled herself in some way in her hair, and one of her ornaments which was made of "new turquoise" fell into the water and sank; she ceased to row, and not herself only, but all the other maidens ceased to row also. When the king saw that the maidens had ceased from their work, he said to them, "Will ye not row?" and they replied, "Our "leader has ceased to row." Then turning to the maiden who had dropped her ornament overboard, he asked her why she was not rowing, whereupon she told him what had happened. On this the king promised that he would get back the ornament for her.

Then the king commanded that Tchatcha-em-ānkh should appear before him at once, and as soon as the sage had been brought into his presence he said to him, "O Tchatcha-em-ānkh, my brother, I have done "according to thy words, and the heart of my Majesty "became glad when I saw how the maidens rowed. But "now, an ornament which is made of new turquoise and "belongeth to one of the maidens who row hath fallen "into the water, and she hath in consequence become "silent, and hath ceased to row, and hath disturbed the "rowing of those in her company. I said to her, 'Why "dost thou not row?' and she replied, 'An ornament "[of mine] made of new turquoise hath fallen into the "water.' Then I said to her, 'I will get it back for "thee.'" Thereupon the priest and writer of books Tchatcha-em-ānkh spake certain words of power (*hekau*), and having thus caused one section of the water of the lake to go up upon the other, he found the ornament lying upon a pot-sherd, and he took it and gave it to the maiden. Now the water was twelve cubits deep, but when Tchatcha-em-ānkh had lifted up one section of the water on to the other, that portion became four and twenty cubits deep. The magician again uttered certain words of power, and the water of the lake became as it had been before he had caused one portion of it to go up on to the other; and the king prepared a feast for all his royal household, and rewarded Tchatcha-em-ānkh with gifts of every kind. Such is a story of the power possessed by a magician in the time of king Khufu (Cheops), who reigned at the beginning of the IVth dynasty, about B.C. 3800. The copy of the story which we possess is older than the period when Moses lived, and thus there can be no possibility of our seeing in it a distorted version of the miracle of the waters of the sea standing like walls, one on the right hand and one on the left; on the other hand Moses' miracle may well have some connexion with that of Tchatcha-em-ānkh.

Among the Greeks and Romans considerable respect was entertained, not only for the "wisdom" of the Egyptians, but also for the powers of working magic which they were supposed to possess. The Greek travellers who visited Egypt brought back to their own country much information concerning its religion and civilization, and, though they misunderstood many things which they saw and heard there, some of the greatest of thinkers among the Greeks regarded that country not only as the home of knowledge and the source of civilization and of the arts, but also as the fountain head of what has been called "white magic," and the "black art." In some respects they exaggerated the powers of the Egyptians, but frequently when the classical writers were well informed they only ascribed to them the magical knowledge which the Egyptian magicians themselves claimed to possess. A striking instance of this is given in the second book of the *Metamorphoses of Apuleius* where, it will be remembered, the following is narrated. The student Telephron arrived one day at Larissa, and as he was wandering about in an almost penniless condition he saw an old man standing on a large block of stone issuing a proclamation to the effect that any one who would undertake to guard a dead body should receive a good reward. When Telephron asked if dead men were in the habit of running away the old man replied testily to the effect that the witches all over Thessaly used to tear off pieces of flesh from the faces of the dead with their teeth, in order to make magical spells by means of them, and to prevent this dead bodies must needs be watched at night. The young man then asked what his duties would be if he undertook the post, and he was told that he would have to keep thoroughly awake all night, to gaze fixedly upon the dead body, to look neither to the right hand nor to the left, and not to close the eyes even to wink. This was absolutely necessary because the witches were able to get out of their skins and to take the form of a bird, or dog, or mouse, and their craftiness was such that they could take the forms of flies and cast sleep upon the watcher. If the watcher relaxed his attention and the body became mutilated by the witches, the pieces of flesh torn away would have to be made good from the body of the watcher. Telephron agreed to undertake the duty for one thousand nummi, and was led by the old man to a house, and, having been taken into the room where the dead body was, found a man making notes on tablets to the effect that nose, eyes, ears, lips, chin, etc., were untouched and whole. Having been provided with a lamp and some oil that night he began his watch, and all went well, notwithstanding that he was greatly afraid, until the dead of night when a weasel came into the chamber and looked confidingly at the watcher; but he drove the animal—which was no doubt a witch—from the room, and then fell fast asleep. In the early morning he was suddenly wakened by the trumpets of the soldiers, and almost immediately the widow of the dead man came to him with seven witnesses, and began to examine the body to see if it was intact; finding that no injury had been done to it she ordered her steward to pay Telephron his fee, and was so grateful to him that she promised to make him one of her household. In attempting to express his thanks, however, he made use of some inauspicious words, and immediately the servants of the house fell upon him, and buffeted him, and plucked out his hair by the roots, and tore his clothes, and finally cast him out of the house. Soon afterwards, whilst wandering about, he saw the funeral procession pass through the forum, and at that moment an old man went to the bier, and with sobs and tears accused the widow of poisoning his nephew so that she might inherit his property and marry her lover. Presently the mob which had gathered together wanted to set her house on fire, and some people began to stone her; the small boys also threw stones at her. When she had denied the accusation, and had called upon the gods to be witnesses of her innocence, the old man cried out, "Let, then, Divine Providence decide the truth, in "answer to her denial. Behold, the famous prophet, "Zaclas the Egyptian, dwelleth among us, and he hath "promised me that for much money he will make the "soul of the dead man to return from the place of death "in the underworld, and to make it to dwell in his "body again for a short time." With these words, he led forward a man dressed in linen, and wearing palm-leaf sandals, who, like all the Egyptian priests, had his head shaved, and having kissed his hands and embraced his legs he implored him by the stars, and by the gods of the underworld, and by the island of the Nile, and by the Inundation, etc., to restore life to the dead body, if only for the smallest possible time, so that the truth of his accusation against the widow might be proved. Thus adjured Zaclas touched the mouth and the breast of the dead man three times with some plant, and having turned his face to the East and prayed, the lungs of the corpse began to fill with breath, and his heart to beat, and raising his head and shoulders he asked why he had been called back to life, and then he begged to be allowed to rest in peace. At this moment Zaclas addressed him, and telling him that he had the power, through his prayers, to cause the fiends to come and torture him, ordered him to make known the means by which he had died. With a groan he replied that the wife whom he had recently married gave him poison to drink, and that he died in consequence. The wife at once contradicted the words of her husband, and of the people who were standing round some took one side and some another. At length the husband declared that he would prove the truth of his own words, and pointing to Telephron, who had attempted to guard his body, told those present that the witches after making many attempts to elude his vigilance had cast deep sleep upon him. They next called upon himself by his name, which happened to be Telephron, like that of his watcher, and whilst he was endeavouring feebly to obey their spells, his watcher rose up unconsciously and walked about. Seeing this the witches forced their way into the room through some unknown place, and having taken off the nose and ears of the watcher they placed models of these members in their places. Those who heard these words looked fixedly at the young man, who at once put up his hands and touched the members, whereupon his nose came off in his hand, and his ears slipped through his fingers on to the ground.

The end of the story does not concern us, and so we pass on to note that the act of touching the mouth which Zaclas performed is, of course, a part of the ceremony of "opening the mouth" which is so often referred to in religious texts, and was considered of extreme importance for the welfare of the dead,[1] and that the power of bringing back the dead to life which Apuleius ascribes to the priest or magician was actually claimed some thousands of years before Christ by the sages of Egypt, as we may see from the following story in the Westcar Papyrus.

A son of king Khufu (or Cheops, who reigned about

[1] See Chapter VI. (Magical Ceremonies).

B.C. 3800) called Herutātāf, who was famous as a learned man and whose name is preserved in the "Book of the Dead" in connection with the "discovery" of certain Chapters of that wonderful compilation,[1] was one day talking to his father, presumably on the subject of the powers of working magic possessed by the ancients. In answer to some remark by Khufu he replied, "Up "to the present thou hast only heard reports concerning "the things which the men of olden time knew, and man "knoweth not whether they are true or not; but now "I will cause thy Majesty to see a sage in thine own "time, and one who knoweth thee not." In reply to Khufu's question, "Who is this man, O Herutātāf?" the young man replied, "It is a certain man called "Teta, who dwelleth in Tet-Seneferu, and is one hundred "and ten years old, and to this very day he eateth five "hundred loaves of bread, and the shoulder of an ox, and "he drinketh one hundred measures of ale. He knoweth "how to fasten on again to its body a head that hath "been cut off; he knoweth how to make a lion follow "him whilst his snare is trailing on the ground; and he "knoweth the number of the *aptet* of the sanctuary of "Thoth." Now Khufu had for a long time past sought out the *aptet* of the sanctuary of Thoth, because he was anxious to make one similar for his own "horizon." Though at the present it is impossible to say what the

[1] Chapters XXX., LXIV., CXXXVII. See my *Chapters of Coming Forth by Day* (text), pp. 97, 141, 309.

*aptet* was, it is quite clear that it was an object or instrument used in connection with the working of magic of some sort, and it is clear that the king was as much interested in the pursuit as his subjects. In reply to his son's words Khufu told him to go and bring the sage into his presence, and the royal barge or boat having been brought, Herutātāf set out for the place where the sage dwelt. Having sailed up the river some distance he and his party arrived at Tet-Seneferu, and when the boats had been tied to the quay the prince set out to perform the rest of the journey, which was overland, in a sort of litter made of ebony, which was borne by men by means of poles of *sesnetchem* wood, inlaid with gold. When he had arrived at the abode of Teta, the litter was set down upon the ground, and the prince came out to greet the sage, whom he found lying upon a basket-work bed or mattress, which had been placed for him in the court-yard of his house, whilst one servant shampooed his head, and another rubbed his feet. After a suitable greeting and reference to the sage's honourable condition had been made, Herutātāf told him that he had come from a great distance in order to bring to him a message from Khufu his father, and the sage bade him "Welcome" heartily, and prophesied that Khufu would greatly exalt his rank. The greetings ended, Herutātāf assisted Teta to rise, and the old man set out for the quay leaning upon the arm of the king's son, and when he had arrived there he asked that a boat might be provided for the transport of his children and his books. Two boats were at once prepared and filled with their complement of sailors, and Teta sailed down the Nile with Herutātāf, while his family followed.

After a time the party arrived at Khufu's palace, and Herutātāf went into the presence of his father, and reported to him that he had brought Teta the sage for him to see; Khufu gave orders that he was to be brought before him quickly, and having gone forth into the colonnade of the palace, Teta was led in to him. Khufu said to him, "How is it, Teta, that I have never "seen thee?" and the sage replied, "O Prince, he who is "called cometh; and since thou hast called me, behold, "here I am." Khufu said to him, "Is it true, according "to what is reported, that thou knowest how to fasten "on again to its body the head which hath been cut "off?" and the sage replied, "Yea, verily, O my lord the "Prince, I do know how to do this thing." And Khufu said, "Let a captive who is shut up in prison be brought "to me so that I may inflict his doom upon him," but Teta made answer, "Nay, my lord the king, let not this "thing be performed upon man, but upon some creature "that belongeth to the sacred animals." Then some one brought to him a goose, and having cut off its head, he laid the body of the goose on the west side of the colonnade, and the head on the east side. Teta then stood up and spake certain words of magical power, whereupon the body began to move and the head likewise, and each time that they moved the one came nearer to the other, until at length the head moved to its right place on the bird, which straightway cackled. After this Teta had a *khet-āa* bird brought to him, and upon it he performed the same miracle which he had wrought upon the goose; and to prove that he had similar power over the animal creation, an ox was brought to him, and having cut off its head, which fell upon the ground, he uttered words of magical power, and the ox stood up and lived as before.

The two stories from the Westcar Papyrus given above are sufficient to prove that already in the IVth dynasty the working of magic was a recognized art among the Egyptians, and everything we learn from later texts indicates that it is well-nigh impossible to imagine a time in Egypt when such was not the case. But the "wisdom" of the Egyptians was of two kinds, that is to say, they were possessed of the two kinds of "wisdom" which enabled them to deal with both the material world and the spiritual world; the nations around, however, confused the two kinds, and misunderstood matters in consequence.

One of the oldest names of Egypt is "Kamt" or "Qemt," a word which means "black" or "dusky," and it was applied to the country on account of the dark colour of the mud which forms the land on each side of the Nile; the Christian Egyptians or Copts transmitted the word under the form Khême to the Greeks, Romans, Syrians, and Arabs. At a very early period the Egyptians were famous for their skill in the working of metals and in their attempts to transmute them, and, according to Greek writers, they employed quicksilver in the processes whereby they separated the metals gold and silver from the native ore. From these processes there resulted a "black" powder or substance which was supposed to possess the most marvellous powers, and to contain in it the individualities of the various metals; and in it their actual substances were incorporated. In a mystical manner this "black" powder was identified with the body which the god Osiris was known to possess in the underworld, and to both were attributed magical qualities, and both were thought to be sources of life and power. Thus, side by side with the growth of skill in performing the ordinary processes of metal-working in Egypt, there grew up in that country the belief that magical powers existed in fluxes and alloys; and the art of manipulating the metals, and the knowledge of the chemistry of the metals and of their magical powers were described by the name "Khemeia," that is to say, "the preparation of the black ore" (or "powder") which was regarded as the active principle in the transmutation of metals. To this name the Arabs affixed the article *al*, and thus we obtain the word Al-Khemeia, or Alchemy, which will perpetuate the reputation of the Egyptians as successful students both of "white magic" and of the "black" art.

But in addition to their skill as handicraftsmen and artisans the Egyptians were skilled in literary composition, and in the production of books, especially of that class which related to the ceremonies which were performed for the benefit of the dead. We have, unfortunately, no means of knowing what early contemporary peoples thought of the Egyptian funeral ceremonies, but it seems to be certain that it was chiefly by means of these that they obtained their reputation as workers of miracles. If by chance any members of a desert tribe had been permitted to behold the ceremonies which were performed when the kings for whom the Pyramids had been built were laid to rest in them, the stories that they took back to their kinsmen would be received as sure proofs that the Egyptians had the power to give life to the dead, to animate statues, and to command the services of their gods by the mere utterance of their names as words of power. The columns of hieroglyphics with which the walls of the tombs were often covered, and the figures of the gods, painted or sculptured upon stelæ or sarcophagi, would still further impress the barbarian folk who always regard the written letter and those who understand it with great awe. The following story from Mas'ûdî[1] will illustrate the views which the Arabs

[1] *Les Prairies d'Or* (ed. by B. de Meynard and P. de Courteille), Paris, 1863, tom. ii. p. 398 f.

held concerning the inscriptions and figures of gods in the temples of Egypt. It seems that when the army of Pharaoh had been drowned in the Red Sea, the women and slaves feared lest they should be attacked by the kings of Syria and the West; in this difficulty they elected a woman called Dalūkah as their queen, because she was wise and prudent and skilled in magic. Dalūkah's first act was to surround all Egypt with a wall, which she guarded by men who were stationed along it at short intervals, her object being as much to protect her son, who was addicted to the chase, from the attacks of wild beasts as Egypt from invasion by nomad tribes; besides this she placed round the enclosure figures of crocodiles and other formidable animals. During the course of her reign of thirty years she filled Egypt with her temples and with figures of animals; she also made figures of men in the form of the dwellers in the countries round about Egypt, and in Syria, and in the West, and of the beasts which they rode. In the temples she collected all the secrets of nature and all the attracting or repelling powers which were contained in minerals, plants, and animals. She performed her sorceries at the moment in the revolution of the celestial bodies when they would be amenable to a higher power. And it came to pass that if an army set out from any part of Arabia or Syria to attack Egypt, the queen made the figures of its soldiers and of the animals which they were riding to disappear beneath the ground, and the same fate immediately overtook the living creatures which they represented, wherever they might be on their journey, and the destruction of the figures on sculptures entailed the destruction of the hostile host. In brief, the large figures of the gods which were sculptured or painted on the walls, and the hieroglyphic inscriptions which accompanied them, were considered by those who could neither understand nor read them to be nothing more nor less than magical figures and formulæ which were intended to serve as talismans.

The historian Mas'ûdî mentions[1] an instance of the powers of working magic possessed by a certain Jew, which proves that the magical practices of the Egyptians had passed eastwards and had found a congenial home among the Jews who lived in and about Babylon. This man was a native of the village of Zurārah in the district of Kūfa, and he employed his time in working magic. In the Mosque at Kūfa, and in the presence of Walīd ibn Ukbah, he raised up several apparitions, and made a king of huge stature, who was mounted upon a horse, gallop about in the courtyard of the Mosque. He then transformed himself into a camel and walked upon a rope; and made the phantom of an ass to pass through his body; and

[1] *Les Prairies d'Or* (ed. B. de Meynard), Paris, 1865, tom. iv. pp. 266, 267.

finally having slain a man, he cut off the head and removed it from the trunk, and then by passing his sword over the two parts, they united and the man came alive again. This last act recalls the joining of the head of the dead goose to its body and the coming back of the bird to life which has been described above.

We have now to describe briefly the principal means upon which the Egyptians relied for working magic, that is to say, magical stones or amulets, magical figures, magical pictures and formulæ, magical names, magical ceremonies, etc., and such portions of the Book of the Dead as bear upon these subjects generally.

# CHAPTER II.

## MAGICAL STONES OR AMULETS.

"AMULET" is a name given to a class of objects and ornaments, and articles of dress and wearing apparel, made of various substances which were employed by the Egyptians, and later by other nations, to protect the human body, either living or dead, from baleful influences, and from the attacks of visible and invisible foes. The word "amulet" is derived from an Arabic root meaning "to bear, to carry," hence "amulet" is "something which is carried or worn," and the name is applied broadly to any kind of talisman or ornament to which supernatural powers are ascribed. It is not clear whether the amulet was intended first of all to protect the living or the dead body, but it seems that it was originally worn to guard its owner from savage animals and from serpents. As time went on the development of religious ideas and beliefs progressed, and as a result new amulets representing new views were invented; and the objects which were able to protect the living were made, by an easy transition in the minds of those who wore them, to protect the dead. Moreover, as the preservation of the corruptible body, with the number of its members complete and intact, was of the most vital importance for the life of the spiritual and incorruptible body which was believed to spring therefrom, under the influence of the new beliefs the dead body became a veritable storehouse of amulets. Each member was placed under the specific protection of some amulet, and a number of objects which were believed to protect the body generally from serpents, worms, mildew, decay and putrefaction were laid with a lavish hand in, and upon, and about it, and between the bandages with which it was swathed. When men in Egypt began to lay amulets on their dead cannot be said, and it is equally impossible to say when the belief in the efficacy of such and such an amulet sprang into being; it seems clear, however, that certain amulets represent beliefs and superstitions so old that even the Egyptians were, at times, doubtful about their origin and meaning.

Amulets are of two kinds: (1) those which are inscribed with magical formulæ, and (2) those which are not. In the earliest times formulæ or prayers were recited over the amulets that were worn by the living or placed on the dead by priests or men set apart to perform religious services by the community; but it was not in the power of every man to employ them, and at a comparatively early date words of magical power and prayers were cut upon the amulets, which thus became possessed of a twofold power, that is to say, the power which was thought to be inherent in the substance of which the amulet was made, and that which lay in the words inscribed upon it. The earliest name for the formulæ found upon amulets is *hekau*, and it was so necessary for the deceased to be provided with these *hekau*, or "words of power," that in the XVIth century B.C., and probably more than a thousand years earlier, a special section[1] was inserted in the Book of the Dead with the object of causing them to come to him from whatever place they were in, "swifter than greyhounds and quicker than light." The earliest Egyptian amulets known are pieces of green schist, of various shapes, animal and otherwise, which were laid upon the breast of the deceased; these are found in large numbers in the pre-historic or predynastic graves at several places in Egypt. It is most unlikely that they were made by the aboriginal inhabitants of Egypt, for, notwithstanding the various conjectures which have been made as to their object and use, it is pretty certain that, as M. J. de Morgan said,[2] they "belong to the cult." According to this writer their use was exceedingly widespread until the end of the neolithic period, but with the advent of the

[1] *I.e.*, Chapter XXIV., which is entitled, "The Chapter of bringing "words of power unto Osiris in the underworld."

[2] *Ethnographie Préhistorique*, p. 144.

people whom we call Egyptians they become very rare. In the subsequent period the animal forms disappear, and their place is taken by plaques of schist, rectangular in shape, upon which are inscribed, in rough outline, figures of animals, etc. The theory that these objects were intended as whetstones, or as slabs upon which to rub down paint, will not hold, for the reasons which M. J. de Morgan has given. Moreover, in the green stone scarab which was laid upon the breast of the deceased in dynastic times, we probably have a survival of the green schist amulet of predynastic times in Egypt, both as regards the object with which it was made and the material. But the custom of writing *hekau*, or words of power, upon papyrus is almost as old as that of writing them upon stone, and we see from the inscription on the walls of the corridors and chambers of the pyramid of Unas, king of Egypt about B.C. 3300, that a "book with words "of magical power" was buried with him.[1] Elsewhere[2] we are told that the book which Teta, king of Egypt about B.C. 3266, had with him "hath effect "upon the heart of the gods"; and there is no doubt that the object of every religious text ever written on tomb, stele, amulet, coffin, papyrus, etc., was to bring the gods under the power of the deceased, so that he might be able to compel them to do his will.

[1] *Unas*, ed. Maspero, line 584.
[2] *Teta*, ed. Maspero, line 351.

### 1. THE AMULET OF THE HEART, 

The heart was not only the seat of the power of life, but also the source of both good and evil thoughts; and it sometimes typified the conscience. It was guarded after death with special care, and was mummified separately, and then, with the lungs, was preserved in a jar which was placed under the protection of the god Tuamutef. Its preservation was considered to be of such importance that a text[1] was introduced into the Book of the Dead at an early period, with the view of providing the deceased with a heart in the place of that which had been removed in the process of mummification. The text reads:—

"May my heart be with me in the House of Hearts! "May my breast[2] be with me in the House of Hearts! "May my heart be with me, and may it rest there, or "I shall not eat of the cakes of Osiris on the eastern "side of the Lake of Flowers, neither shall I have a "boat wherein to go down the Nile, nor another wherein "to go up, nor shall I be able to sail down the Nile "with thee. May my mouth [be given] to me that "I may speak therewith, and my two legs to walk "therewith, and my two hands and arms to overthrow "my foe. May the doors of heaven be opened unto "me; may Seb, the prince of the gods, open wide his

[1] Chapter XXVI., entitled, "The Chapter of giving a heart to the "deceased."

[2] Literally, "pericardium."

"two jaws unto me; may he open my two eyes which "are blindfolded; may he cause me to stretch apart "my two legs which are bound together; and may "Anpu (Anubis) make my thighs to be firm so that "I may stand upon them. May the goddess Sekhet "make me to rise so that I may ascend into heaven, "and may that which I command in the House of the "Ka of Ptah be done. I shall understand with my "heart, I shall gain the mastery over my heart, I shall "gain the mastery over my two hands, I shall gain "the mastery over my legs, I shall have the power to "do whatsoever my *ka* (*i.e.*, double) pleaseth. My "soul shall not be fettered to my body at the gates "of the underworld, but I shall enter in and come "forth in peace."

When the deceased had uttered these words, it was believed that he would at once obtain the powers which he wished to possess in the next world; and when he had gained the mastery over his heart, the heart, the double, and the soul had the power to go where they wished and to do what they pleased. The mention of the god Ptah and of his consort Sekhet indicates that the Chapter was the work of the priests of Memphis, and that the ideas embodied in it are of great antiquity. According to the Papyrus of Nekhtu-Amen, the amulet of the heart, which is referred to in the above Chapter, was to be made of lapis-lazuli, and there is no doubt that this stone was believed to possess certain qualities which were beneficial to those who wore it. It will also be remembered that, according to one tradition,[1] the text of the LXIVth Chapter of the Book of the Dead was found written in letters of lapis-lazuli in the reign of Hesep-ti, king of Egypt about B.C. 4300, and the way in which the fact is mentioned in the Rubric to the Chapter proves that special importance was attached to it.

Nefer-uben-f, a priest, guarding his heart against the destroyer of hearts. (From Naville, *Todtenbuch*, vol. I. plate 39.)

But although a heart might be given to a man by means of the above Chapter, it was necessary for the deceased to take the greatest care that it was not carried off from him by a monster, who was part man and part beast, and who went about seeking for hearts to carry away. To prevent such a calamity no less than seven Chapters of the Book of the Dead (Nos. XXVII., XXVIII., XXIX., XXIXA, XXX., XXXA,

[1] See *Chapters of Coming Forth by Day* (translation, p. 119).

and XXXB) were written. The XXVIIth Chapter was connected with a heart amulet made of a white, semi-transparent stone, and reads :—

"Hail, ye who carry away hearts! Hail, ye who "steal hearts, and who make the heart of a man to go "through its transformations according to its deeds, let "not what he hath done harm him before you! Homage "to you, O ye lords of eternity, ye possessors of ever-"lastingness, take ye not this heart of Osiris[1] into your "grasp, and cause ye not words of evil to spring up "against it; for it is the heart of Osiris, and it belongeth "unto him of many names,[2] the mighty one whose words "are his limbs, and who sendeth forth his heart to dwell "in his body. The heart of Osiris is triumphant, and "it is made new before the gods: he hath gained power "over it, and he hath not been judged according to what "he hath done. He hath gotten power over his own "members. His heart obeyeth him, he is the lord "thereof, it is in his body, and it shall never fall away "therefrom. I, Osiris, victorious in peace, and trium-"phant in the beautiful Amenta and on the mountain "of eternity, bid thee [O heart] to be obedient unto "me in the underworld."

Another Chapter (XXIXB) was connected with a heart amulet made of carnelian, of which so many examples may be found in large museums; the text

[1] *I.e.*, the deceased who was identified with Osiris, the god and judge of the dead.

[2] *I.e.*, Thoth.

reads: "I am the Bennu,[1] the soul of Rā, and the "guide of the gods who are in the underworld. Their "divine souls came forth upon earth to do the will of "their doubles, let therefore the soul of the Osiris come "forth to do the will of his double." The Bennu was also the soul of Osiris, and thus the amulet brought with it the protection of both Osiris and Rā.

But of all the Chapters which related to the heart, the most popular among the Egyptians was that which is commonly known as XXXB, and its importance from a religious point of view cannot be overstated. The antiquity of the Chapter is undoubted, for according to the Papyrus of Nu,[2] a document of the early part of the XVIIIth dynasty, it dates from the time of Hesep-ti, king of Egypt about B.C. 4300, and it seems that it formed a pendant or supplement to the LXIVth Chapter, which professed to give the substance of all the "Chapters of Coming Forth by Day" in a single Chapter. In the rubric to the longer version of the Chapter, given in the same papyrus,[3] Chapter XXXB is connected with Herutātāf, the son of Khufu (Cheops), a man famed for wisdom, and it is there ordered that the words of it be recited over a hard, green stone scarab, which shall be laid in the breast of the deceased where the heart would ordinarily be; this amulet would then perform for him the "opening of the

[1] The Bennu bird is usually identified with the phœnix.

[2] Brit. Mus., No. 10,477, sheet 13. [3] See sheet 21.

"mouth,"[1] for the words of the Chapter would be indeed "words of power." From reciting the words of the Chapter over a scarab to engraving them upon it was but a step, and this step was taken as early as the IVth dynasty. The text is as follows:—

"My heart, my mother; my heart, my mother! My "heart whereby I came into being! May naught stand "up to oppose me at [my] judgment; may there be "no opposition to me in the presence of the sovereign "princes; may there be no parting of thee from me "in the presence of him that keepeth the Balance! "Thou art my double (*ka*), the dweller in my body, "the god Khnemu who knitteth and strengtheneth my "limbs. Mayest thou come forth into the place of "happiness whither we go. May the *Shenit*, who form "the conditions of the lives of men, not make my "name to stink. Let it be satisfactory unto us, and "let the listening be satisfactory unto us, and let there "be joy of heart unto us at the weighing of words. "Let not that which is false be uttered against me "before the great god, the lord of Amentet. Verily "how great shalt thou be when thou risest in triumph."

It was this Chapter which the deceased recited when he was in the Judgment Hall of Osiris, whilst his heart was being weighed in the Balance against the feather symbolic of right and truth. From certain papyri it seems as if the above words should, properly,

[1] See Chapter VI. (Magical Ceremonies).

be said by the deceased when he is being weighed against his own heart, a conception which is quite different from that of the judgment of the heart before the gods.

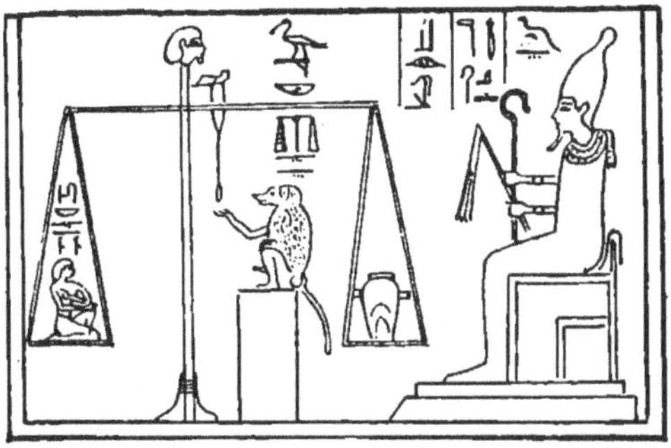

The scribe Nebseni being weighed in a balance against his heart in the presence of Osiris. (From the Papyrus of Nebseni, sheet 4.)

## 2. THE AMULET OF THE SCARAB, 

From what has been said above it will be seen that the amulet of the heart, which was connected with the most important and most popular of the Chapters for protecting the heart, was directed to be made in the form of the scarab at a very early date. We can trace the ideas which the Egyptians held about this insect as far back as the time of the building of the Pyramids,[1] and there is no doubt that they represented beliefs which even at that early period were very old. The

[1] King Teta is said to "live like the scarab" (*Teta*, line 89); and again it is said, "Pepi is the son of the Scarab which is born in "Hetepet under the hair of the northern Iusāas" (*Pepi*, line 422).

Egyptian seems to have reasoned thus: since the physical heart is taken from the body before mummification, and the body has need of another to act as the source of life and movement in its new life, another must be put in its place. But a stone heart, whether made of lapis-lazuli or carnelian, is only a stone heart after all, and even though by means of prayers properly recited it prevents the physical heart from being carried off by "those who plunder hearts," it possesses nothing of itself which can be turned to account in giving new life and being to the body on which it lies. But the scarab or beetle itself possesses remarkable powers, and if a figure of the scarab be made, and the proper words of power be written upon it, not only protection of the dead physical heart, but also new life and existence will be given to him to whose body it is attached. Moreover, the scarab was the type and symbol of the god Khepera, the invisible power of creation which propelled the sun across the sky. The particular beetle chosen by the Egyptians to copy for amulets belongs to the family of dung-feeding Lamellicorns which live in tropical countries. The species are generally of a black hue, but amongst them are to be found some adorned with the richest metallic colours. A remarkable peculiarity exists in the structure and situation of the hind legs, which are placed so near the extremity of the body, and so far from each other, as to give the insect a most extraordinary appearance when walking. This peculiar formation is, nevertheless, particularly serviceable to its possessors in rolling the balls of excrementitious matter in which they enclose their eggs. These balls are at first irregular and soft, but, by degrees, and during the process of rolling along, become rounded and harder; they are propelled by means of the hind legs. Sometimes these balls are an inch and a half or two inches in diameter, and in rolling them along the beetles stand almost upon their heads, with the heads turned from the balls. These manœuvres have for their object the burying of the balls in holes, which the insects have previously dug for their reception; and it is upon the dung thus deposited that the larvæ, when hatched, feed. It does not appear that these beetles have the ability to distinguish their own balls, as they will seize upon those belonging to another, in the case of their having lost their own; indeed, it is said that several of them occasionally assist in rolling the same ball. The males as well as the females assist in rolling the pellets. They fly during the hottest part of the day.[1]

Among the ancients several curious views were held about the scarab, whether of the type *scarabæus sacer* or the *ateuchus Ægyptiorum*,[2] and Ælian, Porphyry,

[1] See J. O. Westwood, *Introduction to the Modern Classification of Insects*, London, 1839, vol. i. p. 204 ff.

[2] See my *Mummy*, p. 233.

and Horapollo declared that no female scarab existed. The last named writer stated that the scarab denoted "only begotten," because it was a creature self-produced, being unconceived by a female. He goes on to say that, having made a ball of dung, the beetle rolls it from east to west, and having dug a hole, he buries it in it for eight and twenty days; on the twenty-ninth day he opens the ball, and throws it into the water, and from it the scarabæi come forth. The fact that the scarab flies during the hottest part of the day made the insect to be identified with the sun, and the ball of eggs to be compared to the sun itself. The unseen power of God, made manifest under the form of the god Khepera, caused the sun to roll across the sky, and the act of rolling gave to the scarab its name *kheper*, *i.e.*, "he who rolls." The sun contained the germs of all life, and as the insect's ball contained the germs of the young scarabs it was identified also with the sun as a creature which produced life in a special way. Now, the god Khepera also represented inert but living matter, which was about to begin a course of existence, and at a very early period he was considered to be a god of the resurrection; and since the scarab was identified with him that insect became at once the symbol of the god and the type of the resurrection. But the dead human body, from one aspect, contained the germ of life, that is to say, the germ of the spiritual body, which was called into being by means of the prayers that were recited and the ceremonies that were performed on the day of the funeral; from this point of view the insect's egg ball and the dead body were identical. Now, as the insect had given potential life to its eggs in the ball, so, it was thought, would a model of the scarab, itself the symbol of the god Khepera, also give potential life to the dead body upon which it was placed, always provided that the proper "words of power" were first said over it or written upon it. The idea of "life" appears to have attached itself to the scarab from time immemorial in Egypt and the Eastern Sûdân, for to this day the insect is dried, pounded, and mixed with water, and then drunk by women who believe it to be an unfailing specific for the production of large families. In ancient days when a man wished to drive away the effects of every kind of sorcery and incantations he might do so by cutting off the head and wings of a large beetle, which he boiled and laid in oil. The head and wings were then warmed up and steeped in the oil of the *āpnent* serpent, and when they had been once more boiled the man was to drink the mixture.[1]

The amulet of the scarab has been found in Egypt in untold thousands, and the varieties are exceedingly numerous. They are made of green basalt, green

[1] See Joachim, *Das älteste Buch über Heilkunde*, Berlin, 1890, p. 160.

granite, limestone, green marble, blue paste, blue glass, purple, blue and green glazed porcelain, etc.; and the words of power are usually cut in outline on the base. In rare instances, the scarab has a human face or head, and sometimes the backs are inscribed with figures of the boat of Rā, of the *Bennu* bird, "the soul of Rā," and of the eye of Horus. The green stone scarabs are often set in gold, and have a band of gold across and

The scribe Ani holding a necklace with pectoral, on which is a figure of the boat of Rā containing a scarab, or beetle, in the presence of Anubis, the god of the dead. (From the *Papyrus of Ani*, plate 15.)

down the back where the wings join; sometimes the whole back is gilded, and sometimes the base is covered with a plate of gold upon which the words of power have been stamped or engraved. Occasionally the base of the scarab is made in the form of a heart, a fact which proves the closeness of the relationship which existed between the amulets of the heart and scarab. In late times, that is to say about B.C. 1200, large funeral scarabs were set in pylon-shaped pectorals, made of porcelain of various colours, upon which the boat of the Sun was either traced in colours or worked in relief, and the scarab is placed so as to appear to be carried in the boat; on the left stands Isis and on the right Nephthys.[1] The oldest green stone funeral scarab known to me is in the British Museum (No. 29,224); it was found at Kûrna near Thebes and belongs to the period of the XIth dynasty, about B.C. 2600. The name of the man for whom it was made (he appears to have been an official of the Temple of Amen) was traced on it in light coloured paint which was afterwards varnished; there are no "words of "power" on this interesting object.

When once the custom of burying scarabs with the bodies of the dead became recognized, the habit of wearing them as ornaments by the living came into fashion, and as a result scarabs of almost every sort and kind may be found by the thousand in many collections, and it is probable that the number of varieties of them was only limited by the ability of those who manufactured them in ancient days to invent new sorts. The use of the scarab amulet passed into Western Asia and into several countries which lay on the Mediterranean, and those who wore it seem to have attached to it much the same idea as its early inventors, the

[1] I have given a summary of the chief varieties of the funeral scarab in my *Papyrus of Ani*, London, 1895, p. 262.

Egyptians. From a Greek magical papyrus translated by Goodwin[1] we may see that certain solemn ceremonies were performed over a scarab before it was worn, even in the period of the rule of the Greeks and Romans. Thus about the "ring of Horus" and the "ceremony of the beetle" we are told to take a beetle, sculptured as described below, and to place it on a paper table, and under the table there shall be a pure linen cloth; under it put some olive wood, and set on the middle of the table a small censer wherein myrrh and kyphi shall be offered. And have at hand a small vessel of chrysolite into which ointment of lilies, or myrrh, or cinnamon, shall be put, and take the ring and lay it in the ointment, having first made it pure and clean, and offer it up in the censer with kyphi and myrrh; leave the ring for three days, and take it out and put it in a safe place. At the celebration let there lie near at hand some pure loaves, and such fruits as are in season, and having made another sacrifice upon vine sticks, during the sacrifice take the ring out of the ointment, and anoint thyself with the unction from it. Thou shalt anoint thyself early in the morning, and turning towards the east shalt pronounce the words written below. The beetle shall be carved out of a precious emerald; bore it and pass a gold wire through it, and beneath the beetle carve the

[1] *Fragment of a Græco-Egyptian Work upon Magic* (Publications of the Cambridge Antiquarian Society, 1852).

holy Isis, and having consecrated it as above written, use it. The proper days for the celebration were the 7th, 9th, 10th, 12th, 14th, 16th, 21st, 24th, and 25th, from the beginning of the month; on other days abstain. The spell to be recited began, "I am Thoth, "the inventor and founder of medicines and letters; "come to me, thou that art under the earth, rise up to "me, thou great spirit."

### 3. The Amulet of the Buckle, 

This amulet represents the buckle of the girdle of Isis, and is usually made of carnelian, red jasper, red glass, and of other substances of a red colour; it is sometimes made of gold, and of substances covered with gold. It is always associated with the CLVIth Chapter of the Book of the Dead, which is frequently inscribed upon it, and which reads:—

"The blood of Isis, and the strength of Isis, and the "words of power of Isis shall be mighty to act as "powers to protect this great and divine being, and to "guard him from him that would do unto him anything "that he holdeth in abomination."

But before the buckle was attached to the neck of the deceased, where the rubric ordered it to be placed, it had to be dipped in water in which *ānkham* flowers had been steeped; and when the words of the Chapter of the Buckle given above had been recited over it, the amulet brought to the deceased the protection of the blood of Isis, and of her words of power. It will be remembered that she raised the dead body of Osiris by means of her words of power, and there is a legend to the effect that she smote the Sun-god Rā with severe sickness by the magical power which she possessed. Another object of the buckle was to give the deceased access to every place in the underworld, and to enable him to have "one hand towards heaven, and one hand "towards earth."

### 4. The Amulet of the Tet, 

This amulet probably represents the tree trunk in which the goddess Isis concealed the dead body of her husband, and the four cross-bars indicate the four cardinal points; it became a symbol of the highest religious importance to the Egyptians, and the setting up of the Tet at Busiris, which symbolized the re-constituting of the body of Osiris, was one of the most solemn of all the ceremonies performed in connexion with the worship of Osiris. The Tet represents neither the mason's table nor a Nilometer, as some have thought. It is always associated with the CLVth Chapter of the Book of the Dead, which reads:—

"Rise up thou, O Osiris! Thou hast thy backbone, "O Still-Heart! Thou hast the fastenings of thy neck "and back, O Still-Heart! Place thou thyself upon

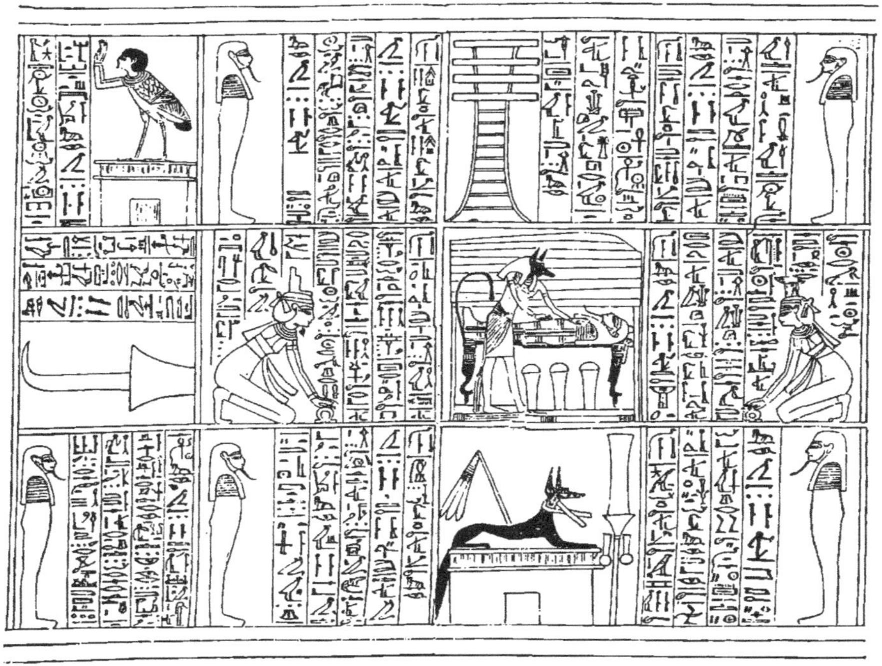

The mummy of Ani the scribe, lying on a bier, attended by Isis, Nephthys, Anubis, the four children of Horus, the *ushabti* figure, his soul, the TET, etc. (From the *Papyrus of Ani*, plates 33, 34.)

"thy base, I put water beneath thee, and I bring unto "thee a Tet of gold that thou mayest rejoice therein."

Like the buckle, the Tet had to be dipped in the water in which *ānkham* flowers had been steeped, and laid upon the neck of the deceased, to whom it gave the power to reconstitute the body and to become a perfect KHU (*i.e.*, spirit) in the underworld. On coffins the right hand of the deceased grasps the buckle, and the left the Tet; both are made of wood, notwithstanding the fact that the rubric to the Chapter of the Te orders the Tet to be made of gold.

### 5. The Amulet of the Pillow, 

This amulet is a model of the pillow which is found placed under the neck of the mummy in the coffin, and its object is to "lift up" and to protect the head of the deceased; it is usually made of hæmatite, and is inscribed with the text of the CLXVIth Chapter of the Book of the Dead, which reads:—

"Thou art lifted up, O sick one that liest prostrate. "They lift up thy head to the horizon, thou art raised "up, and dost triumph by reason of what hath been "done for thee. Ptah hath overthrown thine enemies, "which was ordered to be done for thee. Thou art "Horus, the son of Hathor, . . . who givest back the "head after the slaughter. Thy head shall not be "carried away from thee after [the slaughter], thy head "shall never, never be carried away from thee."

### 6. The Amulet of the Vulture, 𓅐

This amulet was intended to cause the power of Isis as the "divine mother" to be a protection for the deceased, and was made of gold in the form of a vulture hovering in the air with outstretched wings and holding in each talon the symbol of "life" ☥, and was placed on the neck on the day of the funeral. With this amulet the CLVIIth Chapter of the Book of the Dead was associated, and it was ordered by the rubric to it to be recited over it; this text reads:—

"Isis cometh and hovereth over the city, and she "goeth about seeking the secret habitations of Horus "as he emergeth from his papyrus swamps, and she "raiseth up his shoulder which is in evil case. He is "made one of the company in the divine boat, and the "sovereignty of the whole world is decreed for him. "He hath warred mightily, and he maketh his deeds to "be remembered; he hath made the fear of him to "exist and awe of him to have its being. His mother "the mighty lady, protecteth him, and she hath "transferred her power unto him." The first allusion is to the care which Isis shewed for Horus when she was bringing him up in the papyrus swamps, and the second to his combat with Set, whom he vanquished through the might of Isis.

### 7. The Amulet of the Collar of Gold,

This amulet was intended to give the deceased power to free himself from his swathings; it is ordered by the rubric to the CLVIIIth Chapter of the Book of the Dead to be placed on his neck on the day of the funeral, and to be made of gold. The text of the Chapter reads:—"O my father, my brother, my mother Isis, "I am unswathed, and I see. I am one of those who "are unswathed and who see the god Seb." This amulet is very rare, and appears to have been the expression of beliefs which grew up in the period of the XXVIth dynasty, about B.C. 550.

### 8. The Amulet of the Papyrus Sceptre,

This amulet was intended to give the deceased vigour and renewal of youth; it was made of mother-of-emerald, or of light green or blue porcelain, and, when the words of the CLIXth Chapter of the Book of the Dead had been recited over it, it was placed on his neck on the day of the funeral. In the XXVIth dynasty and later it seems as if the amulet represented the power of Isis, who derived it from her father, the husband of Renenet, the goddess of abundant harvests and food. At an earlier period, judging from the text of the CLXth Chapter, the amulet is put by the god

Thoth into the hands of the deceased, who says, "It is "in sound state, and I am in sound state; it is not "injured, and I am not injured; it is not worn away, "and I am not worn away."

### 9. The Amulet of the Soul, 

This amulet was made of gold inlaid with precious stones in the form of a human-headed hawk, and, when the words of the LXXXIXth Chapter of the Book of the Dead had been recited over it, it was directed by the rubric to the Chapter to be placed upon the breast of the deceased. The object of the amulet is apparent from the text in which the deceased is made to say, "Hail, thou god Anniu! Hail, thou "god Pehrer, who dwellest in thy hall! Grant thou "that my soul may come unto me from wheresoever "it may be. If it would tarry, then let my soul "be brought unto me from wheresoever it may be. . . . "Let me have possession of my soul and of my "spirit, and let me be true of voice with them "wheresoever they may be. . . . Hail, ye gods, who "tow along the boat of the lord of millions of years, "who bring it above the underworld, and who make it "to travel over Nut, who make souls to enter into their "spiritual bodies, . . . grant that the soul of the Osiris[1]

[1] *I.e.*, the deceased, who is identified with the god Osiris.

"may come forth before the gods, and that it may be "true of voice with you in the east of the sky, and "follow unto the place where it was yesterday, and "enjoy twofold peace in Amentet. May it look upon "its natural body, may it rest upon its spiritual body, "and may its body neither perish nor suffer corruption "for ever!" Thus the amulet of the soul was intended to enable the soul both to unite with the mummified body, and to be with its spirit (*khu*) and spiritual body at will.

## 10. The Amulet of the Ladder, 

In tombs of the Ancient and Middle Empires small objects of wood and other substances in the form of ladders have often been found, but the signification of them is not always apparent. From the texts inscribed upon the walls of the corridors and chambers of the pyramids of Unas, Teta, Pepi, and other early kings, it is clear that the primitive Egyptians believed that the floor of heaven, which also formed the sky of this world, was made of an immense plate of iron, rectangular in shape, the four corners of which rested upon four pillars which served to mark the cardinal points. On this plate of iron lived the gods and the blessed dead, and it was the aim of every good Egyptian to go there after death. At certain sacred spots the edge of the plate was so near the tops of the mountains that the deceased might easily clamber on to it and so obtain admission into heaven, but at others the distance between it and the earth was so great that he needed help to reach it. There existed a belief that Osiris himself experienced some difficulty of getting up to the iron plate, and that it was only by means of the ladder which his father Rā provided that he at length ascended into heaven. On one side of the ladder stood Rā, and on the other stood Horus,[1] the son of Isis, and each god assisted Osiris to mount it. Originally the two guardians of the ladder were Horus the Elder and Set, and there are several references in the early texts to the help which they rendered to the deceased, who was, of course, identified with the god Osiris. But, with a view either of reminding these gods of their supposed duty, or of compelling them to do it, the model of a ladder was often placed on or near the dead body in the tomb, and a special composition was prepared which had the effect of making the ladder become the means of the ascent of the deceased into heaven. Thus in the text written for Pepi[2] the deceased is made to address the ladder in these words: "Homage to thee, O divine Ladder! Homage to "thee, O Ladder of Set! Stand thou upright, O divine "Ladder! Stand thou upright, O Ladder of Set! Stand "thou upright, O Ladder of Horus, whereby Osiris

[1] *Unas*, line 579. [2] Line 192 f.

"came forth into heaven when he made use of his "magical power upon Rā. . . . For Pepi is thy son, "and Pepi is Horus, and thou hast given birth unto "Pepi even as thou hast given birth unto the god who "is the lord of the Ladder (*i.e.*, Horus); and thou shalt "give unto Pepi the Ladder of the god (*i.e.*, Horus), thou "shalt give unto him the Ladder of the god Set whereby "this Pepi shall come forth into heaven when he shall "have made use of his magical power upon Rā. O "thou god of those whose doubles (*kau*) pass onwards, "when the Eye of Horus soareth upon the wing of "Thoth on the east side of the divine Ladder (*or* "Ladder of God), O men whose bodies [would go] "into heaven, Pepi is the Eye of Horus, and when the "Eye turneth itself to any place where he is, Pepi "goeth side by side with the Eye of Horus, and O "ye who are the brethren of the gods, rejoice ye that "Pepi journeyeth among you. And the brethren of "Pepi who are the gods shall be glad when they meet "Pepi, even as Horus is glad when he meeteth his "Eye. He hath placed his Eye before his father Seb, "and every god and every spirit stretcheth out his "hand towards Pepi when he cometh forth into heaven "from the Ladder. Pepi hath need neither to 'plough "the earth,' nor to 'collect the offering'; and he hath "need neither to go to the Hall which is in Annu "(Heliopolis), nor to the Hall of the Morning which is "in Annu; for that which he seeth and that which he "heareth shall feed him and nourish him when he "appeareth in heaven from the Ladder. Pepi riseth "like the uraeus on the forehead of Set, and every "god and every spirit stretcheth out his hand to Pepi "on the Ladder. Pepi hath gathered together his "bones, he hath collected his flesh, and he hath gone "quickly into heaven by means of the two fingers[1] "of the god of the Ladder (*i.e.*, Horus)." Elsewhere[2] the gods Khonsu, Sept, etc., are invoked to bring the ladder to Pepi, and the ladder itself is adjured to come with its name, and in another place[3] we read, "Homage to thee, O thou Ladder that supportest the "golden vase of the Spirits of Pe and the Spirits of "Nekhen, stretch out thy hand to this Pepi, and let "him take his seat between the two great gods who "are in the place of this Pepi; take him by the hand "and lead him towards Sekhet-Hetep (*i.e.*, the Elysian "Fields), and let him take his seat among the stars "which are in the sky."

In the Theban Recension of the Book of the Dead the importance of the ladder is also seen, for in Chapter CXLIX.[4] the deceased says, "I set up a "Ladder among the gods, and I am a divine being "among them"; and in Chapter CLIII. he says, "The

[1] Compare, "Give thou to Pepi these two fingers which thou hast "given to Nefert, the daughter of the great god, as messengers from "heaven to earth" (*Pepi*, line 422).

[2] *Pepi*, line 200.

[3] *Pepi*, line 471.

[4] See my *Chapters of Coming Forth by Day*, translation, p. 270.

"Osiris Nu shall come forth upon your Ladder which "Rā hath made for him, and Horus and Set shall grasp "him firmly by the hand." Finally, when the custom of placing a model of the ladder in the tomb fell into disuse, the priests provided for the necessity of the dead by painting a ladder on the papyri that were inscribed with the texts from the Book of the Dead and were buried with them.[1]

### 11. The Amulet of the Two Fingers, 

This amulet is intended to represent the two fingers, index and medius, which the god Horus employed in helping his father Osiris up the ladder[2] into heaven, as has been described above; it is found in the interior of mummies and is usually made of obsidian or hæmatite.

### 12. The Amulet of the Eye of Horus, 

The Eye of Horus amulet, or Utchat, is one of the commonest of all, and its use seems to have been universal at all periods. It was made of gold, silver, granite, hæmatite, carnelian, lapis-lazuli, porcelain, wood, etc., although the rubric of a late Chapter of the Book of the Dead[3] directs that the amulet

[1] See the *Papyrus of Ani*, 2nd edition, pl. 22.
[2] See *Pepi*, line 196. [3] *I.e.*, CXL.

should be made either of lapis-lazuli or of *mak* stone. The Utchat is of two kinds, one facing to the left and the other to the right, and together they represent the two eyes of Horus, one of which, according to an ancient text, was white and the other black; from another point of view one Utchat represents the Sun and the other the Moon, or Rā and Osiris respectively. But speaking generally, when the Egyptians wore the Utchat as an amulet they intended it to bring to them the blessings of strength, vigour, protection, safety, good health, and the like, and they had in their minds the Eye of Horus, probably the white one, or the Sun. In religious texts the expression *meh Utchat*, *i.e.*, the "filling of the Utchat," is often used, and from many considerations it is clear that we must understand it to refer to the Sun at the summer solstice; thus the amulet seems to have been intended to bring to its wearer strength and health similar to that of the Sun at the season of the year when it is most powerful. In the CLXVIIth Chapter of the Book of the Dead the deceased is made to say, "The god Thoth hath brought "the Utchat, and he hath made it to rest after it "departed, O Rā. It was grievously afflicted by the "storm, but Thoth made it to rest after it departed "out of the storm. I am sound, and it is sound; I "am sound, and it is sound; and Nebseni, the lord of "piety, is sound." To obtain the full benefit of the Utchat amulet for the deceased it was obligatory to make one in lapis-lazuli and to plate it with gold, and then to offer to it offerings at the summer solstice; another had then to be made of jasper and, if after the specified Chapter (CXL.) had been recited over it, it was laid on any part of the body of the deceased, he would become a god and take his place in the boat of Rā. At this solstice twelve altars[1] had to be lighted, four for Rā-Temu, four for the Utchat, and four for the other gods who had been mentioned in the Chapter. An interesting example of the use of the *utchat* occurs in a Greek spell for the discovery of a thief written as late as the IVth century of our era.[2] In it we are told to "take the herb *khelkbei* and *bugloss*, "press out the juice and burn the crushed leaves and "mix the ashes with the juice. Anoint and write "upon a wall Khoō with these materials. And take "a common piece of wood, and cut a hammer out of "it, and strike with it upon the ear, pronouncing this "spell:—'I adjure thee by the holy names, render up "the thief, who has carried away such [and such] a "thing Khalkhak, Khalkoum, Khiam, Khar, Khroum, "Zbar, Bēri, Zbarkom, Khrē, Kariōb, Pharibou, and by "the terrible names *αεεηηηιιιιοooooυυυυυυωωωωωωω*.'"[3] Following these words we have a picture of the *utchat*

[1] One for each month of the year.

[2] Kenyon, *Catalogue of Greek Papyri*, p. 64.

[3] The seven vowels were supposed in the Gnostic system to contain all the names of God, and were, therefore, most powerful when used as a spell.

with an arrangement of certain vowels on each side of it thus:—

| | | |
|---|---|---|
| ω | | α |
| υυ | | εε |
| ιιι | | ηηη |
| ηηηηη |  | ιιι |
| εεεεεε | | ηηηηη |
| ααααααα | | εεεεεε |
| | | ααααααα |

The spell continues, "'Render up the thief who has "stolen such [and such] a thing: as long as I strike "the ear with this hammer, let the eye of the thief "be smitten and inflamed until it betrays him.' Saying "these words strike with the hammer."[1]

## 13. The Amulet of "Life," ☥ (Ānkh).

The object which is represented by this amulet is unknown, and of all the suggestions which have been made concerning it none is more unlikely than that which would give it a phallic origin. Whatever it may represent, it certainly symbolizes "life"; every god carries it, and it seems, even in the earliest times, to be a conventional representation of some object which in the remotest period had been used as an amulet. In the Papyrus of Ani (2nd edit., plate 2) the Ānkh rises from the Tet, and the arms which project from it support the disk of the sun as here seen. This amulet is made of

[1] See Goodwin, *Fragment of a Græco-Egyptian work upon Magic*, p. 7.

various substances, and was chiefly employed as a pendant of a necklace.

### 14. The Amulet Nefer, 

This amulet signifies "happiness, good luck," etc., and represents a musical instrument; it was made of carnelian, red stone, red porcelain, and the like, and was a very favourite form for the pendants of necklaces and strings of beads.

### 15. The Amulet of the Serpent's Head, 

This amulet was placed on the dead body to keep it from being bitten by snakes in the underworld or tomb. It is made of red stone, red jasper, red paste, and carnelian. As the goddess Isis is often typified by a serpent, and red is a colour peculiar to her, it seems as if the idea underlying the use of this amulet was to vanquish the snakes in the tomb by means of the power of the great snake-goddess Isis. This power had been transferred to it by means of the words of the XXXIVth Chapter of the Book of the Dead, which are often inscribed upon it. The text reads:—
"O Serpent! I am the flame which shineth upon the "Opener of hundreds of thousands of years, and the "standard of the god Tenpu," or as others say, "the standard of young plants and flowers. Depart "ye from me, for I am the divine Lynx." Some

have thought that the snake's head represents the serpent which surmounts the ram's head on the *urhekau* instrument used in performing the ceremony of "Opening the mouth."[1]

The Kher-heb priest touching the statue of the deceased with the *urhekau* instrument to effect the "opening of the mouth." (From the *Papyrus of Ani*, plate 15.)

## 16. The Amulet of the Menat, 𓈙

This amulet was in use in Egypt as early as the VIth dynasty, and it was worn or held or carried with the sistrum by gods, kings, priests, priestesses, etc.; usually it is held in the hand, but it is often worn on the neck. Its object was to bring joy and health to the wearer, and it was believed to possess magical properties; it represented nutrition[2] and

[1] See the description of this ceremony in Chapter VI.

[2] *Menat* is connected with the root from which the word for "nurse" (*menāt*) is derived; see the article by Lefébure, "Le Menat et le Nom "de l'Eunuque" in *Proc. Soc. Bibl. Arch.*, 1891, p. 333 f.

strength, and the might of the male and female organs of generation, mystically considered, was supposed to be united therein. The amulet is made in bronze, stone, porcelain, and other substances, and when laid upon the body of the dead brought to it the power of life and reproduction.

## 17. The Amulet of the Sam, 𓄤

This amulet is probably intended to represent an organ of the human body, and its use is very ancient; it is made of lapis-lazuli and other hard stone substances, and in the late period is often found in the swathings of mummies. Its primary meaning is "union," and refers to animal pleasure.

## 18. The Amulet of the Shen, 𓍶

This amulet is intended to represent the sun's orbit, and it became the symbol of an undefined period of time, *i.e.*, eternity; it was laid upon the body of the dead with the view of giving to it life which should endure as long as the sun revolved in its orbit in the heavens. In the picture of the mummy chamber[1] the goddesses Isis and Nephthys are seen kneeling and resting their hands on *shen*. Figures of the *shen* were

[1] See *Papyrus of Ani*, 2nd edit., plates 33, 34.

painted upon stelæ, coffins, etc.; as an amulet it is commonly made of lapis-lazuli or carnelian. The amulet of the cartouche  has been supposed to be nothing more than *shen* elongated, but it probably refers to the ordinary meaning of  *i.e.*, "name."

## 19. The Amulet of the Steps, 

This amulet seems to have two meanings: to lift up to heaven, and the throne of Osiris. According to one legend, when the god Shu wished to lift up the goddess Nut from the embrace of the god Seb, so that her body, supported by her stretched-out arms and legs, might form the sky, he found that he was not tall enough to do so; in this difficulty he made use of a flight of steps, and having mounted to the top of these he found himself able to perform his work. In the fourth section of the Elysian Fields[1] three such flights of steps are depicted. In the XXIInd Chapter of the Book of the Dead the deceased prays that he "may "have a portion with him who is on the top of the "steps," *i.e.*, Osiris, and in funeral vignettes this god is seen seated upon the top of a flight of steps and holding his usual symbols of sovereignty and dominion. The amulet of the Steps is usually made of green or blue glazed porcelain.

[1] See *Papyrus of Ani*, 2nd edit., plate 35.

## 20. The Amulet of the Frog, 

This amulet is typical of teeming life and of the resurrection. The frog-headed goddess Heqt, the wife of Khnemu, was associated with the resurrection, and this amulet, when laid upon the body of the dead, was intended to transfer to it her power. The frog is often represented on the upper part of the Greek and Roman terra-cotta lamps which are found in Egypt, and on one of them written in Greek is the legend, "I am the "resurrection."[1]

The amulets described above are those which are most commonly found in the tombs and on mummies, but a few others are also known, *e.g.*,  the White crown of the South,  the Red crown of the North,  the horizon, or place where the sun rises,  an angle, typifying protection,  the horns, disk, and plumes,  or  the plummet, etc. Besides these, any ring, or pendant, or ornament, or any object whatsoever, upon which was inscribed the name of a god or his emblem, or picture, became an amulet with protective powers; and it seems that these powers remained active as long as the substance lasted and as long as the name, or emblem, or picture, was not

[1] See Lanzone, *Dizionario*, p. 853.

erased from it. The use of amulets was common in Egypt from the earliest times to the Roman Period, and when the Egyptians embraced Christianity, they, in common with the Gnostics and semi-Christian sects, imported into their new faith many of the views and beliefs which their so-called heathen ancestors had held, and with them the use of the names of ancient Egyptian gods, and goddesses, and demons, and formulæ, which they employed in much the same way as they were employed in the days of old.

# CHAPTER III.

## MAGICAL FIGURES.

It has been said above that the name or the emblem or the picture of a god or demon could become an amulet with power to protect him that wore it, and that such power lasted as long as the substance of which it was made lasted, if the name, or emblem, or picture was not erased from it. But the Egyptians went a step further than this, and they believed that it was possible to transmit to the *figure* of any man, or woman, or animal, or living creature, the soul of the being which it represented, and its qualities and attributes. The statue of a god in a temple contained the spirit of the god which it represented, and from time immemorial the people of Egypt believed that every statue and every figure possessed an indwelling spirit. When the Christianized Egyptians made their attacks on the "idols of the heathen" they proved that they possessed this belief, for they always endeavoured to throw down the statues of the gods of the Greeks and Romans, knowing that if they were once shattered the spirits which dwelt in them would have no place wherein to dwell, and would thereby be rendered homeless and powerless. It will be remembered that it is stated in the Apocryphal Gospels that when the Virgin Mary and her Son arrived in Egypt there "was a movement and quaking throughout "all the land, and all the idols fell down from their "pedestals and were broken in pieces." Then all the priests and nobles went to a certain priest with whom "a devil used to speak from out of the idol," and they asked him the meaning of these things; and when he had explained to them that the footstep of the son of the "secret and hidden god" had fallen upon the land of Egypt, they accepted his counsel and made a figure of this god. The Egyptians acknowledged that the new god was greater than all their gods together, and they were quite prepared to set up a statue of him because they believed that in so doing they would compel at least a portion of the spirit of the "secret and hidden god" to come and dwell in it. In the following pages we shall endeavour to describe the principal uses which the Egyptians made of the figures of gods, and men, and beasts, to which magical powers had been imparted by means of the performance of certain symbolic ceremonies and the recital of certain words of power; and how they could be employed to do both good and evil.

One of the earliest instances of the use of a magical figure is related in the Westcar Papyrus,[1] where we read that Prince Khāf-Rā told Khufu (Cheops) a story of an event which had happened in the time of Neb-ka or Neb-kau-Rā, a king of the IIIrd dynasty, who reigned about B.C. 3830. It seems that this king once paid a visit to one of his high officials called Āba-aner, whose wife fell violently in love with one of the soldiers in the royal train. This lady sent her tire-woman to him with the gift of a chest of clothes, and apparently she made known to him her mistress's desire, for he returned with her to Āba-aner's house. There he saw the wife and made an appointment to meet her in a little house which was situated on her husband's estate, and she gave instructions to one of the stewards of Āba-aner to prepare it for the arrival of herself and her lover. When all had been made ready she went to the house and stayed there the whole day drinking and making love with the man until sunset; and when the evening had come he rose up and went down to the river and the tirewoman bathed him in the water thereof. But the steward, who had made ready the house, declared that he must make the matter known unto his master, and on the following morning as soon as it was light, he went to Āba-aner and related to him everything which had happened. The official made no answer to his

[1] Ed. Erman, pp. 7 and 8.

servant's report, but ordered him to bring him certain materials and his box made of ebony and precious metal. Out of the box he took a quantity of wax, which was, no doubt, kept there for purposes similar to that to which a portion of it was now to be put, and made a model of a crocodile seven spans long, and then reciting certain magical words over it, he said, "When the man cometh down to bathe in "my waters seize thou him." Then, turning to the steward, he gave the wax crocodile to him and said, "When the man, according to his daily wont, "cometh down to wash in the water thou shalt cast "the crocodile in after him"; and the steward having taken the wax crocodile from his master went his way.

And again the wife of Āba-aner ordered the steward who had charge of the estate to make ready the house which was in the garden, "for," she said, "behold, I "am coming to pass some time therein." So the house was made ready and provided with all good things, and she came with the man and passed some time with him there. Now when the evening was come the man went down to the water to wash according to his daily wont, and the steward went down after him and threw into the water the wax crocodile, which straightway turned into a living crocodile seven cubits (*i.e.*, about twelve feet) in length, and seized upon the man and dragged him down in the water.

Meanwhile Āba-aner tarried with his king Neb-kau-Rā for seven days, and the man remained in the depths of the water and had no air to breathe. And on the seventh day Āba-aner the *kher heb*[1] went out with the king for a walk, and invited His Majesty to come and see for himself a wonderful thing which had happened to a man in his own days; so the king went with him. When they had come to the water Āba-aner adjured the crocodile, saying, "Bring hither the man," and the crocodile came out of the water bringing the man with him. And when the king remarked that the crocodile was a horrid looking monster, Āba-aner stooped down and took it up into his hand, when it straightway became a waxen crocodile as it was before. After these things Āba-aner related to the king what had happened between his wife and the man whom the crocodile had brought up out of the water, whereupon the king said to the crocodile, "Take that which "is thine and begone"; and immediately the crocodile seized the man and sprang into the water with him, and disappeared in its depths. And by the royal command Āba-aner's wife was seized, and having been led to the north side of the palace was burnt, and her ashes were cast into the stream. Here then we have already in the IIIrd dynasty the existence of a belief that a wax crocodile, over which certain words

[1] *I.e.*, the priestly official who performed the most important of the funeral ceremonies; he was always a man of great learning, and generally of high rank.

had been said, could change itself into a living reptile at pleasure, and that a man could be made by the same means to live at the bottom of a stream for seven days without air. We may also notice that the great priestly official, the *kher heb,* was so much in the habit of performing such acts of magic that he kept in a room a box of materials and instruments always ready for the purpose; and, apparently, neither himself, nor his king, nor his servant, thought the working of magic inconsistent with his high religious office.

But at the time when Āba-aner was working magic by means of wax figures, probably to the harm and injury of his enemies, the priests were making provision for the happiness and well-being of the dead also by means of figures made of various substances. According to one very early belief the dead made their way to a region called Sekhet-Aaru, where they led a life which was not very different from that which they had led upon earth. From the pictures of this place which are painted on coffins of the XIth dynasty, we see that it was surrounded by streams of water, and that it was intersected by canals, and that, in fact, it was very much like an ordinary well-kept estate in the Delta. The beings who lived in this place, however, had the same wants as human beings, that is to say, they needed both food and drink, or bread-cakes and ale. The existence of bread and ale presupposed the existence of wheat and barley, and the production of these presupposed the tilling of the ground and the work of agricultural labourers. But the Egyptian had no wish to continue the labours of ploughing and reaping and preparing the ground for the new crops in the world beyond the grave, therefore he endeavoured to avoid this by getting the work done vicariously. If words of power said over a figure could make it to do evil, similarly words of power said over a figure could make it to do good. At first a formula[1] was composed, the recital of which was supposed to relieve the deceased from the necessity of doing any work whatsoever, and when the deceased himself had said, "I lift up the hand of the man who is inactive. "I have come from the city of Unnu (Hermopolis). "I am the divine Soul which liveth, and I lead with "me the hearts of the apes," his existence was thought to be without toil. But, since the inhabitants of Sekhet-Aaru needed food and drink, provision must be made for their production, and the necessary labours of the field must, in some manner, be performed. To meet the difficulty a small stone figure of the deceased was buried with him, but before it was laid in the tomb the priests recited over it the words of power which would cause it to do for the deceased whatever work he might be adjudged to perform in the kingdom of Osiris. Later, these words were inscribed upon the figure in hieroglyphics, and later still the figure was

[1] *I.e.*, Chapter V. of the Book of the Dead.

provided with representations of the rope basket, and plough , and flail , such as were employed by the Egyptian labourer in carrying field produce, and in ploughing, and in threshing grain. The formula[1] or words of power which were inscribed on such figures varied at different periods, but one of the oldest, which was in use in the XVIIIth dynasty, makes the deceased say to the figure, which was called "Shabti":—

"O thou Shabti figure of the scribe Nebseni, if I "be called, or if I be adjudged to do any work what-"soever of the labours which are to be done in the "underworld by a man in his turn—behold, any "obstacles (*or* opposition) to thee will be done away "with there—let the judgment fall upon thee instead "of upon me always, in the matter of sowing the fields, "of filling the water-courses with water, and of bringing "the sands from the east to the west." After these words comes the answer by the figure, "Verily I am "here, and [will do] whatsoever thou biddest me to "do." The Egyptians were most anxious to escape the labours of top-dressing[2] the land, and of sowing the seed, a work which had to be done by a man standing in water in the sun, and the toilsome task of working the *shadûf*, or instrument for raising water

[1] *I.e.*, Chapter V. of the Book of the Dead.

[2] This is, I think, the meaning of bringing the sand from the east to the west.

from the Nile and turning it on to the land. In graves not one figure only is found, but several, and it is said that in the tomb of Seti I., king of Egypt about B.C. 1370, no less than seven hundred wooden *ushabtiu* inscribed with the VIth Chapter of the Book of the Dead, and covered with bitumen, were found. The use of the *shabti* figure continued unabated down to the Roman period, when boxes full of ill-shaped, uninscribed porcelain figures were buried in the tombs with the dead.

The next instance worth mentioning of the use of magical figures we obtain from the official account of a conspiracy against Rameses III., king of Egypt about B.C. 1200. It seems that a number of high officials, the Overseer of the Treasury included, and certain scribes, conspired together against this king, apparently with the view of dethroning him. They took into their counsels a number of the ladies attached to the court (some think they belonged to the *harîm*), and the chief abode of these ladies became the headquarters of the conspirators. One official was charged with "carrying abroad their words to their mothers "and sisters who were there to stir up men and to "incite malefactors to do wrong to their lord"; another was charged with aiding and abetting the conspiracy by making himself one with the ringleaders; another was charged with being cognizant of the whole matter, and with concealing his knowledge of it; another with "giving ear to the conversation held by the men con-"spiring with the women of the Per-khent, and not "bringing it forward against them," and so on. The conspiracy soon extended from Egypt to Ethiopia, and a military official of high rank in that country was drawn into it by his sister, who urged him to "Incite "the men to commit crime, and do thou thyself come "to do wrong to thy lord"; now the sister of this official was in the Per-khent, and so she was able to give her brother the latest information of the progress of the disaffection. Not content with endeavouring to dethrone the king by an uprising of both soldiers and civilians, Hui, a certain high official, who was the overseer of the [royal] cattle, bethought him of applying magic to help their evil designs, and with this object in view he went to some one who had access to the king's library, and he obtained from him a book containing formulæ of a magical nature, and directions for working magic. By means of this book he obtained "divine power," and he became able to cast spells upon folk. Having gained possession of the book he next looked out for some place where he could carry on his magical work without interruption, and at length found one. Here he set to work to make figures of men in wax, and amulets inscribed with words of magical power which would provoke love, and these he succeeded in introducing into the royal palace by means of the official Athirmā; and it seems as if those who took them into the palace and those who received them were under the magical influence of Hui. It is probable that the love philtres were intended for the use of the ladies who were involved in the conspiracy, but as to the object of the wax figures there is no doubt, for they were intended to work harm to the king. Meanwhile Hui studied his magical work with great diligence, and he succeeded in finding efficacious means for carrying out all the "horrible things and all the wickednesses "which his heart could imagine"; these means he employed in all seriousness, and at length committed great crimes which were the horror of every god and goddess, and the punishment of such crimes was death. In another place Hui is accused of writing books or formulæ of magical words, the effect of which would be to drive men out of their senses, and to strike terror into them; and of making gods of wax and figures of men of the same substance, which should cause the human beings whom they represented to become paralysed and helpless. But their efforts were in vain, the conspiracy was discovered, and the whole matter was carefully investigated by two small courts of enquiry, the members of which consisted, for the most part, of the king's personal friends; the king's orders to them were that "those who are guilty shall "die by their own hands, and tell me nothing whatever "about it." The first court, which consisted of six members, sat to investigate the offences of the husbands and relatives of the royal ladies, and those of the ladies themselves, but before their business was done three of them were arrested because it was found that the ladies had gained great influence over them, that they and the ladies had feasted together, and that they had ceased to be, in consequence, impartial judges. They were removed from their trusted positions before the king, and having been examined and their guilt clearly brought home to them, their ears and noses were cut off as a punishment and warning to others not to form friendships with the enemies of the king. The second court, which consisted of five members, investigated the cases of those who were charged with having "stirred up men and incited malefactors to do wrong "to their lord," and having found them guilty they sentenced six of them to death, one by one, in the following terms:—"Pentaura, who is also called by "another name. He was brought up on account of the "offence which he had committed in connexion with "his mother Thi when she formed a conspiracy with "the women of the Per-khent, and because he had "intent to do evil unto his lord. He was brought "before the court of judges that he might receive "sentence, and they found him guilty, and dismissed "him to his own death, where he suffered death by "his own hand." The wretched man Hui, who made wax figures and spells with the intent to inflict pain and suffering and death upon the king, was also compelled to commit suicide.[1]

The above story of the famous conspiracy against Rameses III. is most useful as proving that books of magic existed in the Royal Library, and that they were not mere treatises on magical practices, but definite works with detailed instructions to the reader how to perform the ceremonies which were necessary to make the formulæ or words of power efficacious. We have now seen that wax figures were used both to do good and to do harm, from the IIIrd to the XXth dynasty, and that the ideas which the Egyptians held concerning them were much the same about B.C. 1200 as they were two thousand five hundred years earlier; we have also seen that the use of *ushabtiu* figures, which were intended to set the deceased free from the necessity of labour in the world beyond the grave, was widespread. That such figures were used in the pre-dynastic days when the Egyptians were slowly emerging into civilization from a state of semi-barbarism is not to be wondered at, and it need not surprise us that they existed as a survival in the early dynasties before the people generally had realized that the great powers of Nature, which they deified, could not be ruled by man and by his petty words and deeds, however mysterious and solemn. It is, however, very remarkable to find

[1] See Devéria, *Le Papyrus Judiciaire de Turin* in *Journal Asiatique*, 1865; and Chabas, *Le Papyrus Magique Harris*, p. 169 ff.

that the use of wax figures played a prominent part in certain of the daily services which were performed in the temple of the god Amen-Rā at Thebes, and it is still more remarkable that these services were performed at a time when the Egyptians were renowned among the nations of the civilized world for their learning and wisdom. One company of priests attached to the temple was employed in transcribing hymns and religious compositions in which the unity, power, and might of God were set forth in unmistakable terms, and at the same time another company was engaged in performing a service the object of which was to free the Sun, which was deified under the form of Rā, and was the type and symbol of God upon earth, from the attacks of a monster called Āpep!

It will be remembered that the XXXIXth Chapter of the Book of the Dead is a composition which was written with the object of defeating a certain serpent, to which many names are given, and of delivering the deceased from his attacks. In it we have a description of how the monster is vanquished, and the deceased says to him, "Rā maketh thee to turn back, O thou "that art hateful to him; he looketh upon thee, get "thee back. He pierceth thy head, he cutteth through "thy face, he divideth thy head at the two sides of the "ways, and it is crushed in his land; thy bones are "smashed in pieces, thy members are hacked from off "thee, and the god Aker hath condemned thee, O Āpep, "thou enemy of Rā. Get thee back, Fiend, before the "darts of his beams! Rā hath overthrown thy words, "the gods have turned thy face backwards, the Lynx "hath torn open thy breast, the Scorpion hath cast "fetters upon thee, and Maāt hath sent forth thy "destruction. The gods of the south, and of the north, "of the west, and of the east, have fastened chains upon "him, and they have fettered him with fetters; the god "Rekes hath overthrown him, and the god Hertit hath "put him in chains."[1] The age of this composition is unknown, but it is found, with variants, in many of the copies of the Book of the Dead which were made in the XVIIIth dynasty. Later, however, the ideas in it were developed, the work itself was greatly enlarged, and at the time of the Ptolemies it had become a book called "The Book of Overthrowing Āpep," which contained twelve chapters. At the same time another work bearing the same title also existed; it was not divided into chapters, but it contained two versions of the history of the Creation, and a list of the evil names of Āpep, and a hymn to Rā.[2] Among the chapters of the former work was one entitled, "Chapter of putting the "fire upon Āpep," which reads, "Fire be upon thee, "Āpep, thou enemy of Rā! The Eye of Horus prevails "over the accursed soul and shade of Āpep, and the

[1] See *Chapters of Coming Forth by Day*, p. 89.

[2] I have given a hieroglyphic transcript of both works, with translations, in *Archæologia*, Vol. LII.

"flame of the Eye of Horus shall gnaw into that enemy "of Rā; and the flame of the Eye of Horus shall consume all the enemies of the Mighty God, life! "strength! health! both in death and in life. When "Āpep is given to the flame," says the rubric, "thou "shalt say these words of power:—Taste thou death, "O Āpep, get thee back, retreat, O enemy of Rā, fall "down, be repulsed, get back and retreat! I have "driven thee back, and I have cut thee in pieces.

"Rā triumphs over Āpep. Taste thou death, Āpep.
"Rā triumphs over Āpep. Taste thou death, Āpep.
"Rā triumphs over Āpep. Taste thou death, Āpep.
"Rā triumphs over Āpep. Taste thou death, Āpep."

These last sentences were said four times, that is to say, once for each of the gods of the cardinal points. The text continues, "Back, Fiend, an end to thee! "Therefore have I driven flame at thee, and therefore "have I made thee to be destroyed, and therefore have "I adjudged thee to evil. An end, an end to thee! "Taste thou death! An end to thee! Thou shalt never "rise again." Such are the words of power, and these are followed by the directions for performing the ceremony, which read thus:—

"If thou wouldst destroy Āpep, thou shalt say this "chapter over a figure of Āpep which hath been drawn "in green colour upon a sheet of new papyrus, and over "a wax figure[1] of Āpep upon which his name hath been "cut and inlaid with green colour; and thou shalt lay "them upon the fire so that it may consume the enemy "of Rā. And thou shalt put such a figure on the fire "at dawn, and another at noon, and another at even- "tide when Rā setteth in the land of life, and another "at midnight, and another at the eighth hour of the "day, and another towards evening; [and if necessary] "thou mayest do thus every hour during the day and "the night, and on the days of the festivals . . . and "every day. By means of this Āpep, the enemy of Rā, "shall be overthrown in the shower, for Rā shall shine "and Āpep shall indeed be overthrown." And the papyrus and the figure "having been burnt in a fire "made of *khesau* grass, the remains thereof shall be "mixed with excrement and thrown upon a fire; thou "shalt do this at the sixth hour of the night, and at "dawn on the fifteenth day [of the month]. And "when the figure of Āpep is placed in the fire thou "shalt spit upon him several times each hour during "the day, until the shadow turneth round. Thou shalt "do these things when tempests rage in the east of the "sky as Rā setteth, in order to prevent the coming "onward of the storms. Thou shalt do this and so

[1] Theocritus has preserved for us a proof that the Greeks made use of wax figures at an early date. Thus in *Pharmakeutria* (l. 27 ff.) the lady spinning her wheel and addressing the Lynx says, "Even as I "melt this wax, with the god to aid, so speedily may he by love be "molten!" (Lang's *Translation*, p. 12).

"prevent the coming of a shower or a rain-storm, and "thereby shall the sun be made to shine."

In another part of this book the reciter is told to say the following "firmly with the mouth":—"Down "upon thy face, O Āpep, enemy of Rā! The flame "which cometh forth from the Eye of Horus advanceth "against thee. Thou art thrust down into the flame "of fire and it cometh against thee. Its flame is deadly "to thy soul, and to thy spirit, and to thy words of "power, and to thy body, and to thy shade. The lady "of fire prevaileth over thee, the flame pierceth thy "soul, it maketh an end of thy person, and it darteth "into thy form. The eye of Horus which is powerful "against its enemy hath cast thee down, it devoureth "thee, the great fire trieth thee, the Eye of Rā prevaileth "over thee, the flame devoureth thee, and what escapeth "from it hath no being. Get thee back, for thou art "cut asunder, thy soul is shrivelled up, thy accursed "name is buried in oblivion, and silence is upon it, "and it hath fallen [out of remembrance]. Thou hast "come to an end, thou hast been driven away, and "thou art forgotten, forgotten, forgotten," etc. To make these words to be of effect the speaker is told to write the names of Āpep upon a new papyrus and to burn it in the fire either when Rā is rising, or at noon, or at sunset, etc. In another part of the work, after a series of curses which are ordered to be said over Āpep, the rubric directs that they shall be recited by a person who hath washed himself and is ceremonially clean, and when this has been done he is to write in green colour upon a piece of new papyrus the names of all the fiends who are in the train of Āpep, as well as those of their fathers, and mothers, and children. He must then make figures of all these fiends in wax, and having inscribed their names upon them, must tie them up with black hair, and then cast them on the ground and kick them with the left foot, and pierce them with a stone spear; this done they are to be thrown into the fire. More than once is it said, "It "is good for a man to recite this book before the august "god regularly," for the doing of it was believed to give great power "to him, both upon earth and in the "underworld." Finally, after the names of Āpep are enumerated, he who would benefit by the knowledge of them is bidden to "make the figure of a serpent "with his tail in his mouth, and having stuck a knife "in his back, cast him down upon the ground and say, "'Āpep, Fiend, Ḅetet.'" Then, in order to destroy the fiends who are in the train of Āpep, other images or figures of them must be made with their hands tied behind them; these are to be called "Children of "inactivity." The papyrus then continues, "Make "another serpent with the face of a cat, and with a "knife stuck in his back, and call it 'Hemhem' "(Roarer). Make another with the face of a croco-"dile, and with a knife stuck in his back, and call it

"'Hauna-aru-her-hra.' Make another with the face of "a duck, and with a knife stuck in his back, and call it "'Aluti.' Make another with the face of a white cat, and "with a knife stuck in his back, and tie it up and bind "it tightly, and call it 'Āpep the Enemy.'" Such are the means which the Egyptians adopted when they wanted to keep away rain and storm, thunder and lightning, and mist and cloud, and to ensure a bright clear sky wherein the sun might run his course.

Under the heading of "Magical Figures" must certainly be included the so-called Ptah-Seker-Ausar figure which is usually made of wood; it is often solid, but is sometimes made hollow, and is usually let into a rectangular wooden stand which may be either solid or hollow. The three gods or trinity of Ptah, Seker (Socharis), and Ausar (Osiris), are intended to represent the god of the sunrise (Ptah), the god of the night sun (Seker), and the god of the resurrection (Osiris). The name Ptah means "Opener," and is usually applied to the sun as the "opener" of the day; and the name Seker means "He who is shut in," that is to say, the night sun, who was regarded as the sun buried temporarily. Now the life of a man upon earth was identified with that of the sun; he "opened" or began his life as Ptah, and after death he was "shut "in" or "coffined," like it also. But the sun rises again when the night is past, and, as it begins a new life with renewed strength and vigour, it became the type of the new life which the Egyptian hoped to live in the world beyond the grave. But the difficulty was how to obtain the protection of Ptah, Seker, and Osiris, and how to make them do for the man that which they did for themselves, and so secure their attributes. To attain this end a figure was fashioned in such a way as to include the chief characteristics of the forms of these gods, and was inserted in a rectangular wooden stand which was intended to represent the coffin or chest out of which the trinity Ptah-Seker-Ausar came forth. On the figure itself and on the sides of the stand were inscribed prayers on behalf of the man for whom it was made, and the Egyptian believed that these prayers caused the might and powers of the three gods to come and dwell in the wooden figure. But in order to make the stand of the figure as much like a coffin as possible, a small portion of the body of the deceased was carefully mummified and placed in it, and it was thought that if the three gods protected and preserved that piece, and if they revivified it in due season, the whole body would be protected, and preserved, and revivified. Frequently, especially in the late period, a cavity was made in the side of the stand, and in this was laid a small roll of papyrus inscribed with the text of certain Chapters of the Book of the Dead, and thus the deceased was provided with additional security for the resurrection of his spiritual body in the world to come. The little rolls of papyrus are often inscribed with but short and fragmentary texts, but occasionally, as in the case of the priestess Anhai, a fine large papyrus,[1] inscribed with numerous texts and illustrated with vignettes, was placed inside the figure of the god, who in this instance is in the form of Osiris only.[2] It seems that the Ptah-Seker-Ausar figure was much used in the late period in Egypt, for many inscribed examples have been found which are not only illegible, but which prove that the artist had not the remotest idea of the meaning of the things which he was writing. It is possible that they were employed largely by the poor, among whom they seem to have served the purpose of the costly tomb.

Returning once more to the subject of wax figures, it may be wondered why such a very large proportion of the figures of the gods which were worn by the living and attached to the bodies of the dead as amulets are made of almost every kind of substance except wax. But the reason of this is not far to seek: wax is a substance which readily changes its form under heat and pressure, and it is also possible that the fact of its having been employed from time immemorial for making figures which were intended to work harm and not good to man, induced those who made amulets in the forms of the gods to select some other material. As a matter of fact, however, several figures of gods

[1] This papyrus is preserved in the British Museum (No. 10,472).
[2] British Museum, No. 20,868.

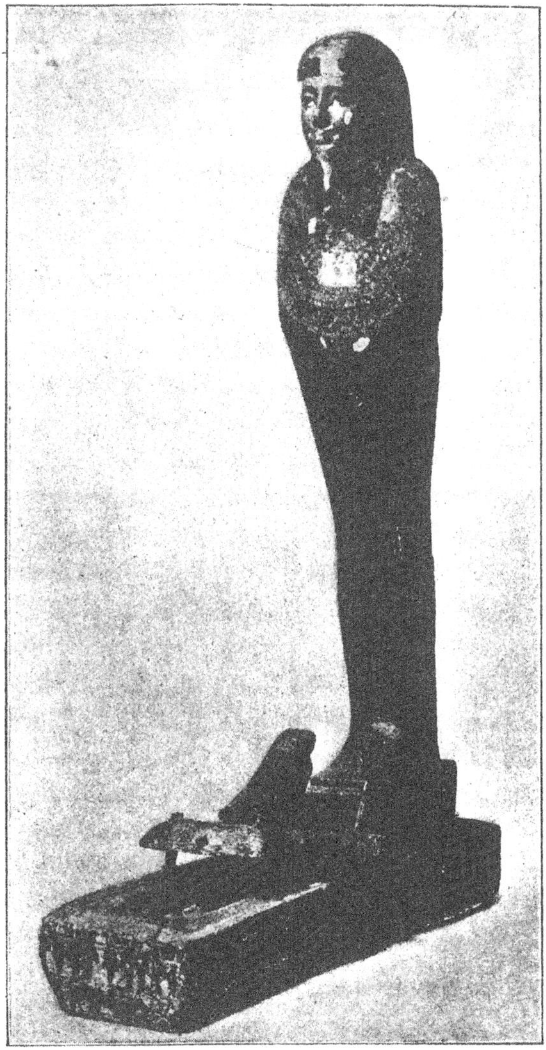

Ptah-Seker-Ausar figure with cavity containing a portion of a human body mummified.
(British Museum, No. 9736.)

made of wax to serve as protective amulets are known, and a set of four, representing the four children of Horus, now preserved in the British Museum, are worthy of notice. The four children of Horus, or the gods of the four cardinal points, were called Mestha, Hāpi, Tuamutef, and Qebhsennuf, and with them were associated the goddesses Isis, Nephthys, Neith, and Serqet respectively. Mestha was man-headed, and represented the south, and protected the stomach and large intestines; Hāpi was dog-headed, and represented the north, and protected the small intestines; Tuamutef was jackal-headed, and represented the east, and protected the lungs and the heart; and Qebhsennuf was hawk-headed, and represented the west, and protected the liver and the gall-bladder. The various internal organs of men were removed from the body before it was mummified, and having been steeped in certain astringent substances and bitumen were wrapped up in bandages, and laid in four jars made of stone, marble, porcelain, earthenware, or wood. Each jar was placed under the protection of one of the four children of Horus, and as it was hollow, and its cover was made in the form of the head of the god who was represented by it, and as the jar by means of the inscription upon it became an abode of the god, it might well be said that the organ of the deceased which was put in it was actually placed inside the god. The custom of embalming the intestines separately is very old, and several examples of it in the XIth dynasty are known; even at that early period the four jars of mummified intestines were placed in a funeral chest, or coffer, which was mounted on a sledge, and drawn along in the funeral procession immediately after the coffin. In later times we find that many attempts were made to secure for the deceased the benefit of the protection of these four gods without incurring the expense of

The Four Children of Horus.

Hāpi. Mestha. Tuamutef. Qebhsennuf.

Osiris rising from the funeral chest holding the symbol of "life" in each hand. (From the *Papyrus of Ani*, plate 8.)

stone jars; this could be done by burying with him four models or "dummy" jars, or four porcelain figures of the four gods, , or four wax ones. For some unknown reason the set referred to above was made of wax.[1] The four children of Horus played a

[1] Nos. 15,563, 15,564, 15,573, and 15,578 in the Second Egyptian Room.

very important part in the funeral works of the early dynasties; they originally represented the four supports of heaven, but very soon each was regarded as the god of one of the four quarters of the earth, and also of that quarter of the heavens which was above it. As the constant prayer of the deceased was that he should be able to go about wherever he pleased, both on earth and in heaven, it was absolutely necessary for his welfare that he should propitiate these gods and place himself under their protection, which could only be secured by the recital of certain words of power over figures of them, or over jars made to represent them.

But of all the Egyptians who were skilled in working magic, Nectanebus, the last native king of Egypt, about B.C. 358, was the chief, if we may believe Greek tradition. According to Pseudo-Callisthenes, and the versions of his works which were translated into Pehlevi, Arabic, Syriac, and a score of other languages and dialects, this king was famous as a magician and a sage, and he was deeply learned in all the wisdom of the Egyptians. He knew what was in the depths of the Nile and of heaven, he was skilled in reading the stars, in interpreting omens, in casting nativities, in telling fortunes, and in predicting the future of the unborn child, and in working magic of every kind, as we shall see; he was said to be the lord of the earth, and to rule all kings by means of his magical powers.

Whenever he was threatened with invasion by sea or by land he succeeded in destroying the power of his enemies, and in driving them from his coasts or frontiers; and this he did by the following means. If the enemy came against him by sea, instead of sending out his sailors to fight them, he retired into a certain chamber, and having brought forth a bowl which he kept for the purpose, he filled it with water, and then, having made wax figures of the ships and men of the enemy, and also of his own men and ships, he set them upon the water in the bowl, his men on one side, and those of the enemy on the other. He then came out, and having put on the cloak of an Egyptian prophet and taken an ebony rod in his hand, he returned into the chamber, and uttering words of power he invoked the gods who help men to work magic, and the winds, and the subterranean demons, which straightway came to his aid. By their means the figures of the men in wax sprang into life and began to fight, and the ships of wax began to move about likewise; but the figures which represented his own men vanquished those which represented the enemy, and as the figures of the ships and men of the hostile fleet sank through the water to the bottom of the bowl, even so did the real ships and men sink through the waters to the bottom of the sea. In this way he succeeded in maintaining his power, and he continued to occupy his kingdom in peace for a considerable period. But it fell out on a day that certain scouts came and informed Nectanebus that a multitude of the nations of the East had made a league together against Egypt, and that their allied forces were at that moment marching against him. When the king heard the news he laughed, and having said some scornful words about his enemies, he went into his private chamber, and pouring water into the bowl began to work magic in the usual way. But when he had spoken the words of power, he looked at the wax figures, and saw, to his dismay, that the gods of Egypt were steering the enemies' ships, and leading their soldiers to war against himself. Now as soon as Nectanebus saw this, he understood that the end of the kingdom of Egypt was at hand, for hitherto the gods had been wont to hold converse with him readily, and to lend him their help whenever he had need of it. He then quitted the chamber hastily, and having shaved off his hair and his beard, and disguised himself by putting on common apparel, he took ship and fled to Pella in Macedonia, where he established himself as a physician, and as an Egyptian soothsayer.

Omitting, for the present, any reference to the contents of the IVth chapter of Pseudo-Callisthenes, in which the casting of the nativity of Olympias by Nectanebus is described, we come to the passage in which the story of the way in which he sent a dream to the queen by means of a wax figure is told. His object was to persuade the queen that the Egyptian god Amen would come to her at night. To do this he left her presence, and going out into the desert he collected a number of herbs which he knew how to employ in causing people to dream dreams, and having brought them back with him he squeezed the juice out of them. He then made the figure of a woman in wax, and wrote upon it the name of Olympias, just as the priest of Thebes made the figure of Āpep ỉn wax and cut his name upon it. Nectanebus then lit his lamp, and, having poured the juice of the herbs over the wax figure of the queen, he adjured the demons to such purpose that Olympias dreamed a dream in which the god Amen came to her and embraced her, and told her that she should give birth to a man-child who should avenge her on her husband Philip. But the means described above were not the only ones known to Nectanebus for procuring dreams, for when he wanted to make Philip of Macedon to see certain things in a dream, and to take a certain view about what he saw, he sent a hawk, which he had previously bewitched by magical words, to Philip as he lay asleep, and in a single night the hawk flew from Macedonia to the place where Philip was, and coming to him told him what things he should see in his dream, and he saw them. On the morrow Philip had the dream explained by an expounder of dreams, and he was satisfied that the child[1] to whom his wife Olympias was about to give birth was the son of the god Amen (or Ammon) of Libya, who was regarded as the father of all the kings who ascended the throne of Egypt, who did not belong to the royal stock of that country.[2]

Here, in connexion with the Egyptian use of wax figures, must be mentioned one or two stories and traditions of Alexander the Great which are, clearly, derived from Egyptian sources. The Arab writer, Abu-Shâker, who flourished in the XIIIth century of our era, mentions a tradition that Aristotle gave to Alexander a number of wax figures nailed down in a box, which was fastened by a chain, and which he ordered him never to let go out of his hand, or at least out of that of one of his confidential servants. The box was to go wherever Alexander went, and Aristotle taught him to recite certain formulæ over it whenever he took it up or put it down. The figures in the box were intended to represent the various kinds of armed forces that Alexander was likely to find opposed to him. Some of the models held in their hands leaden swords which were curved backwards, and some had spears in their hands pointed head downwards, and some had bows with cut strings ; all these were laid face downwards in the box. Viewed by what we

[1] *I.e.*, Alexander the Great.
[2] For further mention of dreams, see the last chapter in this book.

know of the ideas which underlay the use of wax figures by the Egyptians and Greeks, it is clear that, in providing Alexander with these models and the words of power to use with them, Aristotle believed he was giving him the means of making his enemies to become like the figures in the box, and so they would be powerless to attack him.[1]

In the Græco-Roman period[2] wax figures were used in the performance of magical ceremonies of every kind, and the two following examples indicate that the ideas which underlay their use had not changed in the least. If a lover wished to secure the favours of his mistress, he is directed to make a figure of a dog in wax mixed with pitch, gum, etc., eight fingers long, and certain words of power are to be written over the place where his ribs should be. Next it was necessary to write on a tablet other words of power, or the names of beings who were supposed to possess magical powers; on this tablet the figure of the dog must be placed, and the tablet is made to rest upon a tripod. When this has been done the lover must recite the words of power which are written on the dog's side, and also the names which have been inscribed on the tablet, and one of two things will happen: *i.e.*, the dog will either snarl

[1] See my *Life and Exploits of Alexander the Great* (one volume edition), p. xvi.

[2] The Greeks used incantations at an early date, as we may see from Pindar, *Pythia*, iv. 213; this writer lived in the first half of the fifth century before Christ.

and snap at the lover, or he will bark. If he snarls and snaps the lover will not gain the object of his affections, but if he barks the lady will come to him. In the second example the lover is ordered to make two waxen figures; one in the form of Ares, and the other in the form of a woman. The female figure is to be in the posture of kneeling upon her knees with her hands tied behind her, and the male figure is to stand over her with his sword at her throat. On the limbs of the female figure a large number of the names of demons are to be written, and when this has been done, the lover must take thirteen bronze needles, and stick them in her limbs, saying as he does so, "I pierce" (here he mentions the name of the limb) "that she may think of "me." The lover must next write certain words of power on a leaden plate, which must be tied to the wax figures with a string containing three hundred and sixty-five knots, and both figure and plate are to be buried in the grave of some one who has died young or who has been slain by violence. He must then recite a long incantation to the infernal gods, and if all these things be done in a proper manner the lover will obtain the woman's affections.[1]

From Egypt, by way of Greece and Rome, the use of

[1] I owe the facts of these two examples of the use of wax figures and the two spells for procuring visions and dreams (see p. 96), and the example of the use of the sphere of Democritus (p. 230), to Mr. F. G. Kenyon, Assistant Keeper in the Dept. of MSS., British Museum.

wax figures passed into Western Europe and England, and in the Middle Ages it found great favour with those who interested themselves in the working of the "black "art," or who wished to do their neighbour or enemy an injury. Many stories are current of how in Italy and England ignorant or wicked-minded people made models of their enemies in wax and hung them up in the chimney, not too close to the fire, so that they might melt away slowly, and of how the people that were represented by such figures gradually lost the power over their limbs, and could not sleep, and slowly sickened and died. If pins and needles were stuck into the wax figures at stated times the sufferings of the living were made more agonizing, and their death much more painful.

Sharpe relates[1] that about the end of the VIIth century king Duffus was so unpopular that "a company "of hags roasted his image made of wax upon a wooden "spit, reciting certain words of enchantment, and basting "the figure with a poisonous liquor. These women when "apprehended declared that as the wax melted, the body "of the king should decay, and the words of enchant-"ment prevented him from the refreshment of sleep." The two following extracts from Thomas Middleton's *The Witch*[2] illustrate the views held about wax figures in England in the time of this writer.[3]

[1] See C. K. Sharpe, *Witchcraft in Scotland*, London, 1884, p. 21.
[2] London, 1778. [3] Born about 1570, died about 1626.

I.

"*Heccat.* Is the heart of wax
Stuck full of magique needles?
"*Stadlin.* 'Tis done Heccat.
"*Heccat.* And is the Farmer's picture, and his wives,
Lay'd downe to th' fire yet?
"*Stadlin.* They are a roasting both too.
"*Heccat.* Good:
Then their marrowes are a melting subtelly
And three monethes sicknes sucks up life in 'em."

(Act i., scene 2.)

II.

"*Heccat.* What death is't you desire for Almachildes?
"*Duchesse.* A sodaine and a subtle.
"*Heccat.* Then I have fitted you.
Here lye the guifts of both; sodaine and subtle:
His picture made in wax, and gently molten
By a blew fire kindled with dead mens' eyes
Will waste him by degrees."

(Act v., scene 2.)

Mr. Elworthy in his very interesting book "The "Evil Eye"[1] relates some striking examples of the burning of hearts stuck full of pins for magical purposes

[1] London, 1895, pp. 53, 56.

in recent years. Thus an old woman at Mendip had a pig that fell ill, and she at once made up her mind that the animal had been "overlooked"; in her trouble she consulted a "white witch," *i.e.* a "wise" man, and by his orders she acted thus. She obtained a sheep's heart, and having stuck it full of pins[1] set it to roast before a fire, whilst her friends and neighbours sang:—

> "It is not this heart I mean to burn,
> But the person's heart I wish to turn,
> Wishing them neither rest nor peace
> Till they are dead and gone."

At intervals her son George sprinkled salt on the fire which added greatly to the weirdness of the scene, and at length, when the roasting had been continued until far into the night, a black cat jumped out from somewhere and was, of course, instantly declared to be the demon which had been exorcised. Again, in October, 1882, a heart stuck full of pins was found in a recess of a chimney in an old house in the village of Ashbrittle; and in 1890 another was found nailed up inside the "clavel" in the chimney of an old house at Staplegrove.

The art of making such figures King James I. attributes to the "Divell," and says in describing the

[1] In the North Riding of Yorkshire evil influences were averted by means of a living black cock which "was pierced with pins and "roasted alive at dead of night, with every door, window, and cranny "and crevice stuffed up" (see Blakeborough, *Wit, Character, Folk-lore and Customs of the North Riding of Yorkshire*, London, 1898, p. 205).

things which witches are able to "effectuate by the "power of their master[1]":—"To some others at these "times hee teacheth, how to make pictures of waxe "or clay: That by the roasting thereof, the persons "that they beare the name of, may be continually "melted or dried away by continuall sicknesse. . . . "They can bewitch and take the life of men or women, "by roasting of the pictures, as I spake of before, which "likewise is verie possible to their Maister to performe, "for although (as I said before) that instrument of waxe "have no vertue in that turne doing, yet may hee not "very well, even by the same measure that his conjured "slaves, melts that waxe at the fire, may hee not, I say "at these same times, subtily, as a spirite, so weaken "and scatter the spirites of life of the patient, as may "make him on the one part, for faintnesse, so sweate "out the humour of his bodie: And on the other parte, "for the not concurrence of these spirites, which causes "his digestion, so debilitate his stomacke, that this "humour radicall continually sweating out on the one "part, and no new good sucke being put in the place "thereof, for lacke of digestion on the other, he at last "shall vanish away, even as his picture will die at the "fire? And that knavish and cunning workeman, by "troubling him, onely at sometimes, makes a proportion, "so neere betwixt the working of the one and the other,

[1] The following words are put into the mouth of Epistemon in *Dæmonologie, in Forme of one Dialogue*, London, 1603, Second Booke, Chap. V. pp. 44, 45.

"that both shall end as it were at one time." Thus we have seen that the belief in the efficacy of wax figures is at least six thousand years old, and judging from passages in the works of modern writers its existence is not unknown in our own country at the present time.

This chapter may be fittingly ended by a notice of the benefits which accrued to a Christian merchant in the Levant from the use of a wax figure. According to an Ethiopic manuscript in the British Museum[1] this man was a shipowner as well as a merchant, and he was wont to send his goods to market in his own ships; in his day, however, the sea was infested with pirates, and he lost greatly through their successful attacks upon his vessels. At length he determined to travel in one of his own ships with a number of armed men, so that he might be able to resist any attack which the pirates might make, and punish them for their robberies in times past. Soon after he had sailed he fell in with a pirate vessel, and a fight at once took place between his crew and the robbers, in the course of which he was shot in the eye by an arrow; he stopped the combat and then sailed for a port which was situated near a monastery, wherein the Virgin Mary was reported to work miracles by means of a picture of herself which was hung up in it. When the merchant arrived in port he was so ill through the wound in his eye that he could not be moved, and it was found that a portion

[1] Oriental 646, fol. 29*b* ff.

of the arrow which had struck him remained embedded in it; and unless he could obtain the Virgin's help speedily he felt that his death was nigh. In this difficulty a certain Christian came to the ship and made a wax figure of the merchant, and, having stuck in one eye a model of the arrow which had struck him, carried the figure to the monastery, which was some miles off, and caused the monks to allow him to bring it nigh to the picture of the Virgin. When this had been done, and prayers had been made to her, the figure of the Virgin stretched out its hand, and straightway pulled the model of the arrow out of the eye of the wax figure of the merchant in such a way that no broken fragment remained behind. When the wax figure had been taken back to the ship, it was found that the piece of broken arrow had been extracted from the merchant's eye at the very moment when the Virgin had drawn out the arrow from the eye of the wax figure. The merchant's eye then healed, and he recovered his sight.

## CHAPTER IV.

### MAGICAL PICTURES AND FORMULÆ, SPELLS, ETC.

FROM what has been said above it is clear that the Egyptian believed it possible to vivify by means of formulæ and words of power any figure made in the form of a man or animal, and to make it work either on behalf of or against his fellow man. Besides this, he believed greatly in the efficacy of representations or pictures of the gods, and of divine beings and things, provided that words of power properly recited by properly appointed people were recited over them. If this fact be borne in mind a great many difficulties in understanding religious texts disappear, and many apparently childish facts are seen to have an important meaning. If we look into the tombs of the early period we see painted on the walls numbers of scenes in which the deceased is represented making offerings to the gods and performing religious ceremonies, as well as numbers of others in which he is directing the work of his estate and ruling his household. It was not altogether the result of pride that such pictures were painted on the walls of tombs, for at the bottom of his heart the Egyptian hoped and believed that they were in reality representations of what he would do in the next world, and he trusted that the words of his prayers would turn pictures into realities, and drawings into substances. The wealthy Egyptian left behind him the means for making the offerings which his *ka*,

The goddess Hathor giving the scribe Ani meat and drink from out of a sycamore tree which grows by the side of a stream. (From the *Papyrus of Ani*, plate 16.)

or double, needed, and was able to provide for the maintenance of his tomb and of the *ka* chapel and of the priest or priests who ministered to it. It was an article of faith among all classes that unless the *ka* was properly fed it would be driven to wander about and pick up filth and anything else of that nature which it found in its path, as we may see from the LIInd Chapter of the Book of the Dead, in which the deceased says, "That which is an abomination unto me, that "which is an abomination unto me let me not eat. "That which is an abomination unto me, that which is "an abomination unto me is filth; let me not eat of it "instead of the cakes [which are offered unto] the "Doubles (*kau*). Let it not light upon my body; let "me not be obliged to take it into my hands; and let

The scribe Ani and his wife standing in a stream drinking water.
(From the *Papyrus of Ani*, plate 16.)

"me not be obliged to walk thereon in my sandals." And in the CLXXXIXth Chapter he prays that he may not be obliged to drink filthy water or be defiled in any way by it. The rich man, even, was not certain that the appointed offerings of meat and drink could or would be made in his tomb in perpetuity: what then was the poor man to do to save his *ka* from the ignominy of eating filth and drinking dirty water?

To get out of this difficulty the model of an altar in stone was made, and models of cakes, vases of water, fruit, meat, etc., were placed upon it; in cases where this was not possible figures of the offerings were sculptured upon the stone itself; in others, where even the expense of an altar could not be borne by the relatives of the dead, an altar with offerings painted upon it was placed in the tomb, and as long as it existed through the prayers recited, the *ka* did not lack food. Sometimes neither altar, nor model nor picture of an altar was placed in the tomb, and the prayer that sepulchral meals might be given to the deceased by the gods, which was inscribed upon some article of funeral furniture, was the only provision made for the wants of the *ka;* but every time any one who passed by the tomb recited that prayer, and coupled with it the name of the man who was buried in it, his *ka* was provided with a fresh supply of meat and drink offerings, for the models or pictures of them in the inscription straightway became veritable substances. On the insides of the wooden coffins of the XIIth dynasty, about B.C. 2500, are painted whole series of objects which, in still earlier times, were actually placed in the tombs with the mummy; but little by little men ceased to provide the numerous articles connected with the sepulture of the dead which the old ritual prescribed, and they trusted to the texts and formulæ which they painted on the coffin to turn pictures into substances, and besides the pillow they placed little else in the tomb.

About a thousand years later, when the religious texts which formed the Book of the Dead were written upon papyri instead of coffins, a large number of illustrations or vignettes were added to them; to many of these special importance was attached, and the following are worthy of note.

It will be remembered that the CXXVth Chapter of the Book of the Dead contains the so-called "Negative Confession" which is recited in the Hall of Maāti, and a number of names of gods and beings, the knowledge of which is most important for the welfare of the deceased. At the end of the Chapter we find the following statement:—"This chapter shall be said by "the deceased after he hath been cleansed and purified, "and when he is arrayed in apparel, and is shod with "white leather sandals, and his eyes have been painted "with antimony, and his body hath been anointed with "*ānti* unguent, and when he hath made offerings of "oxen, and birds, and incense, and cakes, and ale, and "garden herbs. And behold, thou shalt paint a picture "of what shall happen in the Hall of Maāti upon a "new tile moulded from earth, upon which neither a "pig nor any other animal hath trodden. And if thou "writest upon it this chapter the deceased shall "flourish; and his children shall flourish; and his "name shall never fall into oblivion; and bread, and "cakes, and sweetmeats, and wine, and meat shall be "given unto him at the altar of the great god; and he "shall not be turned back at any door in the under- "world; and he shall be brought in along with the "Kings of the North and South; and he shall be in "the following of Osiris always and for ever." Here, then, we have an excellent example of the far-reaching effects of a picture accompanied by the proper words of power, and every picture in the Book of the Dead was equally efficacious in producing a certain result, that result being always connected with the welfare of the dead.

According to several passages and chapters the deceased was terrified lest he should lack both air and water, as well as food, in the underworld, and, to do away with all risk of such a calamity happening, pictures, in which he is represented holding a sail (the symbol of air and wind and breath) in his hands, and standing up to his ankles in water,[1] were painted on his papyrus, and texts similar to the following were written below them. "My mouth and my nostrils are "opened in Tattu (Busiris), and I have my place of "peace in Annu (Heliopolis) which is my house; it "was built for me by the goddess Sesheta, and the god "Khnemu set it upon its walls for me. . . ." "Hail, "thou god Tem, grant thou unto me the sweet breath "which dwelleth in thy nostrils! I embrace the great "throne which is in Khemennu (Hermopolis), and I

[1] See the vignettes to Chapters LIV.-LX. of the Book of the Dead.

"keep watch over the Egg of the Great Cackler; I "germinate as it germinateth; I live as it liveth; and "my breath is its breath."[1] But yet another "exceed-"ingly great mystery" had to be performed if the deceased was to be enabled to enter into heaven by its four doors at will, and to enjoy the air which came through each. The north wind belonged to Osiris, the south wind to Rā, the west wind to Isis, and the east wind to Nephthys; and for the deceased to obtain power over each and all of these it was necessary for him to be master of the doors through which they blew. This power could only be obtained by causing pictures of the four doors to be painted on the coffin with a figure of Thoth opening each. Some special importance was attached to these, for the rubric says, "Let none "who is outside know this chapter, for it is a great "mystery, and those who dwell in the swamps (*i.e.*, the "ignorant) know it not. Thou shalt not do this in the "presence of any person except thy father, or thy son, "or thyself alone; for it is indeed an exceedingly great "mystery which no man whatever knoweth."[2]

One of the delights coveted by the deceased was to sail over heaven in the boat of Rā, in company with the gods of the funeral cycle of Osiris; this happiness could be secured for him by painting certain pictures, and by saying over them certain words of power. On

[1] See *Chapters of Coming Forth by Day*, p. 106.
[2] *Ibid.*, p. 289.

a piece of clean papyrus a boat is to be drawn with ink made of green *ābut* mixed with *ānti* water, and in it are to be figures of Isis, Thoth, Shu, and Khepera, and the deceased; when this has been done the papyrus must be fastened to the breast of the deceased, care being taken that it does not actually touch his body. Then shall his spirit enter into the boat of Rā each day, and the god Thoth shall take heed to him, and he shall sail about with Rā into any place that he wisheth.[1] Elsewhere it is ordered that the boat of Rā be painted "in a pure place," and in the bows is to be painted a figure of the deceased; but Rā was supposed to travel in one boat (called "Ātet") until noon, and another (called "Sektet") until sunset, and provision had to be made for the deceased in both boats. How was this to be done? On one side of the picture of the boat a figure of the morning boat of Rā was to be drawn, and on the other a figure of the afternoon boat; thus the one picture was capable of becoming two boats. And, provided the proper offerings were made for the deceased on the birthday of Osiris, his soul would live for ever, and he would not die a second time.[2] According to the rubric to the chapter[3] in which these directions are given, the text of it is as old, at least, as the time of Hesepti, the fifth king of the Ist dynasty, who reigned about B.C. 4350, and the custom of painting the boat upon

[1] See *Chapters of Coming Forth by Day*, p. 162.
[2] *Ibid.*, p. 212. [3] *I.e.*, CXXX.

papyrus is probably contemporaneous. The two following rubrics from Chapters CXXXIII. and CXXXIV., respectively, will explain still further the importance of such pictures:—

1. "This chapter shall be recited over a boat four "cubits in length, and made of green porcelain [on "which have been painted] the divine sovereign chiefs "of the cities; and a figure of heaven with its stars "shall be made also, and this thou shalt have made "ceremonially pure by means of natron and incense. "And behold, thou shalt make an image of Rā in "yellow colour upon a new plaque and set it at the "bows of the boat. And behold, thou shalt make an "image of the spirit which thou dost wish to make "perfect [and place it] in this boat, and thou shalt "make it to travel about in the boat [which shall be "made in the form of the boat] of Rā; and he shall "see the form of the god Rā himself therein. Let not "the eye of any man whatsoever look upon it, with the "exception of thine own self, or thy father, or thy son, "and guard [this] with great care. Then shall the "spirit be perfect in the heart of Rā, and it shall give "unto him power with the company of the gods; and "the gods shall look upon him as a divine being like "unto themselves; and mankind and the dead shall "fall down upon their faces, and he shall be seen in "the underworld in the form of the radiance of Rā."

2. "This chapter shall be recited over a hawk

"standing and having the white crown upon his head, "[and over figures of] the gods Tem, Shu, Tefnut, Seb, "Nut, Osiris, Isis, Suti, and Nephthys, painted in yellow "colour upon a new plaque, which shall be placed in "[a model of] the boat [of Rā], along with a figure of "the spirit whom thou wouldst make perfect. These "thou shalt anoint with cedar oil, and incense shall be "offered up to them on the fire, and feathered fowl,

The soul of the scribe Ani visiting his mummified body as it lies on its bier in the tomb. (From the *Papyrus of Ani*, plate 17.)

"shall be roasted. It is an act of praise to Rā as he "journeyeth, and it shall cause a man to have his being "along with Rā day by day, whithersoever the god "voyageth; and it shall destroy the enemies of Rā in "very truth regularly and continually."

Many of the pictures or vignettes carry their own interpretations with them, *e.g.*, the picture of the soul hovering over the dead body which lies beneath it on the bier at once suggests the reunion of the soul with the body; the picture of the deceased walking away from a "block of slaughter" and a knife dripping with blood suggests escape from a cruel death; the picture of a soul and spirit standing before an open door suggests that the soul has freedom to wander about at will; and the picture of the soul and the shadow in the act of passing out through the door of the tomb indicates clearly that these parts of man's economy are

Anubis holding the mummy of the scribe Ani; by the door of the tomb stand the soul and spirit of the deceased in the form of a human-headed hawk and *bennu* bird respectively. (From the *Papyrus of Ani*, plate 16.)

not shut up in the tomb for all eternity. But the ideas which prompted the painting of other vignettes are not so clear, *e.g.*, those which accompany Chapters CLXII.–CLXV. in the late or Säite Recension of the Book of the Dead, although, fortunately, the rubrics to these chapters make their object clear. Thus the picture which stands above Chapter CLXII. is that of a cow having upon her head horns, a disk, and two plumes, and from the rubric we learn that a figure of it was to be made in gold and fastened to the neck of the deceased, and that another, drawn upon new papyrus, was to be placed under his head. If this be done "then shall abundant warmth be in him throughout, "even like that which was in him when he was upon "earth. And he shall become like a god in the under-

The scribe Ani passing through the door of the tomb; outside are his shadow and his soul in the form of a human-headed bird. (From the *Papyrus of Ani*, plate 18.)

"world, and he shall never be turned back at any of "the gates thereof." The words of the chapter have great protective power (*i.e.*, are a charm of the greatest importance) we are told, "for it was made by the cow "for her son Rā when he was setting, and when his "habitation was surrounded by a company of beings of "fire." Now the cow is, of course, Isis-Hathor, and both the words and the picture refer to some event in the life of Rā, or Horus. It is quite evident that the words of power, or charm, uttered by Isis-Hathor delivered the god out of some trouble, and the idea is that as it delivered the god, and was of benefit to him, even so will it deliver the deceased and be of benefit to him. The words of power read :—"O Amen, O Amen, "who art in heaven, turn thy face upon the dead body "of thy son, and make him sound and strong in the "underworld." And again we are warned that the words are "a great mystery" and that "the eye of no "man whatsoever must see it, for it is a thing of "abomination for [every man] to know it. Hide it, "therefore; the Book of the lady of the hidden temple "is its name."

An examination of mummies of the late period shews that the Egyptians did actually draw a figure of the cow upon papyrus and lay it under the head of the deceased, and that the cow is only one figure among a number of others which were drawn on the same papyrus. With the figures magical texts were inscribed and in course of time, when the papyrus had been mounted upon linen, it superseded the gold figure of the cow which was fastened to the neck of the deceased, and became, strictly speaking, an amulet, though its usual name among archæologists is "hypocephalus." The figure on the opposite page well illustrates the object. It will be noticed that the

**Hypocephalus or object placed under the head of the deceased Shai-enen to keep warmth in the body.**

hypocephalus is round; this is due to the fact that it represents the pupil of the Eye of Horus, which from time immemorial in Egypt was regarded as the source of all generative power, and of reproduction and life. The first group of gods are:--Nehebka offering to Horus his Eye, a goddess with the Eye of Horus for a head, the cow of Isis-Hathor described above, the four children of Horus, two lions, a member of the human body, the pylon of heads of Khnemu the god of reproduction, and Horus-Rā. In the second are the boat of the Sun being poled along by Horus, and the boat of the Moon, with Harpocrates in the bow. In the other scenes we have the god Khepera in his boat, Horus in his boat, and Horus-Sept in his boat. The god with two faces represents the double aspect of the sun in setting and rising, and the god with the rams' heads, who is being adored by apes, is a mystical form of Khnemu, one of the great gods of reproduction, who in still later times became the being whose name under the form of Khnumis or Khnoubis occupied such an important position among the magical names which were in use among the Gnostics. The two following prayers from the hypocephalus will illustrate the words of power addressed to Amen, *i.e.*, the Hidden One, quoted above:—1. "I am the Hidden One in the "hidden place. I am a perfect spirit among the com-"panions of Rā, and I have gone in and come forth "among the perfect souls. I am the mighty Soul of "saffron-coloured form. I have come forth from the "underworld at pleasure. I have come. I have come "forth from the Eye of Horus. I have come forth from "the underworld with Rā from the House of the Great "Aged One in Heliopolis. I am one of the spirits who "come forth from the underworld: grant thou unto "me the things which my body needeth, and heaven "for my soul, and a hidden place for my mummy." 2. "May the god, who himself is hidden, and whose "face is concealed, who shineth upon the world in his "forms of existence, and in the underworld, grant that "my soul may live for ever! May the great god in his "disk give his rays in the underworld of Heliopolis! "Grant thou unto me an entrance and an exit in the "underworld without let or hindrance."

Chapter CLXIII. of the Book of the Dead was written to prevent the body of a man mouldering away in the underworld, and to deliver him from the souls which were so unfortunate as to be shut in the various places thereof, but in order to make it thoroughly efficacious it was ordered to be recited over three pictures: (1) a serpent with legs, having a disk and two horns upon its head; (2) an *utchat*,[1] or Eye of Horus, "in the pupil of which shall be a figure of "the God of the lifted hand with the face of a divine "soul, and having plumes and a back like a hawk"; (3) an *utchat*, or Eye of Horus, "in the pupil of which

[1] See above, p. 55

"there shall be a figure of the God of the lifted hand "with the face of the goddess Neith, and having plumes "and a back like a hawk." If these things be done for the deceased "he shall not be turned back at any "gate of the underworld, he shall eat, and drink, and "perform the natural functions of his body as he did "when he was upon earth; and none shall rise up to "cry out against him; and he shall be protected from "the hands of the enemy for ever and ever." [1]

The words of power which form the CLXIVth Chapter to be effectual had to be recited over a figure of the goddess Mut which was to have three heads. The first head was like that of the goddess Pekhat and had plumes; the second was like that of a man and had upon it the crowns of the South and North; the third was like that of a vulture and had upon it plumes; the figure had a pair of wings, and the claws of a lion. This figure was painted in black, green, and yellow colours upon a piece of *anes* linen; in front of it and behind it was painted a dwarf who wore plumes upon his head. One hand and arm of each dwarf were raised, and each had two faces, one being that of a hawk and the other that of a man; the body of each was fat. These figures having been made, we are told that the deceased shall be "like unto a god with the "gods of the underworld; he shall never, never be "turned back; his flesh and his bones shall be like

[1] See *Chapters of Coming Forth by Day*, p. 292.

"those of one who hath never been dead; he shall drink "water at the source of the stream; a homestead shall "be given unto him in Sekhet-Aaru; he shall become "a star of heaven; he shall set out to do battle with "the serpent fiend Nekau and with Tar, who are in the "underworld; he shall not be shut in along with the "souls which are fettered; he shall have power to "deliver himself wherever he may be; and worms "shall not devour him."[1]

Again, the words of power which form the CLXVth Chapter to be effectual were ordered by the rubric to "be recited over a figure of the God of the lifted hand, "which shall have plumes upon its head; the legs "thereof shall be wide apart, and the middle portion of "it shall be in the form of a beetle, and it shall be "painted blue with a paint made of lapis-lazuli mixed "with *qamai* water. And it shall be recited over a "figure with a head like unto that of a man, and the "hands and the arms thereof shall be stretched away from "his body; above its right shoulder shall there be the "head of a ram, and above its left shoulder shall there "be the head of a ram. And thou shalt paint the "figure of the God of the lifted hand upon a piece of "linen immediately over the heart of the deceased, and "thou shalt paint the other over his breast; but let "not the god Sukati who is in the underworld know "it." If these things be done, "the deceased shall

[1] See *Chapters of Coming Forth by Day*, p. 294.

"drink water from the source of the stream, and he "shall shine like the stars in the heavens above." It is probable that Chapters CLXII.–CLXV. were composed at a comparatively late date.

Yet another example of the magical pictures of the Book of the Dead must here be given. The vignette of Chapter CXLVIII. contains pictures of seven cows "and their bull," and of four rudders; the seven cows have reference to the seven Hathor goddesses, the bull is, of course, a form of Rā, and the four rudders refer to the four quarters of the earth and to the four cardinal points. The text of the Chapter contains the names of the cows and of the bull, and of the rudders, and certain prayers for sepulchral offerings. Now the deceased would be provided with "abundance of food "regularly and continually for ever," if the following things were done for him. Figures of the cows and of their bull and of the rudders were to be painted in colours upon a board (?), and when Rā, the Sun-god, rose upon them the friends of the deceased were to place offerings before them; these offerings would be received mystically by the gods and goddesses whom the figures represented, and in return they would bestow upon the deceased all the offerings or gifts of meat and drink which he would require. Moreover, "if this be done," we are told, "Rā shall be a rudder for "the deceased, and he shall be a strength protecting "him, and he shall make an end of all his enemies for "him in the underworld, and in heaven, and upon "earth, and in every place wherever he may enter."

We have seen above, in the description of the amulets which the Egyptians used, how both the substance of the amulet and the words which were inscribed upon it possessed magical powers, but we may learn from several instances given in the papyri that the written words alone were sufficient in some cases to produce remarkable effects. This is, of course, a very natural development, and charms or words of power which needed nothing but to be written on papyrus or linen to produce a magical effect would be popular with all classes of men and women, and especially among the poor and the ignorant. The written word has been regarded in the East with reverence from time immemorial, and a copy of a sacred writing or text is worn or carried about to this day with much the same ideas and beliefs about its power to protect as in the earliest times. In ancient Egypt the whole Book of the Dead, as well as the various sections of it which are usually copied on papyri, consisted of a series of "words of power," and the modern Egyptian looks upon the Koran in the same light as his ancestor looked upon the older work. A curious passage in the text inscribed on the inside of the pyramid of Unas reads (l. 583), "The bone and "flesh which possess no writing are wretched, but, "behold, the writing of Unas is under the great seal, "and behold, it is not under the little seal." It is difficult to explain the passage fully, but there is no doubt that we have here an allusion to the custom of placing writings believed to be possessed of magical powers with the dead. Certain passages or sections of the religious books of ancient nations have always been held to be of more importance than others, and considering the great length of such compositions this is not to be wondered at. Among the Egyptians two forms of the LXIVth Chapter of the Book of the Dead were in use, and there is no doubt whatever that the shorter form, as far back as the Ist dynasty, about B.C. 4300, was intended to be a summary of the whole work, and that the recital of it was held to be as efficacious as the recital of all the rest of it.[1] It is a remarkable fact that this form is called "The Chapter of "knowing the 'Chapters of Coming Forth by Day' in "a single Chapter," and that it is declared to date from the time of Hesepti, a king of the Ist dynasty, about B.C. 4300, whilst the "finding" of the longer form is attributed to the reign of Men-kau-Rā (Mycerinus), a king of the IVth dynasty, about B.C. 3600. It is interesting to note how persistently certain chapters and formulæ occur in funeral papyri of different periods, and the explanation seems to be that a popular selection was made at an early date, and that this selection was

[1] In a similar way the Arabs attach as much importance to the *Fatha*, or opening chapter, and to the chapter which declares the Unity of God (CXII.), as to the rest of the *Koran*.

copied with such additions or omissions as the means of the friends of the deceased allowed or made necessary. One thing is quite certain: every man in Egypt died in the firm belief that in the course of his journey into the next world he would be provided with words of power which would enable him to make his way thither unhindered, and give him abundance of meat and drink. We may see this view which was held concerning words of power from the following passages:—"May Thoth, "who is filled and furnished with words of power, "come and loose the bandages, even the bandages of "Set which fetter my mouth. . . . Now as concerning "the words of power and all the words which may be "spoken against me, may the gods resist them, and "may each and every one of the company of the gods "withstand them."[1] "Behold, I gather together the "word of power from wherever it is, and from any "person with whom it is, swifter than greyhounds and "quicker than light."[2] To the crocodile which cometh to carry off from the deceased his words of power he says, "Get thee back, return, get thee back, thou "crocodile fiend Sui! Thou shalt not advance to me, "for I live by reason of the words of power which I "have with me. . . . Heaven hath power over its "seasons, and the words of power have dominion over "that which they possess; my mouth therefore shall "have power over the words of power which are

[1] See *Chapters of Coming Forth by Day*, p. 70. [2] *Ibid.*, p. 71

"therein."[1] "I am clothed (?) and am wholly pro-"vided with thy magical words, O Rā, the which are "in the heaven above me, and in the earth beneath "me."[2] To the two Sister-Mert goddesses the deceased says, "My message to you is my words of power. I "shine from the Sektet boat, I am Horus the son of "Isis, and I have come to see my father Osiris."[3] "I "have become a spirit in my forms, I have gained the "mastery over my words of power, and it is decreed "for me to be a spirit."[4] "Hail, thou that cuttest off "heads, and slittest brows, thou who puttest away the "memory of evil things from the mouth of the spirits "by means of the words of power which they have "within them, . . . let not my mouth be shut fast by "reason of the words of power which thou hast within "thee. . . . Get thee back, and depart before the words "which the goddess Isis uttered when thou didst come "to cast the recollection of evil things into the mouth "of Osiris."[5] On the amulet of the Buckle we have inscribed the words, "May the blood of Isis, and the "powers (?) of Isis, and the words of power of Isis be "mighty to protect this mighty one," etc., and in the address which Thoth makes to Osiris he says, "I am "Thoth, the favoured one of Rā, the lord of might, who "bringeth to a prosperous end that which he doeth, the "mighty one of words of power, who is in the boat of

[1] See *Chapters of Coming Forth by Day*, p. 81. [2] *Ibid.*, p. 84.
[3] *Ibid.*, p. 87. [4] *Ibid.*, p. 129. [5] *Ibid.*, p. 150.

"millions of years, the lord of laws, the subduer of "the two lands," etc.[1]

From the above passages we not only learn how great was the confidence which the deceased placed in his words of power, but also that the sources from which they sprang were the gods Thoth and Isis. It will be remembered that Thoth is called the "scribe of the "gods," the "lord of writing," the "master of papyrus," the "maker of the palette and the ink-jar," the "lord "of divine words," *i.e.*, the holy writings or scriptures, and as he was the lord of books and master of the power of speech, he was considered to be the possessor of all knowledge both human and divine. At the creation of the world it was he who reduced to words the will of the unseen and unknown creative Power, and who uttered them in such wise that the universe came into being, and it was he who proved himself by the exercise of his knowledge to be the protector and friend of Osiris, and of Isis, and of their son Horus. From the evidence of the texts we know that it was not by physical might that Thoth helped these three gods, but by giving them words of power and instructing them how to use them. We know that Osiris vanquished his foes, and that he reconstituted his body, and became the king of the underworld and god of the dead, but he was only able to do these things by means of the words of power which Thoth had given to him,

[1] See *Chapters of Coming Forth by Day*, p. 340 f.

and which he had taught him to pronounce properly and in a proper tone of voice. It is this belief which makes the deceased cry out, "Hail, Thoth, who madest "Osiris victorious over his enemies, make thou Ani to "be victorious over his enemies in the presence of the "great and sovereign princes who are in Tattu," or in any other place. Without the words of power given to him by Thoth, Osiris would have been powerless under the attacks of his foes, and similarly the dead man, who was always identified with Osiris, would have passed out of existence at his death but for the words of power provided by the writings that were buried with him. In the Judgment Scene it is Thoth who reports to the gods the result of the weighing of the heart in the balance, and who has supplied its owner with the words which he has uttered in his supplications, and whatever can be said in favour of the deceased he says to the gods, and whatever can be done for him he does. But apart from being the protector and friend of Osiris, Thoth was the refuge to which Isis fled in her trouble. The words of a hymn declare that she knew "how to "turn aside evil hap," and that she was "strong of "tongue, and uttered the words of power which she "knew with correct pronunciation, and halted not in her "speech, and was perfect both in giving the command "and in saying the word,"[1] but this description only

[1] Chabas, *Revue Archéologique*, 1857, p. 65 ff.; Ledrain, *Monuments Égyptiens*, pl. xxii. ff.; and for a recent translation see my *First Steps in Egyptian*, pp. 179–188.

proves that she had been instructed by Thoth in the art of uttering words of power with effect, and to him, indeed, she owed more than this. When she found the dead body of her husband Osiris, she hovered about over it in the form of a bird, making air by the beating of her wings, and sending forth light from the sheen of her feathers, and at length she roused the dead to life by her words of power; as the result of the embrace which followed this meeting Horus was born, and his mother suckled him and tended him in her hiding-place in the papyrus swamps. After a time she was persecuted by Set, her husband's murderer, who, it seems, shut her and her son Horus up in a house as prisoners. Owing, however, to the help which Thoth gave her, she came forth by night and was accompanied on her journey by seven scorpions,[1] called respectively Tefen, Befen, Mestet, Mestetef, Petet, Thetet, and Matet, the last three of which pointed out the way. The guide of the way brought her to the swamps of Per-sui,[2] and to the town of the two goddesses of the sandals where the swampy country of Athu begins. Journeying on they came to Teb,[3] where the chief of the district had a house for his ladies; now the mistress of the house would not

[1] The story is told on the famous *Metternichstele*, ed. Golénischeff, Leipzig, 1877.

[2] *I.e.*, Crocodilopolis.

[3] The city of the two sandals. The two sandals were made of leather from the skin of the god Nehes or Set, the opponent of Horus.

admit Isis on account of the scorpions that were with her, for she had looked out of her door and watched Isis coming. On this the scorpions took counsel together and wished to sting her by means of the scorpion Tefen, but at this moment a poor woman who lived in the marshes opened the door of her cottage to Isis, and the goddess took shelter therein. Meanwhile the scorpion had crept under the door into the house of the governor, and stung the son of the lady of the house, and also set the place on fire; no water could quench the fire, and there was no rain to do it, for it was not then the rainy season. Now these things happened to the woman who had done no active harm to Isis, and the poor creature wandered about the streets of the city uttering loud cries of grief and distress because she knew not whether her boy would live or die.

When Isis saw this she was sorry for the child who had been stung, and as he was blameless in the matter of the door of his mother's house being shut in the face of the goddess, she determined to save him. Thereupon she cried out to the distraught mother, saying, "Come "to me, come to me! For my word is a talisman "which beareth life. I am a daughter well known in "thy city also, and I will do away the evil by means "of the word of my mouth which my father hath taught "me, for I am the daughter of his own body." Then Isis laid her hands upon the body of the boy, and in order to bring back the spirit into his body said—

"Come Tefen, appear upon the ground, depart hence, "come not nigh!

"Come poison of Befen, appear upon the ground. I "am Isis, the goddess, the lady of words of power, who "doeth deeds of magic, the words of whose voice are "charms.

"Obey me, O every reptile that stingeth, and fall "down headlong!

"O poison of [Mestet and] Mestetef, mount not "upwards!

"O poison of Petet and Thetet, draw not nigh!

"O Matet, fall down headlong!"

The goddess Isis then uttered certain words of the charm which had been given to her by the god Seb in order to keep poison away from her, and said, "Turn away, get away, retreat, O poison," adding the words "Mer-Rā" in the morning, and "The Egg of the Goose "appeareth from out of the sycamore" in the evening, as she turned to the scorpions. Both these sentences were talismans. After this Isis lamented that she was more lonely and wretched than all the people of Egypt, and that she had become like an old man who hath ceased to look upon and to visit fair women in their houses; and she ordered the scorpions to turn away their looks from her and to show her the way to the marshes and to the secret place which is in the city of

Khebt. Then the words of the cry, "The boy liveth, "the poison dieth! As the sun liveth, so the poison "dieth," were uttered, and the fire in the house of the woman was extinguished, and heaven rejoiced at the words of Isis. When Isis had said that the "son of "the woman had been stung because his mother had "shut the door of her house in her face, and had done "nothing for her," the words of the cry, "The boy "liveth and the poison dieth," were again uttered, and the son of the woman recovered.

Isis then continues her narrative thus:—"I Isis "conceived a child, and was great with child of Horus. "I, a goddess, gave birth to Horus, the son of Isis, "upon an island (*or* nest) in Athu the region of "swamps; and I rejoiced greatly because of this, for "I regarded Horus as a gift which would repay me for "the loss of his father. I hid him most carefully and "concealed him in my anxiety, and indeed he was well "hidden, and then I went away to the city of Am. "When I had saluted the inhabitants thereof I turned "back to seek the child, so that I might give him suck "and take him in my arms again. But I found my "sucking-child Horus, the fair golden one, well nigh "dead! He had bedewed the ground with the water "from his eye and with the foam from his lips, his "body was stiff, his heart was still, and no muscle in "any of his limbs moved.[1] Then I uttered a bitter cry

[1] This is an exact description of the state of an animal which has

"of grief, and the dwellers in the papyrus swamps ran "to me straightway from out of their houses, and they "bewailed the greatness of my calamity; but none of "them opened his mouth to speak, for every one was in "deep sorrow for me, and no man knew how to bring "back life into Horus. Then there came to me a "certain woman who was well known in her city, for "she belonged to a noble family, and she tried to "rekindle the life in Horus, but although her heart "was full of her knowledge my son remained motion-"less." Meanwhile the folk remarked that the son of the divine mother Isis had been protected against his brother Set, that the plants among which he had been hidden could not be penetrated by any hostile being, that the words of power of Temu, the father of the gods, "who is in heaven," should have preserved the life of Horus, that Set his brother could not possibly have had access to where the child was, who, in any case, had been protected against his wickedness; and at length it was discovered that Horus had been stung by a scorpion, and that the reptile "which destroyeth

**been stung by the small black scorpion in Egypt and the Sûdân. I saw Colonel W. H. Drage's dog "Shûbra" bitten at Merâwî in September, 1897, by a black scorpion, and in about an hour she was in the state of Horus as described above, and the whole camp was distressed, for both master and dog were great favourites. When it was no longer possible to administer spirit to her, Major G. R. Griffith and others immersed her body in pails of very hot water for several hours, and at sundown she was breathing comfortably, and she soon afterwards recovered.**

"the heart" had wounded him, and had probably killed him.

At this juncture Nephthys arrived, and went round about among the papyrus swamps weeping bitterly because of the affliction of her sister Isis; with her also was Serqet, the goddess of scorpions, who asked continually, "What hath happened to the child Horus?" Then Nephthys said to Isis, "Cry out in prayer unto "heaven, and let the mariners in the boat of Rā cease "to row, and let not the boat of Rā move further on "its course for the sake of the child Horus"; and forthwith Isis sent forth her cry up to heaven, and made her request come unto the "Boat of millions of years," and the Sun stood still and his boat moved not from its place by reason of the goddess's petition. Out from the boat came the god Thoth provided with magical powers, and bearing with him the great power to command in such wise that the words of his mouth must be fulfilled straightway; and he spake to Isis, saying, "O thou goddess Isis, whose mouth knoweth "how to utter charms (*or* talismans), no suffering shall "come upon thy child Horus, for his health and safety "depend upon the boat of Rā. I have come this day "in the divine boat of the Disk (Aten) to the place "where it was yesterday. When darkness (*or* night) "ruleth, the light shall vanquish it for the health (*or* "safety) of Horus for the sake of his mother Isis— "and similarly shall it happen unto every one who "possesseth what is [here] written (?)." What took place next is, of course, evident. The child Horus was restored to life, to the great joy of his mother Isis, who was more indebted than ever to the god Thoth for coming to deliver her out of her trouble on the death of her son, just as he had done on the death of her husband. Now because Isis had revivified both her husband and her son by the words of power and talismans which she possessed, mortal man thought it was absolutely necessary for him to secure her favour and protection at any cost, for eternal life and death were in her hands. As time went on the Egyptians revered her more and more, and as she was the lady of the gods and of heaven, power equal to that possessed by Rā himself was ascribed to her. Indeed, according to a legend which has come down to us, and which written upon papyrus or linen formed a magical formula against the poison of reptiles of all kinds, she made a bold attempt to wrest the power of Rā from him and to make herself mistress of the universe. The way in which she did this is told in a hieratic papyrus preserved at Turin,[1] from which the following rendering has been made; the merit of first discovering the correct meaning of the text belongs to M. Lefébure.

[1] See Pleyte and Rossi, *Le Papyrus de Turin*, 1869–1876, pll. 31–37, and 131–138; see also Lefébure in *Ægyptische Zeitschrift*, 1883, p. 27 ff.; Wiedemann, *Religion der alten Ægypter*, 1890, p. 29 ff.; and my *Papyrus of Ani*, 1895, p. lxxxix., and *First Steps in Egyptian*, 1895, pp. 241–256.

THE LEGEND OF RĀ AND ISIS.

"The Chapter of the divine god, the self-created "being, who made the heavens and the earth, and the "winds [which give] life, and the fire, and the gods, "and men, and beasts, and cattle, and reptiles, and the "fowl of the air and the fish of the sea; he is the king "of men and of gods, he hath one period of life (?) and "with him periods of one hundred and twenty years "each are but as years; his names are manifold and "unknown, the gods even know them not.

"Now Isis was a woman who possessed words of "power; her heart was wearied with the millions of "men, therefore she chose the millions of the gods, but "she esteemed more highly the millions of the spirits "(*khu*). And she meditated in her heart, saying, 'Cannot I by means of the sacred name of God make "myself mistress of the earth and become a goddess "like unto Rā in heaven and upon earth?' Now "behold, each day Rā entered at the head of his holy "mariners and established himself upon the throne of "the two horizons. Now the divine one (*i.e.*, Rā) had "grown old, he dribbled at the mouth, his spittle fell "upon the earth, and his slobbering dropped upon the "ground. And Isis kneaded it with earth in her "hand, and formed thereof a sacred serpent in the "form of a dart; she did not set it upright before her "face, but let it lie upon the ground in the path "whereby the great god went forth, according to his "heart's desire, into his double kingdom. Now the "holy god arose, and the gods who followed him as "though he were Pharaoh went with him; and he came "forth according to his daily wont; and the sacred "serpent bit him. The flame of life departed from "him, and he who dwelt among the cedars (?) was "overcome. The holy god opened his mouth, and the "cry of his majesty reached unto heaven; his company "of gods said, 'What hath happened?' and his gods "exclaimed, 'What is it?' But Rā could not answer, "for his jaws trembled and all his members quaked; "the poison spread swiftly through his flesh just as the "Nile rusheth through all his land. When the great "god had stablished his heart, he cried unto those who "were in his train, saying, 'Come unto me, O ye who "have come into being from my body, ye gods who "have come forth from me, make ye known unto "Khepera that a dire calamity hath fallen upon me. "My heart perceiveth it, but my eyes see it not; my "hand hath not caused it, nor do I know who hath "done this unto me. Never have I felt such pain, "neither can sickness cause more woe than this. I "am a prince, the son of a prince, the sacred essence "which hath proceeded from God. I am the great "one, the son of the great one, and my father planned "my name; I have multitudes of names and multitudes "of forms, and my being is in every god. I have been "proclaimed by the heralds Temu and Horus, and my "father and my mother uttered my name; but it hath "been hidden within me by him that begat me, "who would not that the words of power of any seer "should have dominion over me. I came forth to look "upon that which I had made, I was passing through "the world which I had created, when lo! something "stung me, but what I know not. Is it fire? Is it "water? My heart is on fire, my flesh quaketh, and "trembling hath seized all my limbs. Let there be "brought unto me my children, the gods, who possess "the words of power and magical speech, and mouths "which know how to utter them, and also powers "which reach even unto the heavens.' Then the "children of every god came unto him uttering cries "of grief. And Isis also came, bringing with her her "words of magical power, and her mouth was full of "the breath of life; for her talismans vanquish the "pains of sickness, and her words make to live again "the throats of those who are dead. And she spake, "saying, 'What hath come to pass, O holy Father? "What hath happened? Is it that a serpent hath "bitten thee, and that a thing which thou hast created "hath lifted up his head against thee? Verily it shall "be cast down by my effective words of power, and I "will drive it away from before the sight of thy sun-"beams.' The holy god opened his mouth and said, "'I was passing along my path, and I was going "through the two regions of my lands according to "my heart's desire, to see that which I had created, "when lo! I was bitten by a serpent which I saw not. "Is it fire? Is it water? I am colder than water, I "am hotter than fire. All my flesh sweateth, I quake, "my eye hath no strength, I cannot see the sky, and "the sweat rusheth to my face even as in the time of "summer.' Then said Isis unto Rā, 'O tell me thy "name, holy Father, for whosoever shall be delivered "by thy name shall live.' And Rā said, 'I have made "the heavens and the earth, I have knit together the "mountains, I have created all that is above them, "I have made the water, I have made to come into "being the goddess Meht-urt, and I have made the "" Bull of his mother," from whom spring the delights "of love. I have made the heavens, I have stretched "out the two horizons like a curtain, and I have placed "the soul of the gods within them. I am he who, if "he openeth his eyes, doth make the light, and, if he "closeth them, darkness cometh into being. At his "command the Nile riseth, and the gods know not "his name. I have made the hours, I have created "the days, I bring forward the festivals of the year, "I create the Nile-flood. I make the fire of life, and "I provide food in the houses. I am Khepera in the "morning, I am Rā at noon, and I am Temu at even.' "Meanwhile the poison was not taken away from his "body, but it pierced deeper, and the great god could "no longer walk.

"Then said Isis unto Rā, 'What thou hast said is "not thy name. O tell it unto me, and the poison "shall depart; for he shall live whose name shall be "revealed.' Now the poison burned like fire, and it "was fiercer than the flame and the furnace, and the "majesty of the great god said, 'I consent that Isis "shall search into me, and that my name shall pass "from me into her.' Then the god hid himself from "the gods, and his place in the Boat of Millions of "Years was empty. And when the time had arrived "for the heart of Rā to come forth, Isis spake unto "her son Horus, saying, 'The god hath bound himself "by oath to deliver up his two eyes (*i.e.*, the sun and "moon).' Thus was the name of the great god taken "from him, and Isis, the lady of words of magical "power, said, 'Depart, poison, go forth from Rā. O "Eye of Horus, go forth from the god, and shine outside "his mouth. It is I who work, it is I who make to fall "down upon the earth the vanquished poison, for the "name of the great god hath been taken away from "him. Let Rā live, and let the poison die! Let the "poison die, and let Rā live!' These are the words "of Isis, the mighty lady, the mistress of the gods, who "knew Rā by his own name."

Now from a few words of text which follow the above narrative we learn that the object of writing it was not so much to instruct the reader as to make a magic formula, for we are told that it was to be recited over figures of Temu and Horus, and Isis and Horus, that is to say, over figures of Temu the evening sun, Horus the Elder, Horus the son of Isis, and Isis herself. Temu apparently takes the place of Rā, for he represents the sun as an old man, *i.e.*, Rā at the close of his daily life when he has lost his strength and power. The text is a charm or magical formula against snake bites, and it was thought that the written letters, which represented the words of Isis, would save the life of any one who was snake-bitten, just as they saved the life of Rā. If the full directions as to the use of the figures of Temu, Isis, and the two Horus gods, were known unto us we should probably find that they were to be made to act in dumb show the scenes which took place between Rā and Isis when the goddess succeeded in taking from him his name. Thus we have ample evidence that Isis possessed marvellous magical powers, and this being so, the issues of life and death, as far as the deceased was concerned, we know from the texts to have been in her hands. Her words of power, too, were a priceless possession, for she obtained them from Thoth, who was the personification of the mind and intelligence of the Creator, and thus their origin was divine, and from this point of view were inspired.

From a papyrus of the Ptolemaïc period we obtain some interesting facts about the great skill in working magic and about the knowledge of magical formulæ which were possessed by a prince called Setnau Khā-em-Uast. He knew how to use the powers of amulets and talismans, and how to compose magical formulæ, and he was master both of religious literature and of that of the "double house of life," or library of magical books. One day as he was talking of such things one of the king's wise men laughed at his remarks, and in answer Setnau said, "If thou wouldst read a book "possessed of magical powers come with me and I will "show it to thee, the book was written by Thoth him-"self, and in it there are two formulæ. The recital of "the first will enchant (or bewitch) heaven, earth, hell, "sea, and mountains, and by it thou shalt see all the "birds, reptiles, and fish, for its power will bring the "fish to the top of the water. The recital of the second "will enable a man if he be in the tomb to take the "form which he had upon earth," etc. When questioned as to where the book was, Setnau said that it was in the tomb of Ptah-nefer-ka at Memphis. A little later Setnau went there with his brother and passed three days and three nights in seeking for the tomb of Ptah-nefer-ka, and on the third day they found it; Setnau recited some words over it, and the earth opened and they went down to the place where the book was. When the two brothers came into the tomb they found it to be brilliantly lit up by the light which came forth from the book; and when they looked they saw not only Ptah-nefer-ka, but his wife Ahura, and Merhu their son. Now Ahura and Merhu were buried at Coptos but their doubles had come to live with Ptah-nefer-ka by means of the magical power of Thoth. Setnau told them that he had come to take away the book, but Ahura begged him not to do so, and related to him the misfortunes which had already followed the possession of it. She was, it seems, the sister of Ptah-nefer-ka whom she married, and after the birth of her son Merhu, her husband seemed to devote himself exclusively to the study of magical books, and one day a priest of Ptah promised to tell him where the magical book described above might be found if he would give him a hundred pieces of silver, and provide him with two handsome coffins. When the money and the coffins had been given to him, the priest of Ptah told Ptah-nefer-ka that the book was in an iron box in the middle of the river at Coptos. "The iron box is in a bronze box, the "bronze box is in a box of palm-tree wood, the palm-"tree wood box is in a box of ebony and ivory, the "ebony and ivory box is in a silver box, the silver box "is in a gold box, and in the gold (*sic*) box lies the book. "The box wherein is the book is surrounded by swarms "of serpents and scorpions and reptiles of all kinds, and "round it is coiled a serpent which cannot die." Ptah-nefer-ka told his wife and the king what he had heard, and at length set out for Coptos with Ahura and Merhu in the royal barge; having arrived at Coptos he went to the temple of Isis and Harpocrates and offered up a sacrifice and poured out a libation to these gods. Five days later the high priest of Coptos made for him the model of a floating stage and figures of workmen provided with tools; he then recited words of power over them and they became living, breathing men, and the search for the box began. Having worked for three days and three nights they came to the place where the box was. Ptah-nefer-ka dispersed the serpents and scorpions which were round about the nest of boxes by his words of power, and twice succeeded in killing the serpent coiled round the box, but it came to life again; the third time he cut it into two pieces, and laid sand between them, and this time it did not take its old form again. He then opened the boxes one after the other, and taking out the gold box with the book inside it carried it to the royal barge. He next read one of the two formulæ in it and so enchanted or bewitched the heavens and the earth that he learned all their secrets; he read the second and he saw the sun rising in the heavens with his company of the gods, etc. His wife Ahura then read the book and saw all that her husband had seen. Ptah-nefer-ka then copied the writings on a piece of new papyrus, and having covered the papyrus with incense dissolved it in water and drank it; thus he acquired the knowledge which was in the magical book. Meanwhile these acts had stirred the god Thoth to wrath, and he told Rā what Ptah-nefer-ka had done. As a result the decree went forth that Ptah-nefer-ka and his wife and child should never return to Memphis, and on the way back to Coptos Ahura and Merhu fell into the river and were drowned; and while returning to Memphis with the book Ptah-nefer-ka himself was drowned also. Setnau, however, refused to be diverted from his purpose, and he insisted on having the book which he saw in the possession of Ptah-nefer-ka; the latter then proposed to play a game of draughts and to let the winner have the book. The game was for fifty-two points, and although Ptah-nefer-ka tried to cheat Setnau, he lost the game. At this juncture Setnau sent his brother Anhaherurau up to the earth to bring him his talismans of Ptah and his other magical writings, and when he returned he laid them upon Setnau, who straightway flew up to heaven grasping the wonderful book in his hand. As he went up from the tomb light went before him, and the darkness closed in behind him; but Ptah-nefer-ka said to his wife, "I will make "him bring back this book soon, with a knife and a "rod in his hand and a vessel of fire upon his head." Of the bewitchment of Setnau by a beautiful woman called Tabubu and of his troubles in consequence thereof we need make no mention here: it is sufficient to say that the king ordered him to take the book back to its place, and that the prophecy of Ptah-nefer-ka was fulfilled.[1]

[1] For translations see Brugsch, *Le Roman de Setnau* (in *Revue*

In connexion with the subject of the magical powers of Isis must be briefly mentioned the curious small stelæ, with rounded tops, on the front of which are inscribed figures of the god Horus standing upon crocodiles: they are usually known as "cippi of Horus." The largest and finest example of this remarkable class of object is the famous "Metternichstele," which was found in the year 1828 during the building of a cistern in a Franciscan monastery in Alexandria, and was presented by Muhammad Ali Pasha to Prince Metternich. We are fortunately enabled to date the stele, for the name of Nectanebus I., the last but one of the native kings of Egypt, who reigned from B.C. 378 to B.C. 360, occurs on it, and we know from many sources that such a monument could have been produced only about this period. From the two illustrations of it here given we see that it is both sculptured and engraved with figures of many of the gods of ancient Egypt, gods well known from the monuments of the earlier dynasties, and also with figures of a series of demons and monsters and animals which have both mythological and magical importance. Many of these are accompanied by texts containing magical formulæ,

*Archéologique*, 2nd series, vol. xvi., 1867, p. 161 ff.); Maspero, *Contes Égyptiens*, Paris, 1882, pp. 45-82; *Records of the Past*, vol. iv., pp. 129-148; and for the original Demotic text see Mariette, *Les Papyrus du Musée de Boulaq*, tom. i., 1871, pll. 29-32; Revillout, *Le Roman de Setna*, Paris, 1877; Hess, *Roman von Sfne Ha-m-us*, Leipzig, 1888.

magical names, and mythological allusions. In the principal scene we see Horus, or Harpocrates, standing upon two crocodiles; on his brow is the uraeus, and he wears on the right side of his head the lock of hair emblematic of youth. In his hands he grasps serpents, a lion, and an antelope, and it is clear by the look on his face that he is in no wise afraid of them. Above his head is a bearded head, which is usually said to represent that of Bes. On his right are:—(1) an *utchat*,[1] with human hands and arms; (2) Horus-Rā, hawk-headed, and wearing the sun's disk and uraeus, and standing on a serpent coiled up; (3) Osiris, in the form of a hawk standing upon a sceptre, and wearing the *atef* crown; (4) The goddess Isis standing upon a serpent coiled up; (5) The goddess Nekhebet, in the form of a vulture, standing upon a papyrus sceptre. On his left are:—(1) An *utchat* with human hands and arms; (2) a papyrus standard with plumes and *menats*[2]; (3) the god Thoth standing upon a serpent coiled up; (4) the goddess Uatchet, in the form of a serpent, standing upon a papyrus sceptre. Now Horus typifies youth and strength and the rising sun, and the head above him is probably intended to represent that of Rā (or Bes) as an old man; the allusion here is clearly to the god who "is old at eventide and who "becomes young again." The *utchats* and the figures of the gods symbolize the solar powers and the deities

[1] See above, p. 55. [2] See above, p. 60.

Cippus of Horus. (See *Metternichstele*, ed. Golénischeff, plate 1.)

who are masters of the words of power, both in the South and in the North, by which the young god Horus vanquishes all hostile animals, reptiles, and creeping things which live in water and on land. Above and about this scene are several rows of figures of gods and sketches of mythological scenes; many of which are evidently taken from the vignettes of the Book of the Dead, and the object of all of the latter is to prove that light overcomes darkness, that good vanquishes evil, and that renewed life comes after death. The texts which fill all the spaces not occupied by figures describe certain incidents of the eternal combat which Horus wages against his brother Set, and tell the story of the wanderings of Isis with her son Horus and of her sufferings in the country of the papyrus swamps, a sketch of which we have given above (see pp. 130–136); besides these, prayers to certain gods are introduced. The whole monument is nothing but a talisman, or a gigantic amulet engraved with magical figures and words of power, and it was, undoubtedly, placed in some conspicuous place in a courtyard or in a house to protect the building and its inmates from the attacks of hostile beings, visible and invisible, and its power was believed to be invincible. There is not a god of any importance whose figure is not on it, and there is not a demon, or evil animal or reptile, who is not depicted upon it in a vanquished state; the knowledge of the ancient Egyptian mythology and the skill shewn by the designer of this talisman are very remarkable. The small cippi of Horus contain nothing but extracts from the scenes and texts which we find on the "Metternichstele," and it, or similar objects, undoubtedly formed the source from which so many of the figures of the strange gods which are found on Gnostic gems were derived. Certain of the figures of the gods on the cippi were cast in bronze in the Ptolemaïc and Roman periods, or hewn in stone, and were buried in tombs and under the foundations of houses to drive away any of the fiends who might come to do harm either to the living or the dead.

The Arab historian Mas'ûdî has preserved[1] a curious legend of the talismans which were employed by Alexander the Great to protect the city of Alexandria whilst it was being built, and as the legend is of Egyptian origin, and dates from a period not greatly removed from that in which the Metternich stele was made, it is worthy of mention. When the foundations of the city had been laid, and the walls had begun to rise up, certain savage animals came up each night from the sea, and threw down everything which had been built during the day; watchmen were appointed to drive them away, but in spite of this each morning saw the work done during the previous day destroyed. After much thought Alexander devised a plan whereby he

[1] See *Les Prairies d'Or*, ed. B. de Meynard and Pavet de Courteille, Paris, 1861, tom. ii. p. 425 ff.

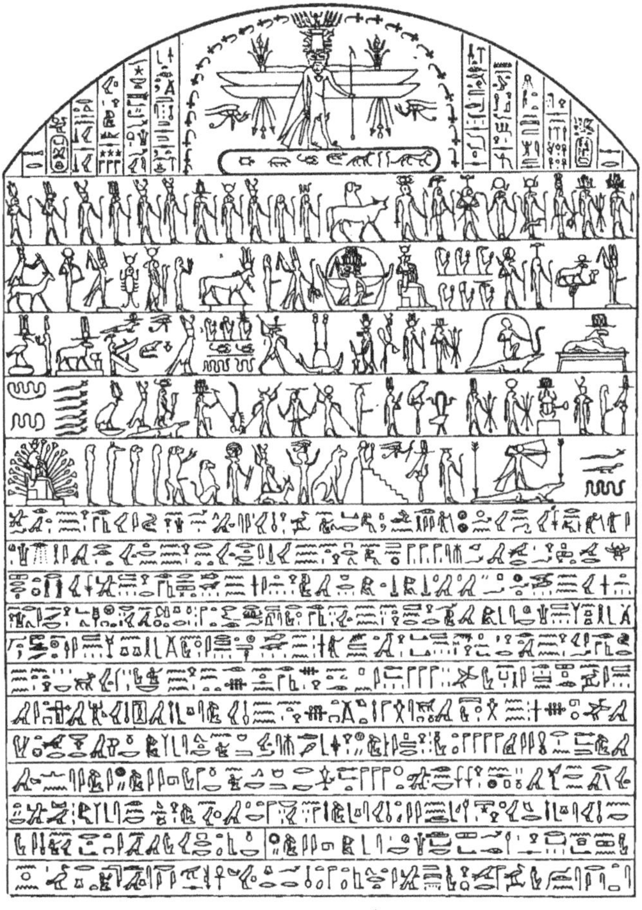

Cippus of Horus. (See *Metternichstele*, ed. Golénischeff, plate 3.)

might thwart the sea monsters, and he proceeded to carry it into effect. He made a box ten cubits long and five cubits wide with sides made of sheets of glass fastened into frames by means of pitch, resin, etc. In this box Alexander placed himself, together with two skilful draughtsmen, and having been closed it was towed out to sea by two vessels; and when weights of iron, lead, and stone had been attached to the under part of it, it began to sink, being guided to the place which Alexander wished it to reach by means of cords which were worked from the ships. When the box touched the bottom of the sea, thanks to the clearness of the glass sides and the water of the sea, Alexander and his two companions were able to watch the various marine monsters which passed by, and he saw that although they had human bodies they had the heads of beasts; some had axes, some had saws, and some had hammers, and they all closely resembled workmen. As they passed in front of the box Alexander and his two draughtsmen copied their forms upon paper with great exactness, and depicted their hideous countenances, and stature, and shape; this done, a signal was made, and the box was drawn up to the surface. As soon as Alexander reached the land he ordered his stone and metal workers to make reproductions of the sea monsters according to the drawings which he and his friends had made, and when they were finished he caused them to be set up on pedestals along the sea-shore, and continued his work of building the city. When the night came, the sea monsters appeared as usual, but as soon as they saw that figures of themselves had been put up on the shore they returned at once to the water and did not shew themselves again. When, however, the city had been built and was inhabited, the sea monsters made their appearance again, and each morning a considerable number of people were found to be missing; to prevent this Alexander placed talismans upon the pillars which, according to Mas'ûdî, were there in his day. Each pillar was in the shape of an arrow, and was eighty cubits in height, and rested upon a plinth of brass; the talismans were placed at their bases, and were in the form of figures or statues of certain beings with suitable inscriptions, and as they were put in position after careful astronomical calculations had been made for the purpose we may assume that they produced the effect desired by the king.

# CHAPTER V.

## MAGICAL NAMES.

THE Egyptians, like most Oriental nations, attached very great importance to the knowledge of names, and the knowledge of how to use and to make mention of names which possessed magical powers was a necessity both for the living and the dead. It was believed that if a man knew the name of a god or a devil, and addressed him by it, he was bound to answer him and to do whatever he wished; and the possession of the knowledge of the name of a man enabled his neighbour to do him good or evil. The name that was the object of a curse brought down evil upon its owner, and similarly the name that was the object of a blessing or prayer for benefits secured for its master many good things. To the Egyptian the name was as much a part of a man's being as his soul, or his double (KA), or his body, and it is quite certain that this view was held by him in the earliest times. Thus in the text which is inscribed on the walls inside[1] the pyramid

[1] Line 169.

of Pepi I., king of Egypt about B.C. 3200, we read, "Pepi hath been purified. He hath taken in his "hand the *māh* staff, he hath provided himself with "his throne, and he hath taken his seat in the "boat of the great and little companies of the gods. "Rā maketh Pepi to sail to the West, he stablisheth "his seat above those of the lords of doubles, and "he writeth down Pepi at the head of those who live. "The doors of Pekh-ka which are in the abyss open "themselves to Pepi, the doors of the iron which "is the ceiling of the sky open themselves to "Pepi, and he passeth through them; he hath his "panther skin upon him, and the staff and whip are "in his hand. Pepi goeth forward with his flesh, Pepi "is happy with his name, and he liveth with his *ka* "(double)." Curiously enough only the body and name and double of the king are mentioned, just as if these three constituted his whole economy; and it is noteworthy what importance is attached to the name in this passage. In the text from the pyramid of another king[1] we have a prayer concerning the preservation of the name, which is of such interest that a rendering of it in full is here given: it reads, "O "Great Company of the gods who dwell in Annu "(Heliopolis), grant that Pepi Nefer-ka-Rā may flourish "(*literally* 'germinate'), and that his pyramid, his ever-"lasting building, may flourish, even as the name of

[1] Pepi II. (ed. Maspero, l. 669, ff. Recueil, tom. xii. 1892, p. 146).

"Temu, the chief of the nine gods, doth flourish. If "the name of Shu, the lord of the upper shrine in "Annu, flourisheth, then Pepi shall flourish, and his "pyramid, his everlasting building, shall flourish! If "the name of Tefnut, the lady of the lower shrine in "Annu, flourisheth, the name of Pepi shall be estab-"lished, and this his pyramid shall be established "to all eternity! If the name of Seb flourisheth "at the 'homage of the earth,' then the name of Pepi "shall flourish, and this his pyramid shall flourish, and "this his building shall flourish unto all eternity! If "the name of Nut in the House of Shenth in Annu "flourisheth, the name of Pepi shall flourish, and this "his pyramid shall flourish, and this his building shall "flourish unto all eternity! If the name of Osiris "flourisheth in the nome of Abydos, then the name of "Pepi shall flourish, and this his pyramid shall flourish, "and this his building shall flourish unto all eternity! "If the name of Osiris Khent-Amentet flourisheth, "then the name of Pepi shall flourish, and this his "pyramid shall flourish, and this his building shall "flourish unto all eternity! If the name of Set, the "dweller in Nubt (Ombos) flourisheth, then the name "of Pepi shall flourish, and this his pyramid shall "flourish, and this his building shall flourish unto all "eternity! If the name of Horus flourisheth, then the "name of Pepi shall flourish, and this his pyramid shall "flourish, and this his building shall flourish unto all "eternity! If the name of Rā flourisheth in the "horizon, then the name of Pepi shall flourish, and "this his pyramid shall flourish, and this his building "shall flourish unto all eternity! If the name of "Khent-merti flourisheth in Sekhem (Letopolis), then "the name of Pepi shall flourish, and this his pyramid "shall flourish, and this his building shall flourish "unto all eternity! If the name of Uatchet in Tep "flourisheth, then the name of Pepi shall flourish, and "this his pyramid shall flourish, and this his building "shall flourish unto all eternity!" The above prayer or formula was the origin of most of the prayers and texts which had for their object the "making the name to germinate *or* flourish," and which were copied so frequently in the Saïte, Ptolemaïc, and Roman periods. All these compositions show that from the earliest to the latest times the belief as to the importance of the preservation of the name never changed in Egypt, and the son who assisted in keeping green his father's name, and in consequence his memory, performed a most meritorious duty. But in the present chapter we are not so much concerned with the ordinary as with the extraordinary uses to which a name might be put, and the above facts have only been mentioned to prove that a man's name was regarded as an essential part of himself, and that the blotting out of the name of an individual was synonymous with his destruction. Without a name no man could be identified in the judgment, and as a man only came into being upon this earth when his name had been pronounced, so the future life could only be attained after the gods of the world beyond the grave had become acquainted with it and had uttered it.

According to the story of the Creation which is related in the Papyrus of Nesi-Amsu,[1] before the world and all that therein is came into being, only the great god Neb-er-tcher existed, for even the gods were not born. Now when the time had come for the god to create all things he says, "I brought (*i.e.*, fashioned) my "mouth, and I uttered my own name as a word of "power, and thus I evolved myself under the evolu- "tions of the god Khepera, and I developed myself out "of the primeval matter which had evolved multitudes "of evolutions from the beginning of time. Nothing "existed on this earth [before me], I made all things. "There was none other who worked with me at that "time." Elsewhere, that is to say, in the other version of the story, the god Khepera says, "I developed "myself from the primeval matter which I made, I "developed myself out of the primeval matter. My "name is 'Osiris,' the germ of primeval matter." Here, then, we have a proof that the Egyptians regarded the creation as the result of the utterance of the name of the god Neb-er-tcher or Khepera by himself. Again, in the story of Rā and Isis, given in the preceding

[1] See my paper in *Archæologia*, Vol. LII., London, 1891.

chapter, we have seen that although Isis was able to make a serpent and to cause it to bite Rā, and to make him very ill, she was powerless to do as she wished in heaven and upon earth until she had persuaded the god to reveal to her his name by which he ruled the universe. In yielding up his name to the goddess he placed himself in her power, and in this example we have a striking instance of the belief that the knowledge of the name of god, or devil, or human being, implied dominion over that being. We have seen elsewhere that Rā, the type and symbol of God, is described as the god of "many names," and in that wonderful composition the XVIIth Chapter of the Book of the Dead,[1] we have the following statement:—"I am the "great god Nu, who gave birth unto himself, and who "made his name to become the company of the gods." Then the question, "What does this mean?" or "Who "is this?" is asked. And this is the answer: "It is "Rā, the creator of the name[s] of his limbs, which "came into being in the form of the gods who are in "the following of Rā." From this we see that all the "gods" of Egypt were merely personifications of the NAMES of Rā, and that each god was one of his members, and that a name of a god was the god himself. Without the knowledge of the names of the gods and devils of the underworld the dead Egyptian would have fared badly, for his personal liberty would have been

[1] See *Chapters of Coming Forth by Day*, p. 49.

fettered, the roads and paths would have been blocked to him, the gates of the mansions of the underworld would have been irrevocably shut in his face, and the hostile powers which dogged his footsteps would have made an end of him; these facts are best illustrated by the following examples :—

When the deceased comes to the Hall of Judgment, at the very beginning of his speech he says, "Homage "to thee, O Great God, thou Lord of Maāti, I have "come to thee, O my Lord, and I have brought myself "hither that I may behold thy beauties. I know thee, "and I know thy name, and I know the names of the "two and forty gods who exist with thee in this Hall "of Maāti."[1] But although the gods may be favourable to him, and he be found righteous in the judgment, he cannot make his way among the other gods of the underworld without a knowledge of the names of certain parts of the Hall of Maāti. After the judgment he acquires the mystical name of "He who is equipped "with the flowers and the dweller in his olive tree," and it is only after he has uttered this name that the gods say "Pass onwards." Next the gods invite him to enter the Hall of Maāti, but he is not allowed to pass in until he has, in answer to questions asked by the bolts, lintels, threshold, fastenings, socket, door-leaves, and door-posts, told their names. The floor of the Hall will not permit him to walk upon it unless he

[1] See *Chapters of Coming Forth by Day*, p. 191.

tells not only its name, but also the mystical names of his two legs and feet wherewith he is about to tread upon it. When all this has been done the guardian of the Hall says to him, "I will not announce thy name "[to the god] unless thou tellest me my name"; and the deceased replies, "'Discerner of hearts and searcher "of the reins' is thy name." In reply to this the guardian says, "If I announce thy name thou must "utter the name of the god who dwelleth in his hour," and the deceased utters the name "Māau-Taui." But still the guardian is not satisfied, and he says, "If I "announce thy name thou must tell me who is he "whose heaven is of fire, whose walls [are surmounted "by] living uraei, and the floor of whose house is a "stream of water. Who is he, I say? (*i.e.*, what is his "name?)" But the deceased has, of course, learnt the name of the Great God, and he replies, "Osiris." The guardian of the Hall is now content, and he says, "Advance, verily thy name shall be mentioned to "him"; and he further promises that the cakes, and ale, and sepulchral meals which the deceased shall enjoy shall come from the "Eye of Rā."

In another Chapter[1] the deceased addresses seven gods, and says, "Hail, ye seven beings who make "decrees, who support the Balance on the night of the "judgment of the Utchat, who cut off heads, who hack "necks in pieces, who take possession of hearts by

[1] See *Chapters of Coming Forth by Day*, p. 123.

"violence and rend the places where hearts are fixed, "who make slaughterings in the Lake of Fire, I know "you, and I know your names; therefore know ye me, "even as I know your names." The deceased, having declared that the seven gods know his name and he their names, has no further apprehension that evil will befall him.

In one portion of the kingdom of Osiris there existed seven halls or mansions through which the deceased was anxious to pass, but each of the gates was guarded by a doorkeeper, a watcher, and a herald, and it required special provision on the part of the deceased to satisfy these beings that he had a right to pass them. In the first place, figures of the seven gates had to be made in some substance (or painted upon papyrus), as well as a figure of the deceased: the latter was made to approach each of the gates and to stand before it and to recite an address which had been specially prepared for the purpose. Meanwhile the thigh, the head, the heart, and the hoof of a red bull were offered at each gate, as well as a very large number of miscellaneous offerings which need not be described in detail. But all these ceremonies would not help the deceased to pass through the gates, unless he knew the names of the seven doorkeepers, and the seven watchers, and the seven heralds who guarded them. The gods of the first gate were:—Sekhet-hra-āsht-aru, Semetu, and Hukheru; those of the second, Tun-hāt, Seqet-hra, and

Sabes; of the third, Am-huat-ent-pehfi, Res-hra, and Uāau; of the fourth, Khesef-hra-āsht-kheru, Res-ab, and Neteka-hra-khesef-atu; of the fifth, Ānkh-em-fentu, Ashebu, and Tebherkehaat; of the sixth, Akentauk-ha-kheru, An-hra, and Metes-hra-ari-she; of the seventh, Metes-sen, Āāa-kheru, and Khesef-hra-khemiu. And the text, which the deceased recites to the Halls collectively, begins, "Hail, ye Halls! Hail, ye who "made the Halls for Osiris! Hail, ye who watch "your Halls! Hail, ye who herald the affairs of the "two lands for the god Osiris each day, the deceased "knoweth you, and he knoweth your names."[1] The names having been uttered, and the addresses duly recited, the deceased went wherever he pleased in the seven Halls of Osiris.

But beside the seven halls the deceased had to pass through the twenty-one hidden pylons of the house of Osiris in the Elysian Fields, and in order to do so he had to declare the names of the pylon and the door-keeper of each, and to make a short address besides. Thus to the first pylon he says, "I have made my way, "I know thee and I know thy name, and I know the "name of the god who guardeth thee. Thy name is "'Lady of tremblings, with lofty walls, the sovereign "lady, the mistress of destruction, who setteth in order "the words which drive back the whirlwind and the "storm, who delivereth from destruction him that

[1] See *Chapters of Coming Forth by Day*, p. 241.

"travelleth along the way'; and the name of thy door-"keeper is Neri." At the second pylon he says, "I "have made [my] way, I know thee, and I know thy "name, and I know the name of the god who guardeth "thee. Thy name is 'Lady of heaven, the mistress of "the world, who devoureth with fire, the lady of "mortals, who knoweth mankind.' The name of thy "doorkeeper is Mes-Ptah," and so on at each of the pylons. In the later and longer version of the chapter which was written to supply the deceased with this knowledge he informs the god of each pylon what purification he has undergone; thus to the god of the first pylon he says, "I have anointed myself with *hāti* "unguent [made from] the cedar, I have arrayed myself "in apparel of *menkh* (linen), and I have with me my "sceptre made of *heti* wood." After the speech the god of the pylon says, "Pass on, then, thou art pure."

When we remember that one of the oldest beliefs as to the future life made it appear that it would be lived by man in the Sekhet-Aaru, or Field of Reeds, a region which, as we know from the drawings of it which have come down to us, was intersected by canals and streams, it is at once clear that in order to pass from one part of it to another the deceased would need a boat. Even assuming that he was fortunate enough to have made his own way into this region, it was not possible for him to take a boat with him. To meet this difficulty a boat and all its various parts were drawn upon the papyrus, upon which the selection of Chapters from the Book of the Dead had been inscribed for him, and a knowledge of the text of the chapter which belonged to it made the drawing to become an actual boat. But before he could enter it, the post to which it was tied up, and every part of the boat itself, demanded that he should tell them their names, thus :—

*Post at which to tie up.* "Tell me my name." D.[1] "Lord of the two lands, dweller in the shrine," is thy name.

*Rudder.* "Tell me my name." D. "Leg of Hāpiu" is thy name.

*Rope.* "Tell me my name." D. "Hairs with which Anpu finisheth the work of my embalmment" is thy name.

*Oar-rests.* "Tell us our name." D. "Pillars of the underworld" is your name.

*Hold.* "Tell me my name." D. "Akau" is thy name.

*Mast.* "Tell me my name." D. "Bringer back of the lady after her departure" is thy name.

*Lower deck.* "Tell me my name." D. "Standard of Ap-uat" is thy name.

*Upper Post.* "Tell me my name." D. "Throat of Mestha" is thy name.

*Sail.* "Tell me my name." D. "Nut" is thy name.

*Leather Straps.* "Tell us our name." D. "Those who

[1] D. = the deceased.

are made from the hide of the Mnevis Bull, which was burned by Suti," is your name.

*Paddles.* "Tell us our name." D. "Fingers of Horus the firstborn" is your name.

*Pump* (?). "Tell me my name. D. "The hand of Isis, which wipeth away the blood of the Eye of Horus," is thy name.

*Planks.* "Tell us our names." D. "Mestha, Hāpi, Tuamutef, Qebhsennuf, Haqau, Thet-em-āua, Maa-an-tef, Ari-nef-tchesef," are your names.

*Bows.* "Tell us our name. D. "He who is at the head of his nomes" is your name.

*Hull.* "Tell me my name." D. "Mert" is thy name.

*Rudder.* "Tell me my name." D. "Āqa" is thy name; "Shiner in the water, hidden beam," is thy name.

*Keel.* "Tell me my name." D. "Thigh of Isis, which Rā cut off with the knife to bring blood into the Sektet boat," is thy name.

*Sailor.* "Tell me my name." D. "Traveller" is thy name.

*Wind.* "Tell me my name." D. "The North Wind, which cometh from Tem to the nostrils of Osiris," is thy name.

And when the deceased had declared to these their names, before he could set out on his journey he was obliged to tell the river, and the river-banks, and the ground their mystical names. This done, the boat admitted him as a passenger, and he was able to sail about to any part of the Elysian Fields at will.

But among the beings whom the deceased wished to avoid in the underworld were the beings who "lay "snares, and who work the nets, and who are fishers," and who would draw him into their nets. It seems as if it were absolutely necessary that he should fall in with these beings and their nets, for a whole chapter of the Book of the Dead was written with the view of enabling him to escape from them unharmed; the god their leader is called "the god whose face is "behind him," and "the god who hath gained the "mastery over his heart." To escape from the net which was worked by "the fishers who lay snares with "their nets and who go round about in the chambers "of the waters," the deceased had to know the names of the net, and of the ropes, and of the pole, and of the hooks, and of each and every part of it; without this knowledge nothing could save him from calamity. We unfortunately understand very few of the allusions to mythological events which are contained in the names of the various parts of the machinery which work the net, but it is quite certain that they have reference to certain events in the lives of the gods who are mentioned, and that these were well known to the writers and readers of religious texts.

From the above descriptions of the means whereby the deceased made his way through the gates and the halls of the underworld and escaped from the fowler and his net, it will be readily understood that the knowledge of the name alone was, in some cases, sufficient to help him out of his difficulties; but in others it was necessary to have the name which was possessed of magical power inscribed upon some object, amulet or otherwise. Moreover, some gods and devils were thought to have the power to assume different forms, and as each form carried with it its own name, to have absolute power over a god of many forms it was necessary to know all his names. Thus in the "Book of Overthrowing Āpep"[1] we are told not only to make a wax figure of the monster, but also to write his name upon it, so that when the figure is destroyed by being burnt in the fire his name also may be destroyed; this is a striking example of the belief that the name was an integral part of the economy of a living creature. But Apep possessed many forms and therefore many names, and unless he could be invoked by these names he still had the power to do evil; the above-mentioned book[2] therefore supplies us with a list of his names, among which occur the following:—"Tutu (*i.e.*, Doubly evil one), Hau-hra (*i.e.*, "Backward Face), Hemhemti (*i.e.*, Roarer), Qetu (*i.e.*, "Evil-doer), Āmam (*i.e.*, Devourer), Saatet-ta (*i.e.*, Dark-"ener of earth), Iubani, Khermuti, Unti, Karauememti,

[1] *Papyrus of Nesi-Amsu*, col. xxiii. l. 6. (*Archæologia*, vol. LII.)
[2] *Ibid.*, col. xxxii. l. 13 f.

"Khesef-hra, Sekhem-hra, Khak-ȧb, Nāi, Uai, Beteshu, "Kharebutu the fourfold fiend," etc. All these names represent, as may be seen from the few of which translations are given, various aspects of Āpep, the devil of thunder, lightning, cloud, rain, mist, storm, and the like, and the anxiety to personify these so that the personifications might be attacked by means of magical ceremonies and words of power seems positively childish.

Passing now to certain chapters of the Book of the Dead which are rich in names of magical power,[1] we notice that the god Amen, whose name meant the "hidden one," possessed numerous names, upon the knowledge of which the deceased relied for protection. Thus he says, "O Amen,[2] Amen; O Re-Iukasa; O "God, Prince of the gods of the east, thy name is "Na-ari-k, or (as others say) Ka-ari-ka, Kasaika is thy "name. Arethikasathika is thy name. Amen-na-an-"ka-entek-share, or (as others say) Thek-share-Amen-"kerethi, is thy name. O Amen, let me make suppli-"cation unto thee, for I, even I, know thy name. "Amen is thy name. Ireqai is thy name. Marqathai "is thy name. Rerei is thy name. Nasaqbubu is thy "name. Thanasa-Thanasa is thy name. Sharesathatha-"katha is thy name. O Amen, O Amen, O God, O "God, O Amen, I adore thy name." In another place[3] the deceased addresses Sekhet-Bast-Rā, saying,

[1] Chapters CLXII., CLXIII., CLXIV., CLXV.

[2] See *Chapters of Coming Forth by Day*, p. 295.

[3] *Ibid.*, p. 293.

"Thou art the fire-goddess Ami-seshet, whose opportunity escapeth her not; thy name is Kaharesapusaremkakaremet. Thou art like unto the mighty flame "of Saqenaqat which is in the bow of the boat of "thy father Harepukakashareshabaiu, for behold, thus "is [the name uttered] in the speech of the Negroes, "and of the Anti, and of the people of Nubia. . . . "Sefiperemhesihrahaputchetef is thy name; Atareamtcherqemturennuparsheta is the name of one of thy "divine sons, and Panemma that of the other." And in yet another chapter[1] the deceased addressing the god Par says, "Thou art the mighty one of names among "the gods, the mighty runner whose strides are mighty; "thou art the god the mighty one who comest and "rescuest the needy one and the afflicted from him "that oppresseth him; give heed to my cry. I am "the Cow, and thy divine name is in my mouth, and "I will utter it; Haqahakaher is thy name; Āurauaaqersaanqrebathi is thy name; Kherserau is thy "name; Kharsatha is thy name. I praise thy name. ". . . . O be gracious unto the deceased, and cause "thou heat to exist under his head, for, indeed, he is "the soul of the great divine Body which resteth in "Annu (Heliopolis), whose names are Khukheperuru "and Barekathatchara."

The examples of the use of names possessing magical powers described above illustrate the semi-religious

[1] See *Chapters of Coming Forth by Day*, p. 289.

views on the subject of names which the Egyptians held, and we have now to consider briefly the manner in which the knowledge of a name was employed in uses less important than those which had for their object the attainment of life and happiness in the world to come. In the famous magical papyrus [1] which Chabas published [2] we find a series of interesting charms and magical formulæ which were written to preserve its possessor from the attacks of sea and river monsters of every kind, of which the following is an example. "Hail, lord of the gods! Drive away from me the "lions of the country of Meru (Meroë ?), and the "crocodiles which come forth from the river, and "the bite of all poisonous reptiles which crawl forth "from their holes. Get thee back, O crocodile Māk, "thou son of Set! Move not by means of thy tail! "Work not thy legs and feet! Open not thy mouth! "Let the water which is before thee turn into a con-"suming fire, O thou whom the thirty-seven gods did "make, and whom the serpent of Rā did put in chains, "O thou who wast fettered with links of iron before "the boat of Rā! Get thee back, O crocodile Māk, "thou son of Set!" These words were to be said over a figure of the god Amen painted on clay; the god was to have four rams' heads upon one neck, under his feet was to be a figure of the crocodile Māk, and

[1] British Museum, No. 10,042.

[2] *Le Papyrus Magique Harris*, Chalon-sur-Saône, 1860.

to the right and left of him were to be the dog-headed apes, *i.e.*, the transformed spirits of the dawn, who sang hymns of praise to Rā when he rose daily.[1] Again, let us suppose that some water monster wished to attack a man in a boat. To avoid this the man stood before the cabin of the boat and, taking a hard egg in his hand, he said, "O egg of the water which "hath been spread over the earth, essence of the "divine apes, the great one in the heaven above and "in the earth beneath, who dost dwell in the nests "which are in the waters, I have come forth with thee "from the water, I have been with thee in thy nest, "I am Amsu of Coptos, I am Amsu, lord of Kebu." When he had said these words he would appear to the animal in the water in the form of the god Amsu, with whom he had identified himself, and it would be afraid and flee. At the end of the papyrus in which the above extracts occur we find a series of magical names which may be read thus:—Atir-Atịsa, Atirkaha-Atisa, Samumatnatmu-Atisa, Samuanemui-Atisa, Samutekaari-Atisa, Samutekabaiu-Atisa, Samutchakaretcha-Atisa, Tāuuarehasa, Qina, Hama, Senentuta-Batetsataiu, Anrehakatha-sataiu, Haubailra-Haari. From these and similar magical names it is quite certain that the Gnostics and other sects which held views akin to theirs obtained the names which they were so fond of

[1] See the scene in the rounded portion of the Metternichstele illustrated on p. 149.

inscribing upon their amulets and upon the so-called magical papyri. The last class of documents undoubtedly contains a very large proportion of the magical ideas, beliefs, formulæ, etc., which were current in Egypt from the time of the Ptolemies to the end of the Roman Period, but from about B.C. 150 to A.D. 200 the papyri exhibit traces of the influence of Greek, Hebrew, and Syrian philosophers and magicians, and from a passage like the following [1] we may get a proof of this:—"I call thee, the headless one, that didst "create earth and heaven, that didst create night and "day, thee the creator of light and darkness. Thou "art Osoronnophris, whom no man hath seen at any "time; thou art Iabas, thou art Iapōs, thou hast dis-"tinguished the just and the unjust, thou didst make "female and male, thou didst produce seeds and fruits, "thou didst make men to love one another and to hate "one another. I am Moses thy prophet, to whom thou "didst commit thy mysteries, the ceremonies of Israel; "thou didst produce the moist and the dry and all "manner of food. Listen to me: I am an angel of "Phapro Osoronnophris; this is thy true name, handed "down to the prophets of Israel. Listen to me.[2] . . ." In this passage the name Osoronnophris is clearly a corruption of the old Egyptian names of the

[1] See Goodwin, *Fragment of a Græco-Egyptian Work upon Magic*, p. 7.

[2] Here follow a number of names of which Reibet, Athelebersthe, Blatha, Abeu, Ebenphi, are examples.

great god of the dead "Ausar Unnefer," and Phapro seems to represent the Egyptian *Per-āa* (literally, "great house") or "Pharaoh," with the article *pa* "the" prefixed. It is interesting to note that Moses is mentioned, a fact which seems to indicate Jewish influence.

In another magical formula we read,[1] "I call upon "thee that didst create the earth and bones, and all "flesh and all spirit, that didst establish the sea and "that shakest the heavens, that didst divide the light "from the darkness, the great regulative mind, that "disposest everything, eye of the world, spirit of spirits, "god of gods, the lord of spirits, the immoveable Aeon, "IAOOUÊI, hear my voice. I call upon thee, the ruler of "the gods, high-thundering Zeus, Zeus, king, Adonai, "lord, Iaoouêe. I am he that invokes thee in the "Syrian tongue, the great god, Zaalaêr, Iphphou, do "thou not disregard the Hebrew appellation Ablana-"thanalb, Abrasilôa. For I am Silthakhōoukh, Lailam, "Blasalōth, Iaō, Ieō, Nebouth, Sabiothar, Bōth, Ar-"bathiaō, Iaoth, Sabaōth, Patoure, Zagourē, Baroukh "Adonai, Elōai, Iabraam, Barbarauō, Nau, Siph," etc. The spell ends with the statement that it "loosens "chains, blinds, brings dreams, creates favour; it may "be used in common for whatever purpose you will." In the above we notice at once the use of the seven vowels which form "a name wherein be contained all Names,

[1] Goodwin, *op. cit.*, p. 21.

"and all Lights, and all Powers."[1] The seven vowels have, of course, reference to the three vowels "Iaō,"[2] which were intended to represent one of the Hebrew names for Almighty God, "Jāh." The names "Adonai, Elōai," are also derived through the Hebrew from the Bible, and Sabaōth is another well-known Hebrew word meaning "hosts"; some of the remaining names could be explained, if space permitted, by Hebrew and Syriac words. On papyri and amulets the vowels are written in magical combinations in such a manner as to form triangles and other shapes; with them are often found the names of the seven archangels of God; the following are examples :—

| No. 1.[3] | No. 2.[4] | No. 3.[5] |
| --- | --- | --- |
| A | αεηιουω | μιχαηλ |
| εε | εηιουωα | ραφαηλ |
| HHH | ηιουωαε | γαβριηλ |
| IIII | ιουωαεη | σουριηλ |
| OOOOO | ουωαεηι | ζαζιηλ |
| ΥΥΥΥΥΥ | υωαεηιο | βαδακιηλ |
| ωωωωωωω | ωαεηιου | συλιηλ |

In combination with a number of signs which owe their origin to the Gnostics the seven vowels were

[1] See Kenyon, *Greek Papyri in the British Museum*, London, 1893, p. 63.

[2] For Iaoouêi we should probably read Iaô ouêi.

[3] British Museum, Gnostic gem, No. G. 33.

[4] Kenyon, *Greek Papyri*, p. 123.

[5] *Ibid.*, p. 123. These names read Michael, Raphael, Gabriel, Souriel, Zaziel, Badakiel, and Suliel.

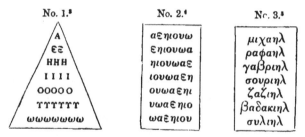

sometimes engraved upon plaques, or written upon papyri, with the view of giving the possessor power over gods or demons or his fellow creatures. The example printed below is found on a papyrus in the British Museum and accompanies a spell written for the purpose of overcoming the malice of enemies, and for giving security against alarms and nocturnal visions.[1]

Amulet inscribed with signs and letters of magical power for overcoming the malice of enemies. (From Brit. Mus., Greek Papyrus, No. CXXIV.—4th or 5th century.)

But of all the names found upon Gnostic gems two, *i.e.*, Khnoubis (or Khnoumis), and Abrasax (or Abraxas), are of the most frequent occurrence. The first is usually represented as a huge serpent having the head of a lion surrounded by seven or twelve rays. Over the seven rays, one on the point of each, are the seven vowels of the Greek alphabet, which some suppose to

[1] Kenyon, *op. cit.*, p. 121.

refer to the seven heavens; and on the back of the amulet, on which the figure of Khnoumis occurs, is usually found the sign SSS, or the triple S and bar. Khnoumis is, of course, a form of the ancient Egyptian god Khnemu, or "Fashioner" of man and beast, the god to whom many of the attributes of the Creator of the universe were ascribed. Khnemu is, however, often depicted with the head of a ram, and in the later times, as the "beautiful ram of Rā," he has four heads; in the Egyptian monuments he has at times the head of a hawk, but never that of a lion. The god Abrasax is represented in a form which has a human body, the head of a hawk or cock, and legs terminating in serpents; in one hand he holds a knife or dagger, and in the other a shield upon which is inscribed the great name ΙΑω, or JĀH. Considerable difference of opinion exists as to the meaning and derivation of the name Abrasax, but there is no doubt that the god who bore it was a form of the Sun-god, and that he was intended to represent some aspect of the Creator of the world. The name was believed to possess magical powers of the highest class, and Basileides,[1] who gave it currency in the second century, seems to have regarded it as an invincible name. It is probable, however, that its exact meaning was lost at an early date, and that it

[1] He of Alexandria, who lived about A.D. 120. He was a disciple of Menander, and declared that he had received the esoteric doctrine of Saint Peter from Glaucias, a disciple of the Apostle.

soon degenerated into a mere magical symbol, for it is often found inscribed on amulets side by side with scenes and figures with which, seemingly, it cannot have any connexion whatever. Judging from certain Gnostic gems in the British Museum, Abrasax is to be identified with the polytheistic figure that stands in the upper part of the Metternich stele depicted on p. 153. This figure has two bodies, one being that of a man, and the other that of a bird; from these extend four wings, and from each of his knees projects a serpent. He has two pairs of hands and arms; one pair is extended along the wings, each hand holding the symbols of "life," "stability," and "power," and two knives and two serpents; the other pair is pendent, the right hand grasping the sign of life, and the other a sceptre. His face is grotesque, and probably represents that of Bes, or the sun as an old man; on his head is a pylon-shaped object with figures of various animals, and above it a pair of horns which support eight knives and the figure of a god with raised hands and arms, which typifies "millions of years." The god stands upon an oval wherein are depicted figures of various "typhonic" animals, and from each side of his crown proceed several symbols of fire. Whether in the Gnostic system Abraxas absorbed all the names and attributes of this god of many forms cannot be said with certainty.

# CHAPTER VI.

## MAGICAL CEREMONIES.

In the preceding pages we have seen how the Egyptians employed magical stones or amulets, and magical words, and magical pictures, and magical names, in the performance of deeds both good and evil; it remains to consider these magical ceremonies in which the skill of the magician-priest was exerted to its fullest extent, and with the highest objects, that is to say, to preserve the human body in a mummified condition, and to perform the symbolic acts which would restore its natural functions. When we think of the sublime character of the life which the souls of the blessed dead were believed to lead in heaven with the gods, it is hard to understand why the Egyptians took such pains to preserve the physical body from decay. No Egyptian who believed his Scriptures ever expected that his corruptible body would ascend into heaven and live with the gods, for they declare in no uncertain manner that it remains upon the earth whilst the soul dwells in heaven. But that the preservation of the body was in some way or for some reason absolutely necessary is certain, for the art of mummification flourished for several thousands of years, and unless there was some good reason, besides the observance of conservative custom and traditional use, why it should do so, king and priest, gentle and simple, and rich and poor, would never have burdened their relatives and heirs with the expense of costly funeral ceremonies, and with the performance of rites which were of no avail. At first sight, too, it seems strange to find the Egyptians studying carefully how best to provide the dead with a regular supply of sepulchral offerings, for when we come to think about it we notice that in arranging for the well-being of the dead nothing whatever was left to chance. For example, a papyrus will contain several prayers and pictures with appropriate formulæ, the object of each of which is to give the deceased meat and drink; any one of these would have been enough for the purpose, but it was thought best in such an important matter to make assurance doubly sure, and if there was the least doubt about the efficacy of one Chapter one or more of the same class were added. Similarly, the tendency of the natural body after death being to decay, the greatest care was taken in mummifying its various members, lest perchance any one of them should be neglected accidentally, and should, either by the omission of the words of power that ought to have been said over it, or through the lax performance of some ceremony, decay and perish. The Egyptian declared that he was immortal, and believed that he would enjoy eternal life in a spiritual body; yet he attempted by the performance of magical ceremonies and the recital of words of power to make his corruptible body to endure for ever. He believed that he would feed upon the celestial and imperishable food whereon the gods lived, but at the same time he spared no effort or expense to provide for his tomb being supplied at stated intervals throughout the year with perishable food in the shape of offerings of oxen, feathered fowl, cakes, bread, and the like. He mummified his dead and swathed them in linen bandages, and then by the performance of magical ceremonies and by the recital of words of power sought to give back to their members the strength to eat, and drink, and talk, and think, and move at will. Indeed, all the evidence now forthcoming seems to prove that he never succeeded in bringing himself to think that the gods could do without his help, or that the pictures or representations of the scenes which took place in the life, and death, and burial, and resurrection of Osiris, upon which he relied so implicitly, could possibly fail to be as efficacious as the actual power of the god himself.

The examination of mummies has shown us with tolerable clearness what methods were adopted in preparing bodies for bandaging and final ornamentation, and the means adopted for disposing of the more corruptible portions of the body are well known from classical and other writers. But for an account of the manner in which the body was bandaged, and a list of the unguents and other materials employed in the process, and the words of power which were spoken as each bandage was laid in its place, we must have recourse to a very interesting papyrus which has been edited and translated by M. Maspero under the title of *Le Rituel de l'Embaumement.*[1] The first part of the papyrus, which probably gave instructions for the evisceration of the body, is wanting, and only the section which refers to the bandaging is at all perfect. The text opens with an address to the deceased in which it is said, "The perfume of Arabia hath been "brought to thee to make perfect thy smell through "the scent of the god. Here are brought to thee "liquids which have come forth from Rā to make "perfect . . . thy smell in the Hall [of Judgment]. "O sweet-smelling soul of the great god, thou dost "contain such a sweet odour that thy face shall neither "change nor perish. . . . Thy members shall become "young in Arabia, and thy soul shall appear over thy "body in Ta-neter (*i.e.*, the 'divine land')." After this the priest or mummifier was to take a vase of liquid which contained ten perfumes, and to smear therewith the body from head to foot twice, taking especial care

[1] In *Mémoire sur quelques Papyrus du Louvre*, Paris, 1875.

to anoint the head thoroughly. He was then to say, "Osiris (*i.e.*, the deceased), thou hast received the per-"fume which shall make thy members perfect. Thou "receivest the source [of life] and thou takest the form "of the great Disk (*i.e.*, Aten), which uniteth itself unto "thee to give enduring form to thy members; thou "shalt unite with Osiris in the great Hall. The "unguent cometh unto thee to fashion thy members "and to gladden thy heart, and thou shalt appear in the "form of Rā; it shall make thee to be sound when thou "settest in the sky at eventide, and it shall spread "abroad the smell of thee in the nomes of Aqert. . . . "Thou receivest the oil of the cedar in Amentet, and "the cedar which came forth from Osiris cometh unto "thee; it delivereth thee from thy enemies, and it pro-"tecteth thee in the nomes. Thy soul alighteth upon "the venerable sycamores. Thou criest to Isis, and "Osiris heareth thy voice, and Anubis cometh unto "thee to invoke thee. Thou receivest the oil of the "country of Manu which hath come from the East, and "Rā riseth upon thee at the gates of the horizon, at the "holy doors of Neith. Thou goest therein, thy soul is "in the upper heaven, and thy body is in the lower "heaven . . . O Osiris, may the Eye of Horus cause "that which floweth forth from it to come to thee, and "to thy heart for ever!" These words having been said, the whole ceremony was repeated, and then the internal organs which had been removed from the body were placed in the "liquid of the children of Horus," so that the liquid of this god might enter into them, and whilst they were being thus treated a chapter was read over them and they were put in the funeral chest. When this was done the internal organs were placed on the body, and the body having been made to lie straight the backbone was immersed in holy oil, and the face of the deceased was turned towards the sky; the bandage of Sebek and Sedi was then laid upon the backbone. In a long speech the deceased is addressed and told that the liquid is "secret," and that it is an emanation of the gods Shu and Seb, and that the resin of Phœnicia and the bitumen of Byblos will make his burial perfect in the underworld, and give him his legs, and facilitate his movements, and sanctify his steps in the Hall of Seb. Next gold, silver, lapis-lazuli, and turquoise are brought to the deceased, and crystal to lighten his face, and carnelian to strengthen his steps; these form amulets which will secure for him a free passage in the underworld. Meanwhile the backbone is kept in oil, and the face of the deceased is turned towards the heavens; and next the gilding of the nails of the fingers and toes begins. When this has been done, and portions of the fingers have been wrapped in linen made at Saïs, the following address is made to the deceased:—"O Osiris, thou receivest thy nails of gold, "thy fingers of gold, and thy thumb of *smu* (or *uasm*) "metal; the liquid of Rā entereth into thee as well "as into the divine members of Osiris, and thou "journeyest on thy legs to the immortal abode. Thou "hast carried thy hands to the house of eternity, thou "art made perfect in gold, thou dost shine brightly in "*smu* metal, and thy fingers shine in the dwelling of "Osiris, in the sanctuary of Horus himself. O Osiris, "the gold of the mountains cometh to thee; it is a holy "talisman of the gods in their abodes, and it lighteneth "thy face in the lower heaven. Thou breathest in "gold, thou appearest in *smu* metal, and the dwellers "in Re-stau receive thee; those who are in the funeral "chest rejoice because thou hast transformed thyself "into a hawk of gold by means of thy amulets (*or* "talismans) of the City of Gold," etc. When these words have been said, a priest who is made to personify Anubis comes to the deceased and performs certain symbolical ceremonies by his head, and lays certain bandages upon it. When the head and mouth and face have been well oiled the bandage of Nekheb is laid on the forehead, the bandage of Hathor on the face, the bandage of Thoth upon the two ears, and the bandage of Nebt-hetep on the nape of the neck. Over the head was laid the bandage of Sekhet, in two pieces, and over each ear, and each nostril, and each cheek was fastened a bandage or strip of linen; over the forehead went four pieces of linen, on the top of the head two, outside the mouth two, and inside two, over the chin two, and over the nape of the neck four large pieces; there were to be twenty-two pieces to the right and to the left of the face passing over the two ears. The Lady of the West is then addressed in these words:—"Grant thou "that breathing may take place in the head of the "deceased in the underworld, and that he may see with "his eyes, and that he may hear with his two ears; "and that he may breathe through his nose; and that "he may be able to utter sounds with his mouth; and "that he may be able to speak with his tongue in the "underworld. Receive thou his voice in the Hall of "Maāti and his speech in the Hall of Seb in the "presence of the Great God, the lord of Amentet." The addresses which follow these words have reference to the delights and pleasures of the future life which shall be secured for him through the oil and unguents, which are duly specified and described, and through the magical figures which are drawn upon the bandages. The protecting properties of the turquoise and other precious stones are alluded to, and after a further anointing with oil and the placing of grains of myrrh and resin, the deceased is declared to have "received "his head," and he is promised that it shall nevermore depart from him. On the conclusion of the ceremonies which concern the head the deceased has the power to go in among the holy and perfect spirits, his name is exalted among men, the denizens of heaven receive his soul, the beings of the underworld bow down before his body, the dwellers upon earth adore him, and the inhabitants of the funeral mountain renew for him his youth. Besides these things, Anubis and Horus make perfect his bandages, and the god Thoth protects his members by his words of magical power; and he himself has learned the magical formulæ which are necessary to make his path straight in the underworld, and also the proper way in which to utter them. All these benefits were secured for him by the use of bandages and unguents which possess both magical names and properties, and by the words of power uttered by the priests who recited the Ritual of Embalmment, and by the ceremonies which the priest who personated Anubis performed beside the body of the deceased in imitation of those which the god Anubis performed for the dead god Osiris in remote days.

Next the left hand of the deceased was mummified and bandaged according to the instructions given in the Ritual of Embalmment. The hand was stretched out on a piece of linen, and a ring was passed over the fingers; it was then filled with thirty-six of the substances which were used in embalming, according to the number of the forms of the god Osiris. This done, the hand was bandaged with a strip of linen in six folds, upon which were drawn figures of Isis and Hāpi. The right hand was treated in a similar way, only the figures drawn upon the bandages were those of Rā and Amsu; and when the appropriate words had been recited over both hands divine protection was assured them. After these things the ceremonies concerning the right and left arms were performed, and these were followed by rubbing the soles of the feet and the legs and the thighs, first with black-stone oil, and secondly with holy oil. The toes were wrapped in linen, and a piece of linen was laid on each leg; on each piece was drawn the figure of a jackal, that on the right leg representing Anubis, and that on the left Horus. When flowers of the *ānkham* plant and other substances had been laid beside and on the legs, and they had been treated with ebony-gum water and holy oil, and appropriate addresses had been said, the ceremony of bandaging the body was ended. Everything that could be done to preserve the body was now done, and every member of it was, by means of the words of power which changed perishable substances into imperishable, protected to all eternity; when the final covering of purple or white linen had been fastened upon it, the body was ready for the tomb.

But the Ritual of Embalmment which has been briefly described above seems to belong to a late period of Egyptian history, and although the ideas and beliefs contained in it are as old as Egyptian civilization itself, it seems as if it was intended to take the place of a much older and more elaborate work which was in use as far back as the period in which the Great Pyramid was built, and which was intended to be recited during the performance of a complex series of ceremonies, some of which are still not completely understood. It seems as if the performance of all the ceremonies would require several days, and it is clear that only the wealthy could afford the expense which must have attended such elaborate obsequies; for the poorer classes of men the various ceremonies must have been greatly curtailed, and at a very early period we find that a shortened form of ritual had taken their place. Of all the ceremonies, the most important was that of the "Opening of the Mouth and Eyes," which was performed either on the mummy itself or upon a statue which represented it. It has already been stated that the Egyptians believed that they could transmit to a statue the attributes of the person in whose image it was made, and similarly that that which was done to the statue of the mummified person was also done to it. The use of a statue instead of the actual mummy has obvious advantages, for the ceremony could be performed at any time and in any place, and the presence of the mummy was unnecessary. As a matter of fact the ceremony was performed in a chamber at the entrance to the tomb, or outside the tomb at a place which had been made ceremonially pure or consecrated, and those who took part in it were:—(1) The *Kher-heb*, or chief officiating priest, who held a roll of papyrus in his hand. (2) The *Sem* priest. (3) The *Smer*, who was, perhaps, some intimate friend of the deceased.

(4) The *Sa-mer-ef*,[1] or man who was either the son of the deceased or his representative. (5) The *Tcherau-ur*, or woman who represented Isis. (6) The *Tcherau-sheraut*, or woman who represented Nephthys. (7) The *Menhu*, or slaughterer. (8) The *Am-asi* priest. (9) The *Am-khent* priest. (10) A number of people who represented the armed guard of Horus. All these became actors in scenes which were intended to represent the events which took place in connexion with the burial of Osiris, with whom the deceased is now identified; the two women took the parts of the goddesses Isis and Nephthys, and the men those of the gods who helped them in the performance of their pious duties. From the scenes[2] which accompany the texts[3] relating to the ceremony of opening the mouth and eyes we see that it began with the sprinkling of water round about the statue or mummy from four vessels, one for each quarter of the earth, and with the recital of addresses to the gods Horus, Set, Thoth, and Sept; this act restored to the deceased the use of his head. The sprinkling of water was followed by a purification by means of incense, also contained in four vases, one for each of the four quarters of the earth. The burning

[1] *I.e.*, "the son who loveth him."

[2] See Dümichen, *Der Grabpalast des Patuamenap*, Leipzig, vol. i., 1884; vol. ii., 1885; vol. iii., 1894; and Champollion, *Monuments*, Paris, 1845, tom. iii., plates 243–248.

[3] See Schiaparelli, *Il Libro dei Funerali degli antichi Egiziani*, Turin, 1882; see also Maspero, *Le Rituel du sacrifice funéraire* (*Revue de l'Histoire des Religions*, tom. xv., p. 159 ff.).

of this sweet-smelling substance assisted in opening the mouth of the deceased and in strengthening his heart. At this stage the *Sem* priest dressed himself in the skin of a cow, and lying down upon a kind of couch pretended to be asleep; but he was roused up by the *Am-asi* priest in the presence of the *Kher-heb* and the *Am-khent* priest, and when the *Sem* priest had seated himself upon a seat, the four men together represented the four children of Horus,[1] or the gods with the heads of a hawk, an ape, a jackal, and a man respectively. The *Sem* priest then said, "I have seen my father in "all his forms," which the other men in turn repeat. The meaning of this portion of the ceremony is hard to explain, but M. Maspero [2] thinks that it was intended to bring back to the body of the deceased its shadow (*khaibit*), which had departed from it when it died. The preliminary purifications being ended, and the shadow having been joined to the body once more, the statue or mummy is approached by the men who represent the armed guard of Horus; and one of their number, having taken upon himself the character of Horus, the son of Osiris and Isis, touches its mouth with his finger. The *Kher-heb* next made ready to perform the sacrifice which was intended to commemorate the slaughter, at some very early period, of the fiends who were the friends of Set. It seems that,

[1] *I.e.*, Mestha, Hāpi, Tuamutef and Qebhsennuf.
[2] *Op. cit.*, p. 168.

the soul of Horus dwelt in an eye, and that Set nearly succeeded in devouring it; but Horus vanquished Set and saved his eye. Set's associates then changed themselves into the forms of animals, and birds, and fish, but they were caught, and their heads were cut off; Set, however, who was concealed in the form of a pig, contrived to escape. The sacrifice consisted of a bull (or cow) or two, two gazelles or antelopes, and ducks. When the bull had been slain, one of the forelegs was cut off, and the heart taken out, and offered to the statue or mummy; the *Sem* priest then took the bleeding leg and touched, or pretended to touch, the mouth and eyes with it four times. The slaughtered gazelles or antelopes and ducks were simply offered before the statue. The *Sem* priest next said to the statue, "I "have come to embrace thee, I am thy son Horus, I "have pressed thy mouth; I am thy son, I love thee. ". . . Thy mouth was closed, but I have set in order "for thee thy mouth and thy teeth." He then brought two instruments, , called "Seb-ur" and "Tuntet" respectively, and touched the mouth of the statue or mummy with them, whilst the *Kher-heb* said, "Thy "mouth was closed, but I have set in order for thee "thy mouth and thy teeth. I open for thee thy mouth, "I open for thee thy two eyes. I have opened for thee "thy mouth with the instrument of Anubis. I have "opened thy mouth with the instrument of Anubis, "with the iron implement with which the mouths of the "gods were opened. Horus, open the mouth! Horus, "open the mouth! Horus hath opened the mouth "of the dead, as he in times of old opened the mouth of "Osiris, with the iron which came forth from Set, with "the iron instrument with which he opened the mouths "of the gods. He hath opened thy mouth with it. The "deceased shall walk and shall speak, and his body "shall be with the great company of the gods in the "Great House of the Aged One in Annu, and he shall "receive there the *ureret* crown from Horus, the lord "of mankind." Thus the mouth and the eyes of the deceased are opened. The *Sem* priest then took in his hand the instrument called *ur hekau*, *i.e.*, the "mighty one of enchantments," a curious, sinuous piece of wood, one end of which is in the form of a ram's head surmounted by a uraeus, and touched the mouth and the eyes of the statue or mummy four times, whilst the *Kher-heb* recited a long address in which he declared that this portion of the ceremony had secured for the deceased all the benefits which accrued to the god Osiris from the actions of Nut, Horus, and Set, when he was in a similar state. It has been said above that every dead man hoped to be provided with the *hekau*, or words of power, which were necessary for him in the next world, but without a mouth it was impossible for him to utter them. Now that the mouth, or rather the use of it, was restored to the deceased, it was all important to give him not only the words of power, but also the ability to utter them correctly and in such wise that the gods and other beings would hearken to them and obey them; four touches of the *ur hekau* instrument on the lips endowed the deceased with the faculty of uttering the proper words in the proper manner in each of the four quarters of the world. When this had been done, several other ceremonies were performed with the object of allowing the "son who "loveth him" or his representative to take part in the opening of the mouth of his father. In order to do this he took in his hand a metal chisel and touched the openings of the mouth and of the eyes, and then the *Sem* priest touched them first with his little finger, and afterwards with a little bag filled with pieces of red stone or carnelian, with the idea, M. Maspero thinks, of restoring to the lips and eyelids the colour which they had lost during the process of mummification. The "son who loves him" then took four objects called "iron of the South, and iron of the "North," and laid each of them four times upon the mouth and the eyes while the *Kher-heb* recited the proper address in which the mummy or statue is said to have had his mouth and lips established firmly. This done, the *Sem* priest brings an instrument called the "Pesh-en-kef," , and touches the mouth of the mummy or statue therewith, and says, "O "Osiris, I have stablished for thee the two jaw-bones "in thy face, and they are now separated"; that is to say, the bandages with which they have been tied up can no longer prevent their movement when the deceased wishes to eat. After the Pesh-en-kef had been used the *Sem* priest brought forward a basket or vessel of some kind of food in the shape of balls, and by the order of the *Kher-heb* offered them to the mouth of the mummy, and when this portion of the ceremony was ended, the *Sem* priest took an ostrich feather, and waved it before its face four times, but with what object is not clear. Such are the ceremonies which it was thought necessary to perform in order to restore to the deceased the functions which his body possessed upon earth. But it must be remembered that hitherto only the "bull of the south" has been sacrificed, and that the "bull of the north" has yet to be offered up; and all the ceremonies which have been already performed must be repeated if the deceased would have the power to go forth at will over the whole earth. From the earliest times the South and the North were the two great sections into which the world was divided, and each section possessed its own special gods, all of whom had to be propitiated by the deceased; hence most religious ceremonies were ordered to be performed in duplicate. In later days each section was divided into two parts, and the four divisions thus made were apportioned to the four children of Horus; hence prayers and formulæ

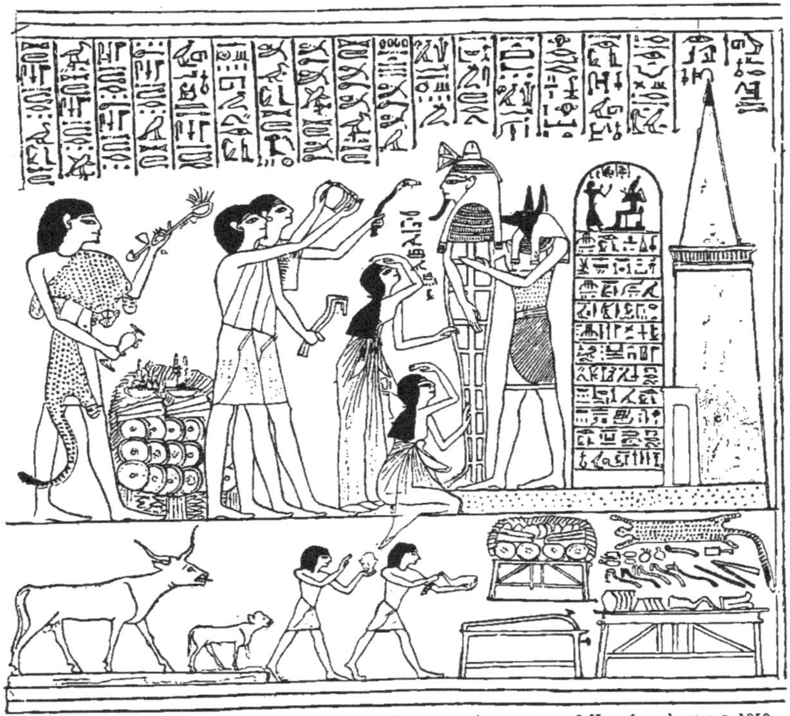

The ceremony of "opening the mouth" being performed on the mummy of Hunefer, about B.C. 1350.
(From the *Papyrus of Hunefer*, sheet 5.)

were usually said four times, once in honour of each god, and the rubrical directions on this point are definite.

In the limited space of this book it is not possible to reproduce all the scenes of the ceremony of opening the mouth and the eyes which are depicted in the tombs and elsewhere, but on page 199 is a general view of the ceremony as it is often given in the papyri of the XVIIIth and XIXth dynasties. On the right we see the pyramidal tomb in the Theban hill with its open door, and by the side of it is the funeral stele with a rounded top inscribed with a figure of the deceased standing in adoration before Osiris, and with a prayer to the god for sepulchral offerings. Anubis, the god of the dead, embraces the mummy, thus indicating his readiness to take the deceased under his protection. Nasha, the wife of the deceased, stands weeping before the mummy, and at his feet kneels another weeping woman, probably his daughter. Anubis and the mummy stand upon a layer of sand which has been placed there with the object of sanctifying the ground. A priest clad in a panther's skin holds a censer containing burning incense in one hand, and a vase, from which he sprinkles water, in the other. One ministrant holds the two instruments "Tun-tet" and "Seb-ur" in the right hand, and the "Ur hekau" instrument in the left; and another offers four vases of unguent. In the lower register are a cow and her

calf, and two men are carrying along to the mummy the haunch which we must assume to have been recently cut from the slaughtered bull, and the heart which has just been taken out of him. On a table we see lying a number of objects, the "Meskhet," and "Pesh-en-kef," and other instruments, two sets of four vases for holding unguents and oil, the bags of colour, the iron of the south and north, etc. The text which runs in short vertical lines above the scene reads:—
"The Chapter of the opening of the mouth of the "statue of Osiris, the royal scribe, Hunefer, which is "to be performed [when] its face [looketh] towards the "south, [and when it is set] upon the sand behind "him. And the Kher-heb shall say four times unto "the *Sem* priest as he goeth round about him bearing "four vases of water: 'Thou art pure with the purifi-"cation of Horus, and Horus is pure with thy purifica-"tion. Thou art pure with the purification of Thoth, "and Thoth is pure with thy purification. Thou art "pure with the purification of Sep, and Sep is pure "with thy purification. Thou art pure with the puri-"fication of Seb, and Seb is pure with thy purification. "Pure. Pure.' [Say] four times. 'Incense hath been "offered unto thee of the incense of Horus, and incense "hath been offered unto Horus of thy incense. Incense "hath been offered unto thee of the incense of Thoth, "and incense hath been offered unto Thoth of thy "incense. Incense hath been offered unto thee of

"the incense of Sep, and incense hath been offered "unto Sep of thy incense. Incense hath been offered "unto thee of the incense of Seb, and incense hath "been offered unto Seb of thy incense.'" The above words are all the text that the scribe considered it necessary to give in the Papyrus of Hunefer, and that he curtailed the representation of the ceremony of opening the mouth and eyes as much as possible is evident.

The performance of the ceremony of opening the mouth was followed by a number of other less important ceremonies which had for their object the providing of the mummy or statue with scents, and unguents, and various articles of wearing apparel; these were not essentials, but sufficient importance was attached to them to make the performance of them almost obligatory. Among the objects presented to the deceased in these ceremonies scents and perfumed unguents play a prominent part, and this is not to be wondered at. To certain kinds of oil, magical properties have been attached from time immemorial in the East, and the important place which they occupied in the ceremonies and rituals of many nations proves that remarkable effects were expected to follow their use. The living made use of oil to soften the skin and to preserve it from the parching heat of the sun, and the dead were anointed with it during the process of mummification so that their skins might, through the magical words which were pronounced whilst it was being rubbed on them, remain soft for all time, and so that the curative properties of the oil might heal the wounds which the mummifiers had made. A glance at the medical papyri of Egypt will shew that oil appears in scores of prescriptions, and it was no less useful to the magician[1] than to the physician in producing good or evil results. It seems to have been used with the idea of effecting transformations by the former, just as it was employed by the priest in the performance of certain important religious ceremonies, and a curious survival of this use is mentioned by Lucian,[2] who relates that a woman transformed herself into a night-raven by its means. The woman first undressed herself, and going to a lamp threw two grains of incense into the flame and recited certain words; she then went to a large chest containing several bottles, and taking out one which, the writer thinks, contained oil, rubbed all her body with the liquid, from head to foot, beginning with the ends of the nails, and suddenly feathers and wings began to grow upon her, and a hooked, horny beak took the place of her nose. In a very short time she resembled a bird in every respect, and when she saw that she was well feathered, she flew upwards and, uttering the cry of a night-

[1] See the description of the ceremony of the beetle, p. 42.

[2] *Lucius sive Asinus*, xlii., 12 (ed. Didot, p. 449). Compare also § 54 (p. 466).

raven, disappeared through the window.[1] In connexion with the recital of certain Chapters of the Book of the Dead a number of interesting ceremonies were performed, but as they only illustrate the beliefs described above they need not be mentioned here.

[1] From the words, *χρίσματι μεμαγευμένῳ ἐπαλείψασα ὄνον ποιήσειε* (see *Lucius sive Asinus*, xlii., 54, ed. Didot, p. 466), it is clear that the person who is speaking believed that he had been transformed into an ass by means of the use of "bewitched oil."

## CHAPTER VII.

### DEMONIACAL POSSESSION, DREAMS, GHOSTS, LUCKY AND UNLUCKY DAYS, HOROSCOPES, PROGNOSTICATIONS, TRANSFORMATIONS, AND THE WORSHIP OF ANIMALS.

THE Egyptians, in common with many other Eastern nations, believed that certain sicknesses and diseases might be cured by certain medicaments pure and simple, but that others needed not only drugs but the recital of words of power to effect their cure. There is good reason for thinking that some diseases were attributed to the action of evil spirits or demons, which had the power of entering into human bodies and of vexing them in proportion to their malignant nature and influence,[1] but the texts do not afford much information on the matter. Incidentally, however, we have one interesting proof that foreign peoples believed that the Egyptians were able to cure the diseases caused by demoniacal possession, and the exercise of their power

[1] As recently as 1895 this belief existed in Ireland, for according to the *Times* of April 2, 3, 6, and 8, Michael Cleary was charged on April 1 at Clonmel with having, on March 14, burnt his wife Bridget, aged 27, for being a witch, thus causing her death, at Baltyvadhen,

on the occasion described was considered to be so noteworthy that the narrative of it was inscribed upon a stele[1] and set up in the temple[2] of the god Khonsu at Thebes, so that all men might read and know what a marvellous cure his priests had effected. It appears that king Rameses II. was in Mesopotamia "according "to his wont, year by year," and all the chiefs of the countries round about came to pay their respects to him, and they sought to obtain his goodwill and protection, probably even an alliance, by bringing to him gifts of gold, and lapis-lazuli, and turquoise, and of every kind of valuable thing which the land produced,

county Tipperary. Johanna Burke swore that boiling herbs out of a saucepan on the fire were forced down the throat of the deceased, her husband asking her in the name of the Father, Son, and Holy Ghost, if she was his wife. He then stripped her naked, threw her on the floor, and pouring paraffin over her, set her on fire. Cleary, assisted by J. Dunne, P. Kennedy, W. Kennedy, and others, next took her to the fire and forced her to sit upon it in order to "drive "out the witch" which possessed her. She was next laid upon the bed and shaken, while her husband recited the words "Away with you," meaning the evil spirit, or spirits, and at six o'clock on the morning of the 15th of March the priest was sent for to exorcise the spirits with which the house was thought to be filled. A herbalist called Denis Ganey was present at the time, being charged as an accessory before the fact. The prisoners were found guilty and were sentenced to terms of imprisonment as follows:—M. Cleary 20 years, J. Dunne 3 years, P. Kennedy 5 years, W. Kennedy 18 months, J. Kennedy 18 months, Boland Kennedy 6 months, Michael Kennedy 6 months.

[1] Originally published by Prisse, *Monuments Égyptiens*, Paris, 1817, pl. 24.

[2] It is now preserved in the Bibliothèque Nationale at Paris; for a full description and translation of it see E. de Rougé, *Étude sur une stèle Égyptienne*, Paris, 1858.

and every man sought to outdo his neighbour by the lavishness of his gifts. Among others there came the Prince of Bekhten, and at the head of all the offerings which he presented to His Majesty he placed his eldest daughter, who was very beautiful. When the king saw her he thought her the most beautiful girl he had ever seen, and he bestowed upon her the title of "Royal spouse, chief lady, Rā-neferu" (*i.e.*, "the "beauties of Rā," the Sun-god), and took her to Egypt; and when they arrived in that country the king married her. One day during the fifteenth year of the king's reign, when His Majesty was in Thebes celebrating the festival of Amen-Rā, a messenger came to the king and reported the arrival of an ambassador from the Prince of Bekhten who had brought rich gifts for the royal lady Rā-neferu. When he had been led into the king's presence, he did homage before him, saying, "Glory and praise be unto thee, O thou Sun of the "nations; grant that we may live before thee!" Having said these words he bowed down and touched the ground with his head three times, and said, "I "have come unto thee, O my sovereign Lord, on behalf "of the lady Bent-ent-resht, the younger sister of the "royal spouse Rā-neferu, for, behold, an evil disease "hath laid hold upon her body; I beseech thy Majesty "to send a physician[1] to see her." Then the king straightway ordered the books of the "double house

[1] *Rekh khet*, "knower of things."

Stele recording the casting out of the devil from the Princess of Bekhten. On the right the king is offering incense to Khonsu Nefer-hetep, and on the left a priest is offering incense to Khonsu, "the great god who driveth away devils." (From Prisse, *Monuments*, plate 24.)

"of life" to be brought and the learned men to appear, and when they had come into his presence he ordered them to choose from among their number a man "wise "of heart and cunning of finger," that he might send him to Bekhten; they did so, and their choice fell upon one Tehuti-em-heb. This sage having come before the king was ordered to set out for Bekhten in company with the ambassador, and he departed; and when they had arrived there the Egyptian priest found the lady Bent-ent-resht to be possessed of a demon or spirit over which he was powerless. The Prince of Bekhten, seeing that the priest was unable to afford relief to his daughter, sent once again to the king, and entreated him to send a god to his help.

When the ambassador from Bekhten arrived in Egypt the king was in Thebes, and on hearing what was asked he went into the temple of Khonsu Nefer-hetep, and besought that god to allow his counterpart Khonsu to depart to Bekhten and to deliver the daughter of the prince of that country from the power of the demon that possessed her. It seems as if the sage Tehuti-em-heb had been sent to Bekhten by the advice of the god, for the king says, in addressing the god, "I have come once again into thy presence"; but in any case Khonsu Nefer-hetep agreed to his request, and a fourfold measure of magical power was imparted to the statue of the god which was to go to Bekhten. The god, seated in his boat, and five other boats with figures of gods in them, accompanied by chariots and horses on the right hand and on the left, set out from Egypt, and after travelling for seventeen months arrived in Bekhten, where they were received with great honour. The god Khonsu went to the place where Bent-ent-resht was, and, having performed a magical ceremony over her, the demon departed from her and she was cured straightway. Then the demon addressed the Egyptian god, saying, "Grateful and "welcome is thy coming unto us, O great god, thou "vanquisher of the hosts of darkness! Bekhten is "thy city, the inhabitants thereof are thy slaves, and "I am thy servant; and I will depart unto the place "whence I came that I may gratify thee, for unto this "end hast thou come thither. And I beseech thy "Majesty to command that the Prince of Bekhten and "I may hold a festival together." To the demon's request Khonsu agreed, and he commanded his priest to tell the Prince of Bekhten to make a great festival in honour of the demon; this having been done by the command of Khonsu the demon departed to his own place.

When the Prince of Bekhten saw that Khonsu was thus powerful, he and all his people rejoiced exceedingly, and he determined that the god should not be allowed to return to Egypt, and as a result Khonsu remained in Bekhten for three years, four months, and five days. On a certain day, however, the Prince was sleeping, and he dreamed a dream in which he saw the god Khonsu come forth from his shrine in the form of a hawk of gold, and having mounted into the air he flew away to Egypt. The Prince woke up in a state of great perturbation, and having inquired of the Egyptian priest was told by him that the god had departed to Egypt, and that his chariot must now be sent back. Then the Prince gave to Khonsu great gifts, and they were taken to Egypt and laid before the god Khonsu Nefer-hetep in his temple at Thebes. In early Christian literatures we find a number of examples of demoniacal possession in which the demon who has entered the body yields it up before a demon of greater power than himself, but the demon who is expelled is invariably hostile to him that expels him, and he departs from before him with every sign of wrath and shame. The fact that it was believed possible for the demon of Bekhten and the god Khonsu to fraternize, and to be present together at a festival made by the Prince of the country, shews that the people of Bekhten ascribed the same attributes to spirits or demons as they did to men. The demon who possessed the princess recognized in Khonsu a being who was mightier than himself, and, like a vanquished king, he wished to make the best terms he could with his conqueror, and to be on good terms with him.

The Egyptians believed that the divine powers frequently made known their will to them by means of dreams, and they attached considerable importance to them; the figures of the gods and the scenes which they saw when dreaming seemed to them to prove the existence of another world which was not greatly unlike that already known to them. The knowledge of the art of procuring dreams and the skill to interpret them were greatly prized in Egypt as elsewhere in the East, and the priest or official who possessed such gifts sometimes rose to places of high honour in the state, as we may see from the example of Joseph,[1] for it was universally believed that glimpses of the future were revealed to man in dreams. As instances of dreams recorded in the Egyptian texts may be quoted those of Thothmes IV., king of Egypt about B.C. 1450, and Nut-Amen, king of the Eastern Sûdân and Egypt, about B.C. 670. A prince, according to the stele which he set up before the breast of the Sphinx at Gîzeh, was one day hunting near this emblem of Rā-Harmachis, and he sat down to rest under its shadow and fell asleep and dreamed a dream. In it the god appeared to him, and, having declared that he was the god Harmachis-Khepera-Rā-Temu, promised him that if he would clear away from the Sphinx, his own image, the drift sand in which it was becoming buried, he would give to him the sovereignty of the lands of the South and of the North, *i.e.*, of all Egypt. In due course the prince became king of Egypt under the title of Thothmes IV., and the stele

[1] See Genesis, Chapters xl., xli.

which is dated on the 19th day of the month Hathor of the first year of Thothmes IV. proves that the royal dreamer carried out the wishes of the god.[1] Of Nut-Amen, the successor of the great Piānkhi who came down from Gebel Barkal and conquered all Egypt from Syene to the sea, we read that in the first year of his reign he one night dreamed a dream wherein he saw two serpents, one on his right hand and the other on his left; when he awoke they had disappeared. Having asked for an interpretation of the dream he was told:—"The land of the South is thine, and thou shalt "have dominion over the land of the North: the White "Crown and the Red Crown shall adorn thy head. "The length and the breadth of the land shall be given "unto thee, and the god Amen, the only god, shall be "with thee."[2] The two serpents were the symbols of the goddesses Nekhebet and Uatchet, the mistresses of the South and North respectively. As the result of his dream Nut-Amen invaded Egypt successfully and brought back much spoil, a portion of which he dedicated to the service of his god Amen.

Since dreams and visions in which the future might be revealed to the sleeper were greatly desired, the Egyptian magician set himself to procure such for his clients by various devices, such as drawing magical pictures and reciting magical words. The following

[1] See Vyse, *Appendix*, London, 1842, vol. iii., p. 114 ff.
[2] See Brugsch, *Egypt under the Pharaohs*, vol. ii., p. 259.

are examples of spells for procuring a vision and dreams, taken from British Museum Papyrus, No. 122, lines 64 ff. and 359 ff.[1]

"To obtain a vision from [the god] Bes. Make a "drawing of Besa, as shewn below, on your left hand, "and envelope your hand in a strip of black cloth that "has been consecrated to Isis (?) and lie down to sleep "without speaking a word, even in answer to a question. "Wind the remainder of the cloth round your neck. "The ink with which you write must be composed of "the blood of a cow, the blood of a white dove, fresh (?) "frankincense, myrrh, black writing-ink, cinnabar, "mulberry juice, rain-water, and the juice of worm-"wood and vetch. With this write your petition before "the setting sun, [saying], 'Send the truthful seer out "of the holy shrine, I beseech thee, Lampsuer, Sumarta, "Baribas, Dardalam, Iorlex: O Lord send the sacred "deity Anuth, Anuth, Salbana, Chambré, Breïth, now, "now, quickly, quickly. Come in this very night.'"[2]

"To procure dreams: Take a clean linen bag and "write upon it the names given below. Fold it up and "make it into a lamp-wick, and set it alight, pouring "pure oil over it. The word to be written is this: "'Armiuth, Lailamchoüch, Arsenophrephren, Phtha, "Archentechtha.' Then in the evening, when you are

[1] See *Catalogue of Greek Papyri*, vol. i. p. 118.

[2] A sketch of the god Besa is given at the end of the papyrus. See the description of the "Metternichstele" above, p. 147 ff.

"going to bed, which you must do without touching food "[or, pure from all defilement], do thus. Approach the "lamp and repeat seven times the formula given below: "then extinguish it and lie down to sleep. The "formula is this: 'Sachmu . . . epaëma Ligotereënch: "the Aeon, the Thunderer, Thou that hast swallowed "the snake and dost exhaust the moon, and dost raise "up the orb of the sun in his season, Chthetho is thy "name; I require, O lords of the gods, Seth, Chreps, "give me the information that I desire.'"

The peculiar ideas which the Egyptians held about the composition of man greatly favoured the belief in apparitions and ghosts. According to them a man consisted of a physical body, a shadow, a double, a soul, a heart, a spirit called the *khu*, a power, a name, and a spiritual body. When the body died the shadow departed from it, and could only be brought back to it by the performance of a mystical ceremony; the double lived in the tomb with the body, and was there visited by the soul whose habitation was in heaven. The soul was, from one aspect, a material thing, and like the *ka*, or double, was believed to partake of the funeral offerings which were brought to the tomb; one of the chief objects of sepulchral offerings of meat and drink was to keep the double in the tomb and to do away with the necessity of its wandering about outside tho tomb in search of food. It is clear from many texts that, unless the double was supplied with sufficient food, it would wander forth from the tomb and eat any kind of offal and drink any kind of dirty water which it might find in its path. But besides the shadow, and the double, and the soul, the spirit of the deceased, which usually had its abode in heaven, was sometimes to be found in the tomb. There is, however, good reason for stating that the immortal part of man which lived in the tomb and had its special abode in the statue of the deceased was the "double." This is proved by the fact that a special part of the tomb was reserved for the *ka*, or double, which was called the "house "of the *ka*," and that a priest, called the "priest of the "*ka*," was specially appointed to minister therein. The double enjoyed the smell of the incense which was offered at certain times each year in the tomb, as well as the flowers, and herbs, and meat, and drink; and the statue of the deceased in which the double dwelt took pleasure in all the various scenes which were painted or sculptured on the walls of the various chambers of the tomb, and enjoyed again all the delights which his body had enjoyed upon earth. The *ka*, or double, then, in very early times was, to all intents and purposes, the ghost of the Egyptians. In later times the *khu*, or "spirit," seems to have been identified with it, and there are frequent allusions in the texts to the sanctity of the offerings made to the *khu*, and to their territories, *i.e.*, the districts in which their mummified bodies lie.

Whether there was any general belief that the *ka*

or *khu* could or did hold intercourse with his relatives or friends whom he left alive upon earth cannot be said, but an instance is known in which a husband complains to his wife, who has been dead for three years, of the troubles which she has brought upon him since her death. He describes his own merits and the good treatment which he had vouchsafed to her when she was alive, and declares that the evil with which she is requiting him is not to be endured. To make his complaint to reach her he first reduced it to writing upon papyrus, then went to her tomb and read it there, and finally tied the papyrus to a statue or figure of his wife which was therein; since her double or spirit lived in the tomb she would, of course, read the writing and understand it.[1] It is a pity that we have no means of knowing what was the result of the husband's complaint. Elsewhere[2] we have a fragment of a conversation which a priest of Amen called Khonsu-em-heb, who was searching for a suitable place in which to build his tomb, holds with the double or spirit of some person whom he has disturbed, and the spirit of the dead tells some details of his life to the living man. The cemeteries were regarded with awe by the ancient Egyptians because of the spirits of the dead

[1] For the text see Leemans, *Monuments Égyptiens*, Partie II., pll. 183, 184, Leyden, 1846, fol.; for a transcript into hieroglyphics see Maspero, *Journal Asiatique*, Sér. 7, tom. 15, May and June, 1880, pp. 365–420.

[2] See Golénischeff in *Recueil de Travaux*, tom. iii., pp. 3–7.

who dwelt in them, and even the Arabic-speaking peoples of Egypt and the Sûdân, if we exclude the "antiquity grubber," have them in great respect for the same reason.[1] The modern peoples of the Sûdân firmly believe that the spirits of those slain in battle dwell on the field where they fell, or where their bodies are buried, and the soldiers in the tenth battalion of Lord Kitchener's army declare that the grave of the gallant Major Sidney, who was shot while charging at the head of his regiment, in the battle of Abū Hamed, August 7th, 1897, "is watched regularly "every night by the ghosts of the native soldiers who "were killed at Abū Hamed, and who mount guard "over their dead commander's tomb, challenging, with "every military detail, all passers-by. So implicitly "is this legend credited by the blacks that none of

[1] When I visited the Pyramids of Meroë in 1898 I took with me the local *shēkh*, and a man and a boy to look after the donkeys. Having come to within half a mile of the pyramids the three stopped and wished me to ride on by myself, and when I asked them why they did not want to come up the hill to the pyramids with me the *shēkh* replied that they had been built by kings whose spirits still dwelt there, and that it would not be seemly for him and his companions to "trouble" them. I pressed him to come, but he answered, "It is not "the custom of our country to go there," so I walked on by myself. When I had been in the pyramid field for about two hours taking photographs and measurements, the *shēkh* arrived with the boy, but nothing would persuade him to walk about there, and having seated himself he recited prayers from the *Koran* in an undertone, and at intervals urged me to return to his straw house on the river bank as soon as possible. He was firmly convinced that the prismatic compass which I used was a talisman, and when he reached home he thanked God fervently that he had not been molested by the spirits of the dead.

"them will, after dusk, approach the grave. Any one "doing so is believed to be promptly halted by a phan- "tom sentry, and even the words (in Arabic), 'Guard, "turn out!' are often (so the story goes) plainly heard "repeated at some distance off across the desert."[1]

[1] See the illustrated paper *The Sketch*, No. 332, June 7, 1899, p. 277. The following from the *Times* of July 7, 1899, is worth quoting:—

"THE GRAVE OF A BRITISH NAVAL OFFICER IN JAPAN.—Recently a "report came to the ears of the British Consul at Hiogo that the grave "of a British naval officer existed near a village on the island of "Hiroshima, in the Inland Sea of Japan—a place rarely visited by "any foreigner—and that, for some reason, it was carefully kept in "order by the peasants in the neighbourhood. The Consul accord- "ingly communicated with the Governor of the prefecture in which "the island is situated; inquiries were made, and the Governor was "able to send to the Consul a history of the lonely grave. The story "was appended by the Governor to a formal despatch of his own, and "was obviously drawn up by the village headman or some equally "humble official, and it is worth giving in full. The *Sylvia*, the "vessel mentioned, was for many years engaged in surveying off the "coasts of Japan:—'In the first year of Meiji, corresponding to "A.D. 1868, H.B.M.S. *Sylvia* was proceeding on a voyage through the "Inland Sea when an officer on board, named Lake, fell ill. He was "landed on the island of Hiroshima, at the village of Hiroshima, in "the district of Naka, province of Sanuki, and prefecture of Kagawa. "The *Sylvia* proceeded along the coast of Hiroshima and cast anchor "at Enoura Bay, to await the officer's recovery. In a few days, how- "ever, he died, and Captain St. John buried his remains in ground "belonging to the temple of Ikwoji above Enoura shrine, and, having "set up a wooden cross to mark the grave, departed. Several years "afterwards, when this monument had almost decayed from the effects "of wind and rain, frost and snow, Awaburi Tokwan, Superior of "Ikwoji Temple, and others said:—"Truly it would be too sad if "the grave of our solitary guest from afar, who has become a spirit "in a strange land, were suffered to pass out of all knowledge." "Thereupon Terawaki Kaemon, head of a village guild, and other "sympathisers, such as Oka Ryohaku, set on foot a scheme for the "erection of a stone monument, and, the shore folk all with one accord

The Egyptians believed that a man's fate or destiny was decided before he was born, and that he had no power whatever to alter it. Their sages, however, professed to be able to declare what the fate might be, provided that they were given certain data, that is to say, if they were told the date of his birth, and if they were able to ascertain the position of the planets and stars at that time. The goddess of fate or destiny was called "Shai," and she is usually accompanied by another goddess called "Renenet," who is commonly regarded as the lady of fortune; they both appear in the Judgment Scene, where they seem to watch the weighing of the heart on behalf of the deceased. But another goddess, Meskhenet, is sometimes present, and she also seems to have had influence over a man's future; in any case she was able to predict what that future was to be. Thus we read that she and Isis, and Nephthys, and Heqet, disguised as women, went to the house of Rā-user, whose wife Rut-Tettet was in travail; when they had been taken into her room they assisted her in giving birth to triplets, and as each child was born Meskhenet declared, "He shall be "a king who shall have dominion over the whole land."

"lending their help, the work was finally brought to completion. "This was on the 7th day of the eleventh month of the fourth year "of Meiji—that is, 1871. Since then nearly 30 winters have passed, "during which time the islanders have not neglected to take good "care of the tomb. In particular, from the 10th to the 16th day of "the seventh month, old style, there are still persons found who every "year clean and sweep the grave, and, offering up flowers and incense, "mourn for and console the spirit of the dead.'"

And this prophecy was fulfilled, for the three boys became three of the kings of the Vth dynasty.[1] The Seven Hathor goddesses also could predict the future of a human being, for in the well-known "Tale of "Two Brothers" it is related that, when the god Khnemu, at the request of Ṛā-Harmachis, had created for Bata a wife "who was more beautiful in her person "than any other woman in all the earth, for the essence "of every god was contained in her," they came to see her, and that they spake with one voice, saying, "Her "death will be caused by the knife." And this came to pass, for, according to the story, when the king whose wife she became heard from her first husband that she had left him and had wrought evil against him, he entered into judgment with her in the presence of his chiefs and nobles, and "one carried out their "decree," *i.e.*, they sentenced her to death and she was executed. Similarly, in another story, the Seven Hathors came to see the son who had been born to a certain king in answer to his prayers to the gods, and when they had seen him they said, "He shall die "by means of a crocodile, or a serpent, or a dog." The story goes on to say how he escaped from the crocodile and the serpent, and though the end is wanting, it is quite clear that he was wounded by an accidental bite of his dog and so died.[2] The moral of all such stories

[1] See Erman, *Westcar Papyrus*, Berlin, 1890, hieroglyphic transcript, pll. 9 and 10.

[2] See Maspero, *Contes Égyptiens*, pp. 29–46.

is that there is no possibility of avoiding fate, and it is most probable that the modern Egyptian has only inherited his ancestors' views as to its immutability.[1] A man's life might, however, be happy or unhappy according as the hour of the day or the day itself was lucky or unlucky, and every day of the Egyptian year was divided into three parts, each of which was lucky or unlucky. When Olympias was about to give birth to Alexander the Great, Nectanebus stood by her making observations of the heavenly bodies, and from time to time he besought her to restrain herself until the auspicious hour had arrived; and it was not until he saw a certain splendour in the sky and knew that all the heavenly bodies were in a favourable position that he permitted her to bring forth her child. And when he had said, "O queen, now thou wilt give birth "to a governor of the world," the child fell upon the ground while the earth quaked, and the lightnings flashed, and the thunder roared.[2] Thus it is quite evident that the future of a child depended even upon the hour in which he was born.

In magical papyri we are often told not to perform certain magical ceremonies on such and such days, the idea being that on these days hostile powers will make them to be powerless, and that gods mightier than

[1] The uneducated Muhammadan believes that man's fate is written upon his skull, and that the sutures are the writing. No man, however, can read them. See the words of Zayn al-Mawasif in Burton's *Alf Laylah wa Laylah*, vol. viii., p. 237.

[2] See Pseudo-Callisthenes, I. 12.

those to which the petitioner would appeal will be in the ascendant. There have come down to us, fortunately, papyri containing copies of the Egyptian calendar, in which each third of every day for three hundred and sixty days of the year is marked lucky or unlucky, and we know from other papyri *why* certain days were lucky or unlucky, and why others were only partly so. Taking the month Thoth, which was the first month of the Egyptian year, and began, according to the Gregorian Calendar, on August 29th, we find that the days are marked as follows:—

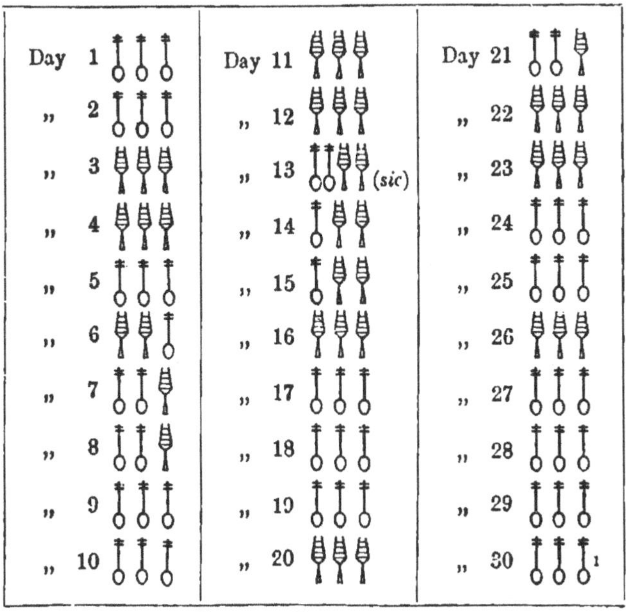


[1] See Brit. Mus. Papyrus, No. 10,474.

Now the sign  means "lucky," and  means "unlucky"; thus at a glance it could be seen which third of the day is lucky or unlucky, and the man who consulted the calendar would, of course, act accordingly. It must be noted that the priests or magicians who drew up the calendar had good reasons for their classification of the days, as we may see from the following example. The 19th day of Thoth is, in the above list, marked wholly lucky, *i.e.*, each third of it is lucky, and the papyrus Sallier IV.[1] also marks it wholly lucky, and adds the reason:—"It is a day of "festival in heaven and upon earth in the presence "of Rā. It is the day when flame was hurled upon "those who followed the boat containing the shrine "of the gods; and on this day the gods gave praises "being content," etc. But in both lists the 26th day is marked wholly unlucky, the reason being, "This was "the day of the fight between Horus and Set." They first fought in the form of men, then they took the form of bears, and in this state did battle with each other for three days and three nights. Isis aided Set when he was getting the worst in the fight, and Horus thereupon cut off his mother's head, which Thoth transformed by his words of power into that of a cow and put on her body. On this day offerings are to be made to Osiris and Thoth, but work of any kind is absolutely forbidden. The calendars of lucky

[1] See Chabas, *Le Calendrier*, p. 24.

and unlucky days do not, however, always agree as to a given day. Thus in the list given above the 20th day of Thoth is marked wholly unlucky, but in the papyrus Sallier IV. it is wholly lucky, but the reader is told not to do any work in it, nor to slay oxen, nor to receive a stranger; on this day the gods who are in the following of Rā slew the rebels. Concerning the fourth day of the next month, Paophi, the papyrus Sallier IV. says, "Go not forth from thy house from any side of it; "whosoever is born on this day shall die of the disease "*aat*." Concerning the fifth day it says, "Go not forth "from thy house from any side of it, and hold no "intercourse with women. This is the day wherein all "things were performed in the divine presence, and the "majesty of the god Menthu was satisfied therein. "Whosoever is born on this day shall die of excessive "venery." Concerning the ninth day it says, "Who-"soever is born on this day shall die of old age," and concerning the fifteenth, "Go not forth from thy "dwelling at eventide, for the serpent Uatch, the son of "the god, goeth forth at this time, and misfortunes "follow him; whosoever shall see him shall lose his "eye straightway." Again, the twenty-sixth day of Paophi was a lucky day for making the plan of a house; on the fifth day of Hathor no fire was to be kindled in the house; on the sixteenth day it was forbidden to listen to songs of joy because on this day Isis and Nephthys wept for Osiris at Abydos;

a man born on the twenty-third day would die by drowning; and so on. But to the three hundred and sixty days given in the calendars of lucky and unlucky days must be added the five epagomenal days which were considered to be of great importance and had each its peculiar name. On the first Osiris was born, on the second Heru-ur (Aroueris), on the third Set, on the fourth Isis, and on the fifth Nephthys; the first, third, and fifth of these days were unlucky, and no work of any kind was to be undertaken on them. The rubric which refers to these days[1] states that whosoever knoweth their names shall never suffer from thirst, that he shall never be smitten down by disease, and that the goddess Sekhet[2] shall never take possession of him; it also directs that figures of the five gods mentioned above shall be drawn with unguent and *ānti* scent upon a piece of fine linen, evidently to serve as an amulet.

From the life of Alexander the Great by Pseudo-Callisthenes[3] we learn that the Egyptians were skilled in the art of casting nativities, and that knowing the exact moment of the birth of a man they proceeded to construct his horoscope. Nectanebus employed for the purpose a tablet made of gold and silver and acacia wood, to which were fitted three belts. Upon the

[1] See Chabas, *op. cit.*, p. 104.

[2] The Eye of Sekhet seems to have taken the form of noxious vapours in the fields at sunrise; see Chabas, *op. cit.*, p. 78.

[3] I. 4.

outer belt was Zeus with the thirty-six *decani* surrounding him; upon the second the twelve signs of the Zodiac were represented; and upon the third the sun and moon.[1] He set the tablet upon a tripod, and then emptied out of a small box upon it models of the seven stars[2] that were in the belts, and put into the middle belt eight precious stones; these he arranged in the places wherein he supposed the planets which they represented would be at the time of the birth of Olympias, and then told her fortune from them. But the use of the horoscope is much older than the time of Alexander the Great, for to a Greek horoscope[3] in the British Museum is attached "an introductory "letter from some master of the art of astrology to "his pupil, named Hermon, urging him to be very "exact and careful in his application of the laws which "the ancient Egyptians, with their laborious devotion "to the art, had discovered and handed down to "posterity." Thus we have good reason for assigning the birthplace of the horoscope to Egypt. In connexion with the horoscope must be mentioned the "sphere" or "table" of Democritus as a means of making predictions as to life and death. In a magical

[1] I quote from my History of *Alexander the Great*, Cambridge, 1889, p. 5.

[2] *I.e.*, Sun, Moon, Zeus, Kronos, Aphrodite, and Hermes; we must add Mars according to Meusel's Greek text.

[3] Published for the first time by Kenyon, *Catalogue of Greek Papyri* vol. i. p. 132 ff.

papyrus[1] we are told to "ascertain in what month the "sick man took to his bed, and the name he received "at his birth. Calculate the [course of] the moon, "and see how many periods of thirty days have "elapsed; then note in the table the number of days "left over, and if the number comes in the upper "part of the table, he will live, but if in the lower "part, he will die."

THE TABLE.

| | | |
|---|---|---|
| 1 | 10 | 19 |
| 2 | 11 | 20 |
| 3 | 13 | 23 |
| 4 | 14 | 25 |
| 7 | 16 | 26 |
| 9 | 17 | 27 |
| 5 | 15 | 22 |
| 6 | 18 | 28 |
| 8 | 21 | 29 |
| 12 | 24 | 30 |

Both from the religious and profane literature of Egypt we learn that the gods and man in the future life were able at will to assume the form of any animal, or bird, or plant, or living thing, which they pleased, and one of the greatest delights to which a man looked forward was the possession of that power. This is proved by the fact that no less than twelve[2] of the chapters of the Book of the Dead are devoted to

[1] *Leyden Pap. V.* (ed. Leemans), col. xi., l. 1 ff.

[2] *I.e.*, Chapters LXXVII. to LXXXVIII.

providing the deceased with the words of power, the recital of which was necessary to enable him to transform himself into a "hawk of gold," a "divine hawk," "the governor of the sovereign princes," "the god who "giveth light in the darkness," a lotus, the god Ptah, a *bennu* bird (*i.e.*, phœnix), a heron, a "living soul," a swallow, the serpent Sata, and a crocodile; and another chapter[1] enabled him to transform himself into "whatever form he pleaseth." Armed with this power he could live in the water in the form of a crocodile, in the form of a serpent he could glide over the rocks and ground, in the form of the birds mentioned above he could fly through the air, and soar up and perch himself upon the bow of the boat of Rā, in the form of the lotus he had mastery over the plants of the field, and in the form of Ptah he became "more "powerful than the lord of time, and shall gain the "mastery over millions of years." The *bennu* bird, it will be remembered, was said to be the "soul of Rā," and by assuming this form the deceased identified himself with Khepera, the great god of creation, and thus acquired the attributes of the soul of the Sun-god. In the Elysian Fields he was able to assume any form and to swim and fly to any distance in any direction. It is noteworthy that no beast of the field or wild animal is mentioned as a type of his possible transformations into animals.

[1] *I.e.*, Chapter LXXVI.

Now the Egyptians believed that as the souls of the departed could assume the form of any living thing or plant, so the "gods," who in many respects closely resembled them, could and did take upon themselves the forms of birds and beasts; this was the fundamental idea of the so-called "Egyptian animal worship," which provoked the merriment of the cultured Greek, and drew down upon the Egyptians the ridicule and abuse of the early Christian writers. But if the matter be examined closely its apparent stupidity disappears. The Egyptians paid honour to certain birds, and animals, and reptiles, because they considered that they possessed certain of the characteristics of the gods to whom they made them sacred. The bull was a type of the strength and procreative power of the god of reproduction in nature, and the cow was the type of his female counterpart; every sacred animal and living thing possessed some quality or attribute which was ascribed to some god, and as each god was only a form of Rā, the quality or attribute ascribed to him was that of the Sun-god himself. The educated Egyptian never worshipped an animal as an animal, but only as an incarnation of a god, and the reverence paid to animals in Egypt was in no way different from that paid to the king who was regarded as "divine" and as an incarnation of Rā the Sun-god, who was the visible symbol of the Creator. The relation of the king to Rā was identical with that of Rā to God. The

Hebrews, Greeks, and Romans never understood the logical conception which underlay the reverence with which the Egyptians regarded certain animals, and as a result they grossly misrepresented their religion. The ignorant people, no doubt, often mistook the symbol for what it symbolized, but it is wrong to say that the Egyptians worshipped animals in the ordinary sense of the word, and this fact cannot be too strongly insisted on. Holding the views he did about transformations there was nothing absurd in the reverence which the Egyptian paid to animals. When a sacred animal died the god whom it represented sought out another animal of the same species in which to renew his incarnation, and the dead body of the animal, inasmuch as it had once been the dwelling-place of a god, was mummified and treated in much the same way as a human body after death, in order that it might enjoy immortality. These views seem strange, no doubt, to us when judged by modern ideas, but they formed an integral part of the religious beliefs of the Egyptians, from the earliest to the latest times. What is remarkable, however, is the fact that, in spite of invasions, and foreign wars, and internal dissensions, and external influences of all kinds, the Egyptians clung to their gods and the sometimes childish and illogical methods which they adopted in serving them with a conservatism and zeal which have earned for them the reputation of being at once the most religious and most superstitious nation of antiquity. Whatever literary treasures may be brought to light in the future as the result of excavations in Egypt, it is most improbable that we shall ever receive from that country any ancient Egyptian work which can properly be classed among the literature of atheism or freethought; the Egyptian might be more or less religious according to his nature and temperament, but, judging from the writings of his priests and teachers which are now in our hands, the man who was without religion and God in some form or other was most rare, if not unknown.

THE END.

# The Demotic Magical Papyrus of London and Leiden

# The Demotic Magical Papyrus of London and Leiden

FRANCIS LLEWELLYN GRIFFITH
HERBERT THOMPSON

# PREFACE

THE MS., dating from the third century A.D., which is here edited for the first time in a single whole, has long been known to scholars. Its subject-matter—magic and medicine—is not destitute of interest. It is closely connected with the Greek magical papyri from Egypt of the same period, but, being written in demotic, naturally does not reproduce the Greek hymns which are so important a feature of those papyri. The influence of purely Greek mythology also is here by comparison very slight—hardly greater than that of the Alexandrian Judaism which has supplied a number of names of Hellenistic form to the demotic magician. Mithraism has apparently contributed nothing at all: Christianity probably only a deformed reference to the Father in Heaven. On the other hand, as might have been expected, Egyptian mythology has an overwhelmingly strong position, and whereas the Greek papyri scarcely go beyond Hermes, Anubis, and the Osiris legend, the demotic magician introduces Khons, Amon, and many other Egyptian gods. Also, whereas the former assume a knowledge of the *modus operandi* in divination by the lamp and bowl, the latter describes it in great detail.

But the papyrus is especially interesting for the language in which it is written. It is probably the latest Egyptian MS. which we possess written in the demotic script, and it presents us with the form of the language as written—almost as spoken—by the pagans at the time when the Greek alphabet was being adopted by the Christians. It must not be forgotten, too, that this is the document which contributed perhaps more than any other to the decipherment of demotic, partly through its numerous Greek glosses.

We have therefore thought that a complete edition, with special reference to its philological importance, would be useful. The vocabulary is extensive, comprising about a thousand words. The present volume, containing the introduction, the transliteration, translation, and notes, will be followed by a complete glossary, with separate indices of Greek words, invocation names, names of animals, plants, and minerals, and a list of the glosses, &c., besides a chapter dealing with the principal grammatical forms met with in the MS., and a hand-copy of the text; the photographic reproduction by Hess of the pages in the British Museum and Leemans' facsimile of those at Leiden will of course preserve their independent value for reference, as, for instance, in judging the condition of the MS. and the precise forms of the signs in particular passages.

There is considerable inconsistency in the spelling of words in the papyrus itself. So much having to be rendered more or less conventionally, while fresh light is thrown daily on the intricacies of demotic, it is probable that there are a good many inconsistencies in our transliterations, translations, and notes, in spite of the watchfulness of the excellent reader at the Clarendon

Press. Those, however, who have dealt with the subject at all will probably not judge these too hardly.

In conclusion, we have to record our gratitude, first, to our predecessors in publication and decipherment of the papyrus—to Reuvens, Leemans, and Hess, to Brugsch, Maspero, Revillout, and W. Max Müller—but for whose varied contributions our task would have been infinitely more laborious even in the present advanced state of the study: and secondly, to the authorities of the Egyptian department in the British Museum, and of the Rijksmuseum in Leiden, for their courtesy in affording every facility for studying the original MS., and more especially to Dr. Boeser of the Leiden Museum for much kindness and assistance.

F. Ll. G.

H. T.

# CONTENTS


| | PAGE |
|---|---|
| INTRODUCTION | |
| I. The History of the MS. | 1 |
| II. Condition of the MS. | 3 |
| III. Contents of the MS. | 5 |
| IV. Previous work on the MS. | 7 |
| V. The Glosses | 8 |
| VI. Date | 10 |
| SYNOPSIS OF CONTENTS | 15 |
| EXPLANATION OF SIGNS | 19 |
| TEXT—RECTO—Transliteration and Translation | 20–169 |
| VERSO—Transliteration and Translation | 170–205 |
| CORRESPONDENCE OF COLUMNS | 207 |

# INTRODUCTION

## I. HISTORY OF THE MS.

THE demotic magical papyrus of London and Leiden was discovered at Thebes with other papyri, principally Greek but dealing with subjects of a like nature, in the early part of the last century, and was bought by Anastasi, who was at that time Swedish consul at Alexandria, and made a large collection of Egyptian MSS. When Anastasi obtained the MS. it must already have been torn into two parts, and it is even probable that he obtained the two parts at different times, since he sold his Egyptian collections, including the Leiden MS., to the Dutch government in 1828, while the London portion was bought at the sale of his later collections at Paris in 1857 for the British Museum (No. 1072 in Lenormant's Catalogue).

The Leiden fragment was made known to the world much earlier than that in the British Museum. Its importance for the deciphering of the demotic script by the help of the numerous glosses in Graeco-Coptic characters was at once perceived by the distinguished scholar Reuvens, at that time Director of the Leiden Museum of Antiquities, who proceeded to study it carefully, and in 1830 published an admirable essay[1] in which he sketched the principal contents of the MS. and indicated its value for the progress of demotic

[1] Lettres à M. Letronne sur les papyrus bilingues et grecs, par C. J. C. REUVENS. Leide, 1830. (Première lettre, Papyrus bilingues.)

studies. He then took in hand its reproduction, and the MS. was lithographed in facsimile under his direction, and he had corrected the proofs of the first plate when he was cut off by a premature death in 1835; his work was carried to completion and published by his successor in the Directorship of the Museum, Leemans, in 1839[1]. Heinrich Brugsch studied it closely, and drew from it most of the examples quoted in his Demotic Grammar published in 1855; but, although later scholars have frequently quoted from it and translated fragments of it, the MS. has hitherto remained without complete translation, commentary, or glossary.

The London MS., however, lay from 1857 onwards almost unnoticed in the British Museum. To the late Dr. Pleyte, Leemans' successor at Leiden, belongs the credit of discovering that the two MSS. originally formed one. He had studied the Leiden portion, and at once recognized the handwriting of its fellow in London. Without publishing the fact, he communicated it to Professor Hess of Freiburg, when the latter was working in Leiden on the MS. there. Professor Hess went on to London, and, having fully confirmed Dr. Pleyte's statement, published in 1892 a reproduction of the British Museum MS. with an introduction, including the translation of one column, and a glossary[2].

Reuvens in his essay dwelt at some length on the 'gnostic' character of the MS. He devoted his attention mainly to the parts which contain the glosses, and those are almost exclusively magical invocations, among which occur the names of gods, spirits, and demons, Egyptian, Syrian, Jewish, &c., strung together in a manner similar

[1] Monuments égyptiens du Musée d'Antiquités des Pays-Bas à Leide: papyrus égyptien démotique à transcriptions grecques I. 383, publié par le Dr. CONRAD LEEMANS. Leide, 1839.

[2] Der gnostische Papyrus von London, Einleitung, Text u. Demotisch-deutsches Glossar von J. J. HESS. Freiburg, 1892.

to those found in gnostic writings and on gnostic gems. He even went so far as to associate them with the name of a particular gnostic leader, Marcus, of the second century, chiefly on the ground of his recorded use of Hebrew and Syriac names in his invocations and the combinations of vowels. In consequence the MS. has acquired the name of the 'Leiden Gnostic,' and the term 'Gnostic' has been passed on to the London MS. But as will be seen from the complete translation here published, there is nothing in the work relating to the gnostic systems—it deals with magic and medicine, and it seems a misnomer to call the MS. gnostic merely because part of the stock-in-trade of the magician and medicine-man were a number of invocation names which he either picked up from the gnostics or derived from sources common to him and them. Hence it has been thought desirable to abandon the epithet 'gnostic,' and to call the work the 'Magical papyrus of London and Leiden' (Pap. mag. LL.).

## II. CONDITION OF THE MS.

The London portion is in far better condition than the Leiden portion. The papyrus is pale in colour and the ink very black; consequently where the MS. has not suffered material damage it is easy to read, as the scribe wrote a beautiful and regular hand.

The Leiden papyrus, on the other hand, has unfortunately suffered much, as Leemans, with a view to protecting the surface, covered both recto and verso with 'vegetable' paper, which probably could not be removed now without serious injury to the MS.; but either the paper or the adhesive matter employed with it has darkened and decayed, rendering the writing illegible in places.

In 1829, while the MS. was still in charge of Reuvens and before it had been subjected to the operation above described, he took a tracing of it which has been preserved, and which, though of little assistance in points of minute detail, may be relied on for filling up with certainty many groups which are now wholly lost in the original.

The main body of the writing is on the recto (horizontal fibres) of the papyrus, while on the verso are written memoranda, medical prescriptions, and short invocations.

The London MS. is Pap. No. 10070 of the British Museum (formerly Anast. 1072).

The Leiden MS. is known as I. 383 (reckoned among the Anastasi MSS. as A. 65).

The London portion forms the initial part of the MS. and joins on to the Leiden portion without a break, the tenth and last column of the London MS. and the first of the Leiden forming one column.

The first London column is imperfect, and it is not possible to say with certainty whether the MS. began with it or whether there was an anterior part now lost. It is quite possible that it began here. On the other hand, it is certain that the MS. is imperfect at the end, since the broken edge of the papyrus at Leiden shows traces of a column of writing succeeding the present final column.

It is impossible to estimate how much is lost, as the MS. is not an original composition on a definite plan, but a compilation of heterogeneous material collected together without any logical order.

The two portions, if joined together, would measure, roughly speaking, some 5 m. (about 16½ feet) in length. In height it averages nearly 25 cm. (10 in.). The writing is in columns, of which there are twenty-nine on the recto, while on the verso are thirty-three small columns or portions of columns; but these are not marked off, as are the recto columns, by vertical and horizontal framing lines[1], nor are they written continuously, but they seem to have been jotted down there on account of their brevity and discontinuous character.

The recto columns vary somewhat in size, but average 20 x 20 cm. (8 in. square). The writing is frequently carried beyond the framing lines.

In each column of the recto the number of lines is on the average about thirty to thirty-three; but the number is very irregular, ranging from forty-three in one column to five in another.

## III. CONTENTS.

As has been stated above, the MS. is a compilation. An analysis of the contents will be found on page 14. From this it will be seen to consist mainly of directions for divination processes involving numerous invocations, together with erotica and medical prescriptions, in which, however, magic plays as large a part as medicine.

The MS. is far from being unique in regard to its contents. Fragments of similar works in demotic exist at Paris (Louvre, No. 3229, published by Maspero, Quelques papyrus du Louvre, 1875), and at Leiden (I. 384 verso, Anast. 75, published by Leemans, Mons. du musée de Leide, 1842, pl. ccxxvi- vii) a MS. partly demotic and partly Greek, the latter portion being published by Leemans in Pap. graeci mus. lugd. bat. 1885, ii. Pap. V, and re-edited by Dieterich, Pap. Mag. Mus. Lugd. Bat. The Greek papyri containing similar texts are numerous, many examples having been pub-

[1] The horizontal lines on the recto are continuous for the whole length of the papyrus.

lished from the museums of Berlin, Leiden, London, and Paris by Goodwin, Parthey, Leemans, Wessely, and Kenyon.

The well-known codex of the Bibliothèque Nationale published by Wessely, Denkschr. Kais. Ak. Wiss. Wien, xxxvi. 1888, contains a few invocations in Old Coptic along with the Greek (cf. Griffith, A. Z. 1901, p. 85, and bibliography, ibid. p. 72).

Magic was from the earliest times largely developed by the Egyptians in relation both to the dead and the living. Under the former head fall both the pyramid texts and other texts found in the tombs, including most of the Book of the Dead, which consists mainly of magical invocations intended to make smooth the path of the deceased in the next world.

Magical texts for the use of the living are found in the Harris magical papyrus (ed. Chabas, 1860), the Metternich stela (ed. Golenischeff, 1877) and kindred stones, the Berlin papyrus edited by Erman (Zaubersprüche für Mutter u. Kind, 1901), &c. Reference may be made to the volume on Egyptian magic by Dr. Wallis Budge, 1899, and to a special study on vessel-divination by E. Lefébure, 'Le vase divinatoire,' in Sphinx, 1902, VI. 61 seq. Cf. also Dieterich, 'Abraxas'; Kenyon in Cat. Greek Pap. in B. M., I. 62 seq.; Miss Macdonald in P. S. B. A., xiii. 160 seq.; Wünsch, Sethianische Verfluchungstafeln aus Rom, &c.

In the closely allied department of medicine, it is sufficient to refer to the Ebers papyrus, the Kahun papyri, and the Berlin medical papyrus (ed. Brugsch, Rec. Mon. pl. 87–107), which offer many parallels. Among the Greek medical writers it is noticeable that Alexander of Tralles seems much more closely allied to the Egyptian school, if that be represented by our MS., than Galen.

But though the subject-matter of the MS. is not without its interest for the history of magic and medicine, its chief claim to publication lies in its philological interest. From the first its numerous glosses have attracted the attention of scholars, and have been the means of fixing the value of a large number of demotic groups. Further it is in date probably the latest known papyrus written in the demotic script; most of the glosses are really Coptic transcriptions, and under this head may likewise be included all the Egyptian words written in cipher; so that the MS. in these furnishes us with a series of very early Coptic words, including several grammatical forms of great interest. Possibly too the text may be of importance in relation to the question of dialects in pagan Egypt; but that is a subject too little worked out at present to allow of definite statements. The vocabulary is very extensive, and includes a number of Greek words, the names of over 100 plants, besides numerous animals and minerals.

## IV. PREVIOUS WORK ON THE MS.

It may be useful to record here the names of those who have dealt with the MS. at greater length than a mere passing reference or quotation, and to whom we are indebted for many suggestions:—

REUVENS. Supra, p. 1.

LEEMANS. Mons. &c., texte; Aegyptische Papyrus in demotischer Schrift, &c. 1839.

MASPERO. Rec. trav., i. 18–40 (1870).

REVILLOUT. Setna, introd. pp. 3–48 (1877); Rev. Égypt., i. 163–172 (1880), ii. 10–15, 270–2 (1881); Poème satyrique (1885).

PLEYTE. P. S. B. A., 1883, 149.

BRUGSCH. Wtb. pass., A. Z., 1884, 18 seq.

MAX MÜLLER. Rec. tr., viii. 172 (1886), xiii. 149 (1890).

HESS. Setna pass. (1888), Zur Aussprache des Griechischen, in the *Indo-germanische Forschungen*, vi. 123; Der gnostische Papyrus von London, Einleitung, Text u. Demotisch-deutsches Glossar, 1892.

GROFF. Mém. de l'Institut Égypt. iii. 337 seq. (1897), and Bulletin du même, 1897, 1898.

As the London portion of the MS., which in the order of contents is the first part, was published fifty years later than the second part at Leiden, it follows that each publication has an independent numbering of the columns, starting from I. In view of the fact that there are many references in demotic literature already to the columns by their numbers as established by the publications of Leemans and Hess, it would have been desirable to retain the existing numbering if possible. But, as will be seen by comparison of the hand copy of the whole MS. which accompanies this edition with the former publications, the changes in the way of consolidation of the columns, and in some cases necessary re-numbering of the lines, have made it compulsory to introduce a new and continuous numbering of the columns. For instance, Hess col. X and Leemans col. I form a single column, and the same is the case with Leemans cols. II and III and cols. IV and V, and with verso, cols. XVI and XVII, XXII and XXIII. A comparative table of the old and new numbers will be found at the end.

## V. THE GLOSSES.

There are about 640 words with transcriptions in Coptic characters in addition to a few inserted in the text.

Besides all the letters of the Greek alphabet we find the following used:—

| | |
|---|---|
| ft (= ⲕ 26/15). | 6 (= ϯ : ϣ 9/11). |
| ح (= ⲕ 7/33, 25/34). | y (= ϥ 2/10, 9/14). |
| h (= ⲗ 25/34, 35 text). | ʌ (= ϩ 9/14, 25/34). |
| ⲯ (= ⲱ 2/13, 5/23, 8/8). | 9 (= ϩ 2/4). |
| 3 (= ϣ 1/25, 8/9, 13, V. 5/9). | ƅ (= ϭ 9/6, 29/10). |
| ⲗ (= ϣ 2/18). | ơ (= ϫ 2/26, 29/10). |

The glosses were undoubtedly written by the same scribe who wrote the demotic text. And it seems that he wrote the glosses before he filled in the rubrics. For the handwriting of the demotic text and of the rubrics is unquestionably the same; and in filling up in red the empty spaces he had left for rubrication, the scribe took occasion to fill in with his red ink occasional lapses in the black writing. In the text this can be observed in e.g. 24/1, the omitted ɹ— of the second *str* (?) has been filled up in red, and also the omitted determinative in the last word of 28/8, an omitted letter in *pḥr* 29/11, an omitted word *šn* interlineated in 29/12, and a plural sign in 25/26; and so too the gloss ⲉⲱⲉ in 28/8, overlooked when the glosses were originally inserted in black ink.

It is a fact that there is often a considerable difference between the Greek letters in the passages written in Greek and in the glosses (e.g. παπιπετου in 15/25 and 15/29), but this may be accounted for by the fact that the former are written in a cursive hand with ligatures, while the glosses are carefully written with separately formed letters without ligatures for distinctness' sake in the narrow space between the lines.

The above considerations, however, only show that the text and glosses were written by the same hand in our existing MS. It does not follow that they were written by the original compiler. Max Müller has argued (Rec. tr., viii. 175) that they must be due to another individual since they are mostly in the Fayumic dialect, while the dialect of the demotic text is 'Untersahidisch' (i. e. Achmimic, so called by Stern). In Rec. tr., xiii. 152 *n.*, he replaces the latter term by a more precise definition: 'Die Mundart steht zwischen Fayumisch u. dem Mittel-ägyptischen von Akhmîm, letzterem näher.' But it is very doubtful whether this distinction between the text and the glosses can be maintained. The only example quoted by Max Müller that distinctly suggests Fayumic is the gloss ⲗⲱ and ⲗ over a group in 16/5 and 25/34, which he reads as = (ⲉ)ⲣⲟⲟⲩ, regarding the interchange of ⲣ and ⲗ as evidence of Fayumic dialect. But the demotic group in question does not read *er-w*, but *mr* as in *mr-ʾḥ* (1/17, 2/7, 14/6, 28), and the gloss ⲗⲱ represents the absolute form of the late Egyptian word which we see in its construct form in Sahidic ⲗⲉⲙⲏⲏϣⲉ and in λεσωνις. From the detailed examination of the dialect (in vol. ii) it appears probable that the dialect of the text does not show any distinction from that of the glosses, and it is not necessary to go behind the scribe of the present MS. and place the compiler earlier. He may well have been one and the same.

## VI. DATE.

Reuvens (u. s. p. 151) placed the date of the MS. in the first half of the third century A. D., and this was repeated by Leemans.

Groff and Hess attributed it on palaeographical grounds to the second century; but in the light of recent additions to the knowledge of Greek palaeography, and the opinions based on them of Kenyon, Grenfell, and Hunt (see A. Z., xxxix. (1901) p. 78), the third century must be accepted as the date of the MS. But this, of course, is the date at which the papyrus was written, and merely furnishes a *terminus ad quem* for deciding as to the date of the contents.

That the whole of the papyrus, in its present state, was written by one and the same scribe—with the possible exception of verso XXVIII—can scarcely be a matter of doubt to any one who has studied closely the handwriting of the original MSS. It must be stated, however, that Reuvens and Leemans were of opinion that the glosses were written by a later hand than that of the body of the text: but this question has been discussed above (p. 9), and apart from the identity of ink, and the material proof given there, it may be added that the hieratic glosses in 27/8 are certainly written by the same hand as the numerous hieratic passages scattered through the text.

The date of the contents is a much more complicated question. Written partly in hieratic, partly in demotic, and partly in Greek, they wear the aspect of a compilation, which is borne out by the varied and disconnected nature of the subject-matter.

It has been suggested that the work is a translation into demotic of a Greek original, and perhaps this is the first question demanding discussion. Prima facie it may be said to be likely, as so many similar works exist in Greek. The introduction of three invocations of considerable length written in Greek characters almost compels us to accept that origin for those particular sections, viz. 4/1–19, 15/24–31, 23/7–20. It seems probable that the translator felt he could transfer to Egyptian the prescriptions and preparations, while the formula of incantation had to be left in the original language. Had these sections been written in Egyptian originally, it is not likely that an incantation in a foreign tongue would be inserted in the place presumably of an Egyptian one.

And in the first named instance there is the additional evidence of two true Greek glosses, i. e. not *Coptic transcriptions* of the demotic words, but Greek equivalents of the two words 'table' and 'goose,' which seem to be inserted clearly to prevent a misunderstanding of the original terms. In the second instance 15/24–31, the original Greek lines 25–28 are immediately followed by a demotic translation of the same passage (ll. 29–31), which points in the same direction. Translation from the Greek is rendered probable, outside the passages already referred to, by the transcription of Greek prescriptions and substances in 24/1–25, and verso I, II, VIII, IX. According to an ingenious suggestion of Max Müller, in verso II the otherwise unintelligible phrase *mʿnes n rm* is almost certainly a mistranslation of *μαγνησία ἀνδρεία*. Max Müller has also (Rec. tr., viii. 175–6) given strong reasons for regarding the passage 25/23–37 as being translated from a Greek original. However, even where there are reasons for believing that the demotic is a translation from the Greek, the original source, in relation to magic at any rate, was probably Egyptian—certainly so in the case of the Greek passage in 15/25–28, which has itself clearly an Egyptian origin.

On the other hand, some of the chief sections of the MS. show no traces of Greek influence, e.g. cols. VI and XV. 1–20; but it would be rash to say that they are older; they may well represent only a purer Egyptian source. Max Müller (Rec. tr., viii. 172) has suggested that some of the magic formulae go back to the period from the Eighteenth to the Twentieth Dynasty. This cannot be true of more than a few phrases. The language indeed is not entirely uniform, but throughout the papyrus the vocabulary and grammar are distinctly not 'Late Egyptian'; they are 'demotic,' and that too of a kind which approaches Coptic much more closely than in any other known papyrus. Certain passages, such as the spell in 13/1–10, show more or less archaism, but in all cases it is mixed with late forms.

The use of hieratic might be thought to indicate some antiquity where it occurs. But the writing is a strange jumble; the hieratic is inextricably though sparingly mixed with the demotic, a single word being often written partly in hieratic, partly in demotic. Where hieratic signs occur the language is not generally more archaic than when the demotic is pure. In 23/24 the word Abrasax is written in hieratic. Now Abrasax is usually regarded as a typical gnostic invocation name, Irenaeus having stated that it was invented by Basilides (fl. 125 A. D.). This statement is now generally regarded as an error, and the name may be earlier; but there is no authority for placing it in pre-Christian times (cf. Hort, s. v. Abrasax, in Smith, Dict. Christ. Biog.; Dieterich, Abrasax, p. 46; C. Schmidt, Gnostische Schriften in Kopt. Spr., 1892, p. 562).

Not many documents written in hieratic have been ascertained to be later than the first century A. D.; but they were plentiful at Tanis amongst the burnt papyri found by Professor Petrie in the house of 'Bakakhuiu' (Asychis), the destruction of which Mr. Petrie was disposed to date to 174 A. D. (Tanis, i. p. 41); and Clemens Alexandrinus (Strom. v. 237) mentions hieratic as still taught in the schools (circa A. D. 160–220). Hieroglyphic inscriptions, with the name of Decius (249–251), are found in the temple of Esneh, and the existence of hieroglyphic almost implies that of hieratic.

Judging by the language, it is difficult to believe that any part of the work in its present redaction is more than a century or two older than the papyrus itself.

The contents of the papyrus may be classified as follows :—

1. Divination—
   (*a*) by the vessel of oil I–III, IX–X. 22, XIV, XVIII. 7–33, XXI. 1–9, XXII (?), XXVIII, verso XXII, verso XXVI.
   (*b*) by a lamp V, VI–VII, VIII. 1–12, XVI, XVII–XVIII. 6, XXV. 1–22, XXVII. 13–36, verso XVIII, verso XXIV, verso XXXI.
   (*c*) by the sun X. 22–end, XXVII. 1–12, XXIX.
   (*d*) by moon XXIII. 21–31.
   (*e*) by the Foreleg constellation (Great Bear) verso XVIII.
   (*f*) by stars ? IV. 23–4.
   (*g*) through the priest Psash (?) VIII. 12–end.
   (*h*) through Imuthes IV. 1–22.
   (*i*) by dreams verso XVII, eye-paint XXI, invocation XXVII ? XXVIII.
   (*k*) for thief-catching III. 29, or shipwreck (?) verso XV.
2. to obtain favour and respect XI, verso XXXII.
   to avert anger of superior XV. 24–31.
3. Erotica—
   by potions XV. 1–21, XXI. 10–43, XXV. 23–XXVI.
   by salves XII, verso III. 14–16, XII–XIII. 9, XIII. 10–11, XIV, XXIII, XXV, XXX, XXXII.
   αγωγιμον verso XVI, XVII, XIX.
   διακοπη XIII. 1–10.
4. Poisons, &c.—
   blinding XIII. 11, XXIV. 30.
   soporifics XXIII. 1–20, XXIV, verso II. 16–III. 3.
   maddening (magic) verso XXIX.
   slaying XXIII. 7, XXIV. 28, verso XXXII.
   uses of the shrew-mouse, &c. (chiefly in erotica) XIII. 11–end and verso XXXII.
5. Healing—
   poison XIX. 10–21.
   sting XX. 1–27.
   dog's bite XIX. 9, 32–40.
   bone in throat XIX. 21–32, XX. 27–33.
   gout and other affections of feet verso VIII–X, XI.
   water in ears verso IV. 1–5.
   ophthalmia (?) verso XX.
   fever verso XXXIII.
   haemorrhage, &c. in woman verso V. 1–3, 9–13, V. 4–8.
   to ascertain pregnancy verso V. 4–8.
6. names or descriptions of plants, drugs, &c. verso I–II. 15, III. 4–13, 17–18, IV. 6–19, V. 14–17.

# SYNOPSIS OF CONTENTS


COLUMN I–III. Divination by vessel with medium.
1/2–3/5 invocation ; 3/5–3/35 directions.

IV. 1–19. Process employed by Imuthes.
1–8 directions ; 9–19 Greek invocation.

IV. 20–22. For a horoscope (?).

IV. 23–24. Eye-paints.

V. 1–2. fragmentary.

3–32. Divination by lamp without medium.
3–8 directions ; 9–23 invocations ; 24–32 prescription for eye-paint and further directions.

VI–VIII. 11. Divination by lamp, with medium and alone.
6/1–11 directions ; 6/11–8/11 invocations.

VIII. 12–18. Divination alone, according to the priest Psash (?).
12–16 invocation ; 16–18 directions.

IX–X. 22. Divination of Chons by vessel.
9/1–10/9 invocation ; 10/9–10/19 directions for use with medium ; 10/20–10/22 for use alone.

X. 22–35. Divination by vessel to see the bark of Ra, alone.
23–30 invocation ; 30–35 directions.

XI. Formula for acquiring praise and honour.
1–21 invocation ; 21–26 directions.

XII. Eroticon.
1–14 directions ; 15–18 invocation ; 18–27 alternative invocation ; 27–31 further directions.

XIII. To separate a man from a woman.
2–9 invocation ; 9–10 directions (? incomplete) ; 11–29 uses of shrew-mouse (?) and other animals, &c., for removing the man and procuring the woman.

XIV. Divination by vessel with medium.
2–16 invocation ; 17–32 directions.

COLUMN XV. 1–20. Eroticon.
1–8 directions; 8–20 invocation.
XV. 21–23. Another eroticon.
XV. 24–31. Formula for averting anger of a superior.
25–28 Greek invocation; 29–31 demotic translation of the same.
XVI. 1–14. Divination by lamp; invocation.
XVI. 15–17. Invocation before the sun for success generally.
XVI. 18–30. Divination by lamp with a medium.
18–19 directions; 20–22 invocation; 22–30 further directions.
XVII. 1–21. Another method of divination by lamp with medium.
1–11 invocation; 11–21 directions.
XVII. 21–23. Another method of the same.
XVII. 24–26. Another method of the same.
XVII. 27–XVIII. 6. Another method of the same.
XVIII. 7–33. Divination by vessel with medium or alone.
8–23 invocation; 24–33 directions.
XIX. 1–9. Formula for the bite of a dog.
1–8 invocation; 8–9 directions.
XIX. 10–21. Formula for extracting poison from the heart of a man who has been made to drink a philtre.
11–19 invocation; 19–21 directions.
XIX. 21–32. Formula for a bone in the throat.
22–28 invocation; 28–32 directions.
XIX. 32–40. Formula for the bite of a dog.
33–39 invocation; 39–40 directions.
XX. 1–27. Formula for the sting of a scorpion (?).
2–13 invocation; 14–27 directions and invocation to the oil.
XX. 27–33. Formula for a bone in the throat.
XXI. 1–9. Divination by vessel through Osiris.
2–8 invocation; 8–9 directions.
XXI. 10–43. Eroticon (a scarab in wine).
10–20 directions; 20–43 invocations.
XXII. 1–5. Divination by vessel for spirit summoning (incomplete).
XXIII. 1–20. Formula to inflict catalepsy and death.
2–8 directions; 9–20 Greek invocation.

COLUMN
XXIII. 21–26. Vessel-divination by the moon.
21–24 directions; 24–26 invocation.
XXIII. 27–31. Another method of the same.
XXIV. Various prescriptions for producing sleep, catalepsy, death, &c.
XXV. 1–22. Divination by lamp with a medium.
2–8 invocation; 9–22 directions.
XXV. 23–31. Eroticon.
XXV. 31–XXVI. 18. Eroticon.
25/31–33 directions; 25/34–37 invocation; 26/1–18 alternative invocation.
XXVII. 1–12. Divination by vessel with medium, for seeing the bark of Ra.
1/9 invocation; 9–12 directions.
XXVII. 13–36. Divination by lamp with medium.
13–19 directions; 20–24 invocation; 24–36 prescription for eye-paint and further directions.
XXVIII. 1–9. Divination by vessel, alone.
1–4 invocation; 4–9 directions.
XXVIII. 10–15. Another method of the same.
XXIX. 1–20. Divination by the sun with medium.
1–4 directions; 5–12 invocation; 12–17 alternative invocation; 17–20 further directions.
XXIX. 20–30. Another method of the same.

## VERSO.

I. Names of plants.
II. 1–15. Names of plants and minerals.
II. 16–20. Prescription for sleeping draught.
III. 1–3. Another.
III. 4–13, 17–18. Names of minerals.
III. 14–16. Eroticon.
IV. 1–5. Prescription for the ears.
IV. 6–19. Names of animals and plants.
V. 1–3, 9–13. Prescriptions for haemorrhage in women.
V. 4–8. Prescription for ascertaining pregnancy.
V. 14–17. Names of plants.

VI–VII. Prescriptions for ailments of women.
VIII–X. Prescriptions for gout.
XI. Prescriptions for ailments of the feet.
XII–XIV. Erotica.
XV. Formula for thief-catching and against shipwreck (?).
XVI. Eroticon.
XVII. Formula for dreams.
XVIII. Divination by lamp, or by the Fore-leg (Great Bear) Constellation.
XIX. Formula for summoning a woman.
XX. Prescription for ophthalmia (?).
XXI. Formula for an eye-paint (?).
XXII. Vessel-divination, alone.
XXIII. Eroticon.
XXIV. Lamp-divination.
XXV. Eroticon.
XXVI. Invocation for use in vessel-divination.
XXVII. Invocation for the same (?).
XXVIII. Directions for spirit-summoning (?).
XXIX. Formula to produce madness.
XXX. Erotica.
XXXI. Invocation for use in lamp-divination.
XXXII. Formula for producing love or death of a woman, and acquiring praise.
XXXIII. Formula for removing fever.

# EXPLANATION OF SIGNS

## TRANSLATION.

RESTORATIONS are placed in *square* brackets [ ]. Lacunae in the original, for which no restoration is suggested, are represented by dots. Words in *round* brackets ( ) are not in the original, but are added by the translators; those between angular brackets ⟨ ⟩ are intended to be omitted.

The second person singular has been rendered by 'thou, thee' in invocations, by 'you' elsewhere. In the very few instances in which the second person plural occurs, it is indicated by the use of 'ye' or 'you' (plur.); (*bis*) following a word indicates that the word is followed in the original by the sign *sp sn*, implying that the word or phrase is to be repeated.

An accurate transcription of the magic names is given in the transliteration; in the translation we have rendered the sound approximately without strict adherence to any one system, generally following the glosses where they exist, as it was thought that this would be the most useful course for such readers as are not Egyptian scholars.

## TRANSLITERATION.

For the system, see note preceding the demotic glossary. Words transliterated with Coptic letters *between asterisks* are written in *cipher* in the original.

## REFERENCES.

In referring to the plates of the papyrus in vol. ii, Col. I. l. 1 is quoted as 1/1 and verso, Col. II. l. 3 as V. 2/3, &c.

# TRANSLITERATION

## Col. I.

1\. . . . . . ḫn p tš n Pr-mze z-mt
2\. . . . . . štte n pe-f ryt ḥtp n Pr- . . . e ḥr-f mw tyk
3\. . . . . . n ʾm t(?) e ne-f(?) sḥ(?)n ʿre·t ʿnḫ·t
4\. . . . . . tkr my p wyn p wstn ḫn pe hn
5\. . . . . . a·wn n-y p t a·wn n-y t ty·t a·wn n-y p nwn
6\. . . . . . ʿo·t n ḥmt n ʾrq-ḥḥ n ntr·w nt n t p·t nt θse ʾm-n
7\. . . . . . wyn p wstn ḫn pe hne pe
8\. . . . . . ḫm-ḫl nte ḥr-f pḫt a py hne (nḥe) my wz

---

### Col. I.

l. 1. Restore from 18/7. The parallel text to ll. 13–17 shows that more than half of the page is lost, but the heading line was probably not of full length. *Pr-mze* is **пемхє** (Oxyrhynchus), capital of the nineteenth nome of Upper Egypt.

l. 2. *Pr- . . . e* (?). The group suggests a reading *Pr-ʾr-ʾmn* for **перемоүн** (Pelusium), but the *ʾr* (?) sign is perhaps too upright, and it is more likely that the two signs following *Pr* are a special group for some divine name. Nothing is known of the religious importance of Pelusium, or even of its name in Egyptian, but the city is mentioned in a Greek invocation quoted below at l. 12.

l. 3. *sḫ* (?). This group, here in the plural, may represent 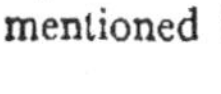 *sʾḥ*, 'toes' (Lange, A. Z., 1896, 76). Cf. Lepsius, Todtenb., c. 42, l. 9 *iw zbʿ·w-i sḫ·w-i m ʿrʿlw* (*sic*) *ʿnḫ·w*, 'my fingers and toes are as rearing serpents.' But the same group recurs in 7/2 as a masc. sing. subst. where the context rather suggests the meaning 'testicles.'

*ʿnḫ·t*, of a serpent, cf. 12/17; in Egyptian Pleyte, Pap. Tur., cxxxii. 4 and (very late) Mar. Pap. Boul., I. Pl. 9, ll. 5–6. It seems to mean 'darting forward for attack.' Similar meanings, 'rise,' &c., are common, esp. in late texts, Br., Wtb., 198–9; cf. also 9/16, 10/7. But in Griffith, Tell el Yahudiyeh, xxv. 15, an enraged serpent *ʿnḫ nf·w-f* 'breathed its vapour' at a god, *ʿnḫ* being there a transitive verb surviving in Sah. **ɑнϣ-тнү** 'breathe,' Bsciai, Rec. tr., vii. 25 (Job ix. 18).

# TRANSLATION

## Col. I.

(1) [A vessel-divination which a physician ?] of the nome of Pemze [gave to me]. Formula: (2) '[O god N.] . . . . . the border of whose girdle (?) rests in Peremoun (?), whose face is like a spark (3) . . . . . . . . . of (?) an obscene (?) cat, whose toes (?) are a rearing uraeus (4) . . . . . . . . . quick[-ly ?]; put light and spaciousness in my vessel (5) . . . . . . . Open to me the earth, open to me the Underworld, open to me the abyss, (6) . . . . . . . . great . . . . . of bronze of Alkhah, ye gods that are in heaven, that are exalted, come ye (7) . . . . . . . . . . [put ?] light and spaciousness in my vessel, my (8) . . . . . . . . [this] boy, whose face is bent over this vessel

l. 4. *p wyn p wstn*, cf. Leyd. Pap. Gr. V. v. 17 (ed. Dieterich) γενεσθω βα(θος) πλα(τος) μη(κος) αυγη in an ονειρου αιτησις.

l. 5. Or perhaps '[Open to me, O heaven !], open to me, O earth !,' &c. Cf. Pap. Bibl. Nat. l. 1180 ανοιγητι (sic) ουρανε.

*ty·t* transcribed ⲧⲏⲓ in Gloss. 17/20, O. C. Par. ⲧⲏ (A. Z., 1883, 94). In II Kham. ii. 10, &c., the judgement of the dead takes place in Tei, which seems convertible with Amenti.

*p nwn*. It is a question whether this is the hieroglyphic . The latter occurs only twice in this papyrus, but in one of the instances it is clearly parallel to *nwn*. Cf. xxi. 33 *nte-k py k km ḥyt 'r pyr n p* 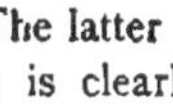 with ix. 15 *'nk p hf 'r pyr n p nwn*.

l. 6. *'rq-ḥḥ*. Brugsch, Dict. Geog., 130, 1121 = [α]λχαι 15/27, O.C. Par. ⲁⲗϫⲁ̄ⲁ̄ (A. Z., 1883, 104), the necropolis at Abydos where the head of Osiris was preserved. It is spelt with *l*, *'lg-ḥḥ* only once in 15/30, cf. the converse in *gh'l'kter* = χαρακτηρ 5/5.

*'m-n*. ⲁⲙⲱⲓⲛⲓ, cf. Müller, A. Z., 1893, 50, who suggests that it is cohortative 1st plur. 'let us come,' or for *'m-w n-y*, 'come ye unto me,' with the *n-y* unaccented being reduced to an enclitic, but cf. 11/16 *'m-n n-y*.

l. 8. *nḥe*, 'oil,' and *hne*, 'vessel,' confused in the writing. Parallel passages authorize either.

9. . . . . . e ze py šn-hne p šn-hne n ᵓS·t pe e-s qte
10. . . . . . ᵓm n-y a ẖn . . . pe ḥtr ze hb nb . . .
11. . . . [nte-]k t wn yr·t-f n py ᶜlw a bl ar-w tre-w
12. . . . . . z ᵓnk pe p pr-ᶜo my-sr sr-my-srpt rn-yt
13. . . . . . [a]r-k ty n p-hw z ᵓnk pe syt-tᵓ-k stm rn-yt stm
14. . . . . . hrenwte lᶜppt-t-thᶜ lᵓksnthᶜ sᶜ
15. . . . . l bwel sp-sn lwtery gᶜsᶜntrᶜ yᶜh-ᶜo
16. . . . . . [p]šft n t p·t ᵓblᶜnᶜthᶜnᶜlbᶜ p srrf
17. . . . . . [e·ᵓr-k] zt-f e·ᵓr-k sq n ẖrw-k p mr-ᵓḥ-nfr pe ḥtr

---

l. 10. *ḥtr* here and elsewhere perhaps 'compeller,' meaning him (here Anubis) who compels the gods to do the magician's will.

l. 11. ⲙⲁ. Note this gloss as a variant or correction of *nte-k ty*, also in l. 18.

l. 12. *z ᵓnk*. For the essentially Egyptian identification of the utterer of the spell with his god see DIETERICH, Abraxas, p. 136 note, and cf. Iambl. de Myst. vi. 6.

*p pr-ᶜo my-sr*, cf. the corrupt *τον μουισδρω τον αναξ* Leyd. Pap. Gr. V. ix. 11–12.

*sr-my-srpt.* The same signs recur grouped together in varying order as a divine appellative in 9/6 and 11/8. The knife and hide are the zodiacal signs of Leo and Aries (BRUGSCH, Nouv. Rech., p. 22); the flower or seed-head is the peculiar determinative of the ⲥⲁⲣⲡⲟⲧ throughout this papyrus. The same divine name, composed of a lotus bud (?) with lion and spelt-out name of ram (*sriw*), occurs in LEPS., Todt., cap. 162, l. 5, variants giving *srpd* for the lotus bud (?) (BR., Wtb., 1265) and *mᵓy* for the lion (Leyd. Lijkpap., No. 16). Cf. also PLEYTE, Chapitres Suppl., Pl. 14 and 131. The group of a lotus leaf, lion, and ram is figured on several hypocephali, the best example being in BUDGE, Lady Meux Cat., 2nd ed., Pl. VI. Cf. PLEYTE, ib. text, Pl. opp. p. 60. Probably none of these instances are earlier than the Persian invasion. Outside our papyrus the normal order is evidently lotus-lion-ram, and Greek versions agree with this: Brit. Mus. Pap. CXXI. l. 499 *εγω ειμι ο εν τω Πηλουσιω καθϊδρυμενος Σερφουθ*: *μουϊσρω*: (so facs.), similarly l. 557; in Leyd. Pap. V. col. 3 a, l. 6, the spelling is varied and corrupt. In each case *σερφοὺθ* is marked off from *μουισρω*, the latter appearing as one word. On a gnostic gem in the Wilson Collection belonging to Aberdeen University is the legend:—*σερφουθ μουισρω λαιλαμ δος μοι χαριν πραξιν νεικην*. In this combination the lotus (ⲥⲁⲣⲡⲟⲧ, see below, 2/17), the lion (ⲙⲟⲩⲓ, see below, 5/11), and the ram (ⲥⲣⲟ, see below, 11/8 and 14/13, and decan names in BR., Wtb. Suppl., 995) probably all represent solar attributes.

*rn-yt.* This abnormal spelling apparently arises from a combination

(oil); cause to succeed (9) . . . . . . . . . . for this vessel-divination is the vessel-divination of Isis, when she sought (10) . . . . . . . come in to me, O my compeller (?), for everything (11) . . . . . . . and cause the eyes of this child to be opened to them all, (12) . . . . . . . for I am the Pharaoh Lion-ram; Ram-lion-lotus is my name (13) . . . . . . . to thee here to-day, for I am Sit-ta-ko, Setem is my name, Setem (14) [is my true name, &c.] Hrenoute, Lapptotha, Laxantha, Sa-(15)[risa, &c.] . . . . . . Bolbouel (*bis*), Louteri, (Klo-)Kasantra, Iaho (16) [is my name, &c., Balkam the] dread (?) one of heaven, Ablanathanalba, the gryphon (17) [of the shrine of God, &c.].' [You] say it, drawling (?) with your

---

of the earlier *rn-y* and the later form found in O. C. Par. ерепт (A. Z., 1900, 89, cf. Boh. еренк Hyv. Actes, 108). Cf. 14/2 *yrt-yt*.

l. 13. Lines 13–17 are repeated with the missing passages complete in verso XXVII, which is written on the back of this and the following column.

*syt-tꜣ-k*. The first element is written as the 'serpent' сіт in the parallel text and *k* is bull (ко, 7/33), but *tꜣ* seems meaningless. It may possibly be 'the impregnator of the cow,' cf. Budge, Nesiamsu, iii. 6, *pꜣ kꜣ sty m kꜣ.wt*. In Parthey, Zwei gr. Zauberpap., i. 252, we have practically the same phrase introduced into an O. C. context which gives an entirely different meaning, 'I am Osiris whom Set destroyed,' пентасит тако(ч); see Erman, A. Z., 1883, 109 note.

*stm*, i. e. 'hearing,' or perhaps 'hearer,' but the personal determinative is absent.

l. 15. *Kasantra* alone without клo appears in the demotic of both texts, suggesting a reminiscence of the prophetess Cassandra.

l. 16. *srrf* the hieroglyphic *sfr* of II Beni Hasan, Pl. IV, a winged quadruped with raptorial beak. The *srrf* is described in Kufi, xv. 1 seq., as 'the image (?) of god (?), the king (?) of all that is in the world, the avenger that cannot (himself) be punished; his beak is that of the falcon, his eyes those of a man, his limbs of a lion, his ears of a . . . , his scales of a water- . . . , his tail a serpent's.' Further, he is the mightiest of beings next to God, has authority over everything on earth like Death, and is the instrument of God's vengeance.

l. 17. *sq*, cf. 6/19 for the complete phrase. The meaning 'drawl' is not quite certain. It must be some artificial way of speaking, such as whining or muttering, cf. 7/32 and Leyd. Pap. Gr. W. col. 1, l. 38, col. 3. l. 2, and φθογγος αναγκαστικος, &c., Brit. Mus. Gr. Pap. CXXI. 765 seq.

18. . . . . . a šnt-k ar-f ty n p-hw nte-k t wn yr·t-f n py ʿ[lw]

19. . . . . . nb nte-k nḥm py ʿlw nte ḥr-f pḥ[t a py]

20. . . . . . n ntr ḥry-t p-sepe-n-p-t ḥry-t . . . .

21. . . . . . ank pe Ḥr ʾMn nt ḥms a py šn-hne ty n p[-hw]

22. . . . . . py šn-hne ty n p-hw mʿryghʿry e·ʾr-k . . . .

23. . . . . . nte-w z pe šn n-y z n-w sp-sn n ntr·w nt wʿb n p nwn

24. . . . . . n t n rn nte n ntr·w n Kmy ḫʿ ḥr n gpe·w

25. . . . . . thʿr z ank tʿ-py-šteh-ʿy n t n rn

26. . . . . . t wz-k p pr-ʿo pešʿm-ʿy nt ḥtp ḥr r

27. . . . . . ny ḫpš·w n nb n mʿ·t t mʿ·t n r-y p ʾbye

28. . . . . . . . thʿ z ank pe stel yʿh-ʿo wn-t

## Col. II.

1. e·ʾr-k z n p ḫm-ḫl z a·wn n yr·t-k e-f wn yr·t-f nte-f nw a p wyn e·ʾr-k t ʾr-f ʿš

2. z ʿw sp-sn p wyn pyr sp-sn p wyn θse sp-sn p wyn ḫy sp-sn p wyn p nt n bl

3. ʾm a ḫn e-f ḫp nte-f wn yr·t-f nte-f tm nw a p wyn e·ʾr-k t ʾr-f ḫtm yr·t-f

---

*p-mr-ʾḥ* pronounced *p-le-ehe*, produces the common Ptolemaic proper name Πελαιας, as is proved by a bilingual (Spiegelberg, Strassb. Pap. No. 21, text, pp. 21–2, the reading *P-ers* to be corrected to *p-mr-ʾḥ*; the Greek nominative shown in Grenf. Amh. Pap. LI. 5). The religious significance of this appellation, 'the good oxherd,' is not clear, nor has it been traced in early texts; from 2/7 it is clearly applied to Anubis, and perhaps dogs were used for herding cattle in Ancient Egypt? It is probably equivalent to Gk. ποιμην, for which see Goodwin, Cambridge Essays, 1852, p. 26, B. M. Gr. Pap. XLVI, l. 31. If the Good Shepherd is the meaning, we may note the Χριστος Ανουβις of Leyd. Pap. Gr. V. vi. 17.

l. 19. *nḥm* written with the lotus bud, cf. Br., Wtb., 796–7.

l. 20. peт. In the writing of the glosses the aspirate is suppressed before p, even in 19/19 πρατ for *p-ḫrt*, so also 16/7 καρρη, 28/9 ροϫορ 29/14 ραϭωτ, V. 33/3 αραει. The initial demotic group *ḥry* is seen in

voice: 'O beautiful oxherd, my compeller, (18) . . . . . . . . . ask thee about here to-day: and do thou cause the eyes of this boy to be opened (19) . . . . . . . . . and do thou protect this boy whose face is bent down [over this (20) vessel] . . . . . of god, lord of earth, the survivor (?) of the earth, lord of earth . . . . (21) . . . . . . . . I am Hor-Amon that sitteth at this vessel-divination here to-day (22) . . . . . . . . . this vessel-divination here to-day; Marikhari, thou . . . . (23) . . . . . . . . . . and that they tell me my inquiry. Say to them (*bis*) "O holy gods of the abyss (24) . . . . . [I am] . . . . of earth by name, under the soles [of] whose [feet?] the gods of Egypt are placed (25) . . . . . . . thar, for I am Ta-pishtehei of earth by name (26) . . . . . . . preserve thee, O Pharaoh, Pashamei that resteth at the mouth (?) (27) . . . . . . . . . . . . . these shoulders of real gold. Truth is in (?) my mouth, honey (28) [is in my lips?] . . . . . . Ma . . . tha for I am Stel, Iaho, Earth-opener."'

## Col. II.

(1) You say to the boy 'Open your eyes'; when he opens his eyes and sees the light, you make him cry out, (2) saying 'Grow (*bis*), O light, come forth (*bis*) O light, rise (*bis*) O light, ascend (*bis*) O light, thou who art without, (3) come in.' If he opens his eyes and does

---

Ptolemaic proper names commencing with Φρι- 'sheikh' = *p-ḥry-*. The pronunciation here would be *ḥri-to* rather than ρετ, unless the spelling is fanciful.

l. 21. Hor-Amon is known in figures of glazed pottery (Lanzone, Diz. Mit., 601).

l. 23. *sp-sn*. It seems probable that this group may be used simply as a mark of emphasis, e.g. after *m šs*, 'exceedingly,' and here after the imperative 'say to them!' It can hardly mean 'say to them twice.'

l. 26. *ḥr r*, or 'opposite,' as in Coptic ϩιρεν-.

l. 27. *'bye*, cf. 9/16: or perhaps, 'The truth of my mouth [is] the honey [of my lips].'

4. e·ʾr-k ʿš ar-f n whm z-mt·t p kke a·ʿl-k n ḥ·t-f p wyn a·ʾny p wyn n-y a ẖn

5. p šʿy nt ẖn p nwn a·ʾny p wyn n-y a ẖn Wsr nt ḥr nšme·t a·ʾny p wyn n-y

6. a ẖn py IV tw nt n bl a·ʾny p wyn n-y a ẖn p nte p šp pa ny wne·t·w n t·t-f a (*sic*)

7. a·ʾny p wyn n-y a ẖn ʾNp p-mr-ʾḥ nfr a·ʾny p wyn n-y a ẖn z e·ʾr-k

8. a t s-ʿo ar-y ty n p-hw z ʾnk Ḥr s ʾS·t p s nfr n Wsr e·ʾr-k a ʾny n ntr·w n t s·t

9. wype e·ʾr-k a t ʾr-w ʾr n pe hb n-se t mšʿe(?) te·t yp·t Ne-tbew e·ʾr-k a ty ʾr-w ʾr nʾm-s

10. z(?) . . . . twrʿm-ne ʿm-ne ʿ·ʿ mes sp-sn ʿo-rnw-ʿo-rf sp-sn ʿo-rnw-ʿo-rf sp-sn pʿh-ʿo-r-f

11. . . . . . pʿh-r-f y-ʿo qwy n stn tw-ḥr my wz py ʿlw nte ḥr-f pḥte a py

12. nḥ[e nte-k(?)] t pḥ(?) n-y Sbk šʿ nte-f pyr stm rn-yt stm pe pe rn n mt z ʾnk

13. l . . [m] . . . . . t twlot tʿt pyntʿt pe rn n mt p ntr ʿo nte ne·ʿw rn-f

---

COL. II.

l. 4. *a·ʿl-k.* The *a* is an addition above the line. *ʿl-k* would be ολ=κ, but the *a* prefixed suggests *αλι=κ on the analogy of αλι, hardly αλο=κ 'cease,' cf. St., § 384. The gloss may of course be incomplete, like some others.

*a·ʾny*, the same formula in O. C. Par. επι cαβαωθ παι εζοπη A. Z., 1900, p. 87.

l. 5. *p šʿy* O. C. Par. πϭοι A. Z., 1883, p. 105: 1900, 92 and ψοι ib. 93 from Pap. Bibl. Nat. l. 1643. A god whose name often occurs in Graeco-Egyptian names, *Σενψαις*, &c. (cf. Spiegelberg, Demot. Stud., i. p. 57*), and in the titles of Antoninus Pius was translated *ἀγαθοδαίμων*. In the older texts (*Šʾy*) he seems to be mainly a god of destiny (Lanz., Diz. Mit., 1185).

*p šʿy nt ẖn p nwn* = *ο μεγας δαιμων ο φνουνοχθονιος*, B. M. Pap. XLVI. 239.

*nšme·t*, the bark of Osiris: see Rec. trav., xvi. 105 seq., esp. p. 121.

l. 6. *šp.* The meaning is very uncertain. It might be 'the ruling star,' cf. Leyd. Pap. Gr. W. col. 9, l. 36 *ἐπικάλου τὸν τῆς ὥρας καὶ τὸν τῆς ἡμέρας θεόν.*

not see the light, you make him close his eyes, (4) you call to him again; formula: 'O darkness, remove thyself from before him (*sic*)! O light, bring the light in to me! (5) Pshoi that is in the abyss, bring in the light to me! O Osiris, who is in the Nesheme-boat, bring in the light to me! (6) these four winds that are without, bring in the light to me! O thou in whose hand is the moment (?) that belongeth to these hours (7) bring in the light to me! Anubis, the good oxherd, bring in the light to me! for thou (8) shalt give protection (?) to me here to-day. For I am Horus son of Isis, the good son of Osiris; thou shalt bring the gods of the place (9) of judgement, and thou shalt cause them to do my business, and they shall make my affair proceed; Netbeou, thou shalt cause them to do it. (10) For [I am ?] Touramnei, Amnei, A-a, Mes (*bis*), Ornouorf (*bis*), Ornouorf (*bis*), Pahorof, (11) . . . . Pahrof, Io, a little (?) king, Touhor; let this child prosper, whose face is bent down to this (12) oil [and thou shalt] escort (?) Souchos to me until he come forth. Setem is my name, Setem is my correct name. For I am (13) L[ot], M[oulo]t, Toulot, Tat,

---

l. 8. ⲥⲱ may be only magical gibberish, but suggests the word for 'protection,' 'amulet.'

l. 9. *wypt*, the gods of the place of judgement are presumably the numerous gods of Egypt who assisted at the judgement of the dead. Cf. V. 33/2.

*Ne-tbew*, a deity (?) unknown except in the proper name Παυετβευς, GRENF. Pap. Tebt. No. 88, l. 20 (B.C. 115–4). There are said to be sixteen of them in V. 33/5 q. v.

*mšᶜ*, of an inanimate object in a transferred sense.

l. 11. *qwy n stn*, perhaps only gibberish, to be pronounced *kouiens* (?).

l. 12. *pḥ* or perhaps *še*.

*Sbk*. It seems curious that the very well-defined god Souchos should be asked for when Anubis is the one really required: doubtless he might be supposed to dwell in the liquid oil.

*rn-yt*, &c. Cf. O. C. Par. ⲉⲣⲉⲛⲧ . . . ⲡⲉ ⲡⲁ ⲣⲉⲛ ⲛ̄ ⲙⲏⲧ (A. Z., 1884, pp. 23–4, 1900, p. 89). το ονομα το αληθινον B. M. Pap. XLVI. 115.

l. 13. Lot Moulot may perhaps be the missing words, cf. 18/13.

14. wnḥ a py ʿlw aph-ʿo-b-ʿo-s ʿpsewst-ʿo-s epʿletsyʿ e·ʾr-k ʿš ny

15. sh̭·w n sp VII e·ʾr-k t ʾr-f wn yr·t-f nte p wyn aʿny nte-f z ʾNp ʾy a h̭n e·ʾr-k ʿš ḥ·t-f

16. z-mt·t ʾy ryz mw ryz ʾy t wr t ʾy py ḥwt nfr a·ms heryew t šr·t n t neme·t

17. ʾm n-y z nte-k py ššn ʾr pyr h̭n t srpt n p nws-t-r nt ʾr wyn a p t tre-f

18. hy ʾNp ʾm n-y p h̭y p zr p ḥry-sšt n na t ty·t p pr-ʿo n na ʾmnt p wr syn

19. . . nfr n Wsr p nh̭t ḥr-f ʾwt n ntr·w e·ʾr-k h̭ʿ n t ty·t ne-ḥr t·t-f n Wsr e·ʾr-k šms

20. [n] by n ʾBt z e-w ʿnh̭ nʾm-k tre·w ny by·w na ty·t tsre·t ʾm a p t wnḥ-k ar-y

---

l. 14. *aph-ʿo-b-ʿo-s*, &c. As the glosses show this is merely a transcription of the Greek words ἀφόβως ἀψεύστως ἐπ' ἀληθείᾳ, and to mark this the determinative of that which is foreign is placed at the end of each word. It is interesting to find the initial letter /, here and in 10/30, representing the Gk. α, and so indicating that that was its normal pronunciation. In Achm. it corresponds to ⲁ, rarely ⲉ, in Sah. and Boh. to ⲉ, rarely ⲁ. ⲉ is probably a wearing down or shortening of the earlier ⲁ.

l. 15. *aʿny*, a peculiar writing (as if *a·ʿn-y*) for ⲁⲛⲁⲓ, occurring also in I Kham. v. 14 *.

16. *ʾy*. The sign represents  and is transcribed ⲏⲓ twice 7/24, 16/9. This can hardly be the pronunciation of the interjection 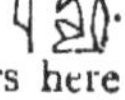. The usual interjection in religious texts is 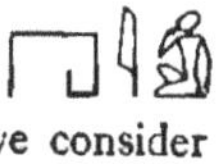 which occurs here frequently spelt , but we consider 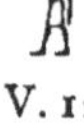 to be distinct from *hy*.

*ryz mw ryz*, cf. 18/13 *lol mw lol*, 27/5 *rw my rw*, V. 12/3 *lyl mw lyl*.

*neme·t* apparently a goddess, perhaps of destruction: usually this

---

* The group for *ʿny* is that which spells *ne-ʿne* (ⲛⲁⲛⲟⲩ⸗) in ordinary texts, but here the *ne* is superfluous, and in this papyrus a false *ne* is always written before *ʿne*, so that ⲛⲁⲛⲟⲩ⸗ has to be written out *ne*(*-ne*)*-ʿne*. In other texts as well as this we find *ne-nfr* with a false *ne-*, probably due to the initial sound of *nfr*, and this may have led to the otiose *ne* before *ʿne* in the present text.

Peintat is my correct name. O great god whose name is great, (14) appear to this child without alarming or deceiving, truthfully.' You utter these (15) charms seven times, you make him open his eyes. If the light is good and he says 'Anubis is coming in,' you call before him (Anubis). (16) Formula: 'O Riz Muriz, O To-ur-to, O this beautiful male born of Herieou, the daughter of the Neme, (17) Come to me, for thou art this lotus-flower that came forth from in the lotus of Pnastor, and that illuminates the whole earth; (18) hail! Anubis, come to me, the High, the Mighty, the Chief over the mysteries of those in the Underworld, the Pharaoh of those in Amenti, the Chief Physician, (19) the fair [son ?] of Osiris, he whose face is strong among the gods, thou manifestest thyself in the Underworld before the hand of Osiris. Thou servest (20) the souls of Abydos, for they all live by thee, these souls (namely) those of the sacred Underworld. Come to the earth, show thyself to me

---

name is attached to the execution-block, but here it has the determinative of fire.

l. 17. Cf. Horus on the lotus at Erment L. D. iv. 61, g. 65; and in Greek papyri, *εχεις μορφην νηπιου παιδος επι λωτω καθημενος* PARTHEY, Zwei gr. Zauberpap., ii. 106; *ο επι του λωτου καθημενος και λαμπυριδων την ολην οικουμενην* Leyd. Pap. Gr. V. iii. 15.

*sšn*, *srpt*, see LORET, Rec. trav., i. 190, for a useful but by no means final discussion of the Egyptian names of the lotus. *srpt* (see 1/12) is a name apparently of late introduction, *sšn* is very ancient, and both words are to be paralleled, with varied meaning, in Semitic languages. From this passage one may conjecture that *srpt* is the lotus bud and *sšn* the flower.

l. 18. *wr syn*, 'chief physician,' an old Egyptian official title (O. K. in P. S. B. A., xi. 306, Persian period BRUGSCH., Thes., 639), but amongst the gods most applicable to Thoth. Apparently Thoth and Anubis are here united, cf. the name Hermanubis and l. 21. *ḥry-sšt*, 'chief over the mysteries,' is another old title appropriate enough for either Thoth or Anubis.

l. 20. 'For they all live by thee.' Apparently Anubis was responsible for the provision of food and attendance on the souls.

21. ty n p-hw nte-k Tḥwt nte-k p e·ʾr pyr n ḥt-f n p šʿy ʿo p yt·w sp-sn n n ntr·w tre·w ʾm a r n r·w

22. n pe hne n p-hw nte-k z n-y wḥ n mt·t mʿ·t ḫr mt·t nb nt e-y šn ḫr-w e·mn mt·t n ʿze nʾm-w z ʾnk ʾS·t

23. t rḫe·t nte n z n r-y ḥp z-mt sp VII e·ʾr-k z n p ḥm-ḥl ze a·zy-s n ʾNp z

24. mšʿ a bl a·ʾny n ntr·w a ḫn e-f mšʿ m-s-w nte-f ʾnyt-w a ḫn e·ʾr-k šn p ʿlw z ḥr n ntr·w

25 ʾy a ḫn e-f z ḥr-w ʾy nte-k nw ar-w e·ʾr-k ʿš ḥ·t-w z-mt·t nhe-k n-y sp-sn p šʿy nhs·t-k merʿ

26. p wr-ty tsytsyw tnnzyw a·ʾry mt ar-y Tḥwt my ʾre qme mḥ p t n wyn hb

27. m ḥr-f šps šps ʿq a p ḥt my t ḥp t mʿ·t p ntr ʿo nte ne·ʿw rn-f z sp VII

28 e·ʾr-k z n p ḥm-ḥl z a·zy-s n ʾNp z a·ʾny wʿ tks a ḫn ḫr n ntr·w my ḥms-w e-w

---

l. 21. *p yt·w sp-sn* is intended to be read *p yt yt·w* as 8/2. Cf. the common appellation προπατωρ in the Gk. papyri. 'Father of the fathers of all the gods' occurs perhaps as early as the N. K. in Boul. Pap. No. 17, p. 7, l. 6 (Hymn to Amon-Re).

l. 22. *nte-k z n-y wḥ*. For this formula cf. O. C. Par. ⲛ̄ⲥⲉϫⲓ ⲟⲩⲱ ⲛⲁⲓ ⲁϥⲱⲃ ⲉⲧⲓϫⲛⲟⲩ ⲙⲙⲟⲟⲩ ⲉⲣⲟⲍ (*sic*) (A. Z., 1900, 89). εισελθε και χρηματισον B. M. Pap. XLVI. 445. *šn*, lit. 'inquire,' is used vaguely, both of the inquiry and of the answer in this papyrus, as χρηματιζειν in Greek. ϣⲓⲛⲓ ϭⲁ in Copt. is 'beg for,' not 'ask a question'; possibly it has such a meaning here.

l. 24. *ḥr n ntr·w ʾy*, &c.=*(ϩ)ⲁⲛⲛⲧⲏⲣ ⲉⲓ . . . *(ϩ)ⲁⲩ ⲉⲓ (see chapter on grammar in vol. ii).

l. 25. 'And you see them' is an addition above the line which does not seem appropriate, as the boy, not the magician, is to see them.

*nhe-k . . . nhs·t-k*: the defective spelling *nhe* is found again in the papyrus, leaving no doubt that it represents *nhse*, 'waken,' 'raise.' The verb is 'iv^tae^ infirmae' according to Sethe, and the suffix form, lost in Coptic, shows here a curious uncertainty as to the retention of the *t*.

l. 26. *wr·ty*. Originally the title of the high priest of Thoth at Hermopolis Magna (Khmun), it was perhaps applied later to the ibis-god himself (e. g. Legrain, Livre des transf., iv. 5). Evidently in connexion with this, Thoth is called 'the god five times great (*ʿo*), the mighty (*wr*) lord of Khmun' (II Mahaffy, Petrie Pap. Pl. 13, II Kham.

(21) here to-day. Thou art Thoth, thou art he that came forth from the heart of the great Agathodaemon, the father of the fathers of all the gods; come to the mouths (22) of my vessel to-day and do thou tell me answer in truth to everything that I shall inquire about, without falsehood therein; for I am Isis (23) the Wise, the words of whose mouth of mine (*sic*) come to pass.' Formula: seven times. You say to the boy 'Speak to Anubis, saying (24) "Go forth, bring in the gods."' When he goes after them and brings them in, you ask the boy, saying 'Have the gods (25) come in?' If he says 'They have come' and you (*sic*) see them, you cry before them. Formula: 'Raise thyself for me (*bis*), Pshoi; raise thyself, Mera (26), the Great of Five, Didiou, Tenziou, do justice to me. Thoth, let creation (?) fill the earth with light; O (thou who art an) ibis in (27) his noble countenance, thou noble one that enters the heart, let truth be brought forth, thou great god whose name is great.' Say seven times. (28) You say to the boy 'Speak to Anubis, saying "Bring in a table for the

---

5, 7). The common Ptolemaic name Πορτις (cf. GRENFELL, Gk. Pap. I, II; Amherst Pap.; WILCKEN, Gr. Ostr.) in the witnesses of the Grey antigraph (Brit. Mus. Gr. Pap. I. Pl. 27) is *P-wr-ty* in the corresponding Berlin demotic Pap. 3119 verso (Berl. Dem. Pap. Pl. 16). Πορτις is no doubt founded on an abbreviated pronunciation of the name which we have here with its full value *P-wer-tiu*. In V. 33/2 we have the normal orthography of the title, varied here and in 22/1.

*my 're qme*. Meaning very uncertain; if the dot after *qme* be taken as closing the phrase, the *'r* must be regarded as passive in meaning 'let a creation (?) be made,' cf. 5/22 *my wn yr·t* and GRIFF., High Priests, p. 87, n. to l. 6, and SETHE, Verb., ii. § 247, and *mḥ* following the dot suggests an imperative. Perhaps *Mareqom* (?) is to be taken as a magical name.

l. 27. *'q a p ḥt*, perhaps may be participial rather than imperative. *'q r ḥt*, lit. 'enter the heart,' is common in early demotic in the sense of 'please.' Cf. ⲁⲕϩⲧⲏⲓ (SPIEGELB., Rec. trav., xxiii. 201) ⲱⲕ ⲛ̄ ϩⲏⲧ (BSCIAI, ib., vii. 27).

29. ḥms e·ʾr-k z a·ʾny wʿ ʾrp a ẖn klp-f a n ntr·w a·ʾny hyn·w t a ẖn my wm-w my swr-w

## Col. III.

1. my wm-w my swr-w my ʾr-w hw nfr e-w wḥ e·ʾr-k z n ʾNp z ʿnn (*sic*) e·ʾr-k šn n-y e-f z t ḥ·t e·ʾr-k z n-f z p ntr nt ne ʾr pe šn

2. n p-hw my ʾr-f ʿḥ e rt-f e-f z ʿḥ-f e·ʾr-k z n-f z a·zy-s n ʾNp z fy n nk n t mte e·ʾr-k ʿš

3. ḥ·t-f ty hte·t z p šʿy n p-hw p nb n p-hw p nte pe-f pe ny wne·t·w e·ʾr-k t ʾr-f zt-s

4. n ʾNp z p ntr nt ne šn n-y n p-hw my ʾr-f z n-y rn-f e-f ʿḥ a rt-f nte-f z rn-f e.ʾr-k šn·t-f

5. a mt·t nb nt e·ʾr-k wẖ-f pe-f swḥ-ʾyẖ ẖr ʾny-k tbe VII nmy e b-ʾr te-w qym nʾm-w a pnʿ-w

6. a p ke ẖr e·ʾr-k fy·t-w e·ʾr-k wʿb n wš n zḥ-w a nte(?) nb n p t nte-k smne·t-w n pe-w ky e·wne-w

7. smne·t nʾm-f ʿn nte-k smne tbe III ẖr p nḥe t k·t tbe·t IV nte-k sʿr-w n p qt n p ẖm-ẖl(?) n wš n

8. zḥ ʿe·t nte-f a p ʾytn nge bʿe VII nte-k ʾr-w n py smte ʿn nte-k ʾny t VII e-w wʿb

9. nte-k sʿr-w n p qte n p nḥe erme tyk VII n ḥm nte-k ʾny wʿ·t bʾtʾne·t nmy nte-k mḥ-s n

---

l. 29. *wʿ ʾrp*, 'a (vessel of) wine,' probably the κεραμιον of the Rosetta stone: cf. the use of *ḥt*, 'silver,' in contracts = *tbn*.

Col. III.

l. 1. *ʾr hw nfr*: from this and other passages it is clear that the actual meaning of this common expression is not to pass a day of pleasure, but simply 'enjoy oneself.'

*ʾNp* would seem to be an error for *p ẖm-ẖl*, 'the boy.'

*t ḥ-t*, probably as we say 'the first thing,' 'at once.'

l. 2. *n t mte*, 'from the midst,' i. e. of the gods seated at the meal.

l. 3. *p-hw . . . ny wne·t·w*, cf. note on 2/6.

l. 5. *swḥ-ʾyẖ*, lit. 'spirit-gathering,' is the title for the material arrangements for divination as to locality, censing, salves, &c., to be employed, not the invocations.

Egyptian bricks are crude. The use of burnt brick was introduced by the Romans and increased to Byzantine times, but crude brick remained throughout the principal building material.

gods, and let them sit."' When they (29) are seated, you say 'Bring in a (jar of) wine, broach it for the gods; bring in some bread, let them eat, let them drink,'

## Col. III.

(1) 'let them eat, let them drink, let them pass a festal day.' When they have finished, you speak to Anubis (*sic*) saying 'Dost thou make inquiry for me?' If he says 'At once,' you say to him 'The god who will make my inquiry (2) to-day, let him stand up.' If he says 'He has stood up,' you say to him (i.e. the child) 'Say to Anubis "Carry off the things from the midst"'; you cry (3) before him (i.e. the god) instantly saying 'O Agathodaemon of to-day, lord of to-day, O thou whose (possession) these moments are!' You cause him (the boy) to say (4) to Anubis 'The god who will inquire for me to-day, let him tell me his name.' When he stands up and tells his name, you ask him (5) concerning everything that you wish.

Its spirit-gathering. You take seven new bricks, before they have been moved so as to turn them (6) to the other face; you take them, you being pure, without touching them against anything on earth, and you place them in their manner in which they were (7) placed, again; and you place three tiles under the oil; and the other four tiles, you arrange them about the child without (8) touching any part of him against the ground; or seven palm-sticks, you treat them in this fashion also. And you take seven clean loaves (9) and arrange them around the oil, with seven lumps of salt,

l. 6. *nte nb.* The reading not quite certain, but extremely probable.

l. 7. *p qt.* The usual group for *qt* is very much abbreviated, and is thus identical with that for *wḫ*, 'wish,' but there can be little doubt of the reading. The meaning must be that the bricks are laid about the boy so that he can stand or sit on them without touching the ground.

l. 9. *tyk* can scarcely be other than Sah. ⲧⲁϭ. The otiose *y* may be

10. nḥe n whe e-f wʿb nte-k t a t bʿtʿne·t ḫm sp-sn n wš n t ḫp hʿyse nte-f ḫp e-f stf

11. m šs sp-sn nte-k ʾny wʿ ḫm-ḫl e-f wʿb e b-ʾr te-f še erme s-ḥm·t e·ʾr-k sze a ḫry ḫn zz-f

12. e-f ʿḥ a rt-f a t ḥ·t z ʿn e-f a ʾr šw n še a p hne e-f ḫp e-f ʾr šw e·ʾr-k t str-f a ḥr ḫe·t-f

13. e·ʾr-k ḥbs-f n wʿ·t šnt·t n ʿyw·t e-s wʿb e·ʾr-k ʿš a ḫry ḫn zz-f e wn wʿ ryt n t ry·t ḥry-f (*sic ?*)

14. n t šnt·t e·ʾr-k ʿš py ʿš nt ḥry a ḫry ḫn zz-f e-f kšp a ḫry nw a ḫn p nḥe šʿ sp VII e yr·t-f

15. ḫtm e·ʾr-k wḥ e·ʾr-k t ʾr-f wn yr·t-f e·ʾr-k šn·t-f a p nte ʾr-k wḥ-f ḫr ʾr-k-f šʿ p nw n p θ VII n p hw

16. p ʿš nte ʾr-k ʿš-w (*sic*) a ḫry ḫn zz-f n ḥ·t a znt-f n ne-f msz·w z ʿn e-f a ʾr šw n še ḫr

17. p hne z-mt·t hb šps nšr bk šps apḥte·t my wʿb-y mw ky hb šps nšr

18. bk šps apḥte·t e·ʾr-k ʿš n·y a ḫry ḫn zz-f šʿ sp VII e·ʾr-k t ʾw ny ḫr

19. mt·t ne-f msz·w e-ḫp nte pe-f msz II mt·t (ne)nfr-f m šs sp-sn e-f ḫp e pe-f msz n

20. wnm(?) pe (ne)nfr-f e-f ḫp e p . . . pe ne-bn-f pḫre·t n pḫr p hne n gtg nte n ntr·w ʾy a ḫn nte-w z

---

compared with that in *byl* for ⲃⲁⲗ 13/12, *P-šylem* (21/3) = O. C. ⲡⲁϭⲁⲗⲱⲙ, and is brought about by such forms as *ʾny·t-k* (root *ʾny*) for *ʾn·t-k*, *my* (ⲙⲟⲓ) ⲙⲁ-, *rn-yt* for *rn-t* (1/12).

l. 10. Oasis oil, cf. 6/2, not mentioned elsewhere; a kind of 'real oil,' but not identical with it 25/12.

*ḫm sp-sn* must be read *ḫmḫm*, C. ϣⲏⲙϣⲏⲙ, cf. 2/21, 18/13, 24/12.

*hʿyse*, meaning quite uncertain: cf. perhaps *ḥsyse* in I Kham. 6/19, II Kham. 6/16.

l. 12. *a ḥr ḫe·t-f*, a curious expression, 'on the face of (?) his belly,' cf. the use of *ḥr* in l. 6.

l. 13. *šnt·t n ʿyw·t* : Boh. ϣⲉⲛⲧⲱ ⲛⲓⲁⲩ (PEYRON), cf. σινδὼν βυσσίνη Hdt. ii. 86. The Egyptian *šnd·t* was the loin-cloth or tunic, and in this papyrus it still seems to signify a dress, though in Coptic it can be used simply for 'cloth.' Cf. Pap. Bibl. Nat. l. 88 (A. Z., 1883, 99) and Brit. Mus. Pap. Gr. No. XLVI. l. 206, for the use of σινδων in magic.

Omit the words 'you call down into his head.'

and you take a new dish and fill it with (10) clean Oasis oil and add to the dish gradually without producing cloudiness (?) so that it becomes clear (11) exceedingly; and you take a boy, pure, before he has gone with a woman, you speak down into his head (12) while he stands, previously, (to learn) whether he will be profitable in going to the vessel. If he is profitable, you make him lie on (?) his belly; (13) you clothe (?) him with a clean linen tunic (?), ⟨you call down into his head⟩, there being a girdle on the upper part (14) of the tunic; you utter this invocation that is above, down into his head, he gazing downwards ⟨looking⟩ into the oil, for seven times, his eyes being (15) closed. When you have finished, you make him open his eyes, you ask him about what you desire; you do it until the time of the seventh hour of the day.

(16) The invocation that you utter down into his head previously to test him in his ears as to whether he will be profitable in going to (17) the vessel. Formula: 'Noble ibis, falcon, hawk, noble and mighty, let me be purified in the manner of the noble ibis, falcon, (18) hawk, noble and mighty.' You utter this down into his head for seven times; when you utter this, then (19) his ears speak. If his two ears speak, he is very good; if it be his right ear, (20) he is good; if it be his left ear, he is bad.

Prescription for enchanting the vessel quickly so that

---

l. 14. Omit 'looking' as corrected by the addition above the line.

l. 15. *n p θ VII*: for the reading *θ*, rather than *θ wne·t*, compare V. 24/6. The phrase is evidently to be connected with the Coptic idiom ⲡⲛⲁⲩ ⲛ̄ ϫⲡ̄ⲯⲓⲧⲉ, 'the ninth hour.' ϫⲡ:ⲁϫⲡ are feminine.

l. 19. *e-ḫp*, probably an unique spelling in demotic instead of the usual *e-f ḫp*, for ⲉϥϣⲱⲡⲉ.

l. 20. The word for left (sinister) cannot yet be transliterated. In Egyptian we have *ỉby* and *smḥ*, in Sah. ϩⲃⲟⲩⲣ and Boh. ϫⲁϭⲏ: in several passages we have *gby'r*, the Achmim. ϭⲃⲓⲣ (Zach. xii. 6, in

21. n-k wḫ n mt·t mʿ·t e·ʾr-k t qwqe n swḥ·t n *ⲙⲥⲉϩ* nge p nt ḫn-s a t st·t ḫr pḫre-f ty hte·t pḫre·t a t ʾr-w

22. sze e·ʾr-k t tp n *ⲕⲣⲟⲩⲣ* a p ʿḫ ḫr ʾr-w sze pḫre·t a ʾny n ntr·w a ḫn n kns e·ʾr-k t sḫy

23. n msḥ ḫr ʿnte sq a p ʿḫ e·ʾr-k wḫ a t ʾr-w ʾy a ḫn n tkr ʿn e·ʾr-k t ḫ n *ⲥⲙⲓⲥ* e p ʿḫ erme t qwqe

24. n swḥ·t nt ḥry ḫr pḫr-f ty hte e·ʾr-k wḫ a ʾny rm e-f ʿnḫ a ḫn e·ʾr-k t gʾlʾgʾntsy a p ʿḫ ḫr ʾw-f a ḫn

25. e·ʾr-k wḫ a ʾny ʾyḫ a ḫn e·ʾr-k t s-wr ḥr ʾny(?) n ylḫ a p ʿḫ ḫr ʾw p ʾyḫ a ḫn e·ʾr-k t ḥt

26. n hyt·t nge wn·t(?) nfr sp·sn e·ʾr-k wḫ a ʾny ḥsy a ḫn e·ʾr-k t gʿlʿb n yʿm a p ʿḫ

27. e·ʾr-k wḫ a ʾny rm e-f mwt a ḫn e·ʾr-k t hs n *ⲉⲟ* ḥr s Nb·t-ḥ·t a p ʿḫ ḫr ʾw-f a ḫn e·ʾr-k

28. wḫ a t še(-w) n-w tre·w e·ʾr-k t hs n *ⲉⲛ* a p ʿḫ ḫr ʾr-w še n-w a pe-w mʿ tre-w nte-k ʿš pe-w r n wt-w ʿn(?)

---

Pap. Rain. Mitth. ii. 266); *gbyr* may possibly be connected with ϩⲃⲟⲩⲣ and with the demotic ligature here; or *ḥmr* may be the reading of the latter.

l. 22. *tp*. Two portions of the body are written *tp* in the demotic of this papyrus. One has the det. of bone as well as that of flesh, and is undoubtedly ⲧⲁⲡ, 'horn,' Eg. . Without the det. of bone we have the *tp* of an ass or a hoopoe, which presumably means the head or skull; in other cases, e.g. 19/26, one may doubt whether horn ⲧⲁⲡ is not intended by the same group.

l. 23. *sq*, written with the crocodile, presumably = ⲥⲓⲕⲉ; see the verb in Brugsch, Rec., iv. Pl. 97, l. 16, and as a participle attached to a word meaning incense, ib., Pl. 85 A, ll. 3, 7, and 11; Pl. 96, l. 6.

ⲥⲙⲓⲥ suggests ⲥⲙⲓⲥⲉ : ⲁⲙⲓⲥⲓ, i.e. 'anise,' or according to some MSS. 'mint,' Loret, Flore Phar., 2nd ed. pp. 53, 71; and it seems possible that the tall dry stalks of the anise (as opposed to the commonly prescribed seeds) should be denoted by *ḫ*, lit. 'wood.'

l. 24. *gʾlʾgʾntsy* with gloss ⲕⲁⲗⲁⲕⲁⲛⲑⲓ suggests κολοκύνθις; but as the determinative here indicates a mineral and not a plant, it must be intended for χαλκάνθη, 'sulphate of copper,' which is written χαλάκανθον in Leyd. Pap. X. 1, 3.

l. 25. *ʾyḫ*, 'spirit' of a dead person, or a 'demon': the Gk. δαίμων, which may be good or bad (Pap. Bibl. Nat. passim). On the Bentresh Stela the demon possessing the princess is *ʾḫ*.

the gods enter and tell (21) you answer truthfully. You put the shell of a crocodile's egg, or that which is inside it, on the flame; it will be enchanted instantly.

Prescription to make them (22) speak: you put a frog's head on the brazier, then they speak.

Prescription for bringing the gods in by force: you put the bile (23) of a crocodile with pounded frankincense on the brazier.

If you wish to make them come in quickly again, you put stalks (?) of anise (?) on the brazier together with the (24) egg-shell as above, then the charm works at once.

If you wish to bring in a living man, you put sulphate of copper on the brazier, then he comes in.

(25) If you wish to bring in a spirit, you put *sa-wr* stone with stone of *ilkh* on the brazier, then the spirit comes in. You put the heart (26) of a hyaena or a hare, excellent (*bis*).

If you wish to bring in a drowned man, you put sea-*karab*-stone (?) on the brazier.

(27) If you wish to bring in a murdered (?) man, you put ass's dung with an amulet of Nephthys on the brazier, then he comes in.

If you (28) wish to make (them) all depart, you put ape's dung on the brazier, then they all depart to their place, and you utter their spell of dismissal also.

---

*ylḫ*. The *ḫ* is written by a sign common enough in other texts, but in this MS. found only here, and in 6/20 *ḫtn* ai l 23/29 *ḫlby*.

l. 26. *ḥsy*, 'approved,' 'deified,' as an expression for one drowned or devoured by a crocodile (19/24), cf. Hdt. ii. 90, and note to l. 31.

*gʿrʿb n yʿm*, 'sea-*karab*,' determined as a mineral can scarcely be κάραβος = 'palinurus vulgaris,' unless its shell be treated as such. Cf. καρκινος ποταμιος in Pap. Bibl. Nat. 2458, 2687. In favour of the sense 'crab' or 'crayfish' we might suppose that it was called 'sea-karab' to distinguish it from the καραβος, 'beetle.'

l. 27. *rm e-f mwt*, ⲣⲉϥⲙⲟⲟⲩⲧ, but perhaps meaning 'murdered man,' not merely a 'dead' man.

l. 28. *še n-w*: this ethical dative adds a certain force to the word, of

29. e·ʾr-k wḫ a ʾny ʿze a ḫn e·ʾr-k t ḫqe n grwgws ḥr ʾbn t a p ʿḫ n sḫ nte ʾr-k ʿš e·ʾr-k šʿne

30. wt-w e pe-w(?) mʿ wt nfr wt rše

31. e·ʾr-k wḫ a t ʾre n ntr·w ʾy n-k a ḫn nte p hn pḫr n tkr e·ʾr-k ʾny wʿ mḫrr nte-k t še-f n ḥsy ḫn p(?) ʾrt n ʾḥ·t km·t

32. nte-k ty-f a p ʿḫ ḫr pḫre-f n t wne·t n rn-s nte p wyn ḫp

33. wʿ s a mr-f a ḫ·t-f n p nt ḫr hne a t ʾr-f pḫr n tktk e·ʾr-k ʾny wʿ swt n ʿyw n ʿy XVI IV·t n ḥt IV·t n [wt ?]

34. IV·t sšt IV·t n ʾtme·t nte-k ʾr-w n wʿ swt nte-k sp-w n snf n qwqwpt nte-k mr-f n wʿ mḫrr n ʿḥ-f n p rʿ

35. ḥsy e-f qs n ḥbs(?) n š-stn nte-k mr-f a ḫe·t-f n p ḫm-ḫl nt ḫr p hn ḫr pḫr-f n tkr e [mn mt·t ?] n p [t . . . .] nʾm-f(?)

## Col. IV.

1. wʿ sš-(?)mšt e·ḫr ʾr-s p ntr ʿo ʾy-m-ḥtp pe-f swḥ-ʾyḫ ḫr ʾny-k wʿ tks n ḫ n zyt

---

withdrawal into or to oneself, an idea naturally associated with sleeping or lying down (*str n-k* 4/8) and best seen with the verb *še*, which by itself means 'go,' while *še n-f* (ϣⲉ ⲛⲁϥ) means 'go away,' 'go home,' 'withdraw.'

l. 29. *ʾny ʿze a ḫn*, probably = *κλεπτην πιασαι* B. M. Pap. XLVI. 172.

*e·ʾr-k šʿne* = ⲉⲕϣⲁⲛ-, an isolated instance at present. The following is the *απολυσις* of the Gk. papyri, B. M. Pap. CXXI. 333.

l. 31. *t še-f n ḥsy* = ϫⲟϥ ⲛϩⲁⲥⲓⲉ, cf. Sah. ⲁⲩϣⲉ ⲛϩⲁⲥⲓⲉ *εναυαγησαν* 1 Tim. i. 19, and ⲃⲱⲕ ⲛϩⲁⲥⲓⲉ 'be drowned' (Peyron). The literal meaning is 'thou shalt cause him to go as one praised (pleasing).' Similarly in I Kham. iv. 9, 14, 20 drowning is expressed by *ʾr-f ḥs·t p Rʿ*, 'He did that which pleased Re (the sun god).' *ḥsy* has det. of sun and in some cases the divine det. 𓊹 prefixed to the word-sign, cf. 15/12. In Gk. our expression is rendered by *ἐκθέωσον*, 'deify,' or possibly 'consecrate,' which proves that the meaning 'blessed dead,' i.e. 'divinised,' was not yet forgotten: *λαβων μυγαλον εκθεωσον πηγαιω υδατι, και λαβων κανθαρους σεληνιακους δυο εκθεωσον υδατι ποταμιω* Pap. Bibl. Nat. l. 2455; *εασον καλαβωτην εις κρινινον εως αν αποθεωθη* B. M. Pap. CXXI. 629; *αποθωσον εις* [*γαλα*, &c.] Berl. Pap. I. 5.

*ḥsy*—as a proper name = *Ασιης* (Spiegelberg, Eigennamen, p. 7*), lit. 'praised' or 'blessed'—is an euphemism for 'drowned.' No other meaning is ascertained in demotic for the word as subst.; and that it

(29) If you wish to bring in a thief, you put crocus powder with alum on the brazier.

The charm which you pronounce when you (30) dismiss them to their place: 'Good dispatch, joyful dispatch!'

(31) If you wish to make the gods come in to you and that the vessel work its magic quickly, you take a scarab and drown it in the milk of a black cow (32) and put it on the brazier; then it works magic in the moment named and the light comes.

(33) An amulet to be bound to the body of him who has the vessel, to cause it to work magic quickly. You take a band of linen of sixteen threads, four of white, four of [green], (34) four of blue, four of red, and make them into one band and stain them with the blood of a hoopoe, and you bind it with a scarab in its attitude of the sun-god, (35) drowned, being wrapped in byssus, and you bind it to the body of the boy who has the vessel and it will work magic quickly; there being nothing [in the world better (?)] than it (?).

## Col. IV.

(1) A scout-spreader (?), which the great god Imuthes makes. Its spirit-gathering. You bring a table of olive-

---

implies that condition is shown by the determinative of water added to the name on mummy tickets (Spiegelberg, l. c.). We may thus be sure of its meaning in l. 26 q.v. and in l. 35, as well as in the numerous parallels to the passage here under discussion. Applied to Osiris, also, the word 'drowned' is quite appropriate, see 6/12.

l. 33. See the same list of the colours in Br., Wtb. Suppl., p. 173.

l. 34. *n ʿḥ-f n p rʿ*, the καυθαρον ηλιακον τον τας ιβ ακτινας εχοντα of Pap. Bibl. Nat. l. 751: i.e. true scarab with front tarsi drawn to edge of thorax, so displaying 12 spines (4 on head and each leg), fancifully compared to sun's rays; cf. hieroglyph of the sun's glory.

l. 35. The reading at the end is very uncertain: perhaps *ar-f*.

Col. IV.

l. 1. Imuthes, cf. Sethe, Untersuch. II, Imhotep. In B. M. Pap. CXXI. 630 he appears as τον εν Μεμφει Ασκληπιον; and in the demotic of Leyd. I.

2. e-f θ rt·t IV e bnp rm nb n p t ḥms ḥr ʾ·t-f a nḥe nte-k ḫʿ-f e-f wʿb a te-k·t qts(?) e·ʾr-k wḫ

3. a ʾr wḫe(?) nʾm-f n mt·t mʿ·t n wš n mt·t n ʿze tey-s pe-f smte e·ʾr-k ḫʿ p tks ḫn wʿ . . . e-f wʿb

4. n t mt·t n p mʿ e-f ḫn a zz-k nte-k ḥbs-f n wʿ·t šnt·t n zz-f a rt-f nte-k ḫʿ tbe·t

5. IV ḫr rt-f n p tks ne-ḥr-f e t wʿ·t n t rʿ·t ḥry·t n t wʿ·t nʾm-w e wn wʿ·t ḫw·t n sʿn ne-ḥr-f nte-k t zbe·t

6. n ḫ n zyt ar-s nte-k t ʿt n sre·t e-f nt·yt ḥr ḫl ḥr qs-ʿnḫ(?) nte-k ʾr-w n bnn·t

7. nte-k t wʿ·t a p ʿḫ nte-k ḫʿ p sp a te-k·t qts(?) nte-k ʿš py ʿš n mt·t wynn(?) ar-f z-mt·t nte-k str n wš n szy

8. wbe rm nb n p t nte-k str n-k ḫr nw-k a p ntr e-f n p smte n wʿ wʿb e-f θ ḥbs(?) n š-stn ḥr ʾ·t-f e-f θ še a rt-f

9. *επεικαλουμαι σε τον εν τω αορατω σκοτει καθημενον και ανα μεσον*

10. *οντα των μεγαλων θεων δυνοντα και παραλαμβανοντα τας ηλιακας*

11. *ακτεινας και αναπεμποντα την φαεσφορον θεαν νεβουτοσουαληθ*

---

384, verso I* he is invoked as 'Imhotp-wer (the Great), son of Ptah and Khretankh,' as at Deir el Medineh, SETHE, ib., 24.

*tks*, elsewhere a 'boat,' but the gloss τραπεσεν defines it as a 'table.' TERTULLIAN, Apol. 23, mentions oracles from tables. *ḥms ḥr ʾt-* in l. 2 can hardly mean anything but 'sit upon,' which rather implies a 'bench,' cf. B. M. Pap. XLVI. 3 βαθρον.

l. 2. *a te-k qt*(?)-*s*, cf. ⲕⲟⲧⲥ, 'circulus,' but *wḫ-s* is a possible reading, and it may be conjectured to mean 'at your convenience,' also in l. 7.

l. 3. *wḫe* with prefixed ⲓ(?), the reading doubtful. For a word *wḫ*, 'letter,' see II Kham. ii. 28, &c. The meaning here seems always to be a *direct* divination without medium. We have *wḫe* (?) *n p ḥbs*, 'lamp divination,' 27/29; *wḫe* (?) *n Manebai*, 'a divination named Manebai,' 27/32; *wḫe* (?) *a ḫrw Pe-sḫ*, 'divination for the voice of Pasash,' 8/12.

*tke* for *tks*, like *nhe* for *nhs* cf. 2/25.

'room (?),' the reading and meaning very uncertain.

l. 5. Or 'one by each of them (the feet),' but the expression hardly admits of this.

l. 6. *sre·t* with gloss ϫⲏⲛⲁⲣⲓⲟⲩ, perhaps a wild goose, cf. BR., Wtb. Suppl., 1082. Note the fem. gender, which apparently distinguishes it

wood (2) having four feet, upon (?) which no man on earth has ever sat, and put it, it being clean, beside (?) you. When you wish (3) to make an inquiry-of-god (?) with it truthfully without falsehood, behold (this is) the manner of it. You put the table in a clean room (?) (4) in the midst of the place, it being near your head; you cover it with a tunic (?) from its head to its feet, and you put four bricks (5) under the table before it, one above another (?), there being a censer of clay before it (the table); and you put charcoal (6) of olive-wood on it (the censer) and put wild-goose fat pounded with myrrh and *qs-ankh*, and make them into balls (7) and put one on the brazier, and lay the remainder at your side (?), and pronounce this spell in Greek (?) speech to it—Formula—and you spend the night without speaking (8) to any one on earth, and you lie down and you see the god in the likeness of a priest wearing fine linen and wearing (a) nose at his feet.

(9) 'I invoke thee who art seated in the invisible darkness and who art in the midst (10) of the great gods sinking and receiving the sun's (11) rays and sending forth the luminous goddess Neboutosoualeth,

---

from the domesticated duck called *sr*, found from the O. K. onwards, which is masc.

l. 7. *wynn*(?), cf. V. 3/12. There as well as here the 'foreign' sign after *mt·t* refers to Greek words. In 27/35 the word is spelt out strangely *wʿyʿny*; *wynn* is the usual demotic spelling, ⲟⲩⲉⲉⲓⲛⲓⲛ the Coptic, but ⲟⲩⲉⲉⲓⲉⲛ is quoted by Peyron in Sah., and perhaps this is the form indicated in 27/35. In 12/25 we have *wʿyʿnʿyne·t* for the fem.

*str n-k*, ethical dative: see note to *še n-w* 3/28.

*szy wbe*, cf. the common phrase in Greek magic *κοιμω μηδενι δους αποκρισιν* B. M. Pap. XLVI. l. 398, CXXI. l. 748, CXXII. 67; *κοιμω αναποκριτος* XLVI. l. 458.

l. 8. *e-f θ še*, apparently as seen in very late sculpture in figures of gods, &c., with jackals' heads on their feet indicating wariness and swiftness (?). Cf. Maspero, Les Origines, p. 149; Pleyte, Chap. Supplem., i. p. 133; in Greek papyri *εν τοις ποσιν εχων την ορασιν* (?).

12. *θεον μεγαν βαρζαν βουβαρζαν ναρζαζουζαν βαρζαβουζαθ*

13. *ηλιον αναπεμπτον μοι εν τη νυκτι ταυτη τον αρχαγγελον σου*

14. *ζεβουρθαυνην· χρηματισον επ' αληθειας αληθως αψευδως αν-*

15. *αμφιλογως περι τουδε πραγματος οτι εξορκιζω σε κατα του εν τη*

16. *πυρινη χλαμυδι καθημενου επι της αρουρεας κεφαλης του αγα-*

17. *θου δαιμονος παντοκρατορος τετραπροσωπου δαιμονος υψιστου σκο-*

18. *τιου και ψυχαουγεου φωξ μη μου παρακουσης αλλα αναπεμψον*

19. *ταχος τη νυκτι ταυτη επιτα . αιην του θεου τουτο ειπας γ'*

20. ḫr ʾr-f sze wbe-k n r-f wbe r-k n mt·t mʿ·t ḫr hb nb e·ʾr-k wḫ-f e-f wḥ e-f še n-f ʿn

21. ḫr ʾr-k wḥ wʿ pyngs n ʿš wne·t(?) ḥr n tbe·tw(?) nte-k wḥ n syw·w ḥr ʾ·t-f nte-k sḫ pe-k ʿs-sḥne a wʿ zʿm nmy

22. nte-k wḥ-f ḫr p pynʿks ḫr ʾr-f t ʾw ne-k syw·w n-k e-w wz ḫr pe-k ʿš-sḥne

23. n wz ḫyb e-f znt swḥ n *ϧⲉⲥ* ḥr ḫl ḫy t a yr·t-k nʾm-f ḫr ʾr-k wz ḫyb·t

24. k·t ʿn tpe ḥnʿ snf n *ⲕⲟⲩⲕⲟⲩⲡ(?)ⲉⲧ* θ-ḫ-w(?) nte-k ʾr-w n pḫre šwy smt yr·t-k nʾm-f ḫr nw-k ar-w ʿn

---

l. 16. *αρουρεας*. Mr. Kenyon suggests that this may possibly be a corruption of *αργυρεας*.

l. 18. *ψυχαουγεου*. Mr. Kenyon, who has kindly looked at this passage in the original MS., writes: 'I think the fourth letter is *α*, not *λ*, . . . and the only thing I can think of is *ψυγαγωγου*. In this case we should again have *γ* and *ο* confused (as in *αρουρεας* = *αργυρεας*?). This leaves *φωξ* unaccounted for, but a nominative (and from its termination it could be nothing else) is out of place here, so that the corruption must in any case be rather extensive. I do not think anything but *επιταγαιην* can be read in l. 19. Probably *ἐπιταγῇ* is meant.' The word *ψυχαγωγου* is probably to be taken as associated with the idea of necromancy.

(12) the great god Barzan Boubarzan Narzazouzan Barzabouzath, (13) the sun; send up to me this night thy archangel (14) Zebourthaunen; answer with truth, truthfully, without falsehood, without (15) ambiguity concerning this matter, for I conjure thee by him (16) who is seated in the flaming vesture on the silver (?) head of the (17) Agathodaemon, the almighty four-faced daemon, the highest (18) darkling and soul-bringing (?) Phox; do not disregard me, but send up (19) speedily in this night an injunction (?) of the god.' Say this three times.

(20) Then he speaks with you with his mouth opposite your mouth in truth concerning everything that you wish. When he has finished, and goes away again, (21) you place a tablet of reading (?) the hours upon the bricks and you place the stars upon it and write your purpose (?) on a new roll (22) and place it on the tablet; then he (?) makes your stars appear which are favourable for your purpose (?).

(23) [A method] of lucky-shadows (?), that is tested: a hawk's egg with myrrh, pound (?), put on your eyes of it, then it makes lucky-shadows (?). (24) Another again: head and blood of a hoopoe; cook (?) them and make them into a dry medicament and paint your eyes with it; then you see them, again.

---

*φωξ* may be an indeclinable magic name, though the customary line has not been drawn over it. Cf. *ο μεγας και ισχυρος θεος φους . . .* B. M. Pap. CXXIV. 20 and *φυξε* below 7/22.

l. 20. *r-f wbe r-k*: *στομα προς στομα* Berl. Pap. I. 39.

l. 23. *wz ḫyb.* The shadow is probably that of the god appearing in the lamp. Cf. 6/6.

l. 24. *θ-ḫ-w*, probably the imperative of some verb *θḫ* (?) followed by the suffix of the object, meaning e. g. 'cook them,' so also Louvre Dem. Mag. vi. 18 *nte-k θ-ḫ-w*.

## Col. V.

1. nte-k ty ʿḥ pe-k(?) . . . . nte-k qlhe a p ʾytn n(?) rt-k n sp VII nte-k ʿš ny sḫ·w a p ḫpš [e ḥr(?)]-k st a mḫty n sp VII

2. nte-k st-k a ḫry nte-k še a wʿ·t ry·t n kke

3. wʿ . . . . . . e-f znt nte-k še-k (*sic*) a wʿ·t ry·t n kke e-s wʿb e ḥr-s wn a p-rs nte-k t wʿb-s n mw

4. n ḥsm nte-k ʾny wʿ ḫbs nmy e-f wbḫ e bnp-w t prš mw n qme ar-f nte-k t wʿ šʿl

5. e-f wʿb ar-f nte-k mḥ-f n nḥe n mʿ·t bn-s sḫ py rn ḥnʿ ny ghʿlʿgter a p šʿl n rʾw ḫl n ḥ·t

6. nte-k wḥ-f ḥr wʿ·t tbe·t nmy ne-zz-k e ḫr-f prḫ n šʿ nte-k ʿš ny sḫ a p ḫbs ʿn n ke sp VII e·ʾr-k t ʾlbwnt a ḥry ne-ḥr

7. p ḫbs e·ʾr-k nw m-s p ḫbs ḫr nw-k a p ntr n p qte n p ḫbs nte-k str n-k ḥr wʿ·t tme·t n qme e bnp-k sze

8. wbe rm nb n p t ḫr z-f n-k wḥ n rswe·t tey-s pe-f ʿš z-mt·t (tey-s sḫ·w nt e·ʾr-k sḫ a p šʿl ḫbs ⲃⲁⲭⲩⲭⲥⲓⲭⲩⲭ)

---

### Col. V.

l. 1. There seem to be traces of writing above this line, at least towards the left end: compare the top line in Col. VIII. Lines 1 and 2 are probably to be read in l. 3, before 'thou goest to a dark niche,' the phrase with which l. 2 ends.

Read *e-ḥr-k* (or *e zz-k* as in l. 32?) *st e mḫty*.

*mḫty*, a word occurring as early as the time of Darius, possibly arising from a confusion of the words *mḥt*, 'north,' and *ḫty*, 'go north.' An instance of careless confusion of *ḥ* and *ḫ* by our scribe, due to both being ϩ, e.g. in Sah., occurs in 21/12, but is on a different footing.

*ḫpš*, lit. the 'foreleg' = the Great Bear. ϣⲱⲡϣ : ϣⲱⲃϣ corresponds to ἀρκτοῦρος in Job ix. 9 (cf. also Zoega, 650). But in the astronomical texts *ḫpš* as consisting of seven stars evidently is ἄρκτος itself (Brugsch, Thes., 123, Aegyptol., 343).

l. 3. *nte-k še-k* should be either *nte-k še* in continuation of other directions (cf. ll. 1–2), or *ḫr še-k*.

l. 4. *prš*, ⲡⲏⲣϣ, either red earth or red lead. The requirement that the lamp used for divination shall be free from red colour (ἀμίλτωτος) is found in Leiden Pap. Gr. V, col. 1, l. 22, and col. 4, l. 25; Parthey, Zwei

## Col. V.

(1) And you set up your [planisphere?] and you stamp on the ground with your foot seven times and recite these charms to the Foreleg, turning (?) to the North seven times (2) and you return down and go to a dark recess.

(3) A question-form, tested. You go to a dark clean recess with its face open to the south and you purify it with (4) natron-water, and you take a new white lamp in which no red earth or gum-water has been put and place a clean wick (5) in it and fill it with real oil after writing this name and these figures on the wick with ink of myrrh beforehand; (6) and you lay it on a new brick before you, its underside being spread with sand; and you pronounce these spells over the lamp again another seven times. You display frankincense in front of (7) the lamp and you look at the lamp; then you see the god about the lamp and you lie down on a rush mat without speaking (8) to any one on earth. Then he makes answer to you by dream. Behold its invocation. Formula: (*In margin*: Behold the spells which you write on the wick: Bakhukhsikhukh, *and figures*)

---

gr. Zauberpap., I. l. 277. As to the use of red earth and gum with pottery cf. the quotation from Sacy, s.v. ϫⲱⲓ, in Peyron, p. 380 a.

l. 5. *r'w ḥl*, 'myrrh ink,' σμυρνομελαν, probably somewhat after the recipe given in Parthey, u. s. II. 34[a].

*gh'l'gter* = χαρακτῆρες, a term. techn. for mystic symbols: cf. Wünsch, Sethian. Verfluchungstafeln, p. 98; Schmidt, Gnostische Schriften, p. 54 seq.

l. 6. *ne-zz-k*. It seems probable that 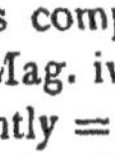 reads *zz*, for apart from any other correspondences we have this compound preposition written out as *ne-zz-* in 14/6 and Louvre Dem. Mag. iv. 19. 22.

*'lbwnt*, *ⲁⲗⲃⲟⲩⲛⲟⲩⲧ* 22/17, evidently = λιβανωτός.

l. 8. ⲃⲁϫⲩϫⲥⲓϫⲩϫ looks like 'Soul of Khukh, son of Khukh.' The magic-name compounds with χουχ, χυχ, χωωχ are very numerous; cf. P. Sophia, § 361, ⲃⲁⲓⲛϫⲱⲱϫ and elsewhere often βαιχυχ. Sethe, Verbum, i. § 417, suggests that the ϫⲟⲩϫ is the elemental god *KK*, 'darkness.'

9. hy ank mwr'y mwry·by b'bel b'-ʿo-th b'-my p šʿy

10. ʿo mwrʿth-ʿo p . . . ẖbr n by nt ḥtp n ḥry ẖn n p·t n p·t·w (*sic*)

11. t'tot sp-sn bwl'y sp-sn my-ẖr . . . sp-sn l'hy sp-sn b-ʿo-lbwel y sp-sn 'ʿ tt sp-sn bwel sp-sn y-ʿo-hel sp-sn p šmsy ḥyt

12. n p ntr ʿo p nt t wyn m šs sp-sn p ẖber n t st·t p nte t st·t n r-f nte b-'re-s ʿẖm p ntr ʿo nt ḥms

13. ẖn t st·t p nt n t mt·t n t st·t nt n p šy n t p·t nte p ʿw erme p nʿš n p ntr n t·t-f wnḥ-k ar-y

14. ty n p-hw mw ky p ky n wnḥ-k a mwses nta e·'r-k 'r-f ḥr p tw nte ḥr-k t ẖp p kke p wyn ne-ḥr-f

15. tg(?)a te-y tbḥ n'm-k nte-k wnḥ-k ar-y ty n py grḥ nte-k sze erme-y nte-k z n-y wḥ n mt·t mʿ·t n wš n mt·t n ʿze z e-y a šʿš-k

16. n 'Bt e-y a šʿšʿ-k n t p·t ne-ḥr p rʿ e-y a šʿšʿ-k ne-ḥr ʿḥ e-y a šʿšʿ-k

17. ne-ḥr p nt ḥr p bḥt nte b-'r-f thm pe p šʿšʿ ʿo petery sp-sn pʿter enphe sp-sn **ενφε β̄**

18. p ntr nt n t rʿ ḥry·t n t p·t nte p šbt nt (ne)ʿne-f n t·t-f 'r t ẖp ntr e bnp ntr t ẖp-f 'm n-y

19. a ẖry a ẖn n t mt·t n ty st·t nt ty ḥ·t-k pa bwel sp-sn nte-k t m'-y p ʿš-sḥne [nt] e-y šll ẖrr-f

20. n py grḥ n mt·t mʿ·t n wš n mt·t n ʿze my m'-s my stm-s p ntr ʿo sysyhowt sp-sn ke-z **αρμιωουθ** 'm

21. a ẖn ẖr zz-y nte-k z n-y wḥ n p nt e-y šn ẖrr-f n mt·t mʿ·t n wš n mt·t n ʿze p ntr ʿo nt ḥr p tw

---

l. 10. Read *ẖn t p·t n n p·tw* or *ẖn p·t p·tw*.

l. 11. In the demotic there is one uncertain sign that may correspond to **ταυι** of the gloss.

l. 12. Lines 12–22 are parallel to 7/8–18, 17/1–10, 17/27–32.

l. 14. Moses was a popular hero with many legends in Jewish circles, both before and after Christ (WIEDEMANN in P. S. B. A. xi. 29, 267). Note that the form of the name employed is Greek and not Hebrew; cf. V. 12/6.

*nta e'r-k*: cf. note to 15/13.

(9) 'Ho! I am Murai, Muribi, Babel, Baoth, Bamui, the great Agathodaemon, (10) Muratho, the . . . form of soul that resteth above in the heaven of heavens, (11) Tatot (*bis*), Bouel (*bis*), Mouihtahi (?) (*bis*), Lahi (*bis*), Bolboel, I (*bis*), Aa, Tat (*bis*), Bouel (*bis*), Yohel (*bis*), the first servant (12) of the great god, he who giveth light exceedingly, the companion of the flame, he in whose mouth is the fire that is not quenched, the great god who is seated (13) in the fire, he who is in the midst of the fire which is in the lake of heaven, in whose hand is the greatness and the power of god; reveal thyself to me (14) here to-day in the fashion of thy revelation to Moses which thou didst make upon the mountain, before whom thou thyself didst create darkness and light, (15)—*insertion*—I pray thee that thou reveal thyself to me here to-night and speak with me and give me answer in truth without falsehood; for I will glorify thee (16) in Abydos, I will glorify thee in heaven before Phre, I will glorify thee before the Moon, I will glorify thee (17) before him who is upon the throne, who is not destroyed, he (= thou) of the great glory, Peteri (*bis*), Pater, Enphe (*bis*), (18) O god who is above heaven, in whose hand is the beautiful staff, who created deity, deity not having created him. Come down ⟨in⟩ to me (19) into the midst of this flame that is here before thee, thou of Boel (*bis*), and let me see the business that I ask about (20) to-night truly without falsehood. Let it be seen (?), let it be heard (?), O great god Sisihoout, otherwise said Armioouth, come (21) in before me and give me answer to that which

---

l. 15. The pointer at the beginning of the line refers to the similar sign at the beginning of ll. 33–4, which offer a variant version of l. 15. One may conjecture that the pointer represents the Eg. *dg'*, Copt. ⲧⲱϭ : ⲧⲱϫ, 'plant,' 'insert,' 'join.'

l. 17. *thm*, a mistake or metathesis for *htm*; cf. 7/12, 17/5, 30. *petery*, &c. See vol. ii, Mythological Index.

22. n ʿtwgy (ⲛⲕⲁⲃⲁⲱⲛ) ghʿbʿh-ʿo ʾm n-y a ḫn my wn yr·t a bl n py grḥ ḥr t mn t mt·t

23. nt e-y šn ḫrr-s n mt·t mʿ·t n wš n mt·t n ʿze a . . . ḫrw (?) n p leʾsphwt nb-lot . . lylʾs sp VII nte-k str n-k

24. n wš n sze p kys nt e·ʾr-k ty-s a yr·t-k e·ʾr-k ʾnnʿy a šn n p ḫbs n šn nb n ḫbs ḥr ʾny-k hyn·w ḥrre n *ⲃⲧⲗ*

25. n *ⲉⲃⲱⲕ* ḥr gm-k-ysw n p mʿ n p s-qlm ke-z p s-trmws e·ʾr-k ʾny·t-w e-w knn e·ʾr-k ty-sw

26. e wʿ lq n yl e·ʾr-k ʿm r-f m šs sp-sn šʿ hw XX n wʿ mʿ e-f hep e-f n kke bn-s hw XX e·ʾr-k

27. ʾny·t-f a ḥry nte-k wn ar-f ḥr gm-k hyn·w ḫry·w ḫn-f erme wʿ mz e·ʾr-k ḫʿ-f šʿ hw XL nte-k ʾny·t-f a ḥry

28. nte-k wn ar-f ḥr gm-k-f e·ḥr-f ʾr snf e·ʾre ḥr ʾr-k ty-f a wʿ nk n yl nte-k t p nk n yl a ḫn wʿ nk

29. n blz n wʿ mʿ e-f hep n nw nb e·ʾr-k wḫ a ʾr . . . . . n p ḫbs nʾm-f n nw nb e·ʾr-k mḥ yr·t-k n py

30. snf nt ḥry eʾr-k ʾnnʿy a ḫn a ʿš sḫ a p ḫbs ḥr nw-k a wʿ sšt n ntr e-f ʿḥ n p bl n p ḫbs nte-f sze

31. wbe-k ḥr p šn nt e·ʾr-k wḫ-f nge nte-k str ḥr ʾw-f n-k a ʾr-f tm ʾy n-k e·ʾr-k nhs e·ʾr-k ʿš pe-f thm

---

l. 22. Atugi with gloss Gabaon: cf. 7/17.

l. 24. Lines 24–30 are repeated in 27/24–29.

l. 25. ⲃⲧⲗ *n* ⲉⲃⲱⲕ = ⲃⲁⲗⲁⲃⲱⲕ, 'raven's eye,' the Greek bean.

*gm-k-ysw*, an extraordinary form; but, it is to be feared, no guide to the real pronunciation, which was probably *gemyoks* or *gemyoksu*; the written *y* is thus superfluous, cf. 3/9 note, or at least misplaced.

*s-qlm*, see note in glossary. 'The place of the garland-seller': does this mean his shop or his garden?

*ty-sw*: the regular form in this papyrus, as it were, *ⲧⲏⲓⲥⲟⲩ. In *gm-k-ysw*, above, the *sw* = Eg. *st*, plur. of the absolute object-pronoun. Here, after the infinitive, it is abnormal, the *s* being inserted before the proper suffix *-w* on false analogy. In Coptic (St., § 342, p. 169, and Piehl, A. Z., 95. 42) the only clear instance of this false form seems to be Sah. ⲥϩⲁⲓⲥⲟⲩ. The similar ⲧⲉⲛⲛⲟⲟⲩⲥⲉ, ⲧⲉⲛⲛⲟⲟⲩⲥⲟⲩ, &c., are also etymologically wrong, but they seem to be helped by the causative with *stm-f*: see Griff., High Priests, p. 85.

l. 26. *yl*: ⲓⲁⲗ : ⲉⲓⲁⲗ probably to be connected with ὕαλος.

I shall ask about, truly without falsehood. O great god that is on the mountain (22) of Atuki (of Gabaon), Khabaho, Takrtat, come in to me, let my eyes be opened to-night for any given thing (23) that I shall ask about, truly without falsehood . . . the voice (?) of the Leasphot, Neblot . . . lilas.' Seven times: and you lie down (24) without speaking.

The ointment which you put on your eyes when you are about to inquire of the lamp in any lamp-divination: you take some flowers (25) of the Greek bean; you find them in the place of the garland-seller, otherwise said of the lupin-seller; you take them fresh and put them (26) in a *lok*-vessel of glass and stop its mouth very well for twenty days in a secret dark place. After twenty days, if you (27) take it out and open it, you find a pair (?) of testicles in it with a phallus. You leave it for forty days and when you take it out (28) and open it, you find that it has become bloody; then you put it on a glass thing and put the glass thing into a pottery thing (29) in a place hidden at all times. When you desire to make inquiry of the lamp with it at any time if you fill your eyes with this (30) blood aforesaid, and if you go in to pronounce a spell over the lamp you see a figure of a god standing behind (?) the lamp, and he speaks (31) with you concerning the question which you wish; or you lie down and he comes to you. If he does not come to

---

*'m.* This group cannot be read *tm*, ⲧⲱⲙ. It must be connected with ⲟⲙⲉ, 'clay.'

l. 27. *ḥyn·w*, 'some,' here and elsewhere suggests the meaning of 'a pair' (Hess, Setne, p. 30).

l. 28. ⲉ(ϩ)ⲁϥⲣ̄ⲥⲛⲟϥ, see the chapter on Grammar.

*e·'re*: probably the Eg. emphasizing particle 𓇋𓂋, cf. 7/1.

The meaning of *ḫr 'r-k*, ϣⲁⲕ, here is not merely consuetudinal but injunctional, equivalent to the old *sdmḫrf*, as used e. g. in Pap. Ebers (Erman, Grammar, 2nd ed. § 221).

32. e·ʾre ḫr ʾr-k str ḥr qme wt e·ʾr-k wʿb a s-ḥm·t e zz-k st a rs e ḥr-k st a mḫty [e] ḥr-f n p ḫbs st a mḫty ḥ-f

33. tg(?) a ḥry te-y tbḥ nʾm-k nte-k wnḥ-k ar-y ty n py grḥ nte-k sze erme-y nte-k z n-y wḥ n mt·t mʿ·t ḫr t mn t mt·t

34. nt e-y šn nʾm-k e-tbe·t[-s ?]

## Col. VI.

1. wʿ šn n p ḫbs ḫr še-k a wʿ·t ry·t n kke e-s wʿb ʾt wyn nte-k šte wʿ qel nmy ḥr wʿ·t zʿe·t

2. ybt nte-k ʾny wʿ ḫbs ḥt e bnp-w t prš mw n qme ar-f e pe-f sʿl wʿb nte-k mḥ-f n nḥe n mʿ·t e-f wʿb n whe

3. nte-k ʿš n sḫ·w n tʾw Rʿ tp twe m ḫʿ-f nte-k ʾny p ḫbs wbe p rʿ e-f mḥ nte-k ʿš n sḫ·w nt ḫry ar-f n sp IV

4. nte-k θy·t-f a ḫn a t ry·t e·ʾr-k wʿb erme p ʿlw nte-k ʿš n sḫ·w a p ʿlw e·bnn-f nw m-s p ḫbs ʿn e yr·t-f

5. ḫtm šʿ sp VII e·ʾr-k t ʾlbwnt a p ʿḥ e-f wʿb e·ʾr-k t·t n pe-k tbʿ a zz-f n p ʿlw e yr·t-f ḫtm

6. e·ʾr-k wḥ e·ʾr-k t ʾr-f wn yr·t-f a ḥr p ḫbs ḫr nw-f a t ḫyb·t n p ntr n p qte n p ḫbs nte-f šn n-k

7. a p nt e·ʾr-k wḥ-f e·ʾre ḫr ʾr-k-f n mre·t n wʿ mʿ e mn-te-f wyn e-f ḫp e·ʾr-k šn ḥr ʾyḫ sšre wʿ sʿl n ht

8. n zy p nt e·ʾr-k ty-f a p ḫbs nte-k mḥ-f n syr e-f wʿb e-f ḫp e ge ʿš-sḥne pe sʿl e-f wʿb ḥr nḥe n mʿ·t e-f wʿb

9. p nt e·ʾr-k ty-f a p ḫbs e-f ḫp e·ʾr-k a ʾr-f a ʾny s-ḥm·t n hwt skne n wrt p nt e·ʾr-k ty-f a p ḫbs e·ʾre ḫr wḥ-k p ḫbs

---

l. 34. *e-tbe·t-s* must be the reading.

Col. VI.

l. 1. A niche in a wall with special orientation for magic utensils, &c., occurs in the nineteenth dynasty; see Naville, Quatre stèles.

l. 3. *Ꜥw Rʿ*, &c. Perhaps the title of some specific religious work, like the hymns to the rising sun prefixed to the New-Kingdom Books of the Dead: or an invocation in an earlier part of the papyrus now lost.

l. 7. *ʾyḫ sšre.* The meaning is not quite clear. In II Kham. ii. 26

you, you rise and pronounce his compulsion. (32) You must lie down on green reeds, being pure from a woman, your head being turned to the south and your face being turned to the north and the face of the lamp being turned northwards likewise.

(33) *insert above*—'I pray thee to reveal thyself to me here to-night and speak with me and give me answer truly concerning the given matter which I ask thee about.'

## Col. VI.

(1) An inquiry of the lamp. You go to a clean dark cell without light and you dig a new hole in an east wall (2) and you take a white lamp in which no minium or gum water has been put, its wick being clean, and you fill it with clean genuine Oasis oil, (3) and you recite the spells of praising Ra at dawn in his rising and you bring the lamp when lighted opposite the sun and recite to it the spells as below four times, (4) and you take it into the cell, you being pure, and the boy also, and you pronounce the spells to the boy, he not looking at the lamp, his eyes being (5) closed, seven times. You put pure frankincense on the brazier. You put your finger on the boy's head, his eyes being closed. (6) When you have finished you make him open his eyes towards the lamp; then he sees the shadow of the god about the lamp, and he inquires for you (7) concerning that which you desire. You must do it at midday in a place without light. If it be that you are inquiring for a spirit damned, a wick of sail-cloth (?) (8) is what you put in the lamp and you fill it with clean butter. If it is some other business, a clean wick with pure genuine oil (9) is that which you put in the lamp; if you will do it to bring

---

there is mentioned a book for *sḫr ʾḫy*, 'overthrowing (or laying) demons'; cf. note 3/25.

l. 9. *skne n wrt*, ροδινον ελαιον, Diosc. i. 53.

10. ḫr wʿ·t tbe·t nmy nte p ʿlw ḥms ḥ-f ḫr ke tbe·t e yr·t-f ḫtm e·ʾr-k ʿš a ḫry ḫn zz-f šʿ sp IV

11. n sḫ·w nt e·ʾr-k ʿš-w a p sʿl a p ḥbs a t ḥʿ·t e b-ʾr te-k ʿš a p ʿlw z-mt·t ʿn nte-k p sʿl wʿt ʿo n t mnḫ·t n Tḥwt

12. ʾn nte-k p ḥbs n š-stn n Wsr p ḥsy ntr n sšne n t·t ʾS·t n msne n t·t Nb·t-ḥ·t

13. ʾn nte-k p ḫrt tp a·ʾr-w n Wsr ḫnt ʾmnt ʾn nte-k p snb ʿo a·fy ʾNp t·t-f erme-f a t ḫe·t n Wsr p ntr wr

14. a·ʾr-y ʾny nʾm-k n p-hw ʾy p sʿl a t nw p ʿlw a ḫn-k nte-k ʾr wḥ a mt·t nb nt e-y šn ḫrr-w ty n p-hw ʾn

15. tm ʾr·y-s p nt e·ʾr-k ʾr-f ʾy p sʿl a·ʾr-y t nʾm-k a t gyz·t n t ʾḥ·t kme·t a·ʾr-y t mḥ nʾm-k ḫn t gyz·t

16. n t ʾḥ·t s-ḥm·t snf n p ḥsy p nt e-y t nʾm-f m-s-k ḫr nḥe t kyz n ʾNp t nt wḥ ar-k n sḫ·w

17. n p wr ḥyq n nt e-y ʿš n-k nʾm-w nte-k ʾny n-y p ntr nte p wḥ-sḫne n t·t-f n p-hw nte-f z n-y wḥ a mt·t nb nt e-y šn

18. ḫrr-w ty n p-hw n mt·t mʿ·t n wš n mt·t n ʿze ʾy Nw·t mw·t mw hy ʾP·t mw·t st·t

---

l. 12. *p ḥsy*, cf. l. 16, and above, note to 3/31. 'Approved,' 'praised' would be a rather unexpected term to apply to Osiris himself, though it could be explained as equivalent to *mʾʿ ḫrw* and 'deified.' The sense 'drowned' is quite applicable, as Osiris' body was at least sunk in the waters, cf. the text of Ptah published by Breasted, A. Z., 1901, Pl. II, ll. 19, 62; and this sense is implied in Brit. Mus. Pap. XLVI. 259–63 *οσπα Εσιηους . . . . τον Εσιη* (ϩⲁⲥⲓⲉ) *τον ενεχθεντα εν τω ρευματι του ποταμου* for three days and three nights. Plutarch's account, De Iside et Osiride, cap. 13 et seqq., hardly needs quotation.

*sšne*, &c. Cf. similar passage in Pap. Boul. I. Pl. 12, l. 1.

*t·t ʾS·t . . . t·t Nb·t-ḥ·t*. In both cases the strong *t* is written at the end of the word for 'hand.' Presumably it is an old dual form.

l. 13. *snb a·fy*, &c., the linen used by Anubis in wrapping the mummy of Osiris.

l. 14. *a·ʾr-y ʾny*, ⲁⲓⲉⲓⲛⲉ, rather than past relative, which would have taken *nʾm-f* instead of *nʾm-k*; so also in l. 15, &c.

*a t*. This is hardly an imperative *a·t*.

a woman to a man, ointment of roses is that which you put in the lamp. You must lay the lamp (10) on a new brick and the boy also must sit on another brick with his eyes closed. You cry down into his head four times. (11) The spells which you recite ⟨to the lamp⟩ to the wick previously before you recite to the boy: formula: 'Art thou the unique great wick of the linen of Thoth? (12) Art thou the byssus robe of Osiris, the divine Drowned, woven by the hand of Isis, spun by the hand of Nephthys? (13) Art thou the original band that was made for Osiris Khentamente? Art thou the great bandage with which Anubis put forth his hand to the body of Osiris the mighty god? (14) I have brought thee to-day—ho! thou wick—to cause the boy to look into thee, that thou mayest make reply to every matter concerning which I ask here to-day. (15) Is it that you will (?) not do it? O wick, I have put thee in the hand of the black cow, I have lighted thee in the hand (16) of the female cow. Blood of the Drowned one is that which I put to thee for oil; the hand of Anubis is that which is laid on thee. The spells (17) of the great Sorcerer are those which I recite to thee. Do thou bring me the god in whose hand is the command to-day and let him give me answer as to everything about which (18) I inquire here to-day truly without falsehood. Ho! Nut, mother of water, ho! Apet, mother of fire,

---

l. 15. ⲁⲛ *ⲧⲙⲁⲓⲥ, lit. 'Is not-doing-it that which you will (?) do?' Cf. l. 37.

*ʾḥ·t kme·t*, black animals are generally prescribed in both Greek and demotic magic. Cf. B. M. Gk. Pap. CXXI. l. 301, &c., &c.

l. 16. *t ʾḥ·t s-ḥm·t*, 'the female cow,' seems curious, but is quite correct, being due to the fact that, except for the gender of the article, there is no distinction in sound between the words for 'ox' and 'cow.' Cf. 7/1, 2.

l. 17. *p wḥ-sḥne.* The 365 gods are mentioned V. 33/6. Probably one of these presided over the course of each day.

l. 18. Nut, goddess of the sky, wife of Geb and mother of Osiris; Apt, probably the birth-goddess, worshipped in a small temple at Karnak, in

19. ʾw(?)n-y Nw·t mw·t mw ʾm·t ʾP·t mw·t st·t ʾw(?)n-y yʿh-ʿo e·ʾr-k zt-f e·ʾr-k sq n ẖrw-k m šs sp-sn

20. e·ʾr-k z ʿn eseks p-ʿo-e e-f ẖtn(?) ke-z ẖt-ʾN sp VII e-f ẖp e . . . . . pe ny n nt e·ʾr-k ʿš-w

21. wʿt-w a p ḥbs nte-k str n-k n wš n sze ʾnn-e ʿw n ḥt ḥp e·ʾr-k nhe e·ʾr-k ʿš

22. pe-f thm nte pe-f ḥtr pe z-mt·t ʾnk p ḥr n srʿw ḥwnw rn-y a·ʾr-w ms·t ẖr p ʾšte šps

23. n ʾBt ʾnk p by n p sr wr nt m ʾBt ank p sʾwte n t ẖe·t ʿo·t nt m ww-pq

24. ank p nte yr·t-f n yr·t n ʿẖm e-f rs a Wsr n grḥ ank tp tw-f ḥr ḥs·t n ʾBt

25. ank nt rs a t ẖe·t ʿo·t nt m tt ʾnk nt rs n . . . . n sẖ·w nt e·ʾr-k sẖ-w a p ḥbs ϧⲁⲭⲩⲭⲥⲓⲭⲩⲭ

26. nt ʿw rn-f ḥep ḥn ḥt-y by by·w rn-f z-mt·t sp VII e-f ẖp e . . . . . pe

27. ny wʿet-w n nt e·ʾr-k ʿš-w e-f ẖp e šn n p ʿlw p nt e·ʾr-k ʾr-f e·ʾr-k ʿš n·y nt ḥry a p ḥbs

28. e b-ʾr te-k ʿš a ḥry ḥn a (*sic*) zz-f n p ʿlw e·ʾr-k st-k e·ʾr-k ʿš py ke ʿš a p ḥbs ʿn z-mt·t ʾy Wsr p ḥbs

29. e-f t nw nʾ·w hw·w ḥr-w ʾw-f t nw nʾ·w ẖr-w

---

the inscriptions of which she is often identified with Nut. Rochementeix, Œuvres, pp. 261, 302.

l. 20. *e-f ẖtn*, &c. The pronunciation of both groups was probably almost identical *ẖetôn*.

l. 23. *ww-pq*, a sacred place at Abydos, cf. Brugsch, Dict. Geog., 226.

l. 24. *ʿẖm*. Perhaps, according to its ancient significance, meaning one of the mummied hawk-figures placed watching at the corners of the coffin, but in Coptic the word ⲁϧⲱⲙ has acquired the meaning 'eagle.'

*n grḥ*: the gloss ⲙ over the *n* is strange, as the group evidently corresponds to Boh. ⲛϫⲱⲣϩ.

*tp tw-f*. The old title of Anubis.

'desert,' probably in the sense of 'necropolis.'

l. 25. The name written with three hieratic signs 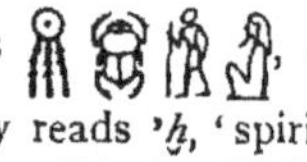, cf. 11/9, 16, is quite uncertain. The first sign probably reads *ʾḫ*, 'spirit,' but might read *wyn*, 'light,' *wbn*, 'shine' or 'rise,' or possibly *šw*, 'light,' or the god 'Shu.' The scarab may read *ḫpr*, 'scarab,' 'become,' the god Khepera, but hardly *t*, 'land': and the last sign *wr*, 'great,' *ʿo*, 'great,' *sr*,

(19) come unto me, Nut, mother of water, come Apet, mother of fire, come unto me Yaho.' You say it drawling (?) with your voice exceedingly. You say again: 'Esex, Poe, Ef-khe-ton,' otherwise said, 'Khet-on,' seven times. If it is a direct (?) inquiry, these alone are the things that you recite (21) to the lamp, and you lie down without speaking. But if obduracy take place, you rise, you recite (22) his summons, which is his compulsion. Formula: 'I am the Ram's face, Youth is my name; I was born under the venerable persea (23) in Abydos, I am the soul of the great chief who is in Abydos; I am the guardian of the great corpse that is in U-pek; (24) I am he whose eyes are as the eyes of Akhom when he watcheth Osiris by night; I am Teptuf upon the desert of Abydos; (25) I am he that watcheth the great corpse which is in Busiris; I am he who watcheth for Light-scarab-noble (?).' (*In margin*) The spells that you write on the lamp, Bakhukhsikhukh (*and figures*) (26) 'whose name is hidden in my heart; Bibiou (Soul of souls) is his name.' Formula, seven times. If it is a direct (?) inquiry, (27) these things alone are what you recite. If it is an inquiry by the boy that you are about, you recite these aforesaid to the lamp (28) before calling down into the head of the boy, you turn round (?), you recite this other invocation to the lamp also. Formula: 'O Osiris, O lamp (29) that giveth vision

'magnate,' *ỉ·w*, 'old.' It is no doubt a solar name (here for Osiris ?), and it occurs in ch. 162 of the Book of the Dead, but unfortunately without variants (Pleyte, Chap. Suppl., Pl. 21, 130)*.

l. 29. *hw·w*. This has evidently been written by mistake for *ḥry·w*, which has been inserted above. The mistake is important as indicating that the *r* of *hrw*, *hw*, 'day,' was retained in the plural (sing. ϩοογ).

* Cf. perhaps the inscription on a hypocephalus at Cairo  , Daressy, Textes Mag., p. 56, and , ib., p. 15 =  Mett., St., l. 39.

θs-pẖr ʾy p ẖbs sp-sn ʾMn mne nʾm-k ʾy p ẖbs sp-sn te-y

30. ʿš n-k e·ʾr-k ʾnnʿ a ḥry ẖr zz p yʿm ʿo p yʿm n [ẖ]r p yʿm n Wsr ʿn e-y z

31. n-k ʾn e·ʾr-k ʾy hb-yt-k ʾy p ẖbs mtr ar-k n-t gm-k Wsr ḥr pe-f rms n zwf tḥn

32. e ʾS·t ne-zz-f e Nb·t-h·t ne-rt-f e n [ntr·w] ḥwt·w n ntr·w s-ḥm·tw n pe-f qte a·zy-s ʾS·t my z-w-s

33. n Wsr e-tbe n mt·tw nt e-y šn ẖrr-w a t ʾw p ntr nte p wḥ-sḥne n t·t-f nte-f z n-y wḥ a mt·t nb nt e-y šn ẖrr-w

34. ty n p-hw e ʾS·t z my ʿš-w n-y a wʿ ntr hb-y-s e n(?) šq-f a n mt·tw nt e-f a še nʾm-s nte-f mnq-s

35. šm-w ʾny-w n-s nte-k p ẖbs p-e·ʾny-w n-s p ẖyt n Sẖm·t te-k.t mw·t erme Ḥke pe-k yt

36. ḥwy ar-k bnn-k mḥ a Wsr erme ʾS·t bnn-k mḥ ʾNp e bnp-k z n-y wḥ a mt·t nb nt e-y šn

37. ẖrr-w ty n p-hw n mt·t mʿ·t n wš n z n-y mt·t n ʿze ʾn tm ʾry-s p nt e·ʾr-k a ʾr-f bn e-y a t n-k nḥe

## Col. VII.

1. bn e-y a t n-k nḥe bn e-y a t n-k ʿt ʾy p ẖbs e·ʾry e-y a t n-k n t ẖe·t n t ʾḥ·t s-ḥm·t nte-y t·t snf

---

l. 31. *hb-yt-k*, note the final *sdm-f*, especially common in the 1 pers. sing. Cf. l. 34.

*n-t* with *sdm-f* = ⲛ̄ⲧⲉⲣⲉ, cf. I Kham. 5/35, II Kham. 6/3 (Griff., High Priests, p. 193).

*rms*, see Griff., High Priests, p. 100. Evidently the πλοιον παπυρινον ο καλειται αιγυπτιστι ρωψ of Leyd. Pap. U. col. 2, l. 6, 7; an *m* before *s* would naturally become *p* in the mouth of a Greek.

l. 32. *n ntr·w ḥwt·w . . . s-ḥm·tw*, O. C. Par. ⲛ̄ⲧⲉⲣ ϩⲥⲓⲙⲉ . . . ⲛⲧⲉⲣ ϩⲟⲟⲩⲧ A. Z., 1900, p. 88. Cf. the same expression in the Hittite treaty, L. D. III. 146, ll. 26, 30.

l. 34. *e n*(?) *šq-f*. Perhaps an adjectival verb of the form ⲛⲁⲛⲟⲩϥ 'he being clever' (or discreet, or swift, &c.).

l. 35. *p ẖyt n . . . ḥwy* seems to be equivalent to ἐξορκίζω σε κατα . . . .

*Ḥke*, cf. Lanzone, Diz. Mit., 851, 859. As a form of the god Shu

of the things ⟨of days⟩ above, that giveth vision of the things below and vice versa; O lamp (*bis*), Amen is moored in thee; O lamp (*bis*) I (30) invoke thee, thou goest up to the shore of the great sea, the sea of Syria, the sea of Osiris. Do I speak (31) to thee? Dost thou come that I may send thee? Ho, lamp, witness (?) to thyself, since thou hast found Osiris upon his boat of papyrus and *teḥen*, (32) Isis being at his head, Nephthys at his feet, and the male and female gods about him. Speak, Isis, let it be told (33) to Osiris concerning the things which I ask about, to cause the god to come in whose hand is the command, and give me answer to everything about which I shall inquire (34) here to-day. When Isis said "Let a god be summoned to me that I may send him, he being discreet (?) as to the business on which he will go and he accomplish it," (35) they went and they brought to her; thou art the lamp that was brought to her. The fury of Sekhmet thy mother and of Heke thy father is (36) cast at thee, thou shalt not be lighted for Osiris and Isis, thou shalt not be lighted for Anubis until thou hast given me an answer to everything which I ask (37) about here to-day truly without telling me falsehood. If thou wilt not do it, I will not give thee oil.

## Col. VII.

(1) 'I will not give thee oil, I will not give thee fat, O lamp; verily I will give thee the body of the female

---

he would be connected with the lion-headed goddess Tefnut, here perhaps assimilated to the lion-goddess Sochmet.

l. 37. *bn e-y a* (sic) *t*. The *a* is false with neg. fut., but occurs commonly in this papyrus. See 7/1, &c.

Col. VII.

l. 1. *e·ʾry* with gloss ⲉⲣⲉ, apparently = Eg. 𓇋𓂋, as *eʾre* in 5/28: here 'verily' or 'but.'

2. n p ʾḥ ḥwt m-s-k nte-y t t·t-k n p ʾswe(?) n ḫft Ḥr a·wn n-y ʾy na t ty·t t tb·t n ḫl nt n t·t-y

3. šp·t a ḫr-tn ʾy n by·w ʾqr·w(?) na bywkm t tyb·t n ʿnte nt ḫr qh IV ʾy p ʾʾe nt e-w

4. z n-f ʾNp n rn nt ḥtp ḥr t tybe·t n ḫl e rt-f smn·t ḥr t tybe·t n ʿnte my ʾw n-y

5. p kys m-s p šre ḫbs nte-f z n-y wḥ ḫr mt·t nb nt e-y šn ḫrr-w ty n p-hw n mt·t mʿ·t e mn mt·t n ʿze nʾm-w

6. y-ʿo tʿbʿ-ʿo swgʿmʿmw ʿkhʿkhʿ·nbw sʿnʿwʿny etsie qm-t

7. geth-ʿo-s bʿsʿe·th-ʿo-ry thmylʿ·ʿkh·khw a·ʾry n-y wḥ a mt·t nb nt e-y šn ḫrr-w ty n p-hw sp VII

8. n sḫ·w n p ʿlw b-ʿo-el b-ʿo-el sp-sn y·y sp-sn ʿ·ʿ sp-sn tt tt sp-sn p nt t wyn m šs sp-sn p ḫber n t st·t

9. p nte t st·t n r-f nte b·ʾr-s ʿḫm p ntr ʿo nt ḥms ḫn t st·t p nt n t mt·t n t st·t p nt n p šy n t p·t

10. nte p ʿw erme p nʿš n p ntr n t·t-f wnḥ-k a py ʿlw nt ḫr pe hne n p-hw nte-f z n-y wḥ n mt·t

11. mʿ·t n wš n mt·t n ʿze e-y a ty ʿy-k n ʾBt e-y a šʿšʿ-k n t p·t ne-ḥr p rʿ e-y a šʿšʿ-k

12. ne-ḥr ʿḥ e-y a šʿšʿ-k n p t e-y a šʿšʿ-k ne-ḥr p nt ḥr p bḥt nte b·ʾr-f htm pe p šʿšʿ

13. ʿo petery petery pʿter enphe enphe p ntr nt n t ry·t ḥry·t n t p·t nte p šbt nt (ne)-

---

l. 2. Referring to the contest between Horus and Set when Horus injured the testicles of Set, and Set, at the same time, put out the eye of Horus. The eye of Horus symbolizes light—hence the threat to the lamp. But the reading and meaning are uncertain. Cf. note to 1/3.

*t tb·t n ḫl* seems to be in apposition to *ty·t*; a similar construction in l. 3.

l. 3. *ʾqr.* The double figure in the underworld formed of the foreparts of two lions or of a lion and a bull. LANZONE, Diz. Mit., p. 5.

*bywkm* seems to be the name of the Arabian desert at the latitude of El Kab, according to BRUGSCH, D. Geogr., 211, 1154, where the lion-

cow and put blood (2) of the male bull into (?) thee and put thy hand to the testicles (?) of the enemy of Horus. Open to me, O ye of the underworld, the box of myrrh that is in my hand; (3) receive me before you, O ye souls of Aker belonging to Bi-wekem, the box of frankincense that hath four corners. O dog, which is (4) called Anubis by name, who resteth on the box of myrrh, whose feet are set on the box of frankincense, let there come to me (5) the ointment for the son of the lamp that he (?) may give me answer as to everything about which I ask here to-day, truly without falsehood therein. (6) Io, Tabao, Soukhamamou, Akhakhanbou, Sanauani, Ethie, Komto, (7) Kethos, Basaethori, Thmila, Akhkhou, give me answer as to everything about which I ask here to-day.' Seven times. (8) The spells of the boy: 'Boel, Boel (*bis*), Ii (*bis*), Aa (*bis*), Tattat (*bis*), he that giveth light exceedingly, the companion of the flame, (9) he in whose mouth is the fire that is not quenched, the great god that sitteth in the fire, he that is in the midst of the fire, he that is in the lake of heaven, (10) in whose hand is the greatness and might of God, reveal thyself to this boy who hath my vessel to-day, and let him give me answer truly (11) without falsehood. I will glorify thee in Abydos, I will glorify thee in heaven before Phre, I will glorify thee (12) before the moon, I will glorify thee on earth, I will glorify thee before him who is upon the throne, who is not destroyed, he of the great glory, (13) Peteri, Peteri, Pater, Enphe, Enphe, the god who is above heaven, in

---

pair Shu and Tefnut were worshipped. Possibly the latter were identified with Aker.

The animal of Anubis was strictly a fox according to its shape, but coloured black.

l. 5. *p šre ḫbs*. Is this an expression for the wick, or for the boy-medium, or for the god?

l. 8. Lines 8–18, cf. 5/12–22.

14. ʿne-f n t·t-f ʾr t ẖp ntr e bnp ntr t ẖp-f ʾm a ẖn n t mt·t n ty st·t nt ty ḥ·t-k pa bwel (ⲁⲛⲓⲏⲗ)

15. nte-k t { mʾ-y p ʿš-sḥne nt e-y šn ẖrr-f ty n p-hw
16. { p zr n n bel·w n p ʿlw nt ẖr pe hne a t

my mʾ-s my stm-s p ntr ʿo }
mʾ-f-s erme ınsz-f a t stm-f p ntr ʿo } s-ʾy-s-ʾy-ḥwt sp-sn

17. (ⲁⲭⲣⲉⲙⲧⲱ) ʾm a ẖn { ẖr zz-y n p-hw nte-k t wn
18. { n t mt·t n ty st·t

yr·t a bl n mt·t nb nt e-y šll ẖrr-w ty n p-hw } p ntr ʿo nt

ḥr p tw n gʾbʾ·wn ghʿbʿh-ʿo (ⲧⲁⲕⲁⲣⲧⲁⲧ) e·ʾr-k ʿš ny

19. šʿ nte p wyn ẖp a·ʾre p wyn ẖp e·ʾr-k st e·ʾr-k ʿš ty ḥ·t(?) sẖ n wḥm ʿn tey-s t ḥ·t n p thm

20. ḥ-s nt e·ʾr-k ʿš-s ʾy a·z(?) n-y sp-sn ths ten-ʿo-r p yt n nḥe z·t p ntr nt ḥr p t tre-f sʿlkm-ʿo

21. bʿlkm-ʿo brʿk nephr-ʿo·b-ʿn-p-rʿ bryʿs sʿry-ntr·w melykhryphs

22. lʿrnknʿnes herephes mephr-ʿo·bryʿs phrgʿ phekse ntsywpšyʿ

23. mʿrmʿreke·t lʿ-ʿo-re·grepšye my nw-y a p wḥ n p šn nt e-y ty e-tbe·t-f my ʾr-w n-y wḥ

24. a mt·t nb nt e-y šn ẖrr-w ty n p-hw n mt·t mʿ·t n wš n mt·t n ʿze ʾy ʾtʿel ʾpthe gh-ʿo·gh-ʿo·m-ʿo-le

25. hesen·myngʿ·nt-ʿo-n ʿo-rth-ʿo·bʿwb-ʿo n-ʿo-ere sere· sere sn-gʿthʿrʿ

26. eresgšyngʿl sʿkgyste n-t-te·gʿgyste ʿkrwr-ʿo·b-ʿo-re g-ʿo-ntere

---

ll. 15, 17. These interlineations are words to be substituted in the case of no medium being employed.

l. 19. *ty k·t* was first written before *sẖ*, and then *ḥ* written upon the *k*: see the Glossary.

l. 20. *ʾy*: after this word the name of the deity invoked would be expected: a vertical line following may indicate an omission. *z n-y sp-sn* would seem to be an imperative with emphasis.

l. 22. *ntsywpšyʿ*. *nt* represents δ and *ts* θ, so *nts* probably represents an aspirated *d*, i. e. *dh*, which is transcribed in the Greek by Δ alone; but *ts* also represents Δ in 2/26.

l. 25. Hesenmigadon, &c. A similar string of names occurs in Brit.

whose hand is the beautiful staff, (14) who created deity, deity not having created him, come into the midst of this fire that is here before thee, he of Boel, Aniel

(15) { cause me to see the business about
(16) and do thou { give strength to the eyes of the boy

{ which I am inquiring here to-day, let it be seen, let
{ who has my vessel, to cause him to see it, and to his

{ it be heard
{ ears to cause him to hear it, } O great god Sisihout,

(17) { before me and cause my eyes
(18) Akhremto, come in { into the midst of this flame,

(17) to be opened to everything for which I pray here to-day, (18) O great god that is upon the hill of ⟨Atugi⟩ Gabaon, Khabaho, Takrtat.' You recite this (19) until the light appear. When the light appears, you turn round (?), you recite this spell-copy a second time again. Behold the spell-copy also (?) of the summons (20) that you recite: 'Ho! speak to me (*bis*) Thes, Tenor, the father of eternity without end, the god who is over the whole earth, Salkmo, (21) Balkmo, Brak, Nephro, Bampre, Brias, Sarinter, Melikhriphs, (22) Largnanes, Herephes, Mephrobrias, Pherka, Phexe, Diouphia, (23) Marmareke, Laore-Krephie, may I see the answer to the inquiry on account of which I am here, may answer be made to me (24) to everything about which I ask here to-day, truly without falsehood. Ho! Adael, Aphthe, Khokhomole, (25) Hesenmigadon, Orthobaubo, Noere, Sere, Sere, San-kathara, (26) Ereskhigal, Saggiste, Dodeka-

---

Mus. Gr. Pap. No. XLVI. l. 424, et seq.; WESSELY, Ephes. Gram., 36, 244–5, 341, 377.

l. 26. Ereshkigal is the Sumerian goddess of the Underworld, cf. LEGGE, P. S. B. A., xxii. 121, lit. 'mistress of the Great Land,' i. e. the infernal regions; see the myth in BUDGE and BEZOLD, Tel-el-amarna Tablets, No. 82, p. 140; the name is found also in an Assyrian text in R. C. THOMPSON, Reports of the Magicians and Astrologers, No. 267 (from

27. e·ʾr-k t ʾr-f wn yr·t-f nte-f nw m-s p ḫbs nte-k šn·t-f a p nt e·ʾr-k wḫ-f a·ʾre ʿw n ḥt ḫp e bnp-f nw a p ntr e.ʾr-k st-k

28. e·ʾr-k ʿš pe-f ḥtr z-mt·t semeʿ·gʿn-tw gen-tw g-ʿo-n-tw geryn-tw ntʿreng-ʿo lekʿwks

29. ʾm n-y gʿnʿb a·ʾry kʿt-ʿy bʿrykʿt-ʿy ʾtn ʿḥ n n ntr-w ʾtn stm ḫrw-y my z-w n-y wḥ

30. a mt·t nb nt e-y šn ḫrr-w ty n p-hw ʾy p ste nsʿlʿbʿḥ-ʿo nʿsyrʿ hʿke twn-f p my sr*i*w

31. my nw-y a p wyn n p-hw erme n ntr·w nte-w z n-y wḥ a mt·t nb nt e-y šn ḫrr-w ty n p-hw n mt·t mʿ·t nʿ·nʿ·nʿ·nʿ rn-k

32. nʿnʿ pe-k rn n mte e·ʾr-k ʿš šmšeke n ḫrw-k e-f ʿy e·ʾr-k ʿš z ʾm n-y yʿh-ʿo yʿ-ʾw

33. yʿh-ʿo ʿwḥ-ʿo yʿh-ʿo hʾy k hw qʾ nʿ-šbt ʾr-py-hpe ʿblʿ-bl-n-bk

34. ḥr n bk ny-ʿbyt thʿtlʿt my-ʾry-bl

## Col. VIII.

1. a [ʾre p ntr (?)] ʾsq a tm ʾy a(?) ḫn e·ʾr-k ʿš

2. my-ʾry-bl·qmlʿ·kykḥ p-yt·yt·w n n ntr·w pḫr wʿ·t yr·t rym k·t sby yʿḥ sp-sn sp-sn ḥʿ·ḥʿ·he

3. st·st·st·st yḥʾ yʿh-ʿo ḥḥ my ʾw n-y p ntr nte p wḥ-sḥne n p-hw n t·t-f nte-f z n-y wḥ a mt·t nb

4. nt e-y šn ḫrr-w ty n p-hw e·ʾr-k z pf-ntr(?) n r-k tne sp nb n e·ʾr-k ʿš te-y ḥwy ḫyt ar-k n p nt ḫt nʾm-k n p nt ʿme nʾm-k

---

information kindly supplied by Mr. Thompson and Mr. Hall, of the British Museum).

l. 28. The names in this line are found in Pap. XLVI above, l. 428, and also on a Gnostic gem described by Goodwin, Cambridge Essays, 1853, p. 54.

l. 30. *twn-f*, 'raise him up!' or with reflexive masc. suffix 'arise!' instead of fem. as in Coptic ⲧⲱⲟⲩⲛⲟⲥ, 'arise!'

Col. VIII.

l. 1. The short heading seems only intended to remind the reader of the subject in hand (see 6/27), and is not a new heading.

kiste, Akrourobore, Kodere.' (27) You make him open his eyes and look at the lamp, and ask him as to that which you wish. If obstinacy appear, he not having seen the god, you turn round (?), (28) you pronounce his compulsion. Formula: 'Semea-kanteu, Kenteu, Konteu, Kerideu, Darenko, Lekaux, (29) come to me, Kanab, Ari-katei, Bari-katei, disk, moon of the gods, disk, hear my voice, let answer be given me (30) as to everything about which I ask here to-day. O perfume of Zalabaho, Nasira, Hake, arise (?) O Lion-ram, (31) let me see the light to-day, and the gods; and let them give me answer as to everything about which I ask here to-day truly. Na, Na, Na, Na, is thy name, (32) Na, Na, is thy true name.' You utter a whisper (?) with your voice loudly; you recite saying, 'Come to me Iaho, Iaeu, (33) Iaho, Auho, Iaho, Hai, Ko, Hoou, Ko, Nashbot, Arpi-Hap (?), Abla, Balbok, (34) Honbek (Hawk-face), Ni, Abit, Thatlat, Maribal.'

## Col. VIII.

(1) If [the god (?)] delay so as not to come in, you cry: (2) 'Maribal, Kmla, Kikh, Father of the fathers of the gods, go round (?), one Eye weeps, the other laughs. Ioh (*bis*, *bis*), Ha, Ha, He, (3) St, St, St, St, Ihe, Iaho, seek (?); let there come to me the god in whose hand is the command to-day, and let him give me reply to everything (4) about which I ask here to-day.' You say, 'Pef-nuti (?)' with your mouth each

---

l. 2. This continues from 6/34, which is short because of meeting the ruling: v. the facsimile.

*my* *'r-y* *bl* is repeated from the end of 6/34. Such repetition is usual where a page ends in the middle of a paragraph (e.g. in Cols. II–III, VI–VII), but there are exceptions as in Cols. IX–X. The sign over *bl* is hieratic for  (= *bl*), as in 11/12.

l. 4. *pf-ntr* (?): possibly an archaic expression, 'that god,' but this and

5. my ꜣre p kke prze a p wyn ne-ḥr-y ꜣy p ntr ḥw-ḥs rʿ·t ẖtm sy sp-sn ꜣw ḥw ꜣw ḥ·t b-ꜣr-y

6. ghꜣ ꜣt rʿ·t šfe bybyw yʿh-ʿo ʿryʿḥʿ sp-sn a·ꜣry n-s e-w a st ḥr bks gs·gs·gs·gs

7. yʿnyʿn e·ꜣr-n e-y bs ks·ks·ks·ks my ꜣw n-y p ntr nte p wḥ-sḥne n t·t-f nte-f z n-y wḥ a mt·t nb nt e-y

8. šn ẖrr-w ty n p-hw ꜣm a ẖn pyꜣ-t·w ẖy-tre·t ꜣy ẖp ẖpe ẖp ʿbrʿ-ḥmė p zf n t yr·t n t wz

9. qmr·qmr·qmr·qmr qm-r a·t ẖp qm·qm wr wt š . . knwš pe-k rn n mte my z-w n-y wḥ

10. a mt·t nb nt e-y šn ẖrr-w ty n p-hw ꜣm n-y bʿkʿksykhekh a·zy n-y wḥ a mt·t nb nt e-y šn ẖrr-w ty n p-hw n mt·t mʿ·t

11. n wš n z n-y mt·t n ʿze z-mt·t sp VII

12. wʿ . . . . a ẖrw pe-sẖ p wʿb n ks e-f z nꜣm-f z e-f znt n sp IX

13. ank r-mšw šw r-mšw p šre n ta p šw n mw·t-f ta p šw e-f ẖp

14. e t mn t mt·t ne ẖp mpr ꜣy n-y n pe-k ḥr n pẖe·t e·ꜣr-k a ꜣy n-y n pe-k ẖbr n wʿb

15. n pe-k sšt n rm ḥ·t-ntr e-f ẖp e bn-e-s a ẖp e·ꜣr-k ꜣy n-y n pe-k smte n gʿlʿšyre

16. *z* ꜣnk r-mšw šw r-mšw p šre n ta p šw n mw·t-f ta p šw a ḥr

---

other expressions that seem to have a meaning, such as 'do for her' *arainas*, 'they shall return' *euesbl*, in l. 6, are likely to be only gibberish ejaculations; cf. δωδεκακιστη in Greek magic.

*ne'r-k* = conjunctive ⲛⲧⲉ, usually written *nte-k* as Boh. ⲛⲧⲉⲕ.

l. 8. *wz*. The  eye is named ους (cf. gen. ουατ-ος), ουατιον B. M. Pap. XLVI. 75 and 92, pointing to the pronunciation ⲟⲩⲁϫⲉ, ⲟⲩⲟϫⲉ (?), cf. ταουατις, 'she of the sacred eye,' in Spiegelb., Eigenn., p. 51*.

l. 12. *pe-sẖ*. There is no determinative to prove that this is a proper name. The previous sign instead of *ẖrw*, 'voice,' might be read as 'foreigner,' or 'Greek,' cf. 4/7, V. 3/12.

time, and you cry, 'I cast fury at thee of him who cutteth thee, of him who devoureth thee. (5) Let the darkness separate from the light before me. Ho! god, Hu-hos, Ri-khètem, Si (*bis*), Aho (?), Ah, Mai (?) ("I do not"?), (6) Kha, Ait, Ri-shfe, Bibiu, Iaho, Ariaha (*bis*), Arainas ("do for her"), Euesetho ("they will turn the face"), Bekes, Gs, Gs, Gs, Gs, (7) Ianian, Eren, Eibs, Ks, Ks, Ks, Ks, let the god come to me in whose hand is the command and give me answer as to everything about which I (8) inquire here to-day. Come in, Piatoou, Khitore; ho! Shop, Shope, Shop, Abraham, the apple (?) of the Eye of the Uzat, (9) Kmr, Kmr, Kmr, Kmr, Kmro, so as to create, Kom, Kom-wer-wot, Sheknush (?) is thy real name, let answer be told to me (10) as to everything about which I ask here to-day. Come to me Bakaxikhekh, tell me answer to everything which I ask about here to-day truly (11) without telling me falsehood.' Formula. Seven times.

(12) A direct (?) inquiry by (?) the voice of Pasash (?) the priest of Kes; he (the informant) tells it, saying it is tested, nine times: (13) 'I am Ramshau, Shau, Ramshau son of Tapshau, of his mother Tapshau, if it be that (14) any given thing shall happen, do not come to me with thy face of Pekhe; thou shalt come to me in thy form of a priest, (15) in thy figure of a servant of the temple. (But) if it shall not come to pass, thou (shalt) come to me in thy form of a Kalashire, (16) for I am Ramshau, Shau, Ramshau, the son of Tapshau, of his

---

*Ks* may be Cusae, or Cynopolis (El Qais), or some other town in Middle Egypt.

'Nine times tried' seems proverbial, cf. 14/31; and for the whole sentence, 29/1.

l. 14. *Pḫe·t*, a feline goddess worshipped at Speos Artemidos near Beni-Hasan in Middle Egypt. LANZONE, Diz. Mit., 234.

l. 15. *gˁlˁšyre*, see the Glossary.

17. p ḫpš n p mḥ III n p wrš e wn wʿ yb n mzwl ḥt n ḫlpe III e wn mḥ-n-tp III

18. n bʿnyp tks nʾm-f nte-k ʿš n·y ar-f n sp VII nte-k ḫʿ·f ne-zz-k ḫr nw-f n-k nte-f sze erme-k

## Col. IX.

1. p šn-hne n Ḫns . . . ḥr-k Ḫns m ws·t nfr ḥtp p syf šps ʾr pyr n p sšn Ḥr nb nw wʿ pw . . .

2. ʾy ḥt nb ḥt ʾy šn-ty·t nb šn-ty·t nb ʾtn p ntr ʿo p k wt p šre n p ʾkš ʾm n-y p syf šps p ntr ʿo nt [ḥn]

3. p ʾtn nte ḥn-w . . . p-ʿo-m-ʿo nt e-w z n-f p k sp-sn wr p ntr ʿo nt ḥn t wz·t ʾr pyr a bl ḥn p IV [ḥn]

4. n z·t p tbe n n ef·w nt e b ʾr-rḫ-w rn-f b ʾr-rḫ-w ky-f b rḫ-w smte-f te-y ʾr-rḫ⟨-w⟩ rn-k te-y ʾr-rḫ⟨-w⟩ ky-k te-y [ʾr-rḫ⟨-w⟩]

5. smte-k ʿo rn-k ʾw rn-k ʾḫ rn-yk ʾmn rn-k wr ntr·w rn-yk ʾmn rn-f a ntr·w nb rn-yk ʿo·m

6. wr ʿm rn-k ntr·w nb rn-yk srpt-my-sr rn-yk l-ʿo-w ʾy nb t·w sp-sn rn-yk ʾmʿḫr n p·t rn-k sšn n syw . . .

---

l. 17. *τριταιας ουσης της σεληνης* Pap. Bibl. Nat. l. 170.

*yb*, lit. 'tooth.' Cf. Lat. 'spica allii.'

### Col. IX.

l. 1. *Ḫns-m-ws·t-nfr-ḥtp*, the title of the principal form of Khons at Thebes, see the Bekhten stela. Khons was a moon-god, son of Amen and Mut. He is here identified with Horus and other gods.

For Horus rising from the lotus-flower see Lanzone, Diz. Mit., ccxiv.

'Lord of time,' as the moon regulating seasons.

l. 2. *ḥt*, 'silver,' the moon-colour.

*šn-ty·t*, 'circuit of the underworld (?).'

*p k wt*, cf. his title 'ein feuriger Stier' in an inscription translated by Brugsch, Religion, p. 360; *wt* is evidently the Eg. *wʾz*.

*p ʾkš*, the Ethiopian, i. e. Amen, who at this time was popularly considered as, above all, the god of Meroe: see V. 20/1 and note.

l. 3. *nte ḥn-w* . . . Cf. ϩⲛⲉ- ϩⲛⲁ⸗ and below l. 10, and with the idea cf. Khons' title *nb ʾw·t ib*, 'lord of joy.'

*p IV ḥn n z·t*, cf. l. 13 with gloss. ϩⲛⲁⲉ. *ḥn* is a vessel below 12/29. Here it may be a 'space' referring to the 'four quarters.' *z·t* may perhaps refer to 'space,' not time. One may also suggest the meaning of 'four boundaries' or 'four seasons,' and in l. 8 *ḥn* seems to mean

mother Tapshau.' [Say it] opposite (17) the Shoulder constellation on the third day of the month, there being a clove of three-lobed white garlic and there being three needles (18) of iron piercing it, and recite this to it seven times; and put it at thy head. Then he attends to you and speaks with you.

## COL. IX.

(1) The vessel-inquiry of Chons. '[Homage ?] to thee, Chons-in-Thebes-Nefer-hotep, the noble child that came forth from the lotus, Horus, lord of time (?), one he is . . . (2) Ho! silver, lord of silver, Shentei, lord of Shentei, lord of the disk, the great god, the vigorous bull, the Son of the Ethiopian, come to me, noble child, the great god that is in (3) the disk, who pleaseth men (?), Pomo, who is called the mighty bull (*bis*), the great god that is in the *Uzat*, that came forth from the four [boundaries ?] (4) of eternity, the punisher of the flesh (?), whose name is not known, nor his nature, nor his likeness (?). I know thy name, I know thy nature, I [know] (5) thy likeness. Great is thy name, Heir is thy name, Excellent is thy name, Hidden is thy name. Mighty one of the gods is thy name, "He whose name is hidden from all the gods" is thy name, Om, (6) Mighty Am is thy name, "All the gods" is thy name, Lotus-lion-ram is thy name, "Loou comes, lord of the lands" (*bis*) is thy name, Amakhr of heaven is thy name, "Lotus-flower of stars (?)

---

a 'cycle.' Cf. τα τεσσαρα μερη του ουρανου και τα τεσσαρα θεμελια της γης, B. M. Pap. CXXI. 552.

l. 4. *p tbe*, cf. note on Petbe in P. S. B. A. xxii. 162.

*te-y ʾr-rḫw*: the written *w* seems meaningless, for *rḫ* is not here in *stm-f* dependent on *te-y*. The latter is the pron. 1st sing. [illegible] followed by inf. or pseudo-part. For *ʾr-rḫ* see GRIFFITH, High Priests, p. 106.

l. 5. *ʾḥ* with gloss [illegible] and therefore not 'spirit,' which would be [illegible]. Perhaps it is the adjective 'beneficial.'

'He whose name is hidden from all the gods,' a phrase current in the New Kingdom for Amenra.

7. ʾy ʾy-y-ʿo ne-ʾy-ʿo rn-yk pe-k sšt mḫrr n ḥr n sre e st-f n bk e bs II ḫrr-f pe-k [ḥfe ḥfe]

8. n z·t pe-k ḥn n wrš pe-k ḫ n ḫ n elle ʾšt pe-k sym n sym n ʾMn pe-k ʾrw n t p·t byn pe-k rym n [p mty ?]

9. lbs km st smn·t ḥr p t yb rn-k n te-k·t ḫe·t n p yʿm pe-k sšt n ʾny a·pyr-k nʾm-f . . .

10. t p·t te-k·t qnḥ·t p t te-k·t hyw·t wn-ne p ḥny a mḥt nʾm-k ty n p-hw z ʾnk ḫʿ(?) mne nw . . . y

11. ʾʾe e bnp-y ʾr-f ḫr ʾsq e bnp-y gm rn-yk p ntr ʿo nte (ne-)ʿy rn-f p ḥry ḫte·t n t p·t a·ʾr-y ʾr-f ʾr [p ḥkr ?]

12. n p t p ʾyb n p mw nte-k nḫt nte-k t wz-y nte-k t n-y ḥs·t mr·t šfe·t a ḥr rm nb z ʾnk pe p k . . .

13. p ntr ʿo nt ḫn t wz·t ʾr pyr a bl ḫn p IV ḥn n z·t ʾnk ḥwne p rn ʿo nt n t p·t nt e-w z n-f . . .

14. ʾm-ph-ʿo-w sp-sn n mʿ·t sp-sn ḥs-f a ʾBt Rʿ Ḥr ḥnn(?) pe pe rn ḥry ntr·w rn-t n mte nḫt my wz-y my ḫpe pe hne . . .

15. a·wn n-y n ʿrq-ḥḥ a ḥr ntr nb rm nb ʾr pyr

---

l. 7. The figure described may be compared with the ram-headed scarabs having hawk's wings which are common on late coffins, on the breast of the figure upon the inner coffins. What *bs* is is not evident. These scarabs often hold two Shen rings, or two sceptres with Maat feathers on the end.

*pe-k [ḥfe ḥfe] n z·t.* There seems to be space in the lacuna for the whole groups spelled out, as in l. 20. The extent of the lacuna, about 2 cm., can be judged by l. 12, where *k[wr]* has to be read. For the *ḥf n z·t*, cf. I Kham. iii. 31; Griff., High Priests, p. 22; and *τον αειζωον οφιν* Pap. Bibl. Nat. 1323.

l. 8. *ʾšt.* The identity of this fruit-tree is very uncertain, v. Loret, Flore Phar., 2nd ed. p. 102.

*rym n [p mty ?].* Cf. I Kham. iii. 13, but the precise wording required is quite uncertain.

l. 9. *lbs.* There is a fish called λεβιας; and there is the modern لبيس. On the latter Mr. G. A. Boulenger kindly furnishes a note, 'the lebis is the Arabic name of Labeo Niloticus, a fish allied to and not unlike our carp. Like the latter, without being absolutely black, it may be of a very dark olive brown above.'

*yb* probably has a definite meaning, but as yet it is obscure.

l. 10. *e ḥn-y.* This reading is possible, see the facsimile.

(7) cometh," Ei-io Ne-ei-o is thy name. Thy form is a scarab with the face of a ram; its tail a hawk's, it wearing (?) two panther-skins (?). Thy [serpent is a serpent ?] (8) of eternity, thine orbit (?) a lunar month, thy tree a vine-tree and persea (?), thy herb the herb of Amen, thy fowl of heaven a heron, thy fish of [the deep (?)] (9) a black *lebes*. They are established on earth. Yb is thy name in thy body in (?) the sea, thy figure of stone in which thou camest forth is a . . .; (10) heaven is thy shrine, the Earth thy fore-court; it was my will (?) to seize thee here to-day, for I am one shining, enduring: my . . . (11) faileth (?) if I have not done it through (?) the delay, I not having discovered thy name, O great god whose name is great, the lord of the threshing-floor (?) of heaven. (But) I have done it, [enduring ?] hunger (12) for bread, and thirst for water; and do thou rescue (?) me and make me prosper and give me praise, love, and reverence before every man. For I am (?) the [mighty] bull, (13) the great god that is in the *Uzat*, that came forth from the four regions (?) of space (?). I am *Hune* (youth), the great name that is in heaven, whom they call . . . (14) Amphoou (*bis*), "True" (*bis*), "He is praised to (?) Abydos," "Ra," "Horus the boy" is my name, "Chief of the gods" is my correct name, preserve me, make me to prosper, make my vessel to become [successful ?]. (15) Open to

---

l. 11. *a·ʾr-y.* The translation is uncertain owing to the lacuna.

l. 12. *ʾnk pe p k* might mean 'I am he of the [mighty] bull'; if not, the magician identifies himself with Khons, see l. 3.

l. 14. *ḥs-f a ʾBt.* The *a* as a separate letter seems certain, v. the facs. The gloss *ḥsef* has the appearance of a construct form, but it may well be for *ḥsaf*. Even so it is difficult to find a meaning for the phrase.

The reading of the group following *R‘-Ḥr* is not certain. The signs are .

l. 15. The 'stone of Ptah' is not otherwise known. For Ptah as a creator see Brugsch, Religion, p. 110; Breasted, A. Z., 1901, 51.

a bl ẖn p ʾny n Ptḥ z ank p ḥf ʾr pyr n p nwn ʾnk . . .

16. bre n ʾkš ʿnẖ n ḥf n nb n mʿ·t a·ʾre ʾbye n sp·t p nt e-y a z·t-f ẖr ẖpe-f twn hy . . .

17. apḥte z ʾnk ʾNp p sst (*sic*) nḥne ʾnk ʾS·t e-y a mr-f ank Wsr e-y a mr-f ank ʾNp [e-y a mr]-f e·ʾr-k a nḥm-t a . . . nb

18. s·t thth nb lsmtnwt lsmʿtot nḫt my wz-y my n-y ḥs·t mr·t šfe·t ẖn pe hne . . .

19. pe swt ty n p-hw ʾm-t n-y ʾS·t t nb ḥyq t wr ḥyq n n ntr·w tre·w Ḥr ḥ·t ʾS·t m-s-y Nb·t-ḥ·t n te grpe

20. wʿ ḥf n šre ʾTm p nt . . . n ʿre·t a zz-y ze p nt e-f a myšt e-f a myš stn Mnt ty n p-hw(?) n wʿ(?) . . .

21. a my-ḥs apḥte a t še a wʿ my n šr my-ḥs a bl e-f qby a·ʾn·t-w n-y sp-sn n by n ntr n by

22. n rm n by n t ty·t n by n t ʾḥy·t n ʾyẖ·w n n·mw·t-w nte-w ⟨my ʾr-w⟩ z n-y n t mʿ·t n p-hw a p nt e-y šn m-s-f z ʾ[nk]

---

The snake as word-sign has six loops here and in 21/4, four loops in l. 16. This agrees with the snake determinative of *šʿy* which has usually four loops, once (19/12) six loops, and twice (3/3, 5/9) two loops, and Shoi is said to be 'in Nun' 2/5. It is thus the snake of Shay. But the sign, meaning distinctly a (sacred) snake, cannot read *šʿy*, which always means distinctly a divinity. *Ḥfe* is perhaps the most probable reading, see esp. 21/4; the det. of that word in 9/20 has only two loops, but in Louvre dem. Mag. iii. 9 five or six loops. *Syt* 14/3, V. 27/1 has four loops, but the head seems to be raised high; *syt* is derived from Eg. *sʾ-tʾ* which is represented by  in late texts, Br., Dict. Geogr., 762.

l. 16. *bre*: cf. ⲃⲱⲱⲣⲉ, 'intumescere,' ⲃⲟⲣⲉ, 'fastuose se gerere,' or better ⲃⲉⲣⲓ, 'juvenis.'

*ʿnẖ* is evidently the serpent word met with in 1/3. Possibly both *bre* and *ʿnẖ* are adjectives, and the construction may resemble the familiar Coptic construction with adjectives, St., § 187.

*t-wn,* apparently an unetymological spelling for ⲛⲧⲟⲩⲛⲟⲩ: cf. 18/21.

l. 17. *sst*, error for *snt*: cf. 18/22.

l. 20. *wʿ ḥf n šre ʾTm*. Atum being a form of Ra, this may refer to the

me Arkhah before every god and every man that hath come forth from the stone of Ptah. For I am the serpent that came forth from Nun, I am a (16) proud (?) Ethiopian, a rearing serpent of real gold, there being honey in my (?) lips; that which I shall say cometh to pass at once. Ho! . . . (17) mighty one, for I am Anubis, the baby creature (?); I am Isis and I will bind him, I am Osiris and I will bind him, I am Anubis [and I will bind] him. Thou wilt save me from every . . . (18) and every place of confusion (?). Lasmatnout, Lesmatot, protect me, heal me, give me love, praise and reverence in my vessel (19), my bandage (?) here to-day. Come to me, Isis, mistress of magic, the great sorceress of all the gods. Horus is before me, Isis behind me, Nephthys as my diadem, (20) a snake of the son(s) of Atum is that which . . . a uraeus-diadem at my head; for he that shall strike (?) me (?) shall strike (?) King Mont here to-day . . . (21) Mihos, mighty one shall send out a lion of the sons of Mihos under compulsion to fetch them to me (*bis*) the souls of god, the souls (22) of man, the souls of the Underworld, the souls of the horizon, the spirits, the dead, so that they tell me the truth to-day concerning that

---

poisonous serpent formed by Isis from the spittle of Ra, to bite him and make him reveal his secret name (texts of New Kingdom). With the construction compare l. 21 *wʿ my n šr my-ḥs*, 10/13 *tbe·t III n tbe·t nmy*, and 10/10 *šʿ n ʾny*.

l. 21. *My-ḥs*, a lion-god, son of Bubastis. For the pronunciation of the name see Spiegelberg, Eigennamen, p. 4*.

*t še a*: the *a* is quite certain, but is very puzzling.

*a·ʾn·t-w n-y sp-sn*. This should be an imperative: see also the parallel l. 35. Possibly *sp-sn* is falsely written here.

*n by*, gloss. ⲛⲃⲁⲓ. The plural sign is often omitted with *by*, and here we see the reason, viz. that the plural had no special form.

l. 22. *n·mw·t-w*, cf. l. 25. The prefixed *n* seems to represent a reduplication of the initial *m*, *n* being regularly assimilated to a following *m*.

Here we have νεκυες και οι δαιμονες of Pap. Bibl. Nat. 1453.

23. Ḥr s ʾS·t e-f ʾnnʿ a mr n ʿrq-ḥḥ a hwy qs·t a ḥr n s·w a t mnḫ·t n p ḥsy

24. p ḥsy nfr n n ḥsy·w e·ʾr-k nhs e·ʾr-k a rpy ḥr r n r·w n pe hne pe swt pe zʿl mt·t . . .

25. nhs nʾm-w n-y [n] ʾyh·w n mt·w nhs pe-w by pe-w sšt n n r·w n pe hne nhs-w nʾm-w n-y . . .

26. erme n mt·w nhs nʾm-w n-y sp-sn nhse(?) pe-w by erme pe-w sšt p ḫyt n py-s s wnte ta ʿrb . . .

27. nhs nʾm-w n-y sp-sn [n wn]te-w n ne-w s·t tbe my ʾr-w sze n r-w my ʾr-w mt·t n spe-w my ʾr-w z p-e·z-y [a p nt]

28. e-y šn ḫrr-f ty n p-hw my ʾr-w mt·t n . . . my ʾre mt·t mʿ·t ḫp n-y mpr t ḥr ḫr ḥr rn ḫr rn n mʿ·t sp-sn(?) [e mn]

29. mt·t n ʿze nʾm-w(?) [ʾy] p mḫrr n ḫstb n mʿ·t nt ḥms ḫr zz p šy n p pr-ʿo Wsr wn-nfr . . .

30. mḥ r-k n mw n(?) . . . kš-f a zz-y erme p nt ne-t·t my wz-y my wz-f θs-pḫr šʿ nte p-e·z[-y ḫp m]y ʾre

31. p-e·z-y ḫp z e·ʾre tm te(?) p-e·z-y ḫp e-y a t qte t st·t n p qte n ty sewe šʿ nte p-e·z-y ḫp z . . .

32. a p t stm-w n-y . . . z-w n-y nte-k nym sp-sn ʾnk ʾTm n p wtn n p rʿ ank ʿryʿttw t št-ʿo·t n(?) . . .

---

l. 23. *a mr·t* in the Khamuas stories means 'on board ship' (High Priests, p. 98), but ⲉⲙⲏⲣ in Coptic is 'across,' 'to the other side,' 'beyond.' *a mr n* may be 'beyond' as a preposition; the same word is used in 15/12 in the same connexion (with the tomb of Osiris at Abydos).

l. 24. *e·ʾr-k.* The gloss is certainly ⲉⲧ, and must be a correction.

*swt* is difficult to understand. The idea must be founded on the use of knots in magic, Lat. 'ligatura.'

*zʿl-mt·t* probably = 'word-seeking,' from Eg. *zʿr*, preserved also in ϫⲏⲣ, &c. Were all these used at once, or were they alternatives?

l. 26. *wnte*: cf. Lanz., Diz. Mit., 165, or better Brugsch, Wtb. Suppl., 322. It would be possible to read *ḥwnte.* From the next line the *wnte* would seem to be souls in torment or else punishing demons.

l. 27. *spe-w*, see Glossary, s. v. *spt.*

after which I am inquiring: for I am (23) Horus son of Isis who goeth on board at Arkhah to put wrappings on the amulets, to put linen on the Drowned one, (24) the fair Drowned one of the drowned (?). They shall rise, they shall flourish at the mouths of my vessel, my bandage (?), my word-seeking (?). (25) Arouse them for me (*bis*), the spirits, the dead; rouse their souls and forms at (?) the mouths of my vessel; rouse them for me (26) with the dead; rouse [them] for me (*bis*); rouse their souls and their forms. The fury of Pessiwont ("Her (whose) son is Wont"), the daughter of Ar . . . (27) rouse them for me (*bis*), the Unti from their places of punishment, let them talk with their mouths, let them speak with their lips, let them say that which I have said, [about that which] (28) I am asking them here to-day; let them speak before (?) me, let truth happen to me; do not substitute a face for a face, a name for a true (*bis*) name [without] (29) falsehood in it. [Ho ?] scarab of true lapislazuli that sitteth at the pool of Pharaoh Osiris Unnefer! (30) fill thy mouth with the water of [the pool ?], pour it on my head together with him who is at my hand; make me prosper, make him prosper, and conversely, until my words [happen ?], let (31) that which I say come to pass; for if that which I have said do not come to pass, I will cause fire to go round about this *Seoue* until that which I have said do come to pass; for [they came] (32) to the earth, they listened to me . . . they said to me, "Who art thou?" (*bis*), I am Atum in the sun-boat of Phre;

l. 28. *n ḥr*(?) *t-y*(?). Perhaps a very incorrect writing for *n ḥ·t-y*, 'before me.'

l. 29. *p šy*. Perhaps the 'lake of U-Peke' in 12/17.

l. 31. *e·'re tm te*, ⲉⲣⲉⲧⲙ̄-, but the *te* is inexplicable.

*sewe*. This seems a threat to burn the bandages or even the mummy of Osiris.

l. 32. *št-ʿo·t*, probably the chest, Eg. *šty·t*, of Osiris, Br., Wtb., 1410.

33. a·e-y kšp a bl ḥʿ[·t-k ?] a nw m-s Wsr p ʾkš e-f ʾn·ʾw a ḫn a zz-y e wn šr ʾNp II ḥ·t-f šr Wpy [II m-s-f]

34. šr rr·t II mne [nʾm-]f z-w n-y nte-k nym sp-sn ank wʿ n py bk II nt rsy a ʾS·t erme Wsr t grp·t t . . .

35. erme py-s ʿw . . . a·ʾny·t-w n-y sp-sn n by n ntr n by n rm by n t ty·t n by n t ʾḫy·t

## Col. X.

1. n ʾyḫ·w n mt·w my ʾr-w z n-y t mʿ·t n p-hw ḥr p nt e-y šn ḫrr-f z ʾnk ʾrtemy(?) . . . mw·t e-f ḥʿ ḥr ybt

2. ʾm n-y a ḫn ʾNp n pe-k ḥr nfr a·ʾr-y ʾy a wšte-k . . . sp-sn ḥ·t sp-sn . . . [rs mḥ]t ʾmnt ybt

3. tw n ʾmnt nb my ʾr-w ḫp e-w šs sp-sn e-w smn·t e-w swtn e-w pḫr e ḫ p ḫyt [n p wr ?] šfe z ʾnk

4. yʿe yʿ-ʿo yʿeʿ yʿ-ʿo sʿbʿ-ʿo-th ʿ-t-ne z te-y ḥwy [ḫyt] ar-k tsye glʿte

5. ʾrkhe y-ʿo-ʿ phʿlekmy yʿ-ʿo mʿkhʿhʿy yee kh-ʿo . . . n kh-ʿo-khrekhy ee-ʿo-th

6. sʿrbyʿqw ygrʿ pšybyeg m-ʿo-mw mwnekh stsyth-ʿo s-ʿo-th-ʿo-n nʿ-ʿo-n khʿrmʿy

7. p ḫyt n ny ntr·w tre-w a·z-y rn-w ty n p-hw nhs nʾm-w n-y sp-sn n ḥsy·w n mt·w ʿnḫe(?) pe-tn by pe-tn sšt n-y

8. a n r·w n pe ḫbs pe swt pe zʿiʿ mt·t my ʾr-f n-y wḥ ḫr mt·t nb nt e-y šn [ḫrr-w] ty n p-hw n mt·t mʿ·t sp-sn e mn mt·t

---

l. 33. 'The Ethiopian,' a curious epithet of Osiris. But he was worshipped in Ethiopia, Hdt. ii. 99, as well as at Philae, and he was dark-coloured, Plut., Is. et Os., c. 22. 33.

Ophois, Eg. *wp-wʾ·wt*, a jackal god.

l. 34. *Rr·t*, the name of the sow, pıp, and of the hippopotamus goddess, but here perhaps a snake goddess. The det. has only two loops.

*grp·t*. The det. is the uraeus, as in *ʿre·t*, l. 20. In 20/6 it seems to be simply a two-looped snake.

Col. X.

l. 1. Possibly the meaning is 'Artemi in the mother's womb.'

I am Ariotatu, the *Shto* of . . . (33) I looked out before . . . to observe Osiris the Ethiopian, he came into my head, there being two sons of Anubis in front of him, [two] sons of Ophois behind him, (34) two sons of Rere mooring him. They said to me "Who art thou?" (*bis*). I am one of those two hawks that watch over Isis and Osiris, the diadem, the . . . (35) with its glory (?) . . . , bring them to me (*bis*), the souls of god, the souls of man, the souls of the Underworld, the souls of the horizon,

## Col. X.

'(1) the spirits, the dead; let them tell me the truth to-day in that about which I shall ask: for I am Artemi . . . se(?)-mau, rising in the East. (2) Come in to me, Anubis with thy fair face, I have come to pray to thee. Woe (?) (*bis*), fire (*bis*), [South, North,] West, East, (3) every breeze of Amenti, let them come into being, proved (*bis*), established, correct, enchanted, like the fury [of the great one] of reverence; for I am (4) Iae, Iao, Iaea, Iao, Sabaoth, Atone; for I cast fury at thee, Thiai, Klatai, (5) Arkhe, Ioa, Phalekmi, Iao, Makhahai, Iee, Kho..n, Khokhrekhi, Aaioth, (6) Sarbiakou, Ikra, Phibiek, Momou, Mounaikh, Stitho, Sothon, Naon, Kharmai, (7) the fury of all these gods, whose names I have uttered here to-day, rouse them for me (*bis*), the drowned (?), the dead; let your (plur.) soul and your (plur.) form live for me (8) at the mouths of my lamp,

l. 2. *wšt*, 'salute with reverence' is the real meaning, not altogether lost in Coptic.

l. 4. *te-y ḥwy ẖyt ar-k* clearly corresponds to ἐξορκίζω σε.

*tsye*, gloss ⲑⲓⲁⲓ. ⲁⲓ is here probably = short ⲉ.

l. 7. *n ḥsy·w* opposed to *n mt·w*. In the Rhind. bil. *'ẖ ḥsy·w*, 'approved spirits,' often, vii. 10, xiii. 9, xvii. 2. So perhaps here 'approved,' not 'drowned.'

*'nẖe*, again with a meaning allied to that in 1/1

l. 8. *ẖbs*. Hitherto it has been the *hin*, 'vessel,' not the lamp.

9. n ᶜze ḫn-w ys sp-sn tkr sp-sn pe-f swḫ-ʾyḫ ḥr še-k a wᶜ pr n kke e [ḥr]-f wn a pr-rs nge pr-ybt

10. n wᶜ mᶜ e-f wᶜb e·ʾr-k prḫ-f n šᶜ e-f wᶜb n ʾny n p yᶜr-ᶜo e·ʾr-k ʾny wᶜ z n ḥmt e-f wᶜb nge

11. wᶜ hne n blz nmy nte-k t wᶜ lq n mw n str nge mw e-f wᶜb a p z ḥnᶜ wᶜ lq n nḥe n mᶜ·t

12. e-f wᶜb nge nḥe wᶜet-f n wš n t mw ar-f nte-k t wᶜ ʾny n qs-ᶜnḫ(?) a ḫn p hne ḥr nḥe nte-k t wᶜ ḥt

13. n pr-nfr n p ʾytn n p hne nte-k t qte tbe·t III n p qte n p hne n tbe·t nmy

14. nte-k ḫᶜ t VII e-w wᶜb ḥr n tbe·tw nt qte a p hne nte-k ʾny wᶜ ḫm-ḫl e-f wᶜb e-f znt

15. n ne-f msz·w a t ḥ·t z e-f [ʾr] šw n še ḥr p hne e·ʾr-k t ḥms-f ḥr [wᶜ·t tbe·t] nmy nte-k ḥms ḥ-k

16. ḥr ke tbe·t e·ʾr-k wḥ pe-f [ḥr ?] ke-z ʾ·t-f nte-k t t·t-k a r yr·t-f [e yr·t-f] ḫtm e·ʾr-k ᶜš a ḫry

17. ḫn t mt·t n zz-f n sp VII [e·ʾr-k] wḥ e·ʾr-k fy t·t-k ḥr r yr·t-f e·ʾr-k . . . . . . . p hne e·ʾr-k t t·t-k

18. a ne-f msz·w e·ʾr-k mḥt nʾm-w n t·t-k ḥ-k e·ʾr-k šn n p ḫm-ḫl z ᶜn aeʾr-k [nw a p ntr ? ᶜo ?] e-f z te-y nw a wᶜ·t

19. kmeme·t e·ʾr-k z n-f ze a·z-ys z te-y nw a pe-k ḥr nfr e·ʾr-k . . . . . p ntr ᶜo ʾNp

---

l. 9. *ys sp-sn tkr sp-sn* = ηδη ηδη ταχυ ταχυ of the Greek papyri.

l. 11. *lq* = ⲗⲟϭ : ⲗⲟⲕ, translating κοτυλη, which in the LXX. translates the Hebrew *log*. Whatever was the precise measure intended by the ⲗⲟⲕ, it seems to have taken the place of the Egyptian *hin* (less than a pint).

*mw n str* : apparently water allowed to stand for the night.

l. 12. *ḥt n pr-nfr*. The Good House is the place of embalming, GRIFF., High Priests, p. 25; but the presence of a plant det. no doubt indicates that it is a plant-name here. *Ḥt* might then be εγκαρδιον, as a botanical term 'core.' More probably the whole expression 'heart of the Good House' is to be taken as the name of a symbolical plant, such as the 'resurrection' plant, *Anastatica hierochuntina*, or something similar. Cf. the story of the flower enclosing the heart of Bata put in a cup of

my bandage (?), my word-seeking (?). Let him make me answer to every word [about] which I am asking here to-day in truth (*bis*) without (9) falsehood therein. Hasten (*bis*), quickly (*bis*).' Its spirit-gathering: You go to a dark chamber with its [face] open to the South or East (10) in a clean place; you sprinkle it with clean sand brought from the great river; you take a clean bronze cup or (11) a new vessel of pottery and put a *lok*-measure of water that has settled (?) or of pure water into the [cup] and a *lok*-measure of real oil (12) pure, or oil alone without putting water into it, and put a stone of *qs-ankh* in the vessel containing oil, and put a 'heart- (13) of-the-good-house' (plant ?) in the bottom of the vessel, and put three bricks round about the vessel, of new bricks, (14) and place seven clean loaves on the bricks that are round the vessel and bring a pure child that has been tested (15) in his ears before, that is, is profitable in proceeding with the vessel. You make him sit on a new [brick] and you also sit (16) on another brick, you being at (?) his face, otherwise said, his back, and you put your hand before [his] eyes, [his eyes being] closed and call down (17) into the middle of his head seven times. When you have finished, you take your hand from before his eyes, you [make him bend over] the vessel; you put your hand (18) to his ears, you take hold of them with your hand also, you ask the child saying, 'Do you [? see . . .]?' If he says, 'I see a (19) darkness,' you say to him 'Speak, saying, "I see thy beautiful face, and do thou [hear my salutation ?], O great god Anubis!"'

---

water to revive, in the story of the Two Brothers. *qs-ʿnḫ* might similarly be 'quicklime.'

l. 19. *wšte* is probably to be restored at the end of the gap, as in ll. 2, 26. The translation may be 'and do thou [pray to] the great god Anubis.'

20. e·ʾr-k wḫ a ʾr-f n hne wʿet-k e·ʾr-k mḥ yr·t-k n py kys e·ʾr-k [ḥms ḥr? p hne?] a ḫ p nt ḥry e yr·t-k

21. ḫtm e·ʾr-k ʿš p ʿš nt ḥry n sp VII e·ʾr-k wn yr·t-k e·ʾr-k šn·t-f a mt·t nb [nt e·ʾr-k wḫ-f? . . .] ḫr ʾr-k-f n θ n p hw

22. n mḥ IV n p wrš šʿ p hw n mḥ XV nte . . . pe e ʿḥ mḥ wz·t [šn hn]e wʿet a nw

23. a p wtn n p rʿ z-mt·t [a·]wn n-y t p·t t mw·t n n ntr·w my [nw-y a p wt]n n p rʿ e-f ḫty-ḫn[t]

24. ḫn-s z ʾnk Gb ʾrpe ntr·w šll p nt e-ẏ ʾr nʾm-f mbḥ p rʿ pe y[t e-tbe] n mt·t·w ʾr še n t·t

25. ʾy ḥkne·t wr·t nb qnḥ·t tʾ-rʿ-št(?) a·wn n-y t nb ʾyḫ·[w a·wn] n-y t p·t ḥy[t]·t my

26. wšte-y n n wpt·w [z] ank Gb ʾrpe ntr·w ʾy p VII stn hy p [VII mnt] k syt nb šfe·t

27. sḥz t by nn(?) hy rw(?) mi rw(?) nn(?) k kke hy ḫnt-ybt·w

28. nwn wr ḫe hy by sre by ʾmnt·w hy [by by·w k] kke k k·w

---

l. 22. *ʿḥ mḥ wz·t*, i.e. at full moon.

*šn hne wʿet* = *σκεψη δια λεκανης αυτοπτον*, Pap. Bibl. Nat. l. 162; *αυθοπτικη λεκανομαντεια*, ib. l. 221; and *αυτοπτ(ικος) λογος*, B. M. Pap. XLVI. 53.

This passage to the end of the column is repeated in 27/1–12.

l. 23. *ḫty ḫn[t]*. The parallel 27/2 gives in hieratic *ḫt* followed by the nose *ḫnt* and the det. of a boat. *ḫt* means 'float down the river,' 'go north,' and *ḫnt*, 'sail up the river,' 'go south.' With this clue it is easy to read in Leemans' facsimile the verb *ḫty* in demotic, written as in the word *mḫty*, V. 1, with its proper det. of water, and following it the verb *ḫnt*, also in demotic, with its proper det. the boat. Thus, though Leemans' facsimile cannot be confirmed owing to the wear of the papyrus, it is clear that we have a compound expression *ḫty-ḫnt*, 'go down and up.' This is the proper order for the two verbs, as is shown by *ḫn m ḫd m ḫnt*, 'rowing to and fro,' in the Westcar Papyrus, V. 4. It of course refers to the sinking to the horizon and rising to the zenith of the sun-boat.

l. 24. *rpʿ ntr·w* is a very ancient title of Geb.

l. 25. *ḥkne·t*, cf. Lanzone, Diz. Mit., 855; Maspero, Rec. tr., i. 21.

l. 26. Whether the number 7 originally acquired its sacred character in Babylonia or not, it had that character in Egypt, cf. Brugsch, Thes.,

(20) If you wish to do it by vessel alone, you fill your eyes with this ointment, you sit (?) [over the vessel ?] as aforesaid, your eyes being (21) closed; you utter the above invocation seven times, you open your eyes, you ask him concerning everything [that you wish (?)]... you do it from the (22) fourth day of the lunar month until the fifteenth day, which is the half-month when the moon fills the *uzat*.

[A] vessel-[inquiry] alone in order to see (23) the bark of Phre. Formula: 'Open to me heaven, O mother of the gods! Let [me see the ba]rk of Phre descending and ascending (24) in it; for I am Geb, heir of the gods; prayer is what I make before Phre my father [on account of] the things which have proceeded from me. (25) O Heknet, great one, lady of the shrine, the Rishtret (?), Open to me, mistress of the spirits, [open] to me, primal heaven, let (26) me worship the Angels! [for] I am Geb, heir of the gods. Hail! ye seven Kings, ho! ye [seven Mônts], bull that engendereth, lord of strength (27) that lighteth the earth, soul of the abyss; ho! lion as lion of (?) the abyss, bull of the night, hail! thou that rulest the people of the East, (28) Noun, great one, lofty one, hail! soul of a ram, soul of the people of the West, hail! [soul of souls, bull] of the night,

---

117 seqq.; LEPS., Todtenb. Vorw., p. 6; Pap. Ebers LIV. 19 (eighteenth dynasty), the 7 Hathors (nineteenth dynasty, Pap. Orb. ix. 8; BR., Thes., 800) and the 42 assessors in the Book of the Dead, ch. 125. The occurrence of 7 spirits in the very ancient chapter 17 of the Book of the Dead is of special importance.

The 7 kings are not elsewhere mentioned. '4 Mônts in their cities' occurs in the text, 'Que mon nom fleurisse' (LIEBLEIN, x. 3, and parallel passages), and 7 is a number associated with Hermonthis, the city of Mônt (BRUGSCH, Relig., 164, 7 Hathors and 7 Horus, L. D., iv. 63 c).

l. 27. The reading of the name 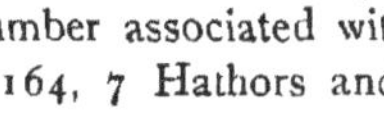 is uncertain. *Rw*, an obscure lion-god (Hieroglyphs, pp. 17, 18).

29. s' nw·t a·wn n-y ank wb-t 'r pr n Gb ḳy [ank y·y·]y e·e·e [he·he·he]

30. h-ʿo h-ʿo h-ʿo ank e-nep-ʿo myryp-ʿo-rʿ mʿ·t(?) 'b thy[by-ʿo 'rw·]wy . . . [yʿh-ʿo]

31. z-mt snf n *ⲥⲙⲟⲩⲛⲉ* snf n *ⲕⲟⲩⲕⲟⲩⲡⲉⲧ* snf n *ⲉ[ⲙⲟⲩⲗϫ]* ʿnḫ-'m·w [snw-p·t]

32. ʿo-'mn qs(?)-ʿnḫ ḫstb n mʿ·t ḫl p-tgs-'S·t nt 'r m bnn·t [nte-k smt yr·t]-k n'm-f t·t(?) [rym ?]

33. n by-ʿo-n-p·t n wʿ ḫ n hr n 'ny nge ḫ n hbyn [nte-k mr-k] a pe-k qte [n wʿ·t]

34. pke n šr-bne·t ḥwt n [wʿ] mʿ e-f θse wbe p rʿ bn-s t . . . . . yr·t-k n . . . .

35. a ḫ p nt sḫ ar-f

## Col. XI.

1. r n t ḥse·t 'm n-y p . . . . . . . . pe-k rn nfr Tḥwt ys sp-sn 'm n-y

2. my m'-y ḥr-k nfr ty n p-hw . . . . . . e-y n ky ʿʿn nte-k šme . . .

3. n ḥs 'e n pe-k ls n . . . . . . stm-]k ḫrw-y n p-hw nḥm-k-t mw 'ḫy nb t·w

4. r bn(?) nb hy p nte ḫbr-f n . . . . . . . . . ḫbr-f ʿo št a·pry ntr ḫr wt·t-f

---

l. 29. 'Son of Nut' might be either Osiris or Set, probably here the former: 'soul (*b'*) of Nut' is a possible reading.

l. 30. Anepo may be 'great Anubis' or 'elder Anubis.'

The gloss ⲧⲟⲩ may be incomplete, in 27/9 it is ⲟⲩϩⲟⲩ: the hieratic probably reads .

l. 32. *p-tgs-'S·t*, pronounced perhaps *pteksese*. Cf. πιτταξις, the fruit of the κρανεια or cornel-tree.

l. 33. *ḫ n hr*, apparently the name of some object made of wood, lit. wood or stick of satisfaction, possibly the kohl-stick.

*'ny*, possibly Eg. *ʿnnw* (Eb.) = *ʿwn* = *wʿn*, 'juniper' (Loret, Fl. Phar., 2nd ed., p. 41), the αρκευθιτις of the Greek papyri. Its juice is used as a writing ink in Louvre dem. Mag. V. 20.

*mr-k a pe-k qte*, the restoration is from the parallel 27/11. The bull (?) of bulls, (29) son of Nut, open to me, I am the Opener of earth, that came forth from Geb, hail! [I am I, I,] I, E, E, E, [He, He, He,] (30) Ho, Ho, Ho; I am Anepo, Miri-po-re, Maat (?) Ib, Thi[bio, Ar]oui, Ouoou, [Iaho.'] (31) Formula: blood of a *smun*-goose, blood of a hoopoe, blood of a n[ightjar], *ankh-amu* plant, [*senepe* plant], (32) 'Great-of-Amen' plant, *qes-ankh* stone, genuine lapis-lazuli, myrrh, 'footprint-of-Isis' plant, pound, make into a ball, [you paint] your [eyes] with it; put (?) a goat's-[tear] (33) in (?) a 'pleasure-wood' of *ani* or ebony wood, [you bind it (?)] around (?) you [with a] (34) strip of male-palm fibre in [an] elevated place opposite the sun after putting [the ointment as above on] your eyes ... (35) according to what is prescribed for it.

## Col. XI.

1. A spell of giving favour: 'Come to me, O....... thy beautiful name. O Thoth, hasten (*bis*); come to me. (2) Let me see thy beautiful face here to-day....... [I stand (?)] being in the form of an ape; and do thou greet (?) me (3) with praise and adoration (?) with thy tongue of... [Come unto me] that thou mayest hearken to my voice to-day, and mayest save me from all things evil (4) and all slander (?). Ho! thou whose form is of .....his great and mysterious form, from whose be-

---

meaning 'to your side' is indicated by 21/12, *mr-k a pe-k ḥr* probably referring to a phylactery or knot tied at a particular place.

Col. XI.

l. 1. *t ḥse·t*, apparently not *t ḫp ḥse·t* as in l. 20. Cf. 12/21.

l. 2. *šme* (?), cf. *šm* 18/9, but with different det. One may perhaps conjecture *šm·t*, 'favour (?) me,' here; it is hardly ϣωⲙ, 'wash,' 'purify' (of clothes, Bsciai, Rec. trav., vii. 27).

l. 3. Cf. ll. 16–17, and Pleyte, Chap. Suppl., Pl. 128, *nḥm-k wi mʿ iḫ·t nb dw* (var. *iḫ·t nb bin dw*) *ḫpr m ʿwy n rm·t ntr·w iḫ·w mt·w*.

l. 4. *r bn* may mean 'evil spell.'

5. nt ḥtp a mt(?) n N ank . . . . . . . . n t srỉ·t(?) ʿo·t nt e pyr Hʿp(?)

6. ḫr-s(?) ank p ḥr n šfe·t ʿo . . . . . . by m s·w-f ank syf šps

7. nt n pr rʿ ank p nem šps nt m tpḥ·t . . . . . . [h]b n s·w n mʿ·t nt ḥtp n ʾN

8. ank p nb ḫrwy ʿo nb *tm mʾ* pḥt m . . . . . . . [rn]-yt (?) ank sre s sre srpt-my-[sr] θs-pḫr

9. rn-yt ʾḫ-ḫpr-sr(?) rn-yt n mʿ·t sp-sn my n-y ḥs mr·t [šfe·t ne-ḥr mn a·ms] mn n p-hw nte-f t n-y ʾḫy nb nfr

10. nte-f t n·y kew tfew nte-f ʾr mt·t nb nt e-y [a wḫ-s nte-k tm t ʾr-f(?)] the a·ʾr-y a ʾr n-y mt·t bn(?) nte-f z n-y mt·t

11. e mst-s m hw pn m grḥ pn m ʾbt pn m rnp·t tn m wne·t(?) . . . . . . e p rʿ a sḫt ḥt-w nte-f knm

12. yr·t-w nte-f t ḫp p kke m ḥr-w z ank byrʿy . . . [rʿ]y ḫre-tn rʿy ank s Sḫm·t

13. ank bygt k lt ank gʿt s gʿt nte . . . . . ty·t nte ḥtp a mt(?) m h·t-ʿo·t m ʾN

14. ank s Ḥkne·t nb mke·t nt ʿrf n ḫne·t . . . . . nte n nḫt·w ʿo apḥt m sw-f

---

l. 5. *ḥtp a mt* (?), cf. l. 13. *mt* (?) is written differently from ⲙⲏⲧⲉ and may well be a masculine word, such as *mt*, 'depth.' It can hardly be ⲙⲏⲣ.

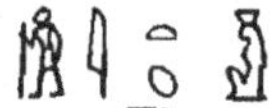 *srỉ·t* seems a possible reading.

*pyr*. The reading of the following words is uncertain. The construction with  (ⲉⲧⲉ) suggests *nt e pyr Ḥp* (cf. V. 5/1) *ḫr-s*, and the facsimile admits of it.

l. 7. *pr rʿ*, 'House of Re,' Heliopolis.

l. 8. *nb ḫrwy*. It seems as if the scribe had substituted 'hostility' for *ḫrwy*, 'testicles,' unless the words here are mere gibberish.

The tail of  *sr* is traceable in the gap after  in the Leiden facsimile.

l. 9. Cf. l. 17 for the restoration.

l. 11. *mst-s*, probably for *mst-y-s*, 'which I hate,' unless it be passive, 'which is hated.' Note the present sense of the *sḏm-f* in a relative clause, apparently confined in demotic to the verbs *mr*, 'love,' and *mst*, 'hate' (see chapter on Grammar).

getting came forth a god, (5) who resteth deep (?) in Thebes; I am ...... of the great Lady, under whom cometh forth the Nile, (6) I am the face of reverence great ......... soul (?) in his protection; I am the noble child (7) who is in the House of Re: I am the noble dwarf who is in the cavern ....... the ibis as a true protection, who resteth in On; (8) I am the master of the great foe, lord of the obstructor (?) of semen, mighty ...... my name (?) I am a ram, son of a ram, Sarpot Mui-Sro (and vice versa) (9) is my name, Light-scarab-noble (?) is my true name (*bis*); grant me praise and love [and reverence from N. son of] N. to-day, and let him give me all good things, (10) and let him give me nourishment and fat things, and let him do for me everything which I [wish for; and let him not] injure me so as to do me harm, nor let him say to me a thing (11) which (I) hate, to-day, to-night, this month, this year, [this] hour (?)... [But as for my enemies ?] the sun shall impede their hearts and blind (12) their eyes, and cause the darkness to be in their faces; for I am Birai... rai, depart ye (?), Rai; I am the son of Sochmet, (13) I am Bikt, bull of Lat, I am Gat, son of Gat, whose ..... the Underworld, who rests deep (?) in the Great Residence in On, (14) I am son of Heknet, lady of the protecting bandage (?), who binds with thongs (?).... [I am the ....] phallus (?) which the great and mighty Powers guard,

---

*knm*. Cf. Brit. Mus. Gr. Pap. XLVI, l. 488, and the early Christian curse invoking blindness (Crum, A. Z., 96. 85).

l. 12. ⲣⲁⲓ̈, with det. of hide, may be the name of the lion (?), but there is a tendency to write ⲁⲓ words with this det. Cf. ϩⲁⲉⲓ, 7/33.

*ḥre-ln rʿy* suggests a fanciful writing for 'be far from me (*a r-y*, ⲁⲣⲁⲓ̈).

'Son of Sochmet,' perhaps Nefertem or Mihos, both being lion gods.

l. 13. The 'Great Residence in On' is the name of the temple of the Sun at Heliopolis.

l. 14. *nht*. Cf. Rit. Pamonth, ii. 8, 'Hear ye, O divine powers of

15. nt ḥtp mw ḫn pr-wbst·t ank p ʿmʿm ntr nt . . . . . ḫn sḫym·t nb ʾy·t nb ʿot(?)

16. rn-yt ʾḫ-ḫpr-sr(?) rn-yt n mʿ·t sp-sn ʾy ny ntr·w tre-w [a·z-y rn-w(?)] ty n p-hw ʾm-n n·y stm-tn n e·z-y n p-hw

17. nḥm-tn[-t] m nene nb ze nb ʾḫy nb t nb m hw pn my n-y ḥs·t mr·t šf[e·t ne-ḥr] t mn p pr-ʿo erme pe-f mšʿ

18. p tw erme ne-f ʾw·w nte-f ʾr mt·t nb nt e-y a zt-w n-f erme(?) [rm nb nt e-w a·nw(?)] a·ʾr-y nt e-y a sze erme-w nt e-w a sze

19. erme-y ḫn ḥwt nb s-ḥm·t nb ḫm-ḫl nb ḫl-ʿo nb ḥr nb . . . . . [n p] t tre-f [nt e-w] a nw a·ʾr-y ḫn ny wne·tw n p-hw

20. nte-w ty ḫp te·t ḥse·t n ḥt-w n mt·t nb nt e-y a . . . . n mne erme n nt e-w a ʾy n-y e sḫr ḫfe(?) nb·w(?)

21. ys sp-sn tkr sp-sn e b-ʾr te-y zt-w nte-y whm zt·w . . . [ʾ]h *ϵϵn* n mnḥ tbt(?) nte-k ty-f

22. a ḫn wʿ(?) sšn ke-z tšps tp nge nḥe n bq e-f . . . . n *ⲛⲉⲛⲉⲃⲉ* ar-f ḥr ʿnt tp ḥnʿ pr·w(?)

---

Bubastis, who have come out of your shrines,' and below, V. 33/5; I Kham. iv. 7; Griff., High Priests, p. 109.

l. 15. *ʿmʿm*. Cf. 13/11, 13, and in cipher ⲉⲙⲙⲙ 24/34, V. 32/2. This must be the shrew-mouse. Here it appears connected with Letopolis, where the shrew-mouse was sacred to the blind Horus (Renouf, P. S. B. A., viii. 155). In 13/11 the animal is prescribed to produce blindness, and in 13/12 and 24/34 it produces death in a man, and in V. 32/2 erotic feeling in a woman. The *ʿmʿm*, with determinative of an animal, is prescribed in Pap. Eb. 91/10; and in Pap. Kah. 7/9 the remains of a determinative will suit very well the picture of a mouse. It is curious that the cipher writing yielding ⲉⲙⲙⲙ (which is certainly the same creature, cf. 13/19–21 with V. 32) makes its name almost identical with Sah. ⲁⲙⲏⲙ, which in Sap. 12/8 corresponds to σφῆκες of LXX. In Coptic, however, the shrew-mouse is ⲁⲗⲓⲗ : ⲁⲗⲓⲗⲓ (Peyr., Lex. and Gramm.). The μυγαλος (*sic*) is prescribed several times in Pap. Bibl. Nat. in ἀγωγαί.

*Sḫym* (Ⲃⲟⲩ-ϣⲏⲙ) and *ʾy·t* are both names of Letopolis in the Delta. The last group in the line looks like *ʿḥ*, but is probably intended for *wʿḥ*.

l. 16. For the restoration cf. 10/7.

(15) which rests in Bubastis; I am the divine shrew-mouse which [resteth with-] in Skhym; lord of Ay, sole (?) lord ... (16) is my name Light-scarab-noble (?) is my true name (*bis*). Ho! all ye these gods, [whose names I have spoken] here to-day, come to me, that ye may hearken to that which I have said to-day (17) and rescue [me] from all weakness (?), every disgrace, everything, every evil (?) to-day; grant me praise, love [and reverence before] such an one, the King and his host, (18) the desert and its animals; let him do everything which I shall say to him together with [every man who shall see] me or to whom I shall speak or who shall speak (19) to me, among every man, every woman, every child, every old man, every person [or animal or thing (?) in the] whole land, [which] shall see me in these moments to-day, (20) and let them cause my praise to be in their hearts of everything which I shall [do] daily, together with those who shall come to me, to (?) overthrow every enemy (?), (21) hasten (*bis*) quickly (*bis*), before I say them or repeat them.' Over an ape of wax.

An oxyrhynchus (?) fish—you put it (22) in prime lily otherwise *tesheps*-oil or moringa (?) oil which [has been ... and you put liquid ?] styrax to it, with prime frank-

---

l. 17. *šfe·t.* In the conspiracy against Rameses III (?) of the twentieth dyn., we hear of a spell to give *nrwy* and *šfe·t*, 'valour and respect.' NEWBERRY, Amherst Pap. II, l. 2.

l. 20. The last words may perhaps be *ḫf nb* (?), 'every enemy,' *nb* being written over the line as a correction of the plural signs. 'Enemy' is written *ḫf* (without *t*) as in I Rhind dem. 2, 3. The passage is very obscure.

l. 21. *'h*, for a similar direction following the invocation, cf. V. 33/8. The fish is here masc., and therefore different from that in 12/31.

l. 22. *sšn*, 'lotus,' may be an error for *skn sšn*, 25/26, σουσινον, DIOSC. i. 62, oil of lilies (κρινα), and ελαιον σουσινον, Pap. Berl. II. 249.

*tšps* as an oil, BR., Wtb., 1602, made from laurus cinnamomum according to LORET, Flore Phar., 2nd ed. p. 51.

*bq.* v. LORET, Rec. trav., vii. 101.

πεπεϐε. v. LORET, Rec. trav., xvi. 148 لُبْنى styrax.

23. wr-mr·t ḫn wᶜ ḥn(?) n thne nte-k ʾny wᶜ ᶜnḫ n . . . . . . ths-f n py nḥe nt ḥry nte-k ᶜš

24. ny [sḫ ?]·w ar-f n sp VII mbḥ p rᶜ n twe e b-ʾr te-k sz[e wbe] rm nb n p t nte-k šty-f nte-k ths ḥr-k nʾm-f

25. nte-k ḫᶜ [p]ᶜnḫ ḫn t·t-k nte-k mšᶜ a mᶜ nb . . . . . ʾwt mšᶜ nb ḫr te-f t ḫp n-k

26. ḥs·t ᶜo·t ʾwt-w m šs sp-sn py sp n sḫ pa p pr-ᶜo [Ntryw (?)]š pe mn p nt (ne-)ᶜne-f ar-f

## Col. XII.

1. [wᶜ ky(?) a t ʾre] s-ḥm·t mr ḥwt hepwbᶜlsᶜmw sttr(?) I hbʾryr(?) . . . . . sttr(?) I

2. qwšt sttr(?) I . . . . . . . . n sty sttr(?) I mrwe sttr(?) I nḥe n mᶜ·t lq II e·ʾr-k nt ny [pḫre·tw(?)]

3. e·ʾr-k ty-sw a wᶜ [ᶜngen(?)] e-f wᶜb nte-k t p nḥe n pe-w ḥr·w ḫr t ḥ·t n p wrš wᶜ hw a·ʾre p w[rš]

4. ḫp e·ʾr-k ʾny wᶜ·t qeš . . . . [k]m(?) e-s ʾr n tbᶜ IX ke-z VII n ḫy·t e yr·t-s šel n ʾwn n [p nt(?)]

---

l. 26. The *pa* is for **ⲡⲁ-**. **ⲡⲉⲣⲟ** in O. C. Par. corresponds to *p pr-ᶜo* in 21/2. So also we have in B. M. Pap. XLVI, l. 113 *εγω ειμι αγγελος του φαπρω οσορουνωφρις*, 'of Pharaoh Osoronnophris,' where *φαπρω* = our *pa p pr-ᶜo*. Undoubtedly the initial letter of *pr-ᶜo* had already been lost by assimilation to the article. The tautology of *του φα-* is precisely the same as in *Αμενωφις του Παaπιος*, 'Amenophis, son of Hapis,' in Josephus, Contra Ap. i. 26.

. . . . š. The only kings whose names end in š are Darius, Xerxes, Artaxerxes, and the native Khebbesh. Of these Darius is doubtless the name to be restored here; cf. Diod. Sic. i. 95, and for his reputation as a magician in particular, *μαγικων διδασκαλος*, Porphyry, de Abstin., iv. 16. That kings, as well as aspirants to the throne, used these arts is suggested by the spell 'of Rameses III' being given to the herdsman Penhuyban in order to give him 'valour and respect.' See note to l. 17 above.

### Col. XII.

l. 1. Restore [*wᶜ ky* (?) *a t ʾre*] *s-ḥm·t* from 25/23, 31.

*hepwbᶜlsᶜmw*: cf. *υποβαλσαμινα* (*ξυλα*) Leyden Pap. W. ix. 21 = *οποβαλσαμον*, 'juice of balsam tree'; cf. Sigismund, Aromata, pp. 14, 15.

**ⲙⲁⲗⲁⲃⲁⲑⲟⲩ** = *μαλαβαθρον*, 'leaf of Laurus Cassia'; Sigismund,

incense together with seeds of (23) 'great-of-love' plant in a metal (?) vase; you bring a wreath of flowers of..... ... and you anoint it with this oil as above, and recite (24) these spells over it seven times before the sun in the morning, before speaking to any man on earth; you extract it, you anoint your face with it, (25) you place the wreath in your hand, and proceed to any place [and be] amongst any people; then it brings you (26) great praise among them exceedingly. This scribe's feat is that of King [Dariu]s (?); there is no better than it.

## Col. XII.

(1) [A method for making] a woman love a man. Opobalsamum, one stater(?); malabathrum, one stater(?). (2) *kusht*, one stater(?); scented ...., one stater(?); *merue*, one stater(?); genuine oil, two *lok*; you pound these [medicaments]. (3) You put them into a clean [vessel], you add the oil on the top of them one day before the lunar period (?); when the lunar period (?) (4) comes, you take a black *Kesh* ... -fish measuring nine fingers—another says seven—in length, its eyes being variegated (?) of

---

Aromata, p. 33, and Lemm., Kopt. Apocr. Apostelacten (Mél. Asiat. t. x. p. 351). It occurs in magic prescriptions, Leyden Pap. W. i. 16, ix. 10. The demotic group *hb* .... corresponding to it is strange in form and difficult to read: there seems to be a gap between the *r* and the measure.

Graphically ⊙, ⊙ (fem.) are hieroglyphic equivalents of the demotic for ⲕⲓⲧⲉ, 'didrachma,' but from 24/15, 18 the former should be a small multiple of the latter. στατηρ (Copt. ⲥⲁⲧⲉⲉⲣⲉ, fem.) is common as a weight = 'tetradrachma,' in Ptolemaic and Roman papyri.

l. 2. *qwšt*, perhaps κοστος (Diosc. i. 15), which follows μαλαβαθρον in a prescription, Pap. Bibl. Nat. l. 2680; cf. Leyd. Pap. W. i. 16, ix. 10.

*lq*. The Hebrew log is ·56 litre, about one pint, and the Coptic ⲗⲟⲕ translates κοτυλη, which in all its varieties is no larger than a pint.

*ny* [*pḫre·tw* (?)]: cf. 29/28, 29.

l. 3. *wꜥ* [*ꜥngen* (αγγειον of l. 11) *e*]-*f* *wꜥb* seems to fill the gap, which is too wide in the Pl. of vol. ii. in this and the following line according to the evidence of the succeeding lines.

4. *qcš* ..., in l. 27 *qš* ..., in both cases broken. In l. 9 it is referred

5. [e·ʾr-k] gm ḥn wʿ mw(?) . , . . . nte-k ty-s a py nḥe nt ḥry n hw II e·ʾr-k ʿš n py ʿš ar-f n twe . . . .

6. e b-ʾr te-k ʾy n p [bl n pe-k(?)] ʿy e b-ʾr te-k sze wbe rm nb n p t a·ʾr p(?) hw II sny [e·ʾr-k]

7. ḫrp a bl n twe e·ʾr[-k še] a wʿ km e·ʾr-k ʾny wʿ šlḥe n elle e b·ʾr te-f wtḥ elle . . . .

8. e·ʾr-k fy·t-f n te-k·t [t·t n] . . . . e·ʾr-k ty-f a te-k·t t·t n wnm e·ʾr-f ʾr n tbʿ VII e·ʾr-k θy·t-f [a pe-k(?)]

9. ʿy nte-k ʾny p [tbt(?)] a ḥry ḥn p nḥe nte-k mr-s (*sic*) a py-s st n tyb n mḥe nte-k ʿyḫ·t-s m-s [zz-f]

10. n p ḫ n elle [nte-k ḫʿ] p nk nt ḫr nḥe ḫrr-s šʿ nte-s zlzl p nt n ḥe·t-s a ḫr[y]

11. e p ʿngen nt ḫr[r-s] ḥr wʿ·t tbe nmy šʿ ke hw III a·ʾre p hw III sny e·ʾr-k [ʾny·t-s]

12. a ḫry e·ʾr-k qs[-s] n ḫl ḥsm ḥbs n š-stn e·ʾr-k ḫʿ-s n wʿ mʿ e-f hep ḥn pe-[k pr]

13. nge e·ʾr-k ʾr ke hw II e·ʾr-k ʿš a p nḥe ʿn a hw VII e·ʾr-k ḥrḥ ar-f e·ʾr[-k wḥ (?)]

14. a t ʾr-f te-f yp·t e[ʾr-k th]s pe-k mt n ḥwt ḥnʿ pe-k ḥr e·ʾr-k str erme t s-ḥm·t nt e·ʾr-k ʾr-f aʾr-s

15. n sḫ nt e·ʾr-k ʿš-w a p nḥe ank šwy(?) glʿbʾn-ʿo ank rʿ ʾnk qm-rʿ ʾnk s rʿ ank

16. syšt s šwy(?) qme(?) n mw n ʾN py srrf nt n ʾBt nte·t tp·t wr·t wr ḥyq

---

to apparently as *p tbt*, 'the fish'; and in l. 31 is written with the fish sign, but with feminine article and termination. It seems characteristically female, the gender of the pronoun changing to fem. ungrammatically immediately after the masculine *tbt*, in l. 9, and no doubt it was sacred to some goddess. The lates niloticus (which according to MM. Lortet and Hugounenq is found of all sizes mummified at Latopolis, and is therefore the Latus, Ann. du Serv. iii. 15) is called in Arabic *qišr*, قشر.

l. 6. *a·ʾr*. The original reads perhaps *a ʾr p*. In either case it is probably a slip for *a ʾre p*.

l. 8. Vice versa of 'Lotus Lion-Ram' is 'Lion-Ram Lotus,' not 'Ram Lion Lotus'; see note to 1/12.

l. 9. *p* [*tbt*]. The remains favour this restoration. The word does

the colour of (?) the . . . (5) [which you (?)] find in a water (?) . . . you put it into this oil above-mentioned for two days; you recite this formula to it (the oil) at dawn . . . (6) before going [out of your] house, and before speaking to any man on earth. When two days have passed [you] (7) rise early in the morning [and go] to a garden; you take a vine-shoot before it has ripened grapes, (8) you take it with your left hand, you put it into your right hand—when it has grown seven digits (in length)—you carry it [into your] (9) house, and you take the [fish] out of the oil, you tie it by its tail with a strip (?) of flax, you hang it up to . . . (10) of (?) the vine-wood. [You place] the thing containing oil under it until it (the fish) pours out by drops that which is in it downwards, (11) the vessel which is under [it] being on a new brick for another three days; when the three days have passed, you [take it] (12) down, you embalm [it] with myrrh, natron, and fine linen; you put it in a hidden place or in [your chamber] (13) You pass two more days; you recite to the oil again for seven days; you keep it; when you [wish] (14) to make it do its work, you anoint your phallus and your face; you lie with the woman for whom you do it. (15) The spells which you recite to the oil, 'I am Shu, Klabano, I am Re, I am Komre, I am son of Re, I am (16) Sisht (?), son of Shu; a reed (?) of the water of On, this gryphon which is in Abydos. Thou (fem.) art Tepe-were (first, great) great of sorcery,

---

not occur elsewhere in the papyrus. For the change of gender in *mr-s* see note to l. 4.

*m-s* [*zz-f*], see l. 29.

l. 12. *pe-*[*k pr*] restored from the parallel l. 31.

l. 13. *nge* here and in l. 31 seems to be placed after the alternative phrase, as is the case with *r-pw* in older Egyptian.

l. 14. *a'r-s* for *ar-s*, **epoc**, 'to her.'

l. 15. *šwy*. The name of the god Shu (cf. l. 20) is here falsely written like **ται**.

17. t ʿre·t ʿnḥ·t nte·t [p w]tn p šy n wʿ-pke my n-y ḥs·t mr·t šfe·t ne-ḥr

18. ʿte·t nb s-ḥm·t nb mr·t pe rn n mte ʿš nte-s ʿn ʾnk šwy(?) klʾkyn-ʿo-k ank yʾrn

19. ʾnk gʿmren ʾnk se . . . . . pe pʾeaypʿf ynpen ntynhs gʿm-r-n mw n ʾN ʾnk

20. šwy(?) šʿbw šʿ . . . . . . šʿbʿh-ʿo lʿh-ʾy-lʿhs(?) lʿh-ʿe·t p ntr ʿo nt ḥr pr-ybt·t

21. lʿbrʿthʿʿ a[nk p] srrf nt n ʾBt ky nʾm-y(?) ʿn(?) a t ḥs·t n ḥwt a ḥr s-ḥm·t θs-pẖr a ḥr . . .

22. nte-t t wr·t t wr ḥyq . . . . ʾkš·t s·t n rʿ t nb ʿre·t nte-t Sẖm ʿo·t nb ʾs·t

23. ʾr sẖme sʿbe nb a . . . . . . t n p rʿ n t wz·t a·ms ʿḥ n t XV·t n grḥ nte-t qm . . . .

24. wr nwn nte-t qm . . . . . . . wr·t nt n ḥ·t-bnbn m(?) ʾN nte-t t yʿl n nb [nte-t t]

25. skte·t p wtn n p rʿ . . . . lʿnzʾ p ẖrt p šr n t wʿyʿnʿyne·t t pyt·t n t . . . . .

26. n gwg ny št-t . . . . n by-wekm t ḥs·t t mr·t nta p rʿ pe-t yt ty-s n-t m[y] . . .

27. n-y a ẖry ẖn py nḥe . . . . . ḥr ḥt yr·t nb s-ḥm·t nb nt e-y ʾn·nʿ a ẖn a ḥr-w a wʿ·t qš . . . .

28. n tbʿ IX e-s km nte[-k ty-s a] ẖn wʿ sknn n wrt nte-k ʾr-s n ḥsy ḥn-f nte-k ʾny·t[-s a ḥry]

---

l. 18. *ʿš nte-s ʿn.* The blank before *ʿš* is perhaps for the insertion of a word (*ke* (?)) in red ink; *nte-s* is ⲛⲧⲁⲥ, St., § 299, and the invocation is still to the fish.

l. 20. *lʿh-ʿe·t.* The plural of *ʿe-t*, 'limbs,' is ⲏⲟⲩ in O. C. Par. The singular may have been *ⲏⲉ.

l. 21. *nʾm-y.* Probably an error for *nʾm-f*, but the facsimile would admit of the reading *nʾm-w ʿn.*

l. 22. Thoueris is generally figured as a hippopotamus.

*ʾs·t* must be the place *ls·t*, dem. *ʾs*, mentioned in Brugsch, Dict. Geogr., pp. 70–71, as being under the rule of Sochmet.

l. 23. *wz·t*: sun or moon as eyes of heaven; cf. 8/8, 10/22, 29/23.

l. 24. *Ḥ·t-bnbn* [*m*] *ʾN* is the best restoration. The 'house of the obelisk' was a famous shrine in the temple of Heliopolis.

(17) the living uraeus, thou art the sun-boat, the lake of Ua-peke; grant to me praise, love, and lordship before (18) every womb, every woman. Love (?) is my true name.' [Another (?)] invocation of it again: 'I am Shu, Klakinok, I am Iarn, (19) I am Gamren, I am Se.... Paer(?)ipaf, Iupen, Dynhs, Gamrou, water of On, I am (20) Shu, Shabu, Sha...., Shabaho, Lahy-lahs, Lahei, the great god who is in the East (21) Labrathaa, I am that gryphon which is in Abydos.'

[Another] form of them (?) again (?) to give favour to a man before a woman and vice versa, before.... 'Thou art Thoueris, the great of sorcery, [cat (?)] of Ethiopia, daughter of Re, lady of the uraeus; thou art Sochmet, the great, lady of Ast, (23) who hast seized every impious person.... [eye-ball (?)] of the sun in the *uzat*, born of the moon at the midmonth at night, thou art Kam (?)..... (24) mighty, abyss, thou art Kam (?).... great one (fem.) who art in the House of the obelisk in On; thou art the golden mirror, [thou art ?] (25) the *sektet*-boat, the sun-boat of Re..... Lanza, the youth, the son of the Greek woman, the Amazon (?) in the ... (26) of dûm-palm fruit (?), these .... of Bywekem; the favour and love which the sun, thy father, hath given to thee, send [them] (27) to me down into this oil, before the heart, and eyes of (?) every woman before whom I come in.' [Invocation] to a *Kesh* ...-fish (28) of nine digits and black; [you put it] in an ointment of roses; you drown it therein; you

---

l. 25. *skte·t.* It is interesting to find this clear spelling, not *smkt·t*, which seems to be that of the Pyramid Texts.

*w'y'n'yne·t*, an extraordinary spelling for **ⲟⲩⲉⲉⲓⲛⲓⲛ**, 'Greek.'

*pyt·t.* *pdty* in Eg. seems to be a foreign soldier or mercenary. This is evidently a feminine derivative.

l. 26. *gwg* = *kwk* in Kufi, p. xx; probably the dûm-nut, as in Kufi it is evidently the fruit of a tree, so not **ϭⲟⲩϭ : ϫⲟⲩϫ**, carthamus.

l. 28. *sknn n wrt*, *μυρον ροδινον* of Pap. Bibl. Nat. l. 759. That it was of a consistency to choke a fish is seen by its use as a lamp-oil in 6/9.

29. nte-k ʿyẖ m-s zz[-f] . . . . . e·ʾr-k wḥ e·ʾr-k ty-s a wʿ ḥn(?) n yl e·ʾr-k (*sic*) wʿ ẖm n mw n sʿsmrem

30. erme wʿ ẖm n s-ʾS·t e-f . . . [e-f] nt nte-k ʿš ny ar-f n sp VII n hw VII wbe t pr n p rʿ e·ʾr-k ths ḥr-k nʾm[-f]

31. n p nw nt e·ʾr-k str erme s-ḥm·t [nte-k] qs t . . . ·t n ẖl ḥsm e·ʾr-k tms-s n pe-k pr n wʿ mʿ e-f hep nge

## Col. XIII.

1. p ky n prz ḥwt a s-ḥm·t s-ḥm·t a py-s hy

2. wy sp-sn ẖo sp-sn ʾr(?) Gb ẖbr-f n k nq-f . . . . mw·t-f Tfn·t m whm . . .

3. mw wwhe(?) p ʾb n yt-f ḥr-f p ẖyt n p nte by-f m st·t e ẖe-f (*sic*) m ʾn nte-f . . .

4. mḥ p t n st·t nte n tw·w syt n sʿl(?) p ẖyt n ntr nb ntr·t nb ʿnẖ wr lʿlʿt(?)

5. bʿrešʿk bel-kš . . . ḥwy mn p šr n t mn . . t mn t šr·t n t mn

6. my t st·t m-s ḥt-f t sḥt·t n pe-f mʿ n str e b(?) . . . . . n st·t n mst . . .

---

l. 29. *t*, or a similar word, has dropped out between *e·ʾr-k* and *wʿ*. Such omissions have often been supplied over the line by the scribe.

*sʿsmrem*, probably sisymbrium, of which there were two sorts, growing respectively on land and on water, Diosc. ii. 154–5. The former being also known as Αφροδιτης στεφανος, herba venerea (ib.), is very appropriate for this ἀγωγή. It may be mentha sylvestris, and the second species is nasturtium (Sprengel). Unfortunately the determinative is lost of our word, so that we cannot be sure that a plant was intended: cf. V. 13/7.

l. 30. *s-[n ?]ʾS·t.* Among the ingredients of a sacred oil, Pap. Boul. I. Pl. 38, col. 1, is a plant called by this name. Here there is no det.

l. 31. *t ẖʾ(?)·t* might mean 'the carcase,' but having no determinative almost certainly represents the *qeš* . . . -fish of ll. 6, 27.

### Col. XIII.

l. 1. For the subject, compare Leyd. Pap. Graec. V. col. 11, l. 15 (see Leemans' ed.), headed *wʿ prz*, διακοπος.

l. 2. The first sentence, as far as *p ẖyt*, is in clumsy archaistic language,

take it [out], (29) you hang it up by [its] head [. . . days (?)]: when you have finished you put it on a glass vessel; you [add] a little water of sisymbrium (30) with a little amulet (?)-of-Isis . . . . . and pounded; you recite this to it seven times for seven days opposite the rising of the sun. You anoint your head with [it] (31) in the hour when you lie with [any (?)] woman. [You] embalm the fish with myrrh and natron; you bury it in your chamber or in a hidden place.

## Col. XIII.

(1) The mode of separating a man from a woman and a woman from her husband. (2) 'Woe! (*bis*), flame! (*bis*); Geb assumed his form of a bull, coivit [cum filia ?] matris suae Tefnet, again . . . . (3) because (?) the heart of his father cursed (?) his face; the fury of him whose soul is as flame, while his body is as a pillar (?), so that (?) he . . . . . . . . . . (4) fill the earth with flame and the mountains shoot with tongues (?):—the fury of every god and every goddess Ankh-uer, Lalat (?), (5) Bareshak, Belkesh, . . . . . . be cast upon (?) N. the son of N. [and (?)] N. the daughter of N., (6) send the fire towards his heart and the flame in his place of

---

employing the obsolete *'b* for heart, *mw* for  or , the suffix with the noun *ḥbr*, the past *sḏm-f*, &c.

*wy sp-sn*: cf. Louvre dem. Mag. iii. 16.

*Geb* is Κρονος, the planet Κρονος being named 'Horus the Bull,' and Nut, daughter of Tefnut, is the heavenly cow in the Destruction des Hommes, &c. The restoration before 'his mother' is, however, very uncertain. Cf. the Greek myth of Κρονος, and Plutarch, de Iside et Or., cap. 12, where 'Ρεα is Nut.

l. 3. *ḥe-f*, 'his body,' must be for *ḥe·t-f*, but this spelling occurs elsewhere in the papyrus. Cf. 21/22.

*'n* might represent the city of On, but the determinative is apparently a stone.

l. 5. *ḥwy a* (?) *mn*, 'is cast upon (?) N.'

There are traces of writing covering 1½ inches at the end of this line, perhaps erased by the original scribe, and wholly illegible now.

7. a ḫn a ḥt-f n hte·t nb šʿ nte-f ḥwy t(?) mn t šr·t mn (*sic*) a bl ḫn ne-f ʿy·w e-s lk(?)

8. mst n ḥt-f e-s ḫr ḫnt(?) n ḥr-f my n-f p wywy p wʿwʿ p ʾhe(?) p ḫnt ʾwt-w

9. n hte·t nb šʿ nte-w prz a ne-w ʾre·w e bnp-w ḥtp a šwe a nḥe ***кмме*** *. . . . **р***

10. *ϣⲉⲗ* nte-k t ʾrp ar-w nte-k ʾr-w n wʿ twt(?) n Gb e wn wʿ ws n t·t-f

11. n p ʿmʿm nt ḫr še-f ar-w e·ʾr-k ʾny wʿ ʿmʿm nte-k ʾr-f n ḥsy ḫn hyn·w ***ммаоⲩ*** nte-k t swr p rm n (*sic*)

12. nʾm-f ḫr ʾr-f ***ϭⲱⲛⲙⲙ*** n p byl II e·ʾr-k nt pe-f ***ммоⲥⲉ*** ḥr nk nb(?) n wm nte-k t wm-f-s p rm ḫr ʾr-f(?)

13. ***ммоⲩⲛⲧⲟ*** nte-f ***ϣⲉϥⲉ*** nte-f ***ммоⲩ*** e·ʾr-k ʾr-f a ʾny s-ḥm·t e·ʾr-k ʾny wʿ ʿmʿm e·ʾr-k ḫʿ-f ḥr wʿ·t blz n

14. ḫr nte-k wḥ-f ḥr t *θ*se n wʿ ʿo nte-k t pe-f st ḫn wʿ·t(?) blz n ḫr nge yl ʿn nte-k wrḥ-f e-f ʿnḫ a ḫn

15. n p r n wʿ·t s·t-eyw n t s-ḥm·t nte-k . . . . -f n nb nte-k qs pe-f st nte-k t ḫl e-f nt ar-f nte-k ty-f a ḫn wʿ·t ʾlykt n nb

---

l. 7. At the end read *e-s ḫr* (?).

l. 9. **кмме** is probably the true native pronunciation of the word for gum, unaffected by the Greek.

l. 10. *twt* (?). The determinative of a star must mean that the planet form *Ḥr-p-k*, a bull-headed man standing with *was*-sceptre, is intended, Br., Thes., p. 68. With regard to the reading, the sign is the det. of *twt* in Bul. Pap. I. Pl. 37, l. 14, and in l. 15 stands for *twt*. *Twt*, 'figure,' seems to be the reading here, and wherever it occurs with the det. of divinity (15/10, &c.); but without det. (16/22, &c.) it means 'style,' 'method,' and is probably to be read *ky*. Max Müller, however (Rec. trav. ix. 26), shows reason for reading it *qte*, comparing Louvre dem. Mag. v. 1, vi. 19; *qte*, though apparently masc., may be the origin of the fem. **ϭⲟⲧ**.

l. 11. *hyn·w* **ммаоⲩ**, some water: cf. 21/13 *hyn·w ʾrt·t*.

l. 12. The word in cipher reads **моⲥⲉ**, a word unknown in Egyptian. Probably it is a mis-writing for **ⲥⲱⲙⲉ** (l. 17) = *swmʿ* (σωμα) of V. 32/5.

sleeping, the . . . of fire of hatred never [ceasing to enter] (7) into his heart at any time, until he cast N. daughter of N. out of his abode, she having (?) (8) hatred to his heart, she having quarrel to his face; grant for him the nagging (?) and squabbling (?), the fighting and quarrelling between them (9) at all times, until they are separated from each other, without agreeing again for ever.' Gum, . . . , (10) myrrh; you add wine to them; you make them into a figure of Geb, there being a *was*-sceptre in his hand.

(11) [The uses (?)] of the shrew-mouse (?) to which it is put (goes). You take a shrew-mouse (?), you drown it in some water; you make the man drink (12) of it; then he is blinded in his two eyes. Grind its body (?) with any piece of food, you make the man eat it, then he makes a (13) . . . and he swells up and he dies. If you do it to bring a woman, you take a shrew-mouse (?), you place it on a Syrian (14) pot, you put it on the back-bone (?) of a donkey, you put its tail in a Syrian pot or in a glass again; you let it loose (?) alive within (15) the door of a bath of the woman, you gild (?) it (*sic*) and embalm its tail, you add pounded myrrh to it, you

---

*wm-f-s p rm*: note the superfluous *f*.

l. 13. **ⲙⲟⲩⲛⲧⲟ**, probably a compound word, **ⲙⲟⲩ-ⲛ-ⲧⲟ**. It might mean 'water of spot (ⲧⲟⲉ)' or 'death of spot,' referring to a disease with spots or blisters.

*blz n ḫr*. Wine was imported from Syria in amphorae, but probably some special ware was denoted by this name.

l. 15. The word for bath is determined with the sign of fire: its name in Coptic is **ⲥⲓⲟⲟⲩⲛⲉ : ⲥⲉⲓⲱⲟⲩⲛⲓ** with variations; in the demotic there is no trace of the **ⲛ**, and it evidently means 'place o fwashings,' ***ⲥⲉ-ⲉⲓⲟⲟⲩⲉ**.

'You gild and embalm its tail' is perhaps the meaning.

l. 15. *ʾlykt* (fem.), an unknown word, apparently the *gswr*, 'ring,' of l. 27. It is perhaps to be connected with ἕλιξ or ἑλικτός. **ϩⲁⲗⲁⲕ**, 'ring,' and **ⲁⲗⲕⲟⲩ**, 'vase,' have been suggested, but these are both masculine, and ignore the *t*, which seems to be firm. The determinative appears to be that of silver, also found in *znf*, &c.

16. nte-k ty-s a pe-k tbʿ bn-s ʿš ny sẖ·w ar-f nte-k mšʿ a mʿ [nb ?] erme-f a(?) s-ḥm·t nb nt e·ʾr-k a mḥt nʾm-s ẖr [wẖ ?]-s m-s-k

17. ẖr ʾr-k-f e ʿḥ mḥ e·ʾr-k ʾr-f a t ʾre s-ḥm·t lyb m-s ḥwt e·ʾr-k fy pe-f *ⲥⲟⲙⲁ* e-f šwy e·ʾr-k nt[-f e·ʾr-k] fy

18. wʿ ḥm nʾm-f erme wʿ ḥm n snf n pe-k tbʿ n mḥ II n p sʿlʿpy[n] n tek·t t·t n . . . . e·ʾr-k tẖ-f erme-f e·ʾr-k ty-f

19. a wʿ z n ʾrp e·ʾr-k ty-f n t s-ḥm·t nte-s swr-f ẖr ʾr-s lyb [m-]s-k e·ʾr-k t pe-f *ⲥⲁϣⲉ* a wʿ ʾrp

20. nte p rm swr-f ẖr *ⲙⲧⲉϥ* ty hte·t nge ty-f a nk nb [n wm] e·ʾr-k t pe-f *ϩⲉⲧ* a wʿ ḥtm(?)

21. n nb nte-k ty-f a t·t-k nte-k mšʿ a mʿ nb ẖr te-f t ḥp n-k [ḥs·t mr·t šfe·]t e·ʾr-k ʾr wʿ *ⲃⲉϭ* n ḥsy ḥn

22. wʿ ʾrp nte-k t swr-s p rm ẖr *ⲙⲧⲉϥ* e·ʾr-k t p *ⲥⲁϣⲉ* n [wʿ gʿl]e n rʿqt a nk nb n wm

23. ẖr *ⲙⲧⲉϥ* e·ʾr-k t wʿ·t *ϩⲁϥⲗⲉⲗⲁ* n st II a p nḥe [nte-k psy·]t-s nte-k ths p rm nʾm-f ẖr . . . .

24. e·ʾr-k wẖ a t ḥp *ⲡⲁⲉⲓϣⲉ* ẖr rm nte-s tm lʿk-s wʿ·t *[ϩ]ⲁⲛⲧⲟⲩⲥ* [erme ?] *ϩⲁϥⲗⲉ[ⲗⲁ]* nte-k psy·t-w ẖr . . . .

25. nte-k zqm p rm nʾm-w e·ʾr-k wẖ a t ʾr-f *ⲧⲟⲩⲣ*(?) e·ʾr-k t . . . . ẖr ʾr-f *ⲧⲟⲩⲣ*(?) e·ʾr-k ty ḥnk(?) . . .

26. a yr·t-f n rm ẖr ʾr-f *ϭⲱⲛⲙ*

---

l. 16. 'The charms' are those at the foot of the column, l. 27 et seqq. There seems scarcely space for the *a* before *s-ḥm·t*, and it should no doubt be omitted.

l. 17. There is a variant version in V. col. 32 of the prescriptions in ll. 17–20.

l. 18. *sʿlʿpyn*. The finger is always thus elaborately described in the pap., the blood being used in erotica as here 15/4, 22, V. 32/7. It is evidently the Boh. ⲥⲉⲗⲟⲩⲡⲓⲛ. البنصر 'middle finger' in Kircher. But Sah. ⲥⲉⲗⲉⲡⲓⲛ is 'heart,' also *ὑποχόνδρια* (cf. 21/25, 33); and that a nerve connected the third (ring-) finger of the left hand with the heart is said

put it in a gold ring (?), (16) you put it on your finger after reciting these charms to it, and walk with it to any place, and any woman whom you shall take hold of, she [giveth herself (?)] unto you. (17) You do it when the moon is full. If you do it to make a woman mad after a man, you take its body, dried, you pound [it, you] take (18) a little of it with a little blood of your second finger, (that) of the heart (?), of your left hand; you mix it with it, you put it (19) in a cup of wine; you give it to the woman and she drinks it; then she has a passion for you. You put its gall into a (measure of) wine (20) and the man drinks it; then he dies at once; or (you) put it into any piece [of food]. You put its heart (?) into a seal-ring (?) (21) of gold; you put it on your hand, and go anywhere; then it brings you [favour, love, and] reverence. You drown a hawk in (22) a (measure of) wine; you make the man drink it, then he dies. You put the gall of an Alexandrian [weasel] into any food, (23) then he dies. You put a two-tailed lizard into the oil and [cook] it, and anoint the man with it; then [he dies (?)]. (24) You wish to produce a skin-disease on a man and that it shall not be healed, a *hantous*-lizard [and (?)] a *hafleele*-lizard, you cook them with [oil (?)], (25) you wash the man with them. If you wish to make it troublesome (?), you put . . . . . , then it is troublesome (?). You put beer (?) . . . . . (26) to the eye of a man, then he is blinded.

---

(Apion, frag. 7, Macrob. Saturn. vii. 13) to be a discovery of Egyptian anatomy. For fingers of the right hand see 16/29, 29/5.

l. 20. *ḫr* ⲙⲧⲉϥ. It is very interesting to obtain the *sḏm-f* form following *ḫr*; but whether it would be *ⲙⲧⲟϥ or *ⲙⲧⲁϥ in Sah. may be a little doubtful. The vowel seems however to represent ⲉ, not ⲁ, and should therefore correspond to ⲁ, not ⲟ, in Sah.; but a Sah. form *ⲙⲧⲉϥ, or even *ⲙⲧⲏϥ, would be conceivable.

l. 21. *t* over the line seems to be a correction of *ḥp*.

27. n sḫ·w nt ḫr ʾr-k ʿš-w a p gswr n p nw nt e·ʾr-k mḥt n(?) t s-ḥm·t nʾm[-f . . . .] yʿh-ʿo ʾbrʿsʿks

28. my ʾre mn a·ms mn mryt my ʾr-s mḥ m-s-y a p myt nte-k zrp(?) . . . . ḫr ʾr-s wḥ-s m-s-k ḫr sḫ-k[-s ?] . . .

29. ʿn a t tys nt ḫr ʾr-k qs p [ʿmʿm(?)] nʾm-f

## Col. XIV.

1. p-e·ze ke rm n-y z a·wn n yr·t sp-sn šʿ sp IV(?)

2. . . . . . . a·wn n yr·t-yt a·wn n yr·t-k θs-pḫr šʿ . . . sp III a·wn tt a·wn nʿp III sp

3. a·wn . . . . III(?) z ʾnk ʾrtʿm-ʿo a·ms ḥme-ʿo p syt ʿo n pr-ybt [nt] ḫʿ erme pe-k yt

4. n twe hy sp-sn ḥḥ(?) a·wn n-y hʿh ḫr z-k-f e·ʾr-k sq n ḫrw-k ʾrtʿm-ʿo a·wn n-y hʿh e·ʾr-k

5. tm a wn n-y hʿh e-y a t ʾr-k wn n-y hʿh hb sp-sn nwzḫ nte nw [a] p ntr ʿo ʾNp p nʿš

6. nt n-ne-zz-y p nʿšt ʿo n wz·t p nʿš ʾNp p mr ʾḥ nfr a·wn nb e·ʾr-y

7. wnḥ-k a·ʾr-y z ʾnk nesthom neszot neshotb b-ʿo-rylʿmmʿy sp-sn

---

l. 27. See l. 16 above for the employment of this spell.

l. 29. *qs*: the only embalming is of the tail of the shrew-mouse in l. 15.

### Col. XIV.

l. 1. This line is merely a gloss on l. 2.

l. 2. The mark over *sp* occurs also in 29/22 and V. 9/8. In 29/22 it is placed over *sp* without any number following, in the other instance over a blank space where a numeral would be expected. Here a number has been written under *sp*, but below the line, as if inserted later, and the inference may be drawn that the sign in question indicates that a number is wanting.

l. 3. *Ham-o* might mean 'great carpenter,' but many Egyptian words in these magic names are no doubt almost meaningless, and it is difficult in translating to decide whether to give English equivalents or to transcribe them phonetically.

l. 5. *tm a wn*. The *a* is a mistake, or at least superfluous.

(27) The charms which you recite to the ring at the time of taking hold of the woman . . . . . 'Yaho, Abrasax, (28) may N. daughter of N. love me, may she burn for me by the way (?).' You . . . . . Then she conveys herself (?) after you; you write it (29) again on the strip with which you wrap up the [shrew-mouse (?)].

## Col. XIV.

(1) That which another man said to me: 'Open my eyes,' unto four times. (2) [A vessel-divination:] 'Open my eyes; open thy eyes,' (and) vice versa, unto three times. 'Open, Tat; Open, Nap,' three times; (3) 'open [unto me?]' three [times?], 'for I am Artamo, born of Hame-o (?), the great basilisk of the East, rising in glory together with thy father (4) at dawn; hail (*bis*), Heh, open to me Hah,' you say it with a drawling (?) voice 'Artamo, open to me Hah; if thou dost (5) not open to me Hah, I will make thee open to me Hah. O Ibis (*bis*), sprinkle (?), that I may (?) see the great god Anubis, the power, (6) that is about (?) my head, the great protector (?) of the Uzat, the power, Anubis, the good ox-herd, at every opening (?) (of the eye?) which I have (?) made, (7) reveal thyself to me; for I am Nasthom,

---

*nwzḫ* is used of sprinkling a floor with water for the reception of visitors.

ⲛⲧⲁ would mean 'that I may,' the demotic equivalent of which is usually written *nte-y*, though the *y* was not pronounced. Here we have *nte* alone written, unless the group be read *nte-w* 3rd pl., which would give the meaning 'that the god may be seen.'

l. 6. *n-ne-zz-y*: the *n* is a doubling of the initial.

'That I may see the god every time I open my eyes (?).' *e-ʾr-y* is only past relative in ordinary demotic, but in early demotic is often future. Possibly it retains this meaning here, but if so it is a very exceptional usage.

Arian is repeated three times, each time with a different epithet, but the reading of the second is uncertain: it might mean 'this bringer of prosperity.'

8. mʿstsynks ʾNp mekyste ʾryʿn p nt ʿy ʿryʿn py n(?)-wzy ʾryʾn

9. p nt n bl hy phryks yks ʿnʿksybr-ʿo-ks ʿmbr-ʿo-ks eb-ʿo-rks ks-ʿo-n

10. nbr-ʿo-khrʿ . . p ḫrt wr ʾNp z ʾnk py mty ne-ʾtef ne-pephnwn mʿsph-ʿo-nege

11. hy my ḫp n-e·z-y nb ty n p-hw ze hy nte-k thʿm thʿmth-ʿo-m thʿmʿth-ʿo-m

12. thʿmʿthwmthʿm thʿmʿthwtsy ʾMn sp-sn pe-k rn n mte nt e-w(?) z rn-f z th-ʿo-m

13. ʾnkth-ʿo-m nte-k yt·th thwtsy rn-yk sythom ʿnythom ʾp-sʾ . . . šʿtn-sr

14. km a·wn n-y n n r·w n pe hne ty n p-hw ʾm n-y a n r·w n pe hne pe swt my ʾre

15. pe ʾpt ʾr p(?) w[be ?] n t p·t my ʾre n wḥr·w n p hwlot t n-y p nt n mʿ·t n p nwn my z-w n-y

16. p nt e-y šn ḫrr-f ty n p-hw n mʿ·t sp-sn e mn mt·t n ʿze nʾm-w ⲁ·ⲉ·ⲏ·ⲓ·ⲟ·ⲩ·ⲱ· mʿkh-ʿo-pnewmʿ

17. z-mt·t ḫr ʾny-k wʿ z n ḥmt nte-k ptḥ wʿ twt n ʾNp ḫn-f nte-k mḥ-f n mw n str n

18. mnt(?) b-ʾr p rʿ gm·t-f nte-k zq ḥr-f n nḥe n mʿ·t nte-k wḥ-f ḥr tb·t nmy e ḫrr-w prḫ

19. n šʿ nte-k t ke tb·t IV·t ḫr p ḫm-ḫl nte-k t ʾre p ḫm-ḫl str a ḥr ḫe·t-f

20. nte-k t ʾr-f(?) wḥ te-f mrt a t tb·t n p hne nte-k t ʾr-f kšp a ḫn p nḥe e wn wʿ ḥbs prḫ a zz-f

---

l. 13. *šʿtn-sr-km* looks like 'sacrifice of black ram.'

l. 15. *wbe* (?). The facsimile gives *e* as the last letter of the word, and so excludes *wyn*. The previous group, apparently written *ʾre*, we have taken as *ʾr p*.

*p hwlot* has the determinative of locality.

l. 18. *mnt* (?), perhaps 'custodian,' as in I Kham. iv. 7. It might represent the name of the god Mônth.

*b-ʾr* with final sense? Cf. I Kham. iv. 12, note, and below 22/3. The facsimile would perhaps admit of a reading *e b ʾr*.

Naszot, Nashoteb, Borilammai (*bis*), (8) Mastinx, Anubis, Megiste, Arian, thou who art great, Arian, Pi-anuzy (?), Arian, (9) he who is without. Hail, Phrix, Ix, Anaxibrox, Ambrox, Eborx, Xon, (10) Nbrokhria, the great child, Anubis; for I am that soldier. O ye of the Atef-crown, ye of Pephnun, Masphoneke; (11) hail! let all that I have said come to pass here to-day; say, hail! thou art Tham, Thamthom, Thamathom, (12) Thamathomtham, Thamathouthi, Amon (*bis*), thy correct name, whom they call Thom, (13) Anakthom; thou art Itth; Thouthi is thy name, Sithom, Anithom Op-sao (?), Shatensro (14) black; open to me the mouths of my vessel here to-day; come to me to the mouths of my vessel, my bandage (?), let (15) my cup make the reflection (?) of heaven; may the hounds of the *hulot* give me that which is just in the abyss; may they tell me (16) that about which I inquire here to-day truly (*bis*), there being no falsehood in them ⲁⲉⲏⲓⲟⲩⲱ, Makhopneuma.' (17) Formula: you take a bowl of bronze, you engrave a figure of Anubis in it; you fill it with water left to settle (?) and (18) guarded (?) lest (?) the sun should reach it; you finish its (sur-)face (of the water) with fine oil, you place it on [three ?] new bricks, their lower sides being sprinkled (19) with sand; you put four other bricks under the child; you make the child lie down upon (?) his stomach; (20) you cause him (?) to place his chin on the brick of the vessel; you make him look into

---

*zq*: reading not quite certain, but probably *zq ḥr-f* means ϫⲱⲕ, 'complete its (sur-)face,' i. e. fill up the vessel with a thin layer of oii on the top of the water.

*tb·t*: the facsimile shows a numeral III (?) following, and 'a brick' is always *wᶜ·t tbe·t*. The plural *ḫr-w* also follows; yet in l. 20 'the brick of the vessel' is spoken of in the singular.

l. 19. *a ḥr ḫe·t-f*, a curious expression, possibly meaning 'on his face-and-stomach.'

21. e wn wᶜ ḫbs e-f θ-r·t ḥr pe-f wnm wᶜ ᶜb ḥr st·t ḥr pe-f . . . . nte-k t wᶜ ḫlp n sym n

22. ʼNp ḥr p ḫbs nte-k t py sty a ḥry nte-k ᶜš ny sḫ·w nt ḥry a p hne n sp VII p sty nt e·ʼr-k t·t-f

23. a ḥry ʼlbwnt mrhe(?) ʼmwnyᶜk trymyᶜmᶜ-t-s bne nt-w ḥr ʼrp nte-k ʼr-w n

24. bnn nte-k t a ḥry nʼm-w e·ʼr-k wḥ e·ʼr-k t ʼre p ḫm-ḫl wn yr·t-f e·ʼr-k šn·t-f ze ne(?) p ntr ʼy a ḫn e-f

25. z ḥr p ntr ʼy [a ḫn] e·ʼr-k ᶜš ḥ·t-f z-mt·t pe-k qʼ mᶜo ʼy ʼNp py . . . oy py gᶜm

26. py km pe(?) . . . . py srytsy sp-sn srytsy sp-sn ʼbrytsy rn-yk n pe-k rn n mte

27. nte-k šn·t-f a p nt e·ʼr-k [wḥ-f] e·ʼr-k wḥ n pe-k šn nt e·ʼr-k šn ḫrr-f e·ʼr-k ᶜš ar-f n sp VII e·ʼr-k wt [p ntr] a pe-f ᶜy pe-f wt z-mt·t

28. wt nfr sp-sn ʼNp p mr ʼḥ nfr ʼNp sp-sn p šr n nw wnš wḥr p(?)[-e·ze ?] ke-zm(?) z p šr n ne te(?)

29. ʼS·t wḥr nʼbryš-ᶜo-tht(?) p gerwb n ʼmnt pr-ᶜo n te . . . . z sp VII e·ʼr-k fy

30. p ḫbs a p ᶜlw e·ʼr-k fy p hne nt ḫr mw e·ʼr-k fy t šnto·t [ḥr] ʼ·t-f ḫr ʼr-k-f ᶜn

31. n šn-hne [wᶜe]t-k nfr sp-sn ʼp e-f znt n sp IX p sym n ʼNp ḫr rt-f n hhe n mᶜ

32. te-f gbe·t m q[ty t] gbe·t [n sym ?] n ḥr e-f θy wbḫ te-f ḥrre m q·t[y t ḥ]rre n ʼnq

---

l. 21. *sym n ʼNp*, the ανουβιαδα την τον σταχυν of Pap. Bibl. Nat. l. 901. Cf. below, l. 31.

l. 22. *t a ḥry* is the regular expression for putting incense on the censer or brazier.

l. 23. *ʼmwnyᶜk trymyᶜmᶜ-t-s* Ἀμμωνιακὸν πόα ἐστὶν ὅθεν τὸ ἀμμωνιακὸν θυμίαμα, Diosc. iii. 98. The very slight alteration of *r* to *h* in the demotic would produce θυμιάματος.

l. 28. *p šr n nw wnš wḥr . . . . . p šr n ne te* (?) *ʼS·t wḥr.* For *te* = τα- cf. 8/13, 'the son of those of (?) a (?) jackal and (?) hound . . ., the son of those of Ta-Ese and (?) hound'; possibly a form of pedigree in breeding animals.

the oil, he having a cloth spread over his head, (21) there being a lighted lamp on his right, and a censer with fire on his left; you put a leaf of (22) Anubis-plant on the lamp, you put this incense on (the fire); you recite these spells, which are above, to the vessel seven times. The incense which you put (23) on (the fire): frankincense (?), wax (?), styrax, turpentine (?), date-stone (?); grind them with wine; you make them into a (24) ball and put them on (the fire). When you have finished, you make the child open his eyes, you ask him, saying, 'Is the god coming in?' If he says (25) 'The god has come in,' you recite before him: formula: 'Thy bull (?) Mao, ho! Anubis, this soldier (?), this Kam, (26) this Kem . . . Pisreithi (*bis*), Sreithi (*bis*), Abrithi is thy name, by thy correct name.' (27) You ask him concerning that which you [desire]; when you have finished your inquiry which you are asking about, you call to him seven times; you dismiss the god to his home. His dismissal: formula: (28) 'Farewell (*bis*) Anubis, the good ox-herd, Anubis (*bis*), the son of a (?) jackal (and ?) a dog . . . another volume saith: the child of . . . (29) Isis (?) (and ?) a dog, Nabrishoth, the Cherub (?) of Amenti, king of those of . . . . .' Say seven times. You take (30) the lamp from (?) the child, you take the vessel containing water, you take the cloth off him. You do it also (31) by vessel-inquiry alone, excellent (*bis*), tried (?), tested nine times.

The Anubis-plant. It grows in very numerous places;

---

l. 29. *gerwb* probably = כְּרוּב. Cf. Pap. Bibl. Nat. l. 3061; Leyd. Pap. Gr. V, col. 9, l. 16.

l. 30. *fy* must refer to the removal of the apparatus.

l. 32. [*sym*] *n ḫr*. There seems hardly room for more than the sign *sym*, and some slight remains agree with it.

The leaves of stachys are λευκά (Diosc. iii. 110), coloris in luteum inclinati (Pliny, N. H., xxiv. 86). The former compares it with the

33. . . . . . e·ʾr-k . . . . yr·t . . . . e b-ʾr te-k . . . . . . p hne

## Col. XV.

1. wʿ t swr e·ʾr-k ʾny wʿ ẖm n ẖẖ n ʿpe·t n wʿ rm e-f mw·t n ẖtb·t

2. erme VII n blbyle·t n yt(?) n tms ẖn wʿ·t be·t n rm e-f mw·t nte-k nt-w erme ʾp·t X·t

3. ke-z IX·t pr·w n zpẖ nte-k t snf n wʿ·t hʿlʿmʿtʿ n wʿ ʾʾe(?) km a ẖ·t-w erme wʿ ẖm n

4. snf n pe-k tbʿ n mḥ II n p sʿlʾpyn n te-k·t t·t n gbyr erme te-k·t mt·t nte-k

5. hm-w n wʿ sp nte-k ty-sw a wʿ z n ʾrp nte-k t·t wtḥ III ar-f n t

6. ḥʿyt·t n p ʾrp e b-ʾr te-k tp-f e b-ʾr te-w wtne ẖn-f nte-k ʿš py ʿš ar-f n sp VII

7. nte-k t swr-s t s-ẖm·t nʾm-f nte-k mr p ẖʿr n p syb nt ḥry n wʿ·t tys n š-stn

8. nte-k mr-s a pe-k znḥ n gbyr pe-f ʿš z-mt·t ʾnk pa(?) ʾBt n mʿ·t n

9. mnqe n ms n rn-s n ʾS·t t sbb hh ta t s·t-sbḥ n p šʿy

10. ʾnk py twt n p rʿ s-tʿme-sr rn-yt ʾnk py twt n mr mšʿ a-pḥt py

---

marrubium, the latter (through misunderstanding of πράσιον) with the leek. Here we have it compared to the *ʾnqe* ενϲ : (ενοτκ ?) κόνυζα, Bsciai, Rec. trav., vii. 25; Loret, Flore Phar., 2nd ed., p. 68. Curiously enough, amongst the synonyms of κονυζα in Diosc. iii. 126 ἀνουβιας occurs. Evidently there is some confusion here with stachys.

*θy wbḥ* probably 'tends to whiteness.'

### Col. XV.

l. 1. *ẖtb·t*: this might represent an Achmimic infinitive ending in ε, but in the Hist. Rom. no. 245 there is a fem. subst. *ẖtby*.

l. 2. *rm e-f mw·t*, no doubt again a man slain or murdered. Parts of the body of those who had suffered a violent death were considered peculiarly efficacious for magical purposes. Cf. P. S. B. A. xiii. 169–70.

l. 3. *pr·w*, a genitive *n* has probably been omitted by mistake.

(32) its leaf is like the leaf of Syrian [plant(?)]; it turns (?) white; its flower is like the flower of conyza.

(33) . . . you . . . eye . . . before you . . . the vessel.

## Col. XV.

(1) A potion. You take a little shaving of the head of a man who has died a violent death, (2) together with seven grains of barley that has been buried in a grave of a dead (?) man; you pound them with ten *oipe*, (3) otherwise nine, (of) apple-seeds (?); you add blood of a worm (?) of a black dog to them, with a little (4) blood of your second finger, (that) of the heart (?), of your left hand, and with your semen (?), and you (5) pound them together and put them into a cup of wine and add three *utch* to it of (6) the first-fruits of the vintage, before you have tasted it and before they have poured out from it; and you pronounce this invocation to it seven times (7) and you make the woman drink it; and you tie the skin of the parasite aforesaid with a band of byssus (8) and tie it to your left arm. Its invocation, formula: 'I am he of Abydos in truth, (9) by formation (?) (and ?) birth in her (?) name of Isis the bringer (?) of fire, she of the mercy-seat of the Agathodaemon. (10) I am this figure of the sun, *Sitamesro* is my name. I am this

---

*hꜥlꜥmꜥtꜥ*, referred to in l. 7 as *syb*. *Syb*, cf. 25/25, 28, = ⲥⲓϥ : ⲥⲓⲛ (Eg. *sp*), the meaning of which seems vague—parasitic worms and insects and even sores. Possibly our word may be connected with ἕλμινς.

*a ḫ·t-w*: see chapter on Grammar.

l. 7. *swr-s*: *s* is duplicated either as the object by *n'm-f* or as the subject by *t s-ḥm·t*.

l. 9. *n mnqe n ms* is difficult.

*n rn-s*: it seems as if Abydos were here personified as Isis, cf. l. 13, or else we may translate 'by the name of Isis'; see 19/16.

ⲧⲁⲛ : ⲧⲁ- represents Eg. *tnt*, to which *τα-* corresponds in Ptolemaic transcriptions of proper names. But possibly the *n* was retained in O. C. in looser combinations.

11. štꜥ py sḫr-ꜥo·t t ḫo ꜥo·t rn-yt ʾnk py twt n Ḥr py štꜥm py štꜥ py

12. sḫr-ꜥo·t rn-t ʾnk py twt n ḥsy-ntr(?) nt mtr n sḫ nt ḥtp a mr ty ḫr

13. t ḥtp·t ꜥo·t n ʾBt nta mtr p snf n Wsr a rn-s n ʾS·t e-w ty-f a ḫry ḫn

14. py z py ʾrp my nʾm-f snf n Wsr te-f n ʾS·t a t ʾr-s wꜥ mr n ḥt-s ar-f

15. n grḥ mre·t n nw nb e mn nw šr my nʾm-f p snf n mn a·ms mn a ty-f

16. n mn a·ms mn ḫn py z py ʾpt n ʾrp n p-hw a t ʾr-s wꜥ mr n ḥt-s ar-f

17. p mr nta ʾr-s ʾS·t a Wsr e-s qte m-s-f a mꜥ nb my ʾr-s mn t šr n mn

18. e-s qte m-s mn p šr n mn a mꜥ nb p pz nta ʾr-s ʾS·t a Ḥr Bḥtt my

19. ʾr-s t mn s(?) mn e-s mr nʾm-f e-s lby m-s-f e-s rqh n t·t-f e-s qte m-s-f

20. a mꜥ nb e wn wꜥ·t ḫo n st·t ḫn ḥt-s n ty-s wne·t n tm nw ar-f

21. ke ky nʾm-f ꜥn p znf n p ḫbys n te-k·t ꜥne·t n pr·w zpḫ ḥnꜥ snf

22. n pe-k tbꜥ nt sḫ a ḥry ꜥn nte-k nt p zpḫ nte-k t snf ar-f nte-k ty-f a p z n ʾrp

23. nte-k ꜥš ar-f n sp VII nte-k t swr-s t s-ḥm·t n p nw n rn-f

---

l. 12. *ḥsy* :  inserted after the *ḥ* seems to be a kind of determinative, also in 19/24. The reference here is, of course, to Osiris.

*a mr* : the geographical significance of this is difficult to grasp, but cf. 9/23.

l. 13. *t a ḫry ḫn*, 'pour into,' of liquids : cf. 19/29.

*nt a* seems to be the form for the relative before *stm-f* in this papyrus when used instead of the old relative form *a·stm-f*. Cf. l. 17, &c.

l. 14. *my nʾm-f* : above this is a letter resembling ⌂ erased by two lines ; the following words are very difficult to understand. *Te-f* may be intended for the past relative *a·te-f*, 'which he gave.'

figure of a Captain of the host, very valiant, this (11) Sword (?), this Overthrower (?), the Great Flame is my name. I am this figure of Horus, this Fortress (?), this Sword (?), this (12) Overthrower (?) is my name. I am this figure of One Drowned, that testifieth by writing, that resteth on the other side (?) here under (13) the great offering-table (?) of Abydos; as to which the blood of Osiris bore witness to her (?) name of Isis when it (the blood) was poured into (14) this cup, this wine. Give it, blood of Osiris (that ?) he (?) gave to Isis to make her feel love in her heart for him (15) night and day at any time, there not being time of deficiency. Give it, the blood of N. born of N. to give it (16) to N. born of N. in this cup, this bowl of wine to-day, to cause her to feel a love for him in her heart, (17) the love that Isis felt for Osiris, when she was seeking after him everywhere, let N. the daughter of N. feel it, (18) she seeking after N. the son of N. everywhere; the longing that Isis felt for Horus of Edfu, (19) let N. born of N. feel it, she loving him, mad after him, inflamed by him, seeking him (20) everywhere, there being a flame of fire in her heart in her moment of not seeing him.'

(21) Another method of doing it again. The paring (?) of your nail's point (?) from an apple-fruit (?), and blood (22) of your finger aforesaid again; you pound the apple and put blood on it, and put it in the cup of wine (23) and invoke it seven times, and make the woman drink it at the moment named.

---

l. 21. *znf*: an obscure word; cf. 25/32, V. 7/1. It occurs also in a Philae inscription (Br., Thes., 1017), perhaps with the meaning of a 'small portion.'

*pr·w*: cf. perhaps Sah. ⲉⲃⲣⲁ, pl. ⲉⲃⲣⲏⲧⲉ. It is not clear whether the fruit or the pips are intended.

l. 22. *a ḥry*. The MS. appears to have the *a*, but it must be a mistake of the scribe.

24. n še ne-ḥr ḥry e-f ⟨sre-w(?)⟩ myḫ erme-k nte-f tm sze ar-k

25. *μη με διωκε οδε· ανοχ παπιπετου μετουβανες· βασταζω*

26. *την ταφην του οσιρεως και υπαγω καταστησαι αυτην εις αβιδος*

27. *καταστησαι εις ταστας και καταθεσθαι εις [α]λχας εαν μοι ο ϙ κοπους*

28. *παρασχη προσρεψω αυτην αυτω* pe-f ʿš n mt·t rm n kmy ʿn pe py nt [ḥr]y

29. mpr ptt m-s-y t mn ank pʿpypetw metwbʿnes e-y fy ḫr t qs·t n Wsr

30. e-y ʾnnʿ a θy·t-s a ʾBt a ty ḥtp-s n ʿLghʿh e-f ḫp nte t mn myḫ erme-y n p-hw

31. e-y a hwy·t-s abl z sp VII

## Col. XVI.

1. ke-zʿm thew ye ʿo-e ʿo-n yʿ wʿ ke-zʿm elon nfr sp-sn

2. n mt·wt n p ḫbs b-ʿo-th thew ye we ʿo-ʿo-e yʿ wʿ pthʿkh el-ʿo-e

3. yʿth e-ʿo-n peryphʿe yew yʿ y-ʿo yʿ ywe ʾm a ḫry

4. a p wyn n py ḫbs nte-k wnḥ a py ʿlw nte-k šn n-y ḫr p nt e-y šn ḫrr-f

---

l. 24. *ḥry* probably means 'Sovereign,' 'king,' but may perhaps only mean a 'superior officer.' *sre-w* would seem to mean 'range soldiers,' 'array battle.'

l. 25. The Greek formula, ll. 25–28, is translated into demotic in ll. 29–31.

*ανοχ*, &c. This passage invites interpretation as Old Coptic, but if it really meant anything it must be corrupt, and the demotic version in l. 29 renders it phonetically as if it consisted of magic names. One may perhaps suggest *ʾnk pe pa p nt ʿo my t wʿb n-s*, 'I am the servant of him that is great; give discharge (ⲙⲁⲧⲟⲩⲃⲟ) (of the fault or the liability) to her' (*sic* for 'to me'?).

l. 26. *ταφην*. At this time *ταφή* in Egypt = 'mummy,' as is seen by the mummy tickets (Pap. Rainer Mitth. V. 14).

(24) [A spell] of going to meet a sovereign (?) when he fights with you and will not parley(?) with you. (25) 'Do not pursue me, thou! I am Papipetou Metoubanes. I am carrying (26) the mummy of Osiris and I am proceeding to take it to Abydos, (27) to take [it] to Tastai (?) and to deposit it in Alkhai; if N. deal blows at me, (28) I will cast it at him.' Its invocation in Egyptian also is this as below: (29) 'Do not pursue me, N., I am Papipetu Metubanes. I am carrying the mummy of Osiris, (30) I am proceeding to take it to Abydos, to cause it to rest in Alkhah. If N. fight with me to-day, (31) I will cast it away.' Say seven times.

## Col. XVI.

(1, 2) The words of the lamp: 'Both, Theou, Ie, Oue, O-oe, Ia, Oua—otherwise, Theou, Ie, Oe, Oon, Ia, Oua—Phthakh, Eloe—otherwise, Elon, excellent (*bis*)—(3) Iath, Eon, Puriphae, Ieou, Ia, Io, Ia, Ioue, come down (4) to the light of this lamp and appear to this boy.

---

l. 27. *ταστας*: an unknown name. This phrase is not translated in the demotic.

[*α*]λ*χας*: the λ is sufficiently recognizable in the facs.; see the note on 1/16. The *ς* of *κοπους* is likewise seen in the facs.

*εαν μοι*, &c. Wünsch, in the Supplement on magic tablets to the Corp. inscript. Attic., quotes in his preface an inscription from the Collections du mus. Alaoui I. p. 57 (publ. also Maspero, Et. myth. arch. ii. 297), a Latin eroticon of the 2nd cent. A.D. from Hadrumetum written in Greek characters: 'Si minus descendo in adytus Osyris et dissolvam *τὴν ταφὴν* et mittam ut a flumine feratur. Ego enim sum magnus decanus magni dei Achrammachalala,' i. e. as Wünsch says, a sepulcro Osiridis arcam illius eripiet et in Nilum coniiciet, idem quod olim Typho fecerat.

Col. XVI.

l. 1. This is only a gloss on the second line.

l. 2. The apparent *n* at the beginning before *n mt·wt* is probably false.

l. 4. *šn*. In this papyrus this word is often used in such a way as to suggest the meaning 'answer' rather than 'inquire.' Perhaps it may mean both 'to inquire' and 'to be inquired of.'

5. ty n p-hw yʿ-ʿo yʿ-ʿo-mr therenth-ʿo psykšymeʿkhe-mr blʿ

6. khʿnsplʿ yʿe we-by bʿrbʿrethw yew ʿrp-ʿo-n·ghnwph

7. bryntʿten-ʿo-phry heʿ gʾrhre bʿlmenthre menebʿry-ʿkhegh yʿ

8. khekh bryn·sk(?) ʾlmʿ ʿrwnsʿrbʿ meseghryph nyptw-mykh

9. mʿ-ʿo-rkhʿrʿm ʾy lʿʿnkhekh ʿo-mph brymbʾynwy-ʿo

10. th sengenbʿy gh-ʿo-wghe lʿykhʿm ʾrmy-ʿo-wth nte-k zt-f

11. e-f wʿb n py smte p ntr nt ʿnḫ p ḫbs nt θ-r·yt tʾgrtʾt pa zt wy

12. b-ʿo-el a ḫn šʿ sp III ʾrbeth bʾy wtsy-ʿo p ntr ʿo ʿo a·(?)wy b-ʿo-el

13. a ḫn tʾt sp-sn a·wy b-ʿo-el a ḫn šʿ sp III tʾgrtʾt pa zt [a·]wy

14. b-ʿo-el a ḫn šʿ sp III bewtsy p ntr ʿo a·wy b-ʿo-el a ḫn sʿ sp III

15. p ʿš nt e·ʾr-k ʿš-f a ḥr p rʿ n ḫrp e b-ʾr te-k ʿš a p ʿlw z a·ʾr p nt e·ʾr-k ʾr-f a ḫp

16. p ntr ʿo tʾbʾ-ʿo bʾswkhʿm ʿm-ʿo ʿkhʿ·ghʿr·khʿn·-grʿbwnsʿ

17. nwny·etsyqme-t gʿthwbʿsʿthwry·thmylʿʿl-ʿo sp VII

18. ke gy nʾm-f ʿn e·ʾr-k twn-k n twe ḥr pe-k klk n ḫrp n p hw nt e·ʾr-k a ʾr-f nʾm-f nge hw nb

19. z a·ʾr p nt e·ʾr-k a ʾr-f nb a mte n t·t-k e·ʾr-k wʿb a bte nb e·ʾr-k ʿš py ʿš a ḥr p rʿ n sp III nge sp VII

20. y-ʿo·tʾ·bʾ-ʿo s-ʿo-khʿm·mwʾ ʿo-kh·ʿo-kh·khʿn·bwnsʿ-nw ʿn

21. yesy eg-ʿo-m-p-t geth-ʿo sethwry thmylʿ ʾlwʾp-ʿo-khry my ʾre hb nb

---

l. 5. The demotic sign corresponding to the glosses λο, λω is identical with that for *r* in *R-qty* = **Ρακοτε**, and with that for *mr-* = **λε-**, 'superintendent'; λο, λω is evidently the absolute form of the construct **λε-**.

and inquire for me about that which I ask (5) here to-day, Iao, Iaolo, Therentho, Psikhimeakelo, (6) Blakhanspla, Iae, Ouebai, Barbaraithou, Ieou, Arponknouph, (7) Brintatenophri, Hea, Karrhe, Balmenthre, Menebareiakhukh, Ia, (8) Khukh, Brinskulma, Arouzarba, Mesekhriph, Niptoumikh, (9) Maorkharam. Ho! Laankhukh, Omph, Brimbainouioth, (10) Segenbai, Khooukhe, Laikham, Armioouth.' You say it, (11) it (*sic*) being pure, in this manner: 'O god that liveth, O lamp that is lighted, Takrtat, he of eternity, bring in (12) Boel!'—three times—'Arbeth-abi, Outhio, O great great god, bring Boel (13) in, Tat (*bis*), bring Boel in!' Three times. 'Takrtat, he of Eternity, bring (14) Boel in!' Three times. 'Barouthi, O great god, bring Boel in!' Three times.

(15) The invocation which you pronounce before Phre in the morning before reciting to the boy, in order that that which thou doest may succeed: (16) 'O great god, Tabao, Basoukham, Amo, Akhakharkhan-kraboun-zanouni-(17)edikomto, Kethou-basa-thouri-thmila-alo.' Seven times.

(18) Another method of it again. You rise in the morning from your bed early in the day on which you will do it, or any day, (19) in order that everything which you will do shall prosper in your hand, you being pure from every abomination. You pronounce this invocation before Phre three times or seven times. (20) 'Io, Tabao, Sokhom-moa, Okh-okh-khan-bouzanau, An-(21) iesi, Ekomphtho, Ketho, Sethouri, Thmila, Alouapokhri,

---

l. 7. *καρρϩε*: the aspiration of the second *ρ* is interesting. Cf. note to 1/20.

l. 11. *e-f wʿb*: the lamp must be pure as described in ll. 22 et seqq.

*a·wy*, sometimes perhaps written *wy*, is ⲁⲩ-, ⲁⲩⲉⲓ⸗, St., § 384, and is synonymous with *a·ʾny*: cf. 17/10, &c.

l. 15. *z a·ʾr* = ϫⲉⲣⲉ, 'final.'

22. nt e-y a θy t·t ar-f ty n p-hw my ʾr-f ẖp pe-f ky ẖr ʾny-k wʿ ẖbs nmy e bnp-w t prš ar-f nte-k (*sic*)

23. wʿ sʿl e-f wʿb ar-f nte-k mḥ-f n nḥe n mʿ·t e-f wʿb nte-k wḥ-f n wʿ mʿ e-f wʿb n mw n ḥsm e-f hep

24. nte-k wḥ-f ḥr wʿ·t tbe·t nmy nte-k ʾny wʿ ʿlw nte-k t ḥms-f ḥr k·t tbe·t nmy e ḥr-f

25. st a p ẖbs nte-k ẖtm n yr·t-f nte-k ʿš ny nt ḥry a ḥry ẖn zz-f n p ʿlw n sp VII e·ʾr-k t ʾr-f wn

26. yr·t-f e·ʾr-k z n-f ʿn e·ʾr-k nw a p wyn e-f z n-k te-y nw a p wyn ẖn t st·t n p ẖbs e·ʾr-k ʿš ty hte z

27. hewe ⲧⲟⲧⲉ n sp IX e·ʾr-k šn·t-f a p nt e·ʾr-k wḥ-f nb bn-s ʿš p ʿš a·ʾr-k t ḥ·t mbḥ p rʿ n ẖrp

28. ẖr ʾr-k-f n wʿ mʿ e r wn a pr(?)-ybt nte-k ẖʿ ḥr-f n p ẖbs e-f st nte-k ẖʿ ḥr-f n p ʿlw

29. e-f·st a ḥr p ẖbs e·ʾr-k ḥr . . . . nʾm-f e·ʾr-k ʿš a ḥry ẖn zz-f e·ʾr-k qlh a zz-f n pe-k tbʿ n mḥ II n p (?) ḥyne (?) n te-k·t t·t

30. n wnm

## Col. XVII.

1. ke ky nʾm-f ʿn nfr sp-sn a p ẖbs e·ʾr-k (z ?) b-ʿo-el sp III y·y·y· ʿ·ʿ·ʿ· tʾt tʾt tʾt p šmsy ḥyt n p ntr ʿo p nt t wyn m šs sp-sn

2. p ẖbr n t st·t nte t st·t n r-f pa t st·t nte my-s htm p ntr nt ʿnḫ nte b-ʾr-f mw p ntr ʿo ⟨p⟩ nt ḥms ẖn t st·t nt n t mt·t n t st·t nt

---

l. 22. *θy t·t a*, 'undertake,' 'apply hand to': cf. 17/26 *θ wʿb a.*
*pe-f ky*: this seems to correspond to *py smt* in l. 11.
*t* has been omitted by the scribe at the end of the line.

l. 28. *f* is omitted after *r* and *pr* is incomplete before *ybt*. The scribe has moreover been confused in describing the positions of the lamp and the boy.

l. 29. Thus the middle finger of the right hand must have had a different name from that of the left, see 13/18 and cf. 29/5 with this passage. *ḥyne* (?) has the det. of flesh and should be some part of the body.

let everything (22) that I shall apply (?) my hand to here to-day, let it happen.' Its method. You take a new lamp in which no minium has been put and you (put) (23) a clean wick in it, and you fill it with pure genuine oil and lay it in a place cleansed with natron water and concealed, (24) and you lay it on a new brick, and you take a boy and seat him upon another new brick, his face being (25) turned to the lamp, and you close his eyes and recite these things that are (written) above down into the boy's head seven times. You make him (26) open his eyes. You say to him, 'Do you see the light?' When he says to you 'I see the light in the flame of the lamp,' you cry at that moment saying (27) 'Heoue' nine times. You ask him concerning everything that you wish after reciting the invocation that you made previously before Phre in the morning. (28) You do it in a place with (its) entrance open to the East, and put the face of the lamp turned (*blank*). You put the face of the boy (29) turned (*blank*) facing the lamp, you being on his left hand. You cry down into his head, you strike his head with your second finger, (that) of the . . . . , of your (30) right hand.

## Col. XVII.

(1) Another method of it again, very good, for the lamp. You (say ?): 'Boel,' (*thrice*), 'I, I, I, A, A, A, Tat, Tat, Tat, the first attendant of the great god, he who gives light exceedingly, (2) the companion of the flame, in whose mouth is the flame which is not quenched,

---

Col. XVII.

l. 1. *e·ʾr-k*. 'Thou art Boel' would need *nte-k*: probably *e·ʾr-k z* was intended.

l. 2. *pa t st·t*: the stroke over the *t* is merely a line separating off the interlineation.

*nte my-s* = ετε ϻεс-, elsewhere (l. 27, &c.) written etymologically *nte b ʾr-s*. Cf. ο ασβεστος λυχνος Pap. Bibl. Nat. l. 1218.

3. n p šy n t p·t nte p ʿw erme p nʿš n p ntr n t·t-f ʾm a ḫn n t mt n ty st·t nte-k wnḥ-k ⟨wnḥ-k⟩ a py ʿlw ty n p-hw nte-k t ʾr-f šn n-y ḥr mt·t nb nt e-y

4. a šn·t-f [a]r-w ty n p-hw z e-y a šʿš-k n t p·t ne-ḥr p rʿ e-y a šʿšʿ-k ne-ḥr ʿḥ e-y a šʿš-k n p t

5. e-y a šʿš-k ne-ḥr p nt ḥr p bḥt nte b-ʾr-f htm pa p šʿš ʿo nte p ʿw erme p nʿš n p ntr n t·t-f pa p

6. šʿš ʿo petery sp-sn pʿter emphe sp-sn p ntr ʿo ʿo nt n t rʿ ḥry·t n t p·t nte p šbt nt ne-(ne-)ʿne-f n t·t-f p-e·ʾr t ḫp ntr e bp ntr

7. t ḫp-f ʾm n-y a ḫn erme b-ʿo-el ʾnyel nte-k t p zr n n byl·w n py ʿlw nt ḫr pe hne

8. n p-hw a t nw-f ar-k a t stm msz-f ar-k e·ʾr-k sze nte-k šn n-f ḥr hb nb mt·t nb nt e-y a šn·t-f ar-w ty n p-hw

9. p ntr ʿo sy·sʾ-ʿo-th ʾkhrem-p-t ʾm a ḫn n t mt·t n ty st·t p nt ḥms ḥr p tw

10. n gʾbʾ-ʿo-n tʾgrtʾt pa zt p nte b-ʾr-f mw nt ʿnḫ šʿ nḥḥ ⟨a·wy⟩ a·ʾny b-ʿo-el a ḫn b-ʿo-el sp-sn

11. ʾrbethbʾy·nwtsy ʿo p ntr ʿo sp-sn ⟨a·(?)wy⟩ a·ʾny b-ʿo-el a ḫn tʾt sp-sn ⟨a·wy⟩ a·ʾny b-ʿo-el a ḫn e·ʾr-k

12. z ny sp VII a ḥry ḫn zz-f n p ʿlw e·ʾr-k t ʾr-f wn yr·t-f e·ʾr-k šn·t-f z ʿn ḥr p wyn ḫp

13. e-f ḫp e bnp p wyn pyr e·ʾr-k t ʾre p ʿlw ḥ-f sze n r-f a p ḫbs z-mt·t ʿw p wyn pr

14. p wyn θs p wyn ḫy p wyn pr p wyn n p ntr wnḥ-k a·ʾr-y p šmsy n p ntr nte p wḥ-sḥne n p-hw [n t·]t-f

15. nt ne šn n-y ḫr ʾr-f wnḥ-f a p ʿlw n p nw n rn-f ḫr ʿš-k ny a ḥry ḫn zz-f n p ʿlw e-f nw

---

l. 12. *ʿn ḥr* = Boh. ⲁⲛ ⲁ- cf. 2/24.

the great god that dieth not, the great god he that sitteth in the flame, who is in the midst of the flame, (3) who is in the lake of heaven, in whose hand is the greatness and might of the god, come within in the midst of this flame and reveal thyself to this boy here to-day; cause him to inquire for me concerning everything about which I shall (4) ask him here to-day; for I will glorify thee in heaven before Phre, I will glorify thee before the Moon, I will glorify thee on Earth, (5) I will glorify thee before him who is on the throne, who perisheth not, he of the great glory, in whose hand is the greatness and might of the god, he of the great glory, (6) Petery (*bis*), Pater, Emphe (*bis*), O great great god, who is above heaven, in whose hand is the beautiful staff, who created deity, deity not having (7) created him, come in to me with Boel, Aniel; do thou give strength to the eyes of this boy who has my vessel (8) to-day, to (?) cause him to see thee, cause his ears to hear thee when thou speakest; and do thou inquire for him concerning everything and every word as to which I shall ask him here to-day, (9) O great god, Sisaouth, Akhrempto, come into the midst of this flame, he who sitteth on the mountain (10) of Gabaon, Takrtat, he of eternity, he who dieth not, who liveth for ever, bring Boel in, Boel (*bis*), (11) Arbethbainouthi, great one, O great god (*bis*) ⟨bring⟩ fetch Boel in, Tat (*bis*) ⟨bring⟩ fetch Boel in.' You (12) say these things seven times down into the head of the boy, you make him open his eyes, you ask him saying, 'Has the light appeared?' (13) If it be that the light has not come forth, you make the boy himself speak with his mouth to the lamp. Formula: 'Grow, O light, come forth (14) O light, rise O light, lift thyself up O light, come forth O light of the god, reveal thyself to me, O servant of the god, in whose hand is the command of to-day, (15) who will ask for me.' Then he reveals himself to the boy in the moment named.

16. m·s p ḫbs mpr t ʾr-f nw m·s ge mʿ m·s p ḫbs wʿe·t-f e-f tm nw m-s-f ḫr ʾr-f htye·t

17. e·ʾr-k ʾr ny tre-w e·ʾr-k wḥ n pe-k šn e·ʾr-k st-k e·ʾr-k t ʾr-f ḫtm yr·t-f e·ʾr-k sze a ḫry ḫn zz-f n py ke

18. ʿš nt ḫry ze a·ʾre n ntr·w še n-w nte p ʿlw lk-f e-f nw ar-w ʾ·rkhe·khem·phe nsew

19. hele sʿtrʿpermt ḥrḥ a py ʿlw nte-k tm t ʾr-f htye·t ḥnwḥe škll·t nte-k t

20. st-f a pe-f myt n ḫrp a·wn ty·t a·wn ty te-y z nʾm-s z ne-(ne-)ʿne py šn-hne n p ḫbs (?)

21. a p ḫrp py smt ʿn pe pe-f ky ḫr ʾny-k wʿ ḫbs nmy e·bp-w t prš ar-f nte-k t wʿ sʿl n

22. ḥbs e·f wʿb ar-f nte-k mḥ-f n nḥe n mʿ·t e-f wʿb nte-k wḥ-f ḥr wʿ·t tbe·t nmy nte-k t ḥms p ʿlw ḥr k·t tbe·t

23. wbe p ḫbs nte-k t ʾr-f ḫtm yr·t-f nte-k ʿš a ḫry ḫn zz-f a ḫ p ke ky ʿn ke ʿš e·ḫr

24. ʾr-k ʿš-f wbe p rʿ n twe n sp III nge sp VII z-mt·t y-ʿo·tʾbe-ʿo s-ʿo-kh-ʿo-mmwʾ ʿo-kh

25. ʿo·kh·khʿn bwnsʿ-nw ʿn yesy eg-ʿo-mth-ʿo geth-ʿo seth-ʿo-ry thmy

26. l(ʿ·ʾ)lwʾp-ʿo·khry my ḫp mt·t nb nt e-y a ʾr-w n p-hw nte-w ḫp e-f ḫp nte-k tṃ θ wʿb ar-f b-ʾr-f ḫp te-f mt·t ʿo·t wʿb ke

27. ʿš a ḫ p nt ḥry ʿn z-mt·t b-ʿo-el sp III ⲓ·ⲓ·ⲓ·ⲁ·ⲓ· ⲓ·ⲓ·ⲁ· tʾt sp III p nt t wyn m šs sp-sn p ḫbr n t st·t pa t st·t nte b-ʾr-s

28. htm p ntr nt ʿnḥ nte b-ʾr-f mw p nt ḥms ḫn t st·t nt n t mt·t n t st·t nt n p šy n t p·t nte p ʿw erme p nʿš

29. n p ntr n t·t-f wnḥ-k a py ʿlw hew ⲧⲟⲧ sp-sn he-ʿo

---

l. 19. *hele* has the Greek symbol of the sun (ἥλιε) above it.

l. 20. The demotic sign for  at the end apparently stands for *ḫbs*, 'lamp.'

l. 26. *θ wʿb a*: cf. 14/32.

*te-f mt·t ʿo·t*: cf. εστιν δε το αγαθον ζωδιον B. M. Pap. XLVI. 171.

You recite these things down into the head of the boy, he looking (16) towards the lamp. Do not let him look towards another place except the lamp only; if he does not look towards it, then he is afraid. (17) You do all these things, you cease from your inquiry, you return, you make him close his eyes, you speak down into his head this other (18) invocation which is below, that is, if the gods go away and the boy ceases to see them: 'Arkhe-khem-phai, Zeou, (19) Hele, Satrapermet, watch this boy, do not let him be frightened, terrified, or scared, and make (20) him return to his original path. Open Teï (the Underworld), open Taï (Here).' I say it that this vessel-inquiry of the lamp is better (21) than the beginning. This is the method again; its form: you take a new lamp in which no minium has been put and you put a wick of (22) clean linen in it; you fill it with genuine clean oil; you place it on a new brick, you make the boy sit on another brick (23) opposite the lamp; you make him shut his eyes, you recite down into his head according to the other method also.

Another invocation which (24) you recite towards Phre in the morning three times or seven times. Formula: 'Iotabao, Sokh-ommoa, Okh-(25)-okh-Khan, Bouzanau, Aniesi, Ekomphtho, Ketho, Sethori, (26) Thmilaalouapokhri may everything succeed that I shall do to-day,' and they will (?) succeed. If it be that you do not apply (?) purity to it, it does not succeed; its chief matter is purity.

Another (27) invocation like the one above again. Formula: 'Boel,' (*thrice*), 'I, I, I, A, I, I, I, A, Tat (*thrice*), he who giveth the light exceedingly, the companion of the flame, he of the flame which does not (28) perish, the god who liveth, who dieth not, he who sitteth in the flame, who is in the midst of the flame who is in the lake of heaven, in whose hand is the greatness and might (29) of the god, reveal thyself to

nte-f šn n-y nte-k ty ʾr-f nw nte-f kšp nte-f stm a mt·t nb nt e-y

30. šn·t-f ar·w z e-y a šʿš-k n t p·t e-y a šʿš-k n p t e-y a šʿš-k ne-ḥr p nt ḥr p bḥt nte b-ʾr-f htm

31. py ʿw petery sp-sn emphe sp-sn p ntr ʿo nt n ḥry (?) n t p·t nte p šbt nt ne-(ne-)ʿne-f n t·t-f ʾr t ẖp ntr

32. e bnp ntr t ẖp-f ʾm a ẖn n t mt·t n ty st·t erme b-ʿo-el ʾnyel nte-k t p zr n n byl·w n hew sp-sn

## Col. XVIII.

1. n hew sp-sn p šr n hew sp-sn z e·f a nw ar-k n yr·t-f nte-k t stm msz-f

2. nte-k sze wbe-f n hb nb e-f a šn·t-k ar-f nte-k z n-y wḥ n mt·t mʿ·t nte-k p ntr ʿo sʿ

3. bʿ-ʿo-th ʾm a ẖry erme b-ʿo-el tʾt sp-sn a·wy b-ʿo-el a ẖn ʾm a ẖn n t mt·t n ty st·t

4. nte-k šn n-y ẖr p nt ne-(ne-)ʿne-f tʾgrtʾt py zt a·wy b-ʿo-el a ẖn šʿ sp III ʾrbth

5. bʿynwtsy-ʿo p ntr ʿo a·wy b-ʿo-el a ẖn sp III e-ʾr-k z ny a ẖry ẖn zz-f n p ʿḷw

6. e-ʾr k t ʾr-f wn yr·t-f e-ʾr-k šn·t-f a mt·t nb a ẖ p ky nt n bl ʿn

7. šn-hne e te-s n-y wʿ syn ẖn p tše n pr-mz ẖr ʾr-k-f ʿn n šn-hne wʿ·t-k

8. sʾbʾ nm nn (?) byrybʾt hy sp-sn p ntr sysyʾh-ʿo nt ḥr p tw n qʾbʾh-ʿo

9. nte t wt·t n p šʿy n t·t-f šm a py ẖm-ẖl my pẖr-f p wyn z ʾnk

---

l. 32. Gloss ϩⲟⲩ ϩⲟⲩ: *the word is spelt in the demotic like* ϩⲏⲟⲩ, 'money,' with the det. of silver.

Col. XVIII.

l. 6. *n bl*: ἔξω in the Revenue Pap., Wilck., Ostr., i. 19 n., 'on the verso,' 'on the other side.' Cf. V. 15/7. The verso columns I and II are on the back of this Col. XVIII, but they do not contain the passage here indicated.

this boy, Heou (*bis*), Heo, that he may inquire for me, and do thou make him see and let him look and let him listen to everything which I (30) ask him, for I will glorify thee in heaven, I will glorify thee on earth, I will glorify thee before him who is on the throne, who does not perish, (31) he of greatness, Peteri (*bis*), Emphe (*bis*), O great god who is above heaven, in whose hand is the beautiful staff, who created deity, (32) deity not having created him, come into the midst of this flame with Boel, Aniel, and give strength to the eyes of Heu (*bis*).

## Col. XVIII.

'(1) Of Heu (*bis*), the son of Heu (*bis*), for he shall see thee with his eyes, and thou shalt make his ears to hear, (2) and shalt speak with him of everything; he shall ask thee about it, and thou shalt tell me answer truly; for thou art the great god (3) Sabaoth; come down with Boel, Tat (*bis*); bring Boel in, come into the midst of this flame (4) and inquire for me concerning that which is good; Takrtat, he of eternity, bring Boel in,' three times, 'Arbeth, (5) Bainouthio, O great god, bring Boel in,' three times. You say these things down into the head of the boy, (6) you make him open his eyes, you ask him as to everything according to the method which is outside, again.

(7) [Another ?] vessel-inquiry which a pnysician in the Oxyrhynchus nome gave me; you (can) also make it with a vessel-inquiry alone by yourself: (8) 'Sabanem, Nn, Biribat, Ho! (*bis*) O god Sisiaho who (art) on the mountain of Kabaho, (9) in whose hand is the creation of the Shoy, favour (?) this boy, may he enchant the

---

l. 9. *t wt·t n p šꜥy*: 'the generation of the Agathodaemon' probably signifies 'the fortune produced by the god of Fate.'

10. ḥr ʿnw pe p ze k-zʿm z ʾnk ḥr nwn n twe hʾlʾ-ḥr n mre·t ʾnk

11. ʾh n ḥr rhwe ʾnk p rʿ p ḫrt šps nt e-w z n-f gʾrtʾ n rn ank p-e·ʾr pyr a bl

12. ḫr p znḥ n t rpy·t n pr-ybt ʾnk ʿo sp-sn rn-yt ʿo pe pe rn n mte ʾnk . . . .

13. rn-yt ʾw pe pe rn n mte ank l-ʿo-t mw l-ʿo-t pe p ʾr-y gʿm sp-sn p nte te-f

14. gʿm·t ḫn t st·t pa py qlm n nb nt n zz-f th-ʾy-yt sp-sn t sp-sn

15. hʿtrʿ sp-sn p ḥr n ʾʾe sp-sn hy ʾNp p pr-ʿo n t ty·t my še n-f p kke

16. a·ʾny p wyn n-y a ḫn a pe šn-hne z ʾnk Ḥr s Wsr a·ms ʾS·t

17. p ḫrt šps nte mr-s ʾS·t nt šn m-s pe-f yt Wsr wn-nfr hy ʾNp

18. p pr-ʿo n t ty·t my še n-f p kke a·ʾny p wyn n-y a ḫn a pe šn-hne

19. pe swt ty n p-hw my wz-y my wz p nte ḥr-f pḫt a py hne ty n p-hw

20. šʿ nte n ntr·w ʾy a ḫn nte-w z n-y wḥ n mt·t mʿ·t ḫr pe šn nt e-y šn

21. e-tbe·t-f ty n p-hw n mt·t mʿ·t n wš n mt·t n ʿze twn hy ʾNp

22. p snt nḫne mšʿ a bl ty wne·t a·ʾny n-y n ntr·w n ty bk·t erme

23. p ntr nt θ wḥ n p-hw nte-f z n-y pe šn nt e-y šn ḫrr-f n p-hw n sp IX

24. e·ʾr-k wn yr·t-k nge p ḫm-ḫl nte-k nw a p wyn e·ʾr-k ʿš a p wyn z ʾwe·t-f

---

l. 10. *ḥr ʿnw* possibly means 'ape-headed'; the word *šm* (l. 9) occurs with the name of the ape also in 11/2. The copula usually follows *ʾnk* and *nte-k* immediately in this papyrus, but is separated here as in l. 13 *ʾnk l-ʿo-t mw l-ʿo-t pe*.

l. 12. *t rpy·t*: either the goddess Triphis or possibly the constellation Virgo.

light, for I am (10) Fair-face'—another roll says, 'I am the face of Nun—in the morning, Halaho at midday, I am (11) Glad-of-face in the evening, I am Phre, the glorious boy whom they call Garta by name; I am he that came forth (12) on the arm of Triphis in the East; I am great, Great is my name, Great is my real name, I am Ou, Ou (13) is my name, Aou is my real name; I am Lot Mulot, I have prevailed (?) (*bis*), he whose (14) strength is in the flame, he of that golden wreath which is on his head, They-yt (*bis*), To (*bis*), (15) Hatra (*bis*), the Dog-face (*bis*). Hail! Anubis, Pharaoh of the underworld, let the darkness depart, (16) bring the light in unto me to my vessel-inquiry, for I am Horus, son of Osiris, born of Isis, (17) the noble boy whom Isis loves, who inquires for his father Osiris Onnophris. Hail! Anubis, (18) Pharaoh of the underworld, let the darkness depart, bring the light in unto me to my vessel-inquiry, (19) my knot (?) here to-day; may I flourish, may he flourish whose face is bent down to this vessel here to-day (20) until the gods come in, and may they tell me answer truly to my question about which I am inquiring (21) here to-day, truly without falsehood forthwith (?). Hail! Anubis, (22) O creature (?), Child, go forth at once, bring to me the gods of this city and (23) the god who gives answer (?) to-day, and let him tell me my question about which I am asking to-day.' Nine times.

(24) You open your eyes or (those of) the boy and you see the light. You invoke the light, saying, 'Hail,

---

**ⲟⲩ ⲟⲩ**: the hieratic (?) symbols below are of uncertain meaning.

l. 13. *p 'r-y*. It is difficult to make sense of this as it stands. Possibly the *p* may be a copyist's error for *e*, in which case the meaning could be that given above.

*g'm sp-sn* read *g'mg'm* = **ϫⲉⲙϫⲟⲙ**, cf. 3/10.

l. 17. *nte mr-s*: perhaps present relative, see chapter on Grammar.

l. 23. *nt θ wḥ n p-hw* seems to correspond to *nte p wḥ sḥne n t-t-f n p-hw* 6/17, &c., and so may mean 'who governs to-day': see 21/2.

25. p wyn pr sp-sn p wyn θs sp-sn p wyn ʿw sp-sn p wyn p nt n bl ʾm a ḫn e·ʾr-k z·t-f n sp IX

26. šʿ nte p wyn ʿw nte ʾNp ʾy a ḫn a·ʾre ʾNp ʾy a ḫn nte-f smne nʾm-f

27. e·ʾr-k z n ʾNp z twn mšʿ a bl a·ʾny n-y n ntr·w n ty bk·t tym

28. a ḫn ḫr še-f a bl n t hte·t n rn-s nte-f ʾny n ntr·w a ḫn e·ʾr-k rḫ-s

29. z a n ntr·w ʾy a ḫn e·ʾr-k z n ʾNp z a·ʾny wʿ tks a ḫn ḫr n ntr·w

30. nte-w ḥms e-w ḥms e·ʾr-k z n ʾNp a·ʾny wʿ ʾrp(?) a ḫn erme hyn·w t·w my wm-w my swr-w

31. e-f t wm-w nte-f t swr-w e·ʾr-k z n ʾNp z n se ne šn n-y n p-hw e-f z se ʿn e·ʾr-k z n-f z

32. p ntr nt ne šn n-y my ʾr-f t ʿḥʿ t·t-f n-y nte-f z n-y rn-f e-f z rn-f n-k e·ʾr-k

33. šn·t-f a p nt e·ʾr-k wḫ-f e·ʾr-k wḥ e·ʾr-k šn ḫr p nt e·ʾr-k wḫ-f e·ʾr-k wt-w

## Col. XIX.

1. [r (?)] n mt·t a p phs n p wḥr

2. a·ʾr-y ʾy a bl n ʾrq-ḥḥ e r-y mḥ n snf n ʾʾe(?) km

3. e-y syt nʾm-f p(?) tšer(?) n whr py whr nt ḫn p X n whr

4. nte wn-te ʾNp s-f n ḫet-f šte n te-k·t mt·t ʿl n pe-k zʾk nʾm-y(?) ʿn

5. e·ʾr-k tm šte n te-k·t mt·t nte-k ʿl n pe-k zʾk e-y a θy·t-k

6. a ḥry a p ḥft-ḥ n Wsr pe nw e-y a ʾr n-k n p-e-ʾr-e-p-e ge·t(?) ʾpt·w(?)

---

l. 27. *bk·t tym*: cf. Matt. ix. 35, x. 11, 14.

l. 31. *se*, lit. 'they' (are so), = ϲⲉ, 'yes.'

Col. XIX.

l. 1. Supply *r*, 'spell,' before *n mt·t*: cf. l. 32.

(25) O light, come forth (*bis*) O light, rise (*bis*) O light, increase (*bis*) O light, O that which is without, come in.' You say it nine times, (26) until the light increases and Anubis comes in. When Anubis comes in and takes his stand, (27) then you say to Anubis, 'Arise, go forth, bring in to me the gods of this city (or?) village,' (28) then he goes out at the moment named and brings the gods in. When you know (29) that the gods have come in, you say to Anubis, 'Bring in a table for the gods (30) and let them sit down.' When they are seated, you say to Anubis, 'Bring a wine-jar in and some cakes; let them eat, let them drink.' (31) While he is making them eat and making them drink, you say to Anubis, 'Will they inquire for me to-day?' If he says 'Yes' again, you say to him, (32) 'The god who will ask for me, let him put forth his hand to me and let him tell me his name.' When he tells you his name, you ask him as to that which you desire. When you have ceased asking him as to that which you desire, you send them away.

## Col. XIX.

(1) [Spell] spoken to the bite of the dog. (2) 'I have come forth from Arkhah, my mouth being full of blood of a black dog. (3) I spit it out, the . . . of a dog. O this dog, who is among the ten dogs (4) which belong to Anubis, the son of his body, extract thy venom, remove thy saliva (?) from me (?) again. (5) If thou dost not extract thy venom and remove thy saliva (?), I will take thee (6) up to the court of the temple of Osiris, my watch-tower (?). I will do for thee the *parapage* (?) of

l. 4. *šte* seems to mean 'extract' rather than 'enchant.'

l. 6. *p-e-ʾr-e-p-e ge·t* might mean 'that which he of *ge·t* did.'

*ge·t*, perhaps 'sort,' II Kham. vii. 7.

*ʾpt·w*. Reuvens has clearly *ʾptḥ·w*, the *ḥ* being apparently inserted by error between *t* and the determination of birds.

7. a ḫ p ḫrw n ʾS·t t šte·t t nb šte nt šte n nt nb nte b-ʾr-w šte

8. n-s n rn-s n ʾS·t t šte·t nte-k nt *ϩϫⲁⲛ* ḥr *ϭⲙⲟⲩ*

9. nte-k ty-f a t tm·t n p phs n p whr nte-k mt·t ar-f n mne šʿ nte-f (ne-)nfr

10. [r (?)] n mt·t a šte n t mt·t ḥr ḥt-f n rm e·ḥr-w t swr-f pḫre·t nge (?)

11. zw·t ʾwe·t-f sp-sn yʾblw p z n nb n Wsr

12. e swr ʾS·t Wsr p šʿy ʿo n ḫe·t-k e swr-w p III ntr·w e swr-y

13. m-s-w ḥ·t ze n-k t ʾr-y tḫ n-k t ʾr-y byk n-k t ʾr-y hy

14. a bl n-k t ʾr-y hbrbr n-k t ʾr-y the n ḥt n-k t ʾre r-y

15. z wʿ my wz-y a krʿo (?) mw-bn mtw·t nb a·e-w ḫt (?)-w a ḥt-y

16. e-y swr-k my te-y hwy·t-w a ḥry n rn-s n sʿrbythʿ t šr·t

17. n p šʿy z ʾnk sʾbrʿ bryʾthʿ brysʿrʾ her

18. rn-yt ank Ḥr šʿ-r-n (?) e-f n·ʾw n p θ ʾwe·t-f yʿh-ʿo

19. p ḫrt rn-yt n pe rn n mte a wʿ z n ʾrp

20. nte-k t *ⲃⲉϣⲟⲩϣ* e-f knn nte-k ty-f ar-f nte-k mt·t ar-f n sp VII nte-k t swr-f

21. p rm n twe e b-ʾr te-f wm [r (?)]n mt·t a p rm e wn qs zthe

22. ḥr te-f šnbe·t nte-k pe šlʾte lʿte bʿlʿte

---

l. 7. *ʾS·t tʾ šd·t* is figured on a stela of Horus and the crocodiles in the British Museum, Budge, Mummy, p. 359; Wilkinson, Anc. Eg., 3rd ed., vol. iii. Pl. 33. For *šte* see note to l. 4.

l. 8. *πρασον* is prescribed for *θηριοδηκτοις*, Diosc., ii. 178.

ϭⲙⲟⲩ (ϭⲙⲟϩ ?): cf. *kmw*, Br., Wtb. Suppl., 1245; or *qmḥ*, *kmḥ*, ib., Suppl., 1249; Wtb., 1455, 1495 = קֶמַח, 'fine meal.'

l. 9. *tm·t*, 'wound'; the word is best known in the Eg. *ḫr dm·t* = person stung, bitten, or wounded, written out in the Metternich stela, l. 32.

birds (?) (7) like the voice of Isis, the sorceress (?), the mistress of sorcery (?), who bewitches (?) everything and is not bewitched (?) (8) in her name of Isis the sorceress (?).' And you pound garlic with *kmou* (?) (9) and you put it on the wound of the bite of the dog; and you address it daily until it is well.

(10) [Spell] spoken for extracting the venom from the heart of a man who has been made to drink a potion or (?) (11) . . . 'Hail to him! (*bis*) Yablou, the golden cup of Osiris. (12) Isis (and) Osiris (and) the great Agathodaemon have drunk from thee; the three gods have drunk, I have drunk (13) after them myself; for, dost thou make me drunk? dost thou make me suffer shipwreck? dost thou make me perish? (14) dost thou cause me confusion? dost thou cause me to be vexed of heart? dost thou cause my mouth (15) to speak blasphemy? May I be healed of all poison, pus (and) venom which have been . . . . ed to my heart; (16) when I drink thee, may I cause them to be cast up in the name of Sarbitha, the daughter (17) of the Agathodaemon; for I am Sabra, Briatha, Brisara, Her (18) is my name. I am Horus Sharon (?) when he comes from receiving acclamation (?), Yaho, (19) the child is my name as my real name.' (Pronounced) to a cup of wine (20) and you put (*sic*) fresh rue and put it to it; and you make invocation to it seven times, and make (21) the man drink it in the morning before he has eaten.

[Spell] spoken to the man, when a bone has stuck (22)

---

l. 15. *krᵉo* (?): the reading is very uncertain, and the remains will admit of reading *glᵉo*, i. e. κλο.

*a·e-w*, perhaps for εaϣ, or simply εϣ.

l. 16. *n rn-s*: there is no fem. word preceding to which this can be attached. Apparently the pronoun is explained by the subsequent *Sᶜrbytha*, and the passage may be translated 'by the name of Sarbitha.'

l. 20. Seeds or leaves of rue as an antidote to poison, &c., Dıosc., 3/45. *knn* is a word applied to leaves and flowers in this papyrus.

23. p msḥ wbḫ nt ḫr t stp-p·t(?) n p yʿm n h-ʿo-h nte ḫe·t-f

24. mḥ n qs n ḥsy nb hʿy e·ʾr-k a syt n py qs n-y a ḥry n p-hw e-f ʾr

25. qs e-f ʾr wšym (?) e-f ʾr l . . . s n tys·t e-f ʾr nge nb e mn n

26. ge šre z ʾnk wʿ ḥʿ·t n my ank wʿ tp n sr ank wʿ šʿl

27. n ʾbyw srrf pe pe rn n mte z Wsr p nt m t·t p rm n rn-f

28. p nt . . . . . sp VII nte-k mt·t a wʿ ḫm n *ⲛⲉϩ* nte-k

29. t ḥr-f n p rm a ḥry nte-k ty-f a ḫry ḫn r-f nte-k ḥn pe-k tbʿ erme

30. te-k·t ʿne mwt II n te-f šnbe·t nte-k t ʾr-f ʿm p nḥe nte-k t

31. twn-f-s n ḫtp nte-k t p nḥe nt ḫn te-f šnbe·t a bl ty hte·t

32. ḫr ʾw p qs a ḥry erme p *ⲛⲉϩ* r n mt·t a p phs n p whr

33. p ḫyt(?) n ʾMn t rp·t z ʾnk py hkr nḫt šlʿmʿlʿ mʿlet št(?)

34. a-pḥt št-ʿe·t grš-ʿe·t grš-ʿe nb rnt tʿhne(?) bʿhne(?) py ʾʾe(?)

35. py km p ʾʾe(?) ʾr(?) št(?) py ʾʾe(?) pa ty IV·t ʿlw·t p wnš n šr wpy

36. p šr n ʾNp glz n pe-k šʿl ḫʿ n pe-k ryt a ḫry e·ʾr-k n ḥr

37. n St a Wsr e·ʾr-k n ḥr n ʿpp a p rʿ Ḥr s Wsr a·ms ʾS·t nta e·ʾr-k mḥ r-k ar-f

---

l. 25. Copies and the original seem to admit the reading *wšym*, which may be connected with Eg. *wšm*, meaning perhaps a fine point; and *qs* in Egyptian is a harpoon-head.

l. 26. *ʾnk*, perhaps possessive 'mine is'; *tp*, parallel to *šʿl*, may here be 'horn': see 3/22.

in his throat. 'Thou art Shlate, Late, Balate, (23) the white crocodile, which is under (?) the . . . of the sea of fire, whose belly (24) is full of bones of every drowned man. Ho! thou wilt spit forth this bone for me to-day, which acts (?) [as] (25) a bone, which . . . . ., which . . . . . as (?) a bandage, which does everything without (26) a thing deficient; for I am (?) a lion's fore-part, I am a ram's head (?), I am a leopard's tooth; (27) Gryphon is my real name, for Osiris is he who is in my hand, the man named (28) is he who gives (?) my . . . . .' Seven times. You make invocation to a little oil. You (29) put the face of the man upwards and put it (the oil) down into his mouth; and place your finger and (30) your nail [to the ?] two muscles (?) of his throat; you make him swallow the oil and make him (31) start up suddenly, and you eject the oil which is in his throat immediately; (32) then the bone comes up with the oil.

Spell spoken to the bite of the dog. (33) The exorcism (?) of Amen (and ?) Thriphis; say: 'I am this Hakoris (?) strong, Shlamala, Malet, secret (?) (34) mighty Shetei, Greshei, Greshei, neb Rent Tahne Bahne (?) this [dog ?] (35) this black [one], the dog which hath bewitched (?), this dog, he of these four bitch-pups (?), the jackal (?) being (?) a son of Ophois. (36) O son of Anubis, hold on (?) by thy tooth, let fall thy humours (?); thou art as the face (37) of Set against Osiris, thou art as the face of Apop against the Sun; Horus the son of Osiris, born of Isis (is he ?) at whom thou didst fill thy

---

l. 27. *m t·t*, or 'beside me,' ⲛⲧⲟⲟⲧ.

l. 31. *n ḫtp*: in older demotic *n ḫp*, II Kham. 3/18; possibly the *t* may be an error.

l. 33. *ḫyt* (?): cf. 21/30.

*hkr* is determined with the signs of a foreigner and a man. It is perhaps the same word that constituted the name of king Akoris (*Hgr*) of the twenty-ninth dynasty.

l. 37. Apop, the dragon-enemy of the sun.

38. mn a·ms m[n nta (?)] e·ʾr-k mḥ r-k ar-f stm n py sze Ḥr ʾr t ʿlk ḫmm ʾr še a p nwn

39. ʾr snt p t stm p yʿh-ʿo sʿbʿh-ʿo ʾbyʾh-ʿo n rn e·ʾr-k lšlš (?) t tm·t e·ʾr-k nt

40. ḥm ʾh tt t ar-f ke e·ʾr-k nt bšwš ḥr ʾby t ar·f nte-k z·t-f ʿn a wʿ z n mw nte-k t swr-f-s

## Col. XX.

1. n mt·t a t plege

2. ʾnk pe s stn wr tp ʾNp te mw Sḫm·t ʾS·t (?) ʾre-s (?) ʾy m-s-y

3. a bl a p t n ḫr a p sbt n p t n ḥḥ a p tš n ny wm-rm z

4. ys sp-sn tkr sp-sn pe šr s stn wr tp ʾNp z twn·t-k nte-k ʾy

5. a Kmy z pe-k yt Wsr e-f n pr-ʿo ⟨a⟩ n Kmy e-f n wr a (*sic*) p

6. t tre-f n ntr·w tre·w n Kmy swh a θ t grep·t n t·t-f

7. t wne·t n z ny a·ʾre-s fy n-y n wʿ·t fks·t hy te nmte·t a·ʾr·y

---

l. 38. This seems to imply an original chaos of burning.

l. 39. *p* seems distinct, *stm* is extremely doubtful.

*lšlš* (?): the reading is from Reuvens' copy. τογβο, 'purify,' is determined by  in 5/3, and 'cleanse' fits the sense here.

### Col. XX.

l. 1. *plege* = πληγή, as Max Müller, Rec. tr., viii. 174. πληγη is used especially of the sting of a scorpion, B. M. Gr. Pap. CXXI, l. 193, &c., but also of bites and stings of venomous animals in general, Diosc., Περὶ ἰοβολ. 19, and of wounds in general. Except that it bleeds (l. 14) there is little here to show what is meant by *plege* so long as ll. 7–8 remain unintelligible.

l. 2. According to this Anubis was the eldest son of Osiris (l. 5), and his mother was Sekhemt-Isis, called in l. 9 Isis. The liaison of Osiris with Nephthys (cf. Plutarch) is referred to in the O. C. of Pap. Bibl. Nat.

*nte-s*(?)*ʾy* is a possible reading, *a·ʾr-s* is not possible.

l. 3. *wm-rm*: there were Anthropophagi and Cynamolgi caninis capitibus (cf. 21/7) associated in Africa, apparently on the Upper Nile, Plin.,

mouth (i.e. bite), (38) N. son of N. (is he) (?) at whom thou hast filled thy mouth; hearken to this speech. Horus who didst heal burning pain (?), who didst go to the abyss, (39) who didst found the Earth, listen, O Yaho, Sabaho, A'biaho by name.' You cleanse (?) the wound, you pound (40) salt with . . . ; apply it to him. Another: you pound rue with honey, apply it; you say it also to a cup of water and make him drink it (?).

## Col. XX.

(1) [Spell] spoken to the sting: (2) 'I am the King's son, eldest and first, Anubis. My mother Sekhmet-Isis (?), she came (?) after me (3) forth to the land of Syria, to the hill of the land of Heh, to the nome of those cannibals, saying, (4) "Haste (*bis*), quick (*bis*) my child, King's son, eldest and first, Anubis," saying, "Arise and come (5) to Egypt, for thy father Osiris is King of Egypt, he is ruler over (6) the whole land; all the gods of Egypt are assembled to receive the crown from his hand." (7) The moment of saying those things she brought me a blow (?),

---

H. N., 6. 35 ad fin. Northward, Anthropophagi were placed in Syria, ib. 7. 2, or in Parthia (Robinson, Apocr. Gosp., p. 23, and Preface): cf. Rec. tr., xxv. 41. The land of Hah (Millions) is not known.

l. 5. *a n Kmy . . . a p t* must be for *n Kmy . . . n p t*. Possibly the Faiyumic pronunciation ϵ for ⲛ̄ has produced this exceptional writing.

l. 7. The following may be suggested as an alternative translation for this difficult passage: 'At the moment when she said this, a wasp (?) flew to me, my spittle (?) fell down upon me (from fright); it (the wasp) drew near (or gathered itself together) to me, coming unto me with a sting.' Here *a·'re-s* is taken as a relative attached to *z* as regularly in other demotic texts (I Kham. v. 1, &c.); the *n* before *fks·t* is omitted. *fy* is taken in the sense of 'fly' (see Griff., H. Priests, p. 178, note to l. 19), and *fks·t* as possibly an Egyptian rendering of σφήξ. The Coptic ϥⲟⲩⲕⲁⲥⲓ, meaning an aquatic (?) animal of some kind, can hardly be the same word for phonetic reasons; for the form of the *f* see l. 21. The word recurs in 21/7.

*nmte·t* as 'power' = ⲛⲟⲙϯ: this makes no sense. Cf. Kufi, xii. 30, 'he swallowed his *nmty·t*' (of the monkey when terrified).

8. a·ʾr-s swḥ a·e-s ʾy n-y n nw plege a·e-y ḥms a ẖry a·e-y

9. rym ḥms ʾS·t te mw·t n pe mte a bl e-s z n-y mpr

10. rym sp-sn pe šr s stn wr tp ʾNp lkh n ls·t-k a ḥt-k θs-pẖr

11. šʿ n r·w n t ẖt-s (?) lkh n n r·w n t ẖt-s (?) šʿ n r·w n te-k·t

12. nmte·t p nt e·ʾr-k a lkh-f e·ʾr-k ʿm-f bn pʿy nʾm-f a p t z pe-k

13. ls p ls n p šʿy pe-k sʿl pa ʾTm

14. nte-k lkh-f n pe-k ls e-f ẖr snf ty hte·t m-s-s e·ʾr-k mt·t a wʿ ẖm

15. n nḥe nte-k mt·t ar-f n sp VII e·ʾr-k t nʾm-f a t plege m-mne e·ʾr-k

16. sp wʿ·t tys n ʿyw e·ʾr-k ty-s ar-f

17. nt e·ʾr-k zt-f a p nḥe a ty-f a t plʾge m-mne

18. ḥms ʾS·t e-s mt·t a p nḥe ʿbʿrtʿt ẹ-s tyt a p nḥe

19. n mʿ·t z e·ʿr-k ḥsy te-y ne ḥys·t-k p nḥe te-y ne ḥys

20. nʾm-k e·ʾr-k ḥse n t p šʿy e·ʾr-k mẖy n t·t ḥ·t te-y ne ḥys-k

21. šʿ zt p nḥe sp-sn n sym ke-z mʿ·t p fty n p šʿy p s n Gb ʾS·t t nt

22. mt·t a p nḥe p nḥe n mʿ·t t tltyle·t n hwm-p·t p zlẖ n Ḥr-št

---

l. 10. *ls·t-k.* This form seems due to a confusion in endeavouring to write in archaic style. The *t* is quite unwarranted by Egyptian. We may compare the *t* added before the object pronouns following *stm-f*: cf. also note to l. 20. We have here a passage in which very modern forms ⲙⲡⲁⲙⲧⲟ ⲉⲃⲟⲗ are mixed with older forms *ḥms ʾS·t* (past *stm-f*) and this *ls·t-k.*

l. 12. *nmte·t*: if this means 'tail' we may compare Pist. Sophia, p. 323 ⲧⲧⲁⲡⲣⲟ ⲙⲡⲥⲁⲧ, 'the point of the tail of the dragon.'

*bn pʿy*: the Achmimic vetitive ⲙⲛ = ⲙⲡⲣ, cf. 21/23, probably derived from the old vetitive *m.* It occurs in Eg. as *bn*, Pap. Mag. Harris 8/7.

fell my tail (?) upon me. (8) It (?) gathered together (?), it (?) coming to me with a sting (?): I sat down and (9) wept. Isis, my mother, sat before me, saying to me, "Do not (10) weep (*bis*), my child, King's son, eldest and first, Anubis; lick with thy tongue on thy heart, repeatedly (?) (11) as far as the edges of the wound (?); lick the edges of the wound (?) as far as the edges of thy (12) tail (?). What thou wilt lick up, thou swallowest it; do not spit it out on the ground; for thy (13) tongue is the tongue of the Agathodaemon, thy tongue (?) is that of Atum."'

(14) And you lick it with your tongue, while it is bleeding, immediately; thereafter, you recite to a little (15) oil and you recite to it seven times, you put it on the sting daily; you (16) soak a strip of linen, you put it on it.

(17) [The spell] which you say to the oil to put it on the sting daily: (18) 'Isis sat reciting to the oil Abartat and lamenting (?) to the true oil, (19) saying, "Thou being praised, I will praise thee, O oil, I will praise (20) thee, thou being praised by the Agathodaemon; thou being applauded (?) by me myself, I will praise thee (21) for ever, O herb-oil—otherwise true oil—O sweat of the Agathodaemon, amulet (?) of Geb. It is Isis who (22) makes invocation to the oil. O true oil, O drop of

---

l. 17. *pʾge*: the word has been extensively corrected; *p*, originally ʾ, and *g* and *e* being written above the line—see the facsimile.

l. 18. *tyt* = τοειτ, plangere. The songs at funerals both in ancient and modern Egypt are in praise of the deceased, so the word may really mean, or at least imply, 'pronounce eulogy.'

l. 19. *ḥys-t-k*, and in l. 20 *ḥys-k*. It seems as if in one case the *t* was preserved and in the other lost. Compare the fact that this τ of verbs iiiae inf., is often preserved in Sah. when lost in Boh.

l. 21. *nḥe n sym* = νεϩ νсιм, i. e. ῥαφάνινον, Diosc. i. 45 and Peyr. Lex.

*fty*, cf. 21/16, is the reading = ϥωτε, not *šty*, ϣϯ. For the form of *š* in this papyrus see *šty* in 19/7, 8; *f* over another sign has the tail very short.

l. 22. *zlḥ* means to pump, draw water.

23. nt ʾn·ʾw a ḫry n p wtn n twe e·ʾr-k a ʾr p nfr n t yt·t n twe a hwy

24. t p·t a p ʾytn a ḥr šn nb e·ʾr-k a t nfr t ʿe·t ʾr wḥ (?) e·ʾr-k a ʾr pḫret

25. a p nt ʿnḫ z e-y a bk-k a t plege n s stn wr tp ʾNp pe šr

26. z e·ʾr-k a mḥ-s n e·ʾr-k t nfr-s z e-y a bk-k a plege n mn a·ms mn

27. z e·ʾr-k a mḥ-s n e·ʾr-k t nfr-s sp VII r n mt·t a ʾny qs a bl ḫn šnbe·t

28. ʾnk p nte zz-f *θ*y n t p·t e rt·t-f *θ*y a p nwn ʾr nhe n py msḥ mrh (?) ḫn pr-zm (?)

29. n N z ʾnk sʾ syme tʾmʿh-ʿo pe pe rn n mte ʿnwg sp-sn z swḥ·t n bk

30. p nt n r-y swḥ·t n hb p nt n ḫe·t z qs n ntr qs n rm qs n hʿlet qs n rym

31. qs n ʾw qs n nk nb e mn nk ge z p nt n ḫe·t-k my ʾw-f a ḥt-k p nt n ḥt-k

32. my ʾw-f a r-k p nt n r-k my ʾw-f a t·t ty n p-hw z ʾnk p nt ḫn t VII n p·t nt smne·t

33. ḫn t VII n qnḥ·t z ʾnk p šr n p ntr nt ʿnḫ a wʿ z n mw n sp VII nte-k t swr-s t s·ḥm·t

---

l. 24. *ʾr wḥ*, past part. perhaps of ⲟⲩⲱ, cessare, or of ⲟⲩⲱϩ, permanere.

l. 25. *bk* would seem here to mean 'employ,' 'apply.'

l. 27. *a bl*: or *a ḫry* would be a possible reading.

l. 28. *θy n . . θy a*: cf. note to l. 5.

*ʾr nhe n py msḥ* meaning very uncertain; perhaps 'who has risen, ⲛⲁϩⲥⲉ, as this crocodile,' or, if *nhe* = ⲛⲟⲩϩⲉ, 'who has expelled this crocodile.' Cf. note to 2/25.

*pr-zm*. This, though usually written without the *pr*, must be the ϫⲏⲙⲉ, situated on the west bank of the Nile at Thebes, and well known in Coptic literature. The name *zm* may be written with the figure of a crocodile.

rain, O water-drawing of the planet Jupiter (23) which cometh down from the sun-boat at dawn, thou wilt make the healing effect(?) of the dew of dawn which heaven hath cast (24) on to the earth upon every tree, thou wilt heal the limb which is paralysed (?), thou wilt make a remedy (25) for him that liveth; for I will employ thee for the sting of the King's son, eldest and first, Anubis, my child, (26) that thou mayest fill it; wilt thou not make it well? For I will employ thee for (the ?) sting of N. the son of N., (27) that thou mayest fill it; wilt thou not make it well?"' Seven times.

Spell spoken to fetch a bone out of a throat.

(28) 'I am he whose head reaches the sky and his feet reach the abyss, who hath raised up (?) this crocodile . . . in Pizeme (?) (29) of Thebes; for I am Sa, Sime, Tamaho, is my correct name, Anouk (*bis*), saying, hawk's-egg (30) is that which is in my mouth, ibis-egg is that which is in my belly; saying, bone of god, bone of man, bone of bird, bone of fish, (31) bone of animal, bone of everything, there being nothing besides; saying, that which is in thy belly let it come to thy heart; that which is in thy heart, (32) let it come to thy mouth; that which is in thy mouth, let it come to my hand here to-day; for I am he who is in the seven heavens, who standeth (33) in the seven sanctuaries; for I am the son of the god who liveth.' (Say it) to a cup of water seven times: thou causest the woman (*sic*) to drink it.

---

l. 29. Egg of ibis and hawk, the same collocation in B. M. Pap. XLVI. 241.

l. 31. *e mn nk ge*, 'there being nothing else,' i. e. nothing not included in my words—a curious expression: cf. *emn nge šre*, 19/26.

## Col. XXI.

1. p šn-hne n Wsr

2. ʾwe·t-f Wsr p pr-ʿo n t ty·t p nb n t qs·t p nte zz-f n Tny e rt·t-f n N p nt θ wḥ n ʾBt

3. e te-f ʾwhe·t pr-šylem p nt ḥr p nbs n mrwe p nt ḥr p tw n p-ʿo-rʿnws p nt ḥr pe pr šʿ nḥe

4. p pr n Ne-tbew šʿ z·t p nte ḥr-f m sn n ḥr n bk n š-stn a-pḥte·t nte pe-f st n st n ḥf(?)

5. e te-f ʾ·t n ʾ·t n mnt(?) e te-f gyz n rm nt elθ(?) n py mzḥ n ryt nte py bʿ n wḥ-sḥne n te-f gyz

6. ʾwe·t-f yʿhw sʿbʿh-ʿo ʾt-t-ne mystemw yʿwyw ʾwe·t-f mykhʿel sʿbʾel

7. ʾwe·t-f ʾNp n p tše n n ḥr-n-ʾʾe(?)·w p nte pe-f pe py qh p nt fy fks ḥr t rt·t wʿt·t

8. hp p kke n t mt·t a·ʾny p wyn n-y a ẖn ʾm n-y a ẖn a·z·y n-y p wḥ n p nt e-y šn ẖrr-f ty n p-hw n sp IX

9. šʿ nte p ntr ʾy nte p wyn ẖp ẖr ʾr-k-f a ẖ p ky n p sp nt ⟨bl⟩ ḥry ʿn e ḥr-f n p ʿlw a pr-ybt e ḥr-k ḥ-k a pr-ʾmnt e·ʾr-k ʿš a ẖry ẖn zz-f

---

### Col. XXI.

l. 1. The first lines of this column have been made the subject of special study in connexion with the Old Coptic texts of Paris (written on the first pages of the Pap. Bibl. Nat., edited by Wessely), which contain a variant version of them: Erman, A. Z., 1883, 89; Griffith, A. Z., 1900, 85; 1901, 86.

l. 2. Parallel to this line the O. C. (A. Z., 1883, Pl. 3) gives **ⲉⲟⲩⲱⲧϥ ⲟⲩⲥⲓⲣⲉ. ⲡⲉⲣⲟⲡ̄ⲧⲏ ⲡⲛⲏⲃ̄ ⲡ̄ⲧⲕⲁⲏⲥⲉ ⲡⲉⲧⲡ̄ⲡⲣⲏⲥⲡ̄ⲧⲓⲛ ⲉⲧ+ⲓⲟⲩⲱ ⲡ̄ⲉⲃ̄ⲱⲧ ⲡⲉⲧϩⲁ ϩⲫ̄ⲁ ⲡⲛⲟⲩⲃ̄ⲥ. ⲡ̄ⲡⲉⲣⲟϯⲉ. ⲉⲧⲉ ⲡⲉϥ. ⲉ̀ⲟⲟⲩ ⲡ̄ ⲡⲁ ϭⲁⲗⲱⲙ.** The notes to the foregoing in A. Z., 1900, 86 seq., may be consulted by those who wish to study its connexion with the demotic text.

*Tny.* The Edfu geographical list (Br., Dict. Geogr., 1359) states that the head of Osiris was preserved at Abydos (in the nome of This) and a *sbq*, 'foot (?),' at Thebes.

*θ wḥ*, O. C. **ϫⲓⲟⲩⲱ**: cf. 18/23.

l. 3. *ʾwhe·t* has the determinative of wood: cf. *ʾwhy*, Kufi, xi. 21.

*pr-šylem*, **ⲡⲁϭⲁⲗⲱⲙ**, perhaps Jerusalem, or Siloam. Probably *n pr-šylem* is to be read.

## Col. XXI.

(1) The vessel-inquiry of Osiris. (2) 'Hail to him! Osiris, King of the Underworld, lord of burial, whose head is in This, and his feet in Thebes, he who giveth answer (?) in Abydos, (3) whose . . . . is (in ?) Pashalom, he who is under the *nubs* tree in Meroë, who is on the mountain of Poranos, who is on my house to eternity, (4) the house of Netbeou for ever, he whose countenance is as the resemblance (?) of the face of a hawk of linen, mighty one whose tail is the tail of a serpent, (5) whose back is the back of a crocodile (?), whose hand is a man's, who is girded (?) with this girdle of bandage, in whose hand is this wand of command, (6) hail to him Iaho, Sabaho, Atonai, Mistemu, Iauiu; hail to him, Michael, Sabael, (7) hail to him, Anubis in the nome of the dog-faces, he to whom this earth belongs, who carries a wound (?) on one foot, (8) hide the darkness in the midst, bring in the light for me, come in to me, tell me the answer to that about which I am inquiring here to-day.'— Nine times, (9) until the god come and the light appear. You must do it in the manner of the remainder as above again; the boy's face being to the East and your own face to the West; you call down into his head.

---

*p nbs n mrwe*: cf. Maspero in P. S. B. A., xiii. 496. Cf. *n pr-wt* in l. 36.

*p-ʿo-rʿnws*, perhaps *οὐρανός*, in the sense of Olympus.

l. 4. *Ne-tbew*: see note on 2/9.

*ḥf*: a 'snake's' head or tail is regularly described as *n ḥf* in Eg.: cf. Leyd. I. 384, V. II*. 12.

l. 5. *mnt*: some monster or reptile with spiny back, perhaps a crocodile, to judge by the determinative, for which cf. 3/23. It may mean a guardian (**ⲙⲛⲟⲩⲧ**) dragon, as in I Kham. iv. 7.

*nt elθ* (?): very obscure, though the writing is clear.

l. 7. *ḥr-n-ʾʾe·w*: cf. **ϩⲟⲛⲟⲩϩⲱⲣ**, Z., 235, and see the note to 20/3 and A. Z., 1900, 88 (Hdt. iv. 191).

*t rt·t wʿt·t*, **ⲟⲩⲉ-ⲣⲏⲧⲉ** is thus perhaps one foot as opposed to dual **ⲣⲁⲧ-**.

l. 9. *nt n bl* and *nt ḥry* have both been written.

10. n p mḫrr n p z n ʾrp a t (*sic*) s-ḥm·t mr ḥwt e·ʾr-k ʾny wʿ mḫrr n ḥr (?)  ★ nte py mḫrr ḫm pe nte mn-te-f tp e-f θ n III n ʾkym

11. ḥr t ḥ·t n zz-f ḥr gm-k pe-f ḥr e-f šm a bl nge p nt θ tp II ʿn e·ʾr-k ʾny·t-f n t pr n p rʿ e·ʾr-k mr-k n wʿ ḥbs(?) n p ḥrw n ʾ·t-k

12. nte-k mr-k a pe-k ḥr n wʿ·t pke·t n šr-bne·t e p mḫrr ḥr t ḫ·t n t·t-k nte-k mt·t ar-f a ḥr p rʿ e-f a pr n sp VII e·ʾr-k wḥ e·ʾr-k θ-f n ḥsy

13. ḫn hyn·w ʾrt n ʾḥ·t kme·t e·ʾr-k ḫn a zz-f n wʿ . . . n ḫ n zyt e·ʾr-k ḫʿ-f šʿ rhwe ḫn p ʾrte a·ʾre rhwe ḫp e·ʾr-k

14. ʾn·t-f a ḥry e·ʾr-k prḫ ḫrr-f n šʿ nte-k t wʿ·t mnfre(?) n ḥbs (?) ḫrr-f ḥr p šʿ šʿ hw IV e·ʾr-k ʾr ʿnte ʾh st·t mbḥ-f a·ʾre p hrw IV sny nte-f šwy

15. e·ʾr-k ʾn·t-f ne(?)-rt·t-k e wn wʿ ḥbs (?) prḫ ḫrr-f e·ʾr-k prz-f n te-f mt·t n wʿ tk n ḥmt e·ʾr-k fy te-f pše·t n wnm erme ne-k yb·w n t·t-k rt·t-k n wnm

16. e·ʾr-k zfzf-w ḥr wʿ·t blz n ššw nmy n ḫ n elle e·ʾr-k nt-w ḥr IX·t n blbyle·t n zpḫ erme te-k·t mt·t nge te-k·t fty n wš n nḥe

17. n t s·t-eyw·t nte-k ʾr-f n wʿ·t bnn·t nte-k ty-f a p ʾrp nte-k mt·t ar-f n sp VII nte-k t swr-s t s-ḥm·t nte-k fy te-f ke pše·t n . . . . ḥnʿ · e-k yb·w n t·t-k

18. rt·t-k n . . . ʿn nte-k mr-w n wʿ·t tys n š-stn ḥr

---

l. 10. *a t s-ḥm·t mr*: supply *ʾre* after *t*; cf. 25/31, V. 3/14, 13/10.

'Fish-faced (?)': possibly the weevil as having the oxyrhynchus' snout. In Horap. the weevil (?) is *μονόκερως καὶ ἰδιό-* (*ἰβιό-?*)*μορφος*.

*tp*: cf. 3/22; *ʾkym* probably = Eg. *ỉkm*, 'shield.'

l. 11. *p nt θ tp II* = 'stag-beetle (?).' Cf. Pap. Bibl. Nat. l. 65 *κανθαρον τον ταυρομορφον*, and see Horap. I. 10 for Scarabaeidae, Lucanidae (*δίκερως καὶ ταυροειδής*) and Rhynchophora.

l. 12. *mr* sometimes means 'wrap,' but see 11/33.

*ḫ·t* must be a mistake for *ḥ·t*, probably through confusion of the sounds *ḫ* and *ḥ*.

*θ-f*, not from ϫⲓ : ϭⲓ, which would give *θy·t-f*, but a false writing for *t še-f* above 3/31 = *ϫⲟϥ from ϫⲟ : ϭⲟ.

(10) [The method] of the scarab of the cup of wine, to make a woman love a man. You take a fish-faced (?) scarab, this scarab being small and having no horn, it wearing three plates (11) on the front of its head; you find its face thin (?) outwards—or again that which bears two horns—. You take it at the rising of the sun; you bind (?) yourself with a cloth on the upper part of your back, (12) and bind (?) yourself on (?) your face with a strip of palm-fibre, the scarab being on the front (?) of your hand: and you address it before the sun when it is about to rise, seven times. When you have finished, you drown it (13) in some milk of a black cow; you approach (?) its head with a hoop (?) of olive wood; you leave it till evening in the milk. When evening comes, you (14) take it out, you spread its under part with sand, and put a circular strip of cloth under it upon the sand, unto four days; you do frankincense-burning before it. When the four days have passed, and it is dry, (15) you take it before you (lit. your feet), there being a cloth spread under it. You divide it down its middle with a bronze knife; you take (?) its right half, and your nails of your right hand and foot; (16) you cook them on a new potsherd with vine wood, you pound them with nine apple-pips together with your urine or your sweat free from oil (17) of the bath; you make it into a ball and put it in the wine, and speak over it seven times, and you make the woman drink it; and you take its other half, the left one, together with your nails of your left hand (18) and foot also, and bind them in a strip of fine linen, with myrrh and saffron, and bind them to your

---

l. 15. *ne-rt·t-k*: a strange spelling.

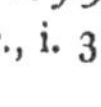 *fy*: so also in l. 17.

l. 16. *fly*, &c. ῥύπος βαλανείων was actually prescribed as a drug, Diosc., i. 34.

ẖl grwgws nte-k mr-w a pe-k znḥ n gbyr nte-k str erme t s-ḥm·t e-w mr ar-k

19. e-f ẖp e·ʾr-k wẖ a ʾr-f ʿn n wš n še-f n ḥsy ẖr ʾr-k-f ʿn n p mḥ III n p wrš e·ʾr-k ʾr n py smte nt ḥry n-f ʿn e·ʾr-k ʿš pe-f ʿš ar-f a ḥr p rʿ n twe e·ʾr-k zfzf

20. e·ʾr-k prz-f e·ʾr-k ʾr-f a ẖ p nt ḥry ʿn n mt·t nb nt e·ʾr-k ʿš-f ar-f mbḥ p rʿ n twe nte-k pe p mẖrr n ẖstb n m·ʿt a·ʾn-y·t-k a bl n p r n pe ʾrpe e·ʾr-k

21. θy(?) zmyz ḥmt a šy·t-k nta rẖ wm p sym e-f hm p sʾẖʿt e-f gmʿ a n sšt(?)·w ʿy·w n na Kmy e-y hb nʾm-k a mn a·ms mn

22. a myẖ·t-s n ḥt-s a ẖe-s sp-sn a ty-s mẖt sp-sn a ty-s ʿte·t z nte-s p-e·ʾr ʾr ty-s mʾ·t a ẖr p rʿ n twe e-s z n p rʿ

23. z bn pr n p ʿḥ z bn wbn n p mw z bn ʾy n na Kmy n t sẖ·t z bn wlʿlʿ n šn·w ʿy·w n na Kmy z bn wtwt

24. e-y hb nʾm-k a mn a·ms mn a šʿkʿ-s n ḥt-s a ẖe-s sp-sn a ty-s mpt (*sic*) sp-sn a ty-s ʿte·t nte-s wḥ-s a p myt m-s mn a·ms mn n nw nb(?)

25. nt e·ʾr-k ʿš-f ar-f e-f ẖn p ʾrte a·wy ʿo sp-sn a·wy pe ʿo sp-sn a·wy nwn-f(?) a·wy mr-f p mẖrr sp-sn nte-k t yr·t n p rʿ p sʾlʿpyn

26. n Wsr t sẖn-t·t(?) n šwy e·ʾr-k nʿy n py ky nta Wsr pe-k yt še nʾm-f e-tbe mn a·ms mn šʿ nte-w t t st·t m-s ḥt-s t ẖo·t

27. m-s ny-s ef-w šʿ nte·s ⟨ne⟩ še mn a·ms mn a mʿ

---

l. 23. Read (*n*) *n šn·w.*

l. 24. *mpt* (*sic*) for *mẖt.*

The last group is  *n nw nb*: cf. l. 43; but in 27/10 we have *stm* written similarly.

l. 25. *sʾlʿpyn*, see note to 13/18.

l. 26. *sẖn-t·t* looks like a compound with *sẖ*, 'the toes' collectively, or 'a toe.' *sẖ-n-t·t* may therefore mean the toes, or the fingers (collectively) of Shu, referring perhaps to his hands which support the sky. The eyes of Ra and Atum were the most important instruments of their rule.

*py ky*, i. e. the condition of one drowned, Ϩⲁⲓⲏⲉ, cf. 6/12.

left arm, and lie with the woman with them bound upon you. (19) If you wish to do it again without its being drowned, then you do it again on the third of the lunar month. You do it in this manner that is above for it again. You pronounce its invocation to it before the Sun in the morning, you cook (it), (20) you divide it, you do it according to that which is above again in everything. [The invocation] which you pronounce to it before the Sun in the morning: 'Thou art this scarab of real lapis-lazuli; I have taken thee out of the door of my temple; thou carriest (?) (21) . . . . . of bronze to thy nose (?), that can eat (?) the herbage that is trampled (?), the field-plants (?) that are injured for the great images of the men of Egypt. I dispatch thee to N. born of N. (22) to strike her from her heart to her belly (*bis*), to her entrails (*bis*), to her womb; for she it is who hath wept (?) before the Sun in the morning, she saying to the Sun, "Come not forth," to the Moon, "Rise not," to the water, "Come not to the men of Egypt," to the fields, "Grow not green," and to the great trees of the men of Egypt, "Flourish not." (24) I dispatch thee to N. born of N. to injure her from her heart unto her belly (*bis*), unto her entrails (*bis*), unto her womb, and she shall put herself on the road (?) after N. born of N. at every time (?).'

(25) [The spell] that you pronounce to it, while it is in the milk. 'Woe (?), great (*bis*), woe (?), my (?) great, woe (?) his (?) Nun, woe (?) his (?) love. O scarab (*bis*), thou art the eye of Phre, the heart (?) (26) of Osiris, the open-hand (?) of Shu, thou approachest in this condition in which Osiris thy father went, on account of N. born of N. until fire is put to her heart and the flame (27) to

l. 27. *ne*. This group occurs in a similar phrase in l. 41 and in l. 32, if the reading in the latter instance be correct. If it stands, then *ne* is difficult to explain; it looks like a preposition 'to,' but if l. 32

nb nt e-f n'm-w      nt e·'r-k ʿš-f ar-f e·'r-k kk n'm-f hy pe ḫrt nfr p syf n wm·w(?) nḫe(?)

28. p-e·'r syt nt syt 'wt n ntr·w tre-w py nta p nt n ḫm erme p nt ʿy gm·t-f ʿwt t p't(?) ʿo·t II·t ḥr pr-ybt n Kmy

29. e-f pr n nw mḫrr km ḥr wʿ·t bw n qme zwf te-y 'r-rḫ n pe-k rn te-y 'r-rḫ n te-k·t ḥm·t(?) t yp·t n syw II(?) rn-k

30. te-y ḥwy ḥyt(?) ar-k n p-hw nphʿlʿm bʿllʿ bʿlkhʿ y-ʿo-phphe z zf nb ḫmm nb sḫt nb nt e·'r-k n'm-w

31. n p-hw e·'r-k-sw ḫn p ḥt p wef p mws p nyš t ʿte·t p mḫt ʿo p mḫt ḫm n spyr·w n ef·w n qs·w n ʿe nb

32. n p ḫʿr n mn a·ms mn šʿ nte-s še(?) ne(?) mn a·ms mn a mʿ nb nt e-f n'm-w      nt e·'r-k ʿš- ar-f ḫn p 'rp      p mḫrr sp-sn nte-k pe p mḫrr

33. n ḫstb n mʿ·t nte-k t yr·t n p rʿ nte-k p byl n 'Tm t sḫn-t·t(?) n šwy p s'lʿpyn n Wsr nte-k py k km ḥyt 'r pyr n p nwn

34. e p nfr n 'S·t erme-k nte-k rʿks rʿpʿrʿks p snf n py ''š ḥwt a·'n-w-f n p t n ḫr a Kmy ḥr p bl(?) a p 'rp(?)

---

be left out of the question, the fact that both in 21/27 and 21/41 š is written over *ne*, as if by an afterthought, suggests that *ne*, which is identical in spelling with **ⲛⲁ** the auxiliary of the future, must be the verb **ⲛⲁ**, 'go' (attaching itself to **ⲛⲟⲩ : ⲛⲟⲩⲓ**, 'futurus esse'), as opposed to **ⲛⲏⲟⲩ**, 'come' (which is qualitative of **ⲉⲓ**; see KABIS, A. Z., 75. 107). **ⲛⲁ** is practically the qualitative of **ϣⲉ** (STERN, § 348). The correction of *ne* to š in both passages would therefore be particularly remarkable. Although, according to STEINDORFF, § 251, the qualitative is admissible in the conjunctive it seems difficult after **ϣⲁⲛⲧⲉ-** : hence no doubt the correction; but if it be possible, the meaning would be 'until she be going,' while š expresses 'until she go.' It would seem that the scribe was puzzled by the *ne*, hence the mistakes and corrections. The following table of forms of the verbs 'come' and 'go' may be useful:—

| | | Inf. | Inf. | | Qual. | Stm-f. |
|---|---|---|---|---|---|---|
| 'go' | Copt. | **ϣⲉ : ϣⲉⲓ** | **ⲛⲟⲩ : ⲛⲟⲩⲓ,** | **ⲛⲁ-** | **ⲛⲁ** | **(ⲧ)ⲉⲛⲛⲟ(ⲟⲩ)?** |
| | Dem. | š | *nʿ* | *ne-* | *ne* (?) | *nʿ-f* |
| 'come' | Copt. | **ⲉⲓ : ⲓ** | — | | **ⲛ-ⲛⲏⲟⲩ** | **(ⲧ)ⲁⲩⲟ** |
| | Dem. | *'y* | — | | *'n-'w* | *'w-f* |

her flesh, until she shall follow (?) N. born of N., unto every place in which he is.' [The spell] which you utter to it when you cook it: 'O my beautiful child, the youth of oil-eating (?), (28) thou who didst cast semen and who dost cast semen among all the gods, whom he that is little (and ?) he that is great found among the two great enneads in the East of Egypt, (29) who cometh forth as a black scarab on a stem of papyrus-reed; I know thy name, I know thy . . . . "the work of two stars" is thy name, (30) I cast forth fury upon thee to-day: Nephalam, Balla, Balkha (?), Iophphe; for every burning, every heat, every fire that thou makest (31) to-day, thou shalt make them in the heart, the lungs, the liver (?), the spleen, the womb, the great viscera, the little viscera, the ribs, the flesh, the bones, in every limb, (32) in the skin of N. born of N. until she follow (?) N. born of N. to every place in which he is.'

[The spell] that you pronounce to it in the wine: 'O scarab (*bis*), thou art the scarab (33) of real lapis-lazuli, thou art the eye of Phre, thou art the eye of Atum, the open-hand (?) of Shu, the heart (?) of Osiris, thou art that black bull, the first, that came forth from Nun, (34) the beauty of Isis being with thee; thou art Raks, Raparaks, the blood of this wild boar (?) which they brought from the land of Syria unto Egypt . . . . . .

---

l. 28. *p'l ʿo·t.* It is very rarely that the Ennead is written without the addition of the word 'gods.' The double Ennead of eighteen gods is frequently mentioned from the earliest times onwards.

l. 29. **ⲡⲟ.** Can this gloss represent a qualitative of ⲡⲓⲣⲉ as ⲟ of ⲉⲓⲣⲉ? The usual qual. is ⲡⲟⲣⲉ.

*n nw mḫrr* for *n wʿ mḫrr*: cf. 14/28, 20/8.

*ḥm·t* (?), 'trade,' 'art' (?).

l. 30. *ẖyt.* In spite of its peculiar form this word can scarcely be other than *ẖyt*, both on account of its meaning and of its association with *ḥwy*. We may translate 'fury of Phalam,' &c.

l. 31. *mws*, O. C. **ⲙⲁⲟⲩⲥ**, probably from Eg. fem. *mis·t*, 'liver' or 'kidneys.' *p mḫt ḥm* named *p ky mḫt* in Pap. Rhind. iv. 6.

35. e-y hb-k n e·ʾr-k nʿ n pe hb n e·ʾr-k a ʾy·f ḫr-k hb·t a p ʾb nte-w tḫm-f a t ḥny·t nte-w t šwy-s a p šʿ n p snyt nte-w ḫḫ-f n wš

36. n tw p zwf n(?) pr-wt nte-w t p ḥmt m-s-f e Ḥr wz n ʾS·t n ḫyrḫr·w ʿy·w n na Kmy nte-w tm ḫʿ ḥwt s-ḥm·t n te-w mt·t e-y hb

37. n·ʾm-k yn a ny e-y hb nʾm-k a ḫry a p ḥt n mn a·ms mn nte-k ʾr st·t n ḫe-s sḥt ḫn ny-s mḫt my p lyb m-s ḥt-s

38. p trwš m-s ny-s ef·w my ʾr-s m qte n p ḫpš m-s t ryr·t my ʾr-s

39. n [p?] mšʿ n p ḫy m-s t ḫyb·t e-s qte m-s mn a·ms mn a mʿ nb nt e-f nʾm-w e-s mr nʾm-f e-s lby m-s-f e b-ʾr-rḫ-s mʿ n p t

40. e-s nʾm-f θy ty-s qt n grḥ my n-s p ʾhm p rwš n mre·t mpr t wm-s mpr t swr-s mpr t str-s mpr t ḥms-s ḫr

41. t ḫyb·t n ny-s ʾy·w šʿ nte-s ⟨ne⟩ še n-f a mʿ nb nt e·f nʾm-w e ḥt-s ʾbḫ e yr·t-s ḥl e ny-s nw pnʿ e·b-ʾr-rḫ-s mʿ

42. n p t e-s nʾm-f šʿ nte-s nw ar-f e yr·t-s m-s yr·t-f ʾb-s m-s ʾb-f t·t-s m-s t·t-f e-s t n-f ty . . . nb my ḥr t ḥ·t n rt·t-s

43. m-s ne-f tbs·w n p [ḫ]yr n nw nb e mn nw šr ys sp-sn tkr sp-sn

## Col. XXII.

1. tey-s n(?) p rn n wr-ty nt e-w ʿš-w a ʾyḫ nb e mn p nte

---

l. 35. *ʾy-f* here and in V. 12/5–8 must represent the infinitive form of *ʾr*, 'do,' with suffix ⲁⲁϥ : ⲁⲓϥ.

*ḫr-k*: cf. V. 33/3.

*tḫm* seems to be the actual reading in the original, but if so it must be an error for *ʿḫm*.

*ḥny·t*: cf. ⲗⲉ-ϩⲱⲛⲉ, Crum, Pap. Fay. No. 34.

l. 37. ⲉⲓⲛⲉ : ⲓⲛⲓ, 'be like,' takes ⲛ in Coptic, but here is used with *a*.

l. 38. The reading is uncertain: perhaps *my ʾr-s p qte*, or more likely the plural *n qte*. The Shoulder and Hippopotamus are the two well-known constellations: cf. Brugsch, Thes., i. 126–7; Maspero, Les Origines, p. 94.

l. 39. The first words may be *n n mšʿ*, hardly *n p mšʿ*.

to the wine, (35) I send thee; wilt thou go on my errand? Wilt thou do it? Thou sayest, "Send me to the thirsty, that his thirst may be quenched, and to the canal that it may be dried up, and to the sand of the *snyt* that it may be scattered without (36) wind, and to the papyrus of Buto that the blade may be applied to it, while Horus is saved for (?) Isis, catastrophes grow great for the Egyptians, so that not a man or woman is left in their midst." I (37) send thee; do like unto these; I send thee down to the heart of N. born of N. and do thou make fire in her body, flame in her entrails, put the madness to her heart, (38) the fever (?) to her flesh; let her make the pursuit of the "Shoulder"-constellation after the "Hippopotamus"-constellation; let her make (39) the movements of the sunshine after the shadow, she following after N. born of N. to every place in which he is, she loving him, she being mad for him, she not knowing the place of the earth in which (40) she is. Take away her sleep by night; give her lamentation and anxiety by day; let her not eat, let her not drink, let her not sleep, let her not sit under (41) the shade of her house until she follow (?) him to every place in which he is, her heart forgetting, her eye flying, her glance turned (?), she not knowing the place (42) of the earth in which she is, until she see him, her eye after his eye, her heart after his heart, her hand after his hand, she giving to him every . . . . . Let fly (?) the tip of her feet (43) after his heels in the street at all times without fail at any time. Quick (*bis*), hasten (*bis*).'

## COL. XXII.

(1) Behold! (spell ?) of the name of the Great-of-Five which they pronounce to every spirit. There is none

---

COL. XXII.

l. 1. No more than the heading has been written. It can hardly refer to the spell in 2/25.

2. n-nḫt-f ar-w(?) ḫr n zʿm·w e·ʾr k ʿš ny sḫ·w a hne nb

3. b-ʾre n ntr·w še n-w e bnp-k šn·t-w a mt·t nb nte-w z n·k

4. p wḥ ḫr t p·t p t t ty·t šn e-f wwy p mw

5. t sḫ·t sḫ e-f n t·t-f n rm a ʿš-f

## Col. XXIII.

1. wʿ r a t hy . . . . z-mt·t

2. ḫr ʾny-k wʿ tp n ʿo nte-k smn·t-f ʾwt rt-k wbe p rʿ n twe e-f a pr

3. wbe-f ʿn n rhwe e-f ʾn·nʿ a p ḥtp nte-k ths te-k·t rt·t n wnm n st

4. n ḫr te-k·t rt·t n . . . . n sʿn n ʿršyn(?)·w n te-k pt ʿn nte-k smn te-k·t wnm

5. ḥr t ḥ·t te-k·t . . . . ḥr pḥ e p tp n te-w mte·t nte-k ths t·t-k n te-k·t t·t II·t n snf n

6. ʿo ḥnʿ t fnz II·t n r-k nte-k ʿš ny sḫ·w a ḥr p rʿ n twe rhwe n hw IV ḫr

7. str-f e·ʾr-k wḫ a t ʾr-f *ⲙⲟⲩ* e·ʾr-k ʾr-f n hw VII e·ʾr-k ʾr pe-f θ-ʾwe·t e·ʾr-k mr wʿ·t ʿy n šr-

8. bne·t a t·t-k wʿ·t pk n šr-bne ḥwt a ḥn·t-k ḥnʿ zz-k nfr nfr pw py(?) (p ?) ʿš nt e·ʾr-k ʿš-f a ḥr p rʿ

9. *επικαλουμαι σε τον εν τω κενεω πνευματι δεινον αορατον*

10. *παντοκρατορα θεον θεων φθοροποιον και ερημοποιον ο μισων*

---

l. 2. Reading *n-nḫt-f e·ʾr-w* (?).

l. 3. Or final 'that the gods depart not.'

l. 5. Probably this spell was never copied out, the remainder of the page having been left blank.

Col. XXIII.

l. 1. . . . . (?). The signs are 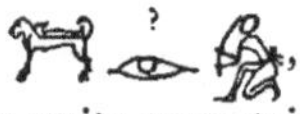, suggesting catalepsy or an evil dream, but the reading is quite uncertain. The result is sleep (l. 7), and, if further prolonged, death.

l. 5. *ḫr bl* or *ḫr pḥ* (?).

*t·t-k n te-k·t t·t II·t*: probably meaning 'your two hands.' Cf. V. 10/4, 5, of the feet.

that is (2) stronger than it in the books. If you pronounce these charms to any vessel, (3) then the gods depart not before you have questioned them concerning every word and they have told you (4) the answer about heaven, earth, and the underworld, a distant inquiry (?), water, (5) (and) the fields. A charm which is in the power (?) of a man to pronounce.

## Col. XXIII.

(1) A spell to inflict (?) catalepsy (? Formula. (2) You take an ass's head, and you place it between your feet opposite the sun in the morning when it is about to rise, (3) opposite it again in the evening when it goes to the setting, and you anoint your right foot with *set*-stone (4) of Syria, and your left foot with clay, the soles (?) of your foot also: and place your right hand (5) in front and your left hand behind, the head being between them. You anoint your hand, of your two hands, with ass's blood, (6) and the two *fnz* of your mouth, and utter these charms towards the sun in the morning and evening of four days, then (7) he sleeps. If you wish to make him die, you do it for seven days, you do its magic, you bind a thread of palm-fibre (8) to your hand, a mat (?) of wild palm-fibre to your phallus and your head; very excellent. This is the invocation which you utter before the sun: (9) 'I invoke thee who art in the void air, terrible, invisible, (10) almighty, god of gods, dealing destruction and making desolate, O thou

l. 6. *fnz*: possibly the corners of the mouth.

l. 7. *ḥ-ʾwe·t* seems to mean literally 'taking pledge,' ϫι-ⲉⲟⲩⲱ : ϭι-ⲁⲟⲩⲱ, so as to get power over a man or god; hence 'magic.' See I Kham. iv. 32.

l. 9. See a very similar invocation in διακοπαί, Leyd. Gr. Pap. V. 11/17, 15/21.

11. *οικιαν ευσταθουσαν ως εξεβρασθης εκ της Αιγυπτου και εξω*

12. *χωρας επενομασθης ο παντα ρησσων και μη νικωμενος*

13. *επικαλουμαι σε τυφων σηθ τας σας μαντειας επιτελω*

14. *οτι επικαλουμαι σε το σον αυθεντικον σου ονομα εν οις ου δυνη*

15. *παρακουσαι ιω ερβηθ ιωπακερβηθ ιωβολχωσηθ ιωπαταθναξ*

16. *ιωσωρω ιωνεβουτοσουαληθ ακτιωφι ερεσχιγαλ νεβοποσοαληθ*

17. *αβεραμενθωου λερθεξαναξ εθρελυωθ νεμαρεβα αεμινα*

18. *ολον ηκε μοι και βαδισον και καταβαλε τον ⚴ η την ⚴ ριγει και πυ*

19. *ρετω αυτος ηδικησεν με και το αιμα τουφυωνος εξεχυσεν παρ εαυ*

20. *τω η αυτη δια τουτο ταυτα ποιω κοινα*

21. a šn wbe ʿḥ e·ʾr-k ʾr·f n šn hn wʿe·t nge ḫm-ḫl e-f ḫp e nte-k nt ne šn e·ʾr-k mḥ yr·t-k

22. n wyt mstme e·ʾr-k ʿḥ ḥr zz wʿ mʿ e-f θse ḥr zz pe-k pr e·ʾr-k sze wbe ʿḥ e-f mḫ

23. wz·t n . . . . . e·ʾr-k wʿb n hw III e·ʾr-k ʿš py ʿš wbe ʿḥ n sp VII nge sp IX šʿ nte-f wnḥ ar-k

24. nte-f sze wbe-k hʾy s-ʿks ʾMn s(t)-ʿks ʿbrʿ-s(t)-ʿks ze nte-k ʿḥ

25. p wr n n syw·w p-e·ʾr ms·t-w stm m-s n-e·z-y mšʿ m-s na r-y wnḥ-k a·ʾr-y tʾhʾnw

26. tʾheʾnwnʿ tʾhnwʿthʿ pfe pe rn n mtr IX n z·t-s šʿ nte-s wnḥ-s ar-k

---

l. 13. *σηθ*: the name of the brother of Osiris is usually written in the Greek papyri with the line over it. Cf. B. M. Pap. CXXI. 965, &c.

l. 15. Cf. Brit. Mus. Gr. Pap. CXXI. l. 893 *ονομασιν σου α ου δυνασαι παρακουσαι.*

l. 18. Frost and fire—probably ague and fever, as REVILLOUT suggests. Cf. *ῥιγοπύρετος* GALEN; *ριγοπυρετιον* Brit. Mus. Gr. Pap. CXXI. l. 218.

l. 19. Read *τυφωνος* (?).

l. 20. *κοινα*: cf. WESSELY, N. gr. Zauberpap., numerous references in index.

l. 22. *sze wbe* is not *ἀποκρίνεσθαι* here.

that hatest (11) a household well established. When thou wast cast out of Egypt and out of (12) the country thou wast entitled, " He that destroyeth all and is unconquered." (13) I invoke thee, Typhon Set, I perform thy ceremonies of divination, (14) for I invoke thee by thy powerful name in (words?) which thou canst not (15) refuse to hear: Io erbeth, Iopakerbeth, Iobolkhoseth, Iopatathnax, (16) Iosoro, Ioneboutosoualeth, Aktiophi, Ereskhigal, Neboposoaleth, (17) Aberamenthoou, Lerthexanax, Ethreluoth, Nemareba, Aemina, (18) entirely(?) come to me and approach and strike down Him or Her with frost and (19) fire; he has wronged me, and has poured out the blood of Typhon (?) beside (?) him (20) or her: therefore I do these things.' Common form.

(21) To divine, opposite the moon. You do it by vessel-inquiry alone or (with) a child. If it is you who will inquire, you fill your eye (22) with green eye-paint (and) stibium, you stand on a high place, on the top of your house, you address the moon when it fills (23) the *uzat* on the 15th day, you being pure for three days; you pronounce this invocation to the moon seven or nine times until he appear to you (24) and speak to you: 'Ho! Sax, Amun, Sax, Abrasax; for thou art the moon, (25) the chief of the stars, he that did form them, listen to the things that I have (?) said, follow the (words) of my mouth, reveal thyself to me, Than, (26) Thana, Thanatha, otherwise Thei, this is my correct name.' Nine (times) of saying it until she (*sic*) reveal herself to thee.

---

l. 24. The acrophonic use of the group  *st* in ⲁϫ is remarkable.

l. 26. 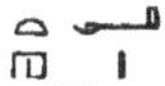 is read first ⲑⲁ and then ⲑⲏⲓ.

After IX probably *sp* should be supplied.

*nte-s wnḥ-s*: it seems as if the feminine referred to the Greek moon σελήνη, the Egyptian being masculine.

27. ke ky n'm-f ʿn a ʿš-f wbe ʿḥ e-ʾr-k smt yr·t-k n py smt e-ʾr-k a ḥry a ḥr ʿḥ e-f mḥ wz·t ḥr nw-k a p sšt n p ntr ḥn t wz·t

28. e-f sze wbe-k ʾnk hʿh qʿ ʿm(?)-r mʿ-ʿmt mtė pe pe rn z ʾnk . . . by s-ʿo ʿgʾnʿgwp

29. mlḫ ʾḫ(?) ʾḫ(?) hy mlḫ rn-yt n mʿ·t sp-sn . . . z·t ank ḫl(?)-by stt ḫn(?) m nfr rn-yt sr ʿo šnbt pe rn n mte

30. z m sp IX e-ʾr-k ʿḥ wbe ʿḥ e yr·t-k mḥ n py kys wy(t) mstme nt ḥr ʾby n ḥr nte-k t wʿ sḫy n wʿ ppy

31. ʿo ar-f nte-k ty-f a wʿ nk n yl nte-k ḫʿ-f n-k n wʿ mʿ e-f hep šʿ p nw nt e-ʾr-k a ʿḥ n-f ḫr ʾr-k-f ʿn a ḫ p nt ḥry

## Col. XXIV.

1 *a*. a . . . . k·t

2 *a*. nyt n bne ḥwt

3 *a*. e-f šʾkh n ʾrte

4 *a*. *ⲉ(?)ⲕⲓⲗ*

5 *a*. nte-k ʾr-w n wʿ m bnn t a p ʾrp(?)

1. pḫre·t e-ʾr-k wḫ a . . . . . *ⲣⲱⲙⲉ* e-f znt
2. *ⲥⲕⲁⲙⲙⲟⲩⲛⲁ ⲣⲓⲛ* (δραχμή) I
3. *ⲟⲡⲓⲟⲩ* (δραχμή) I nt ḥr ʾrte
4. nte-k ʾr-f n bnn nte-k ty-f a wʿ *ⲕⲛⲟⲩⲙ*
5. e-f zf(?) nte-f *ⲟⲩⲁⲙϥ* ḫr ʾr-f *ⲙⲕⲁϩ*
6. k·t e-ʾr-k wḫ a t str rm n hw II
7. *ⲙⲁⲛⲇⲣⲁⲕⲟⲣⲟⲩ ⲣⲓⲍⲁ* (οὐγκία) I
8. *ⲙⲉⲗⲁⲛⲕⲣⲉⲧⲓⲕⲟⲩ* (οὐγκία) I

---

l. 29. The group before *z·t* is difficult to read.

l. 31. *ʿḥ n-f*, 'wait for, be ready for, it.'

Col. XXIV.

l. 1 *a*. The five short lines at the top corner have been taken first and numbered 1 *a*, &c.

l. 1. *e-f znt* seems to belong to ⲣⲱⲙⲉ, but may perhaps be loosely attached, like *nfr* in l. 17 to *pḫre·t*, without reference to its gender.

l. 2. Convolvulus scammonia, Diosc. iv. 168, found chiefly in Syria

(27) Another form of it again, to be pronounced to the moon. You paint your eye with this paint, you (going?) up before the moon when it fills the *uzat*, then you see the figure of the god in the *uzat* (28) speaking unto you. 'I am Hah, Qo, Amro, Ma-amt, Metc is my name; for I am . . . bai, So, Akanakoup, (29) Melkh, Akh, Akh, Hy, Melkh is my true (*bis*) . . . . eternity, I am Khelbai, Setet, Khen (?)-em-nefer is my name, Sro, Oshenbet, is my correct name.' (30) Say it nine times. You stand opposite the moon, your eye being filled with this ointment :—green eye-paint (and) stibium, grind with Syrian honey and put the gall of a chick (31) full grown to it, and put it on a thing of glass, and lay it (by) for yourself in a hidden place till the time when you are ready for it; then you do it again as above.

## Col. XXIV.

(1 *a*) For catalepsy (?)—another: (2 *a*) flour of wild dates (3 *a*) which has been beaten up (?) with milk, (4 *a*) . . . . (5 *a*) you make them up together into a ball, (and) put in the wine.

(1) A medicament, when you wish to drug (?) a man—tested :—(2) scammony root, 1 drachm, (3) opium, 1 drachm; pound with milk, (4) you make it into a ball and put it into some food (?), (5) which is cooked (?), and let him eat it; then he is upset.

(6) Another, when you wish to make a man sleep for two days :—(7) mandragora root, 1 ounce, (8) liquorice (?),

---

and Asia Minor; a strong cathartic, very griping. The root is used, and from it is obtained a gum resin (Brit. Pharmacop.). **pııı** is probably a mistake for **pıϩ** *ῥίζα*, *σκαμβωνίας ῥίζα* occurring amongst the synonyms in Diosc., l. c.

l. 7. Mandragora, Diosc. iv. 76.

l. 8. **μελακρετικοϒ** might be *μῆλα κρητικά* (?) (*κυδώνια*), meaning quinces.

9. *ⲩⲟⲥⲕⲩⲁⲙⲟⲩ* (*οὐγκία*) I

10. *ⲕⲓⲥⲥⲟⲩ* (*οὐγκία*) I

11. e·ʾr-k nt-w a ḫ wꜥ lq n ʾrp e·ʾr-k wḫ ʾr.f n mt·t rm-rḫ

12. e·ʾr-k t ḥt(?) IV·t a p wꜥ sp-sn nʾm-w erme(?) wꜥ wth n ʾrp nte-k

13. ⟨nte-k⟩ tḫb-w n θ n twe šꜥ rhwe nte-k stf-w

14. nte-k t swr-w-s nfr sp-sn k·t III·t *ⲕⲉⲩⲟⲣ*

15. *ⲝⲡⲟϩ* sttr·t(?) I qt I t nꜥ ḥr *ϣⲱⲧⲓ*

16. nte-k ʾr-f n *ⲥⲁⲥⲓ* nte-k t wm-s p rm nt e·ʾr-k wḫ-f

17. pḫr·t a t ʾre rm ʾn-q⟨te⟩tk nfr sp-sn

18. pr·w *ⲝⲡⲱϩ* sttr·t(?) I ½qt·t I nn·t n mꜥntrꜥgwrw IV·t ½qt·t

19. gyss-ꜥo-s IV·t ½qt·t nt n wꜥ sp nte-k t

20. wth n ʾrp XV ar-f nte-k ty-f a wꜥ·t glyt·t n yl

21. nte-k ḥrḥ ar-f e·ʾr-k wḫ a ty-f e·ʾr-k t wꜥ ḫm a wꜥ z n ʾrp

22. e·ʾr-k ty-f n p rm p gyss-ꜥo-s ḥr rt-f ḫn n km·w

23. te-f gbe·t m qty gbe·t n škʾm e-s prz n III ḫlp

24. m qty gbe·t n elle ḥr ʾr-s šp I n ḫy te-f ḥrre

25. m qty ḥt ke-z nb k·t sḫy n *ⲥⲁⲗⲉ* n Rꜥqt

26. nte-k (?)t a nk nb n wm k·t wꜥ·t *ϩⲁϥⲗⲉⲗⲉ ⲕⲥⲉⲧ* II

27. pḫre a . . . . . sḫy n fy pr·w zpḥ n pr-ʾmnt sym(?) n *ⲕⲗⲟ*

28. nt-w n wꜥ sp ʾr m bnn t a p wm(?)

---

But more probably it is the *μελίκρητον*, 'honey and water,' of Hipp., Aph. v. 41 &c.; cf. also *γλυκὺ κρητικόν*, Galen, de Antid. i. 12, &c., 'liquorice.'

l. 9. Hyoscyamus, henbane, Diosc. iii. 69, used as hypnotic, &c., Brit. Pharm.

l. 10. *κισσος*, Diosc. ii. 210.

l. 11. *a ḫ*: a curious usage.

*mt·t rm-rḫ*: cf. I Kham. iv. 37.

l. 12. The meaning may be that you take each of the four ingredients separately and soak it in wine. Perhaps the four *uteh* of wine make the *lok*.

1 ounce, (9) hyoscyamus, 1 ounce, (10) ivy, 1 ounce; (11) you pound them like (*sic*) a *lok*-measure of wine. If you wish to do it cleverly (?) (12) you take four portions to each one of them with an *uteh* of wine, (13) you moisten them from morning to evening; you clarify them, (14) you make them drink it; very good.

Another, the fourth (?):—pips (?) [of ?] (15) apple, 1 stater (?), 1 *kite*, pound with flour. (16) You make it into a cake (?); you make the man eat it, whom you wish.

(17) A medicament for making a man sleep; very good:—(18) pips (?) of apple, 1 stater (?), 1 drachma, mandragora root, 4 drachmas, (19) ivy, 4 drachmas; pound together; you put fifteen (20) *uteh* of wine to it; you put it into a glass *glyt*; (21) you keep it. If you wish to give it, you put a little into a cup of wine, (22) you give it to the man.

Ivy: it grows in gardens; (23) its leaf is like the leaf of *shekam*, being divided into three lobes (24) like a vine-leaf; it (the leaf) is one palm in measurement; its blossom (25) is like silver—another says gold.

Another: gall of an Alexandrian weasel, (26) you add it to any food.

Another: a two-tailed lizard.

(27) A medicament for catalepsy (?): gall of cerastes, pips (?) of western apples, herb of *klo*, (28) pound them together; make into a pill, put (it) into the food (?).

---

*wꜥ sp-sn* = ⲟⲩⲁ ⲟⲩⲁ.

l. 14. *t swr-w-s*, 'let them absorb it,' or 'let the patient (?) drink it.'

l. 18. ½*ql-t*. This group of the *kite*, written with the sign for ½ either over it, as twice in this line, or preceding it, as in l. 19 and V. 7/5, 9/3, doubtless represents the Coptic ϭⲓⲥⲕⲓⲧⲉ : ϫⲉⲥⲕⲓϯ, which is also a fem. word, meaning half a didrachma, or drachma.

l. 26. *nte-k* seems superfluous, see note on plate.

ll. 27–28. A parallel passage, V. 3/1–3.

l. 27. *ⲕⲗⲟ*: Lemm., Kl. Kopt. Stud. x. (Bull. St. Pet. xiii. 12) has shown that ⲕⲗⲟ was the name of a vegetable arrow poison.

29. k·t e·ʾr-k t snf n *ϭⲉⲙⲟⲩⲓ(?)ⲗ* ḥr snf n rm e-f mw·t

30. a p ʾrp nte·k t swr-f p rm ẖr *ⲙⲧⲉϥ*

31. k·t e·ʾr-k t snf n ʾmwlz a *ⲓⲉⲧϥ* ẖr ʾr-f *ϭⲱⲛⲙ*

32. k·t e·ʾr-k t snf n *ϭⲉⲛϭⲗⲱ* py smt ʿn pe

33. k·t e·ʾr-k ʾr wʿ *ⲃⲉϭ* n ḥsy ẖn wʿ ʾrp nte-k t swr-f p rm

34. ẖr ʾr-f te-f yp·t wʿ *ⲉⲙⲓⲙ* n py smt ʿn ẖr ʾr-f

35. te-f yp·t ʿn pe-f *ⲥⲉϩⲉ* ʿn e·ʾr-k ty-s a p ʾrp

36. ẖr ʾr-f te-f yp·t m šs e·ʾr-k t *ⲥⲉϩⲓ* n

37. gʿle·t n Rʿqt a nk nb n wm ẖr ʾr-f te-f yp·t e·ʾr-k t wʿ·t

38. *ϩⲁϥⲗⲉⲗⲉ* n st II a p nḥe nte-k st(?)·t-s erme-f nte-k ths

39. p rm nʾm-f ẖr ʾr-f te-f yp·t

## Col. XXV.

1. n mt·tw n p ḥbs a šn n p ʿlw

2. z-mt·t te·te yg tʿtʿk thethe

3. sʿty sʿn·tʿskl kr-ʿo-mʿkʿt

4. pʿtʿksurʿy kʿlew·pʿnkt ʿ·ʿ·tsyewy

5. mʿkt·sytʿkʿt ḥt-y ḥt r y-ʿo-y

6. ḥʿ·w (?) y my z-w n-y wḥ ⟨a⟩ n mt·t nb nt e-y šn ẖrr-w ty n p-hw

7. z ʾnk Ḥr p ẖrt ḥr ʾb tt z ank ʾS·t t rẖ·t

8. n n z n r-y ẖp z sp VII ḥr ʾny-k wʿ·t mšprt·t (?) nmy

9. nte-k t wʿ sʿl n ḥbs (?) e-f wʿb ar-s n ʾny a bl ẖn ḥ·t-ntr nte-k

10. smn·t-s ḥr wʿ·t tbe·t nmy n ʾny n p myẖl e-s wʿb e bnp

---

l. 30. *t swr-f* (*sic*) *p rm*: so also l. 33.

l. 35. *ty-s* for *ty-f*.

l. 38. *st-s*: can *ps·t-s* be intended? Cf. 27/14.

(29) Another: you put camel's blood with the blood of a dead man (30) into the wine; you make the man drink it; then he dies.

(31) Another: you put a night-jar's blood into his eye; then he is blinded.

(32) Another: you put a bat's blood; this is the manner of it again.

(33) Another: you drown a hawk in a jar of wine; you make the man drink it; (34) then it does its work. A shrew-mouse (?) in the same way; it does (35) its work also. Its gall also, you add it to the wine, (36) then it does its work very much. You put the gall (37) of an Alexandrian weasel into any food; then it does its work. You put a (38) two-tailed lizard into the oil and you cook it with it; you anoint (39) the man with it; then it does its work.

## Col. XXV.

(1) The words of the lamp for inquiry of the boy. (2) Formula: 'Te, Te, Ik, Tatak, Thethe, (3) Sati, Santaskl, Kromakat, (4) Pataxurai, Kaleu-pankat, A-a-tieui, (5) Makat-sitakat, Hati, Hat-ro, E-o-e, (6) Hau (?), E; may they say to me an answer to everything concerning which I ask here to-day, (7) for I am Harpocrates in Mendes, for I am Isis the Wise; (8) the speech of my mouth comes to pass.' Say seven times. You take a new lamp (?), (9) you put a clean linen wick into it brought from a temple, (10) and you set it on a new brick, brought from the mould (?) and clean, on which

---

Col. XXV.

l. 6. ⲧⲁⲧ: the demotic group is probably a ligature for some divine name.

l. 8. *n n z*, probably for ⲉⲛϫⲱ, pronounced ⲛ̄ⲛ̄ϫⲱ.

*mšprḫt*: here and in l. 11 the first sign might be *ḫ* as in the facs.

l. 10. *myḫl*, possibly ⲙⲁϩⲟⲩⲗ, المنقر, in any case probably means the brick-maker's mould; *my* may well represent ⲙⲁ, as in imperative ⲙⲁ-.

11. rm ʿly ar-s nte-k t ʿḥ-s a rt-s nte-k smn t mšprt·t
12. ḥr ʾt-s nte-k t nḥe n mʿ·t ar-s nge nḥe n whe
13. nte-k smn tbe·t II·t nmy ḫrr-k nte-k ḫʿ p ʿlw ʾwt
14. rt-k nte-k ʿš n sḫ·w nt ḥry a ḥry ḫn zz-f n p ʿlw
15. e t·t-k ḥr r yr·t-f nte-k t ḫl a ḥry ḥr gbe·t n twre·t
16. ne-ḥr p ḫbs ḫr ʾr-k-f n wʿ mʿ e·f n kke e-f (*sic*) pe-f r
17. wn a pr-ybt nge p rs e mn ʿy n p ʾytn ḫrr-f
18. nte-k tm ḫʿ wyn a ʾy a ḫn a p mʿ n rn-f nte-k s·wʿb p mʿ n rn-f a t ḥ·t
19. nte-k ḥwy ʾ·t-f n p ʿlw a p r n t ry·t e·ʾr-k wḥ e·ʾr-k ʿš sḫ
20. e·ʾr-k fy t·t-k ḥr r yr·t-f wʿ ʿlw e b-ʾr te-f še erme s-ḥm·t
21. [p] nt e·ʾr-k t še-f ne-t·t-f nte-k šn·t-f z ʾḫ p nt e·ʾr-k nw ar-f
22. ḫr mt·t-f erme-k n mt·t nb nt e·ʾr-k šn·t-f a·ʾr-w
23. wʿ ky a t ḥt s-ḥm·t m-s ḥwt ʾr n wʿ·t wne·t nte-f ḫp ty hte·t ḫr ʾny-k
24. wʿ·t *ϩⲉϣ(?)ⲉ* ⟨e-s ʿnḫ⟩ erme *ⲕⲟⲩⲕⲟⲩⲡ(?)ⲁⲧ* e-w ʿnḫ kys n ʾr n-w
25. snfe n ʿo ḥwt snf n syb n ʾḥ·t km nte-k ths ne-w
26. ʿpe·t·w n skn sšn nte-k ʿš wʿ skp a ḥr p rʿ n te-f wne·t n ḫʿ
27. e·ʾr-k ḫt(?) zz-w n t II·t e·ʾr-k ʾny pe-w ḥt a bl n ne-w spyr n wnm
28. n t II·t nte-k ths-f n p snf n ʿo ḥnʿ p snfe (?) n syb n ʾh·t km·t
29. nt ḥry e·ʾr-kt y-sw a ḫn wʿ ḫʿr n ʿo e·ʾr-k ḫʿ-w n p rʿ šʿ nte-w

---

l. 11. *ʿly* would seem to represent ⲁⲗⲉ : ⲁⲗⲏⲓ ; the gloss ⲁⲗⲟ is strange.

*a rt-s* presumably means 'set it up on end.'

l. 17. *ʿy n p ʾytn*, probably to be taken together, meaning 'cellar.'

(11) no man has mounted (?); you set it upright, you place the lamp (?) (12) on it; you put genuine oil in it, or Oasis oil, (13) and you set two new bricks under you; you place the boy between (14) your feet; you recite the charms aforesaid down into the head of the boy, (15) your hand being over his eyes; you offer myrrh upon a willow leaf (16) before the lamp. You do it in a dark place, the door of it (17) opening to the East or the South, and no cellar being underneath it. (18) You do not allow the light to come into the place aforesaid; you purify the said place beforehand. (19) You push the boy's back to the opening of the niche. When you have finished, you recite a charm, (20) bringing your hand over his eyes. A boy who has not yet gone with a woman, (21) is he] whom you make come before you (?); you question him, saying, 'What do you see?' (22) then he tells you about everything that you ask him.

(23) A method to put the heart of a woman after a man; done in one moment (?), and it comes to pass instantly. You take (24) a swallow (?) alive, together with a hoopoe, (both) alive. Ointment made for them: (25) blood of a male ass, blood of the tick (?) of a black cow; you anoint (26) their heads with lotus ointment; you utter a cry before the sun in his moment of rising; (27) you cut off the heads of the two; you take the heart out of the right ribs (28) of both of them; you anoint it with the ass's blood and the blood of the tick (?) of a black cow, (29)

---

l. 21. Read [*p*] *nt e·ʾr-k*, which is required by the space and the meaning.

*ne-t·t-f*: either *-f* must refer to the lamp, or to the action in general, or else it is a slip for *-k*.

l. 23. *wʿ·t wne·t*: the preparation of the materials would take several days, but they could be kept ready for immediate use.

l. 24. **Внне** seems a likely word, but there is no authority for reading the third sign in the cipher word as н.

*e-w ʿnḫ* does not mean that several hoopoes were required. There were only two birds: see l. 27.

30. šewy n hw IV a·ʾre (?) p hw IV sny e·ʾr-k nt-w e·ʾr-k ty-sw a wʿ

31. ʾrkyʿ e·ʾr-k ḫʿ-f n pe-k ʾy e·ʾr-k wḫ a t ʾre s-ḥm·t mr ḥwt e·ʾr-k θy

32. p znf n wʿ ḫ n hr e·ʾr-k ʿš ny rn·w n mte a ḥr-w

33. e·ʾr-k ty-f a wʿ z n ʾrp nge ḥnke e·ʾr-k ty-f n t s-ḥm·t nte-s swr-f

34. ank byrʿ·ʿqhl lʾ·ʾqh sʾsmryʾ-mr

35. pls·plwn ank ʿo-ʿn-ne sʾbʾʾthl sʾswpw

36. nythy my ḥt mn a·ms mn m-s mn a·ms mn ḫn

37. ny wne·t·w n p-hw sp VII ḫr ʾr-k-f n p mḥ XIV n p wrše nfr sp-sn

## Col. XXVI

1. ke ʿš ʿn n py z n ʾrp
2. byrʿgetht
3. sʿmʿrʿ
4. pylpywn
5. yʿhwt
6. sʿbʿwth
7, 8. sʿypwnythʿs
9. ke ʿš nte-f ʿn ḥr ke-zm
10. ank byrʿgʿtht
11. lʿtht
12. sʿsmyrʿ
13. plyprn
14. ʿo-hw
15. sʿbʿqht
16. sʿswpwnythʿ
17. my ḥt mn m-s

## Col. XXVII.

1. ke šn-hne wʿe·t a nw a p wtn n p rʿ p ʿš nt e·ʾr-k ʿš-f a·wn n-y t p·t t mw·t n n ntr·w

2. my nw-y a p wtn n p rʿ e-f ḫt-ḫnt ḫn-s z ʾnk Gb ʾrpe ntr·w šll p nt e-y ʾr nʾm-f mbḥ p rʿ pe yt

as aforesaid; you put them into an ass's skin; you lay them in the sun until they (30) are dry for four days; when the four days have passed, you pound them, you put them into a (31) box; you lay it in your house.

When you wish to make a woman love a man, you take (32) the shaving (?) of a pleasure-wood (?); you recite these correct names before them; (33) you put it into a cup of wine or beer; you give it to the woman and she drinks it. (34) 'I am Bira, Akhel, La-akh, Sasmrialo(?), (35) Ples-plun, Ioane, Sabaathal, Sasupu, (36) Nithi, put the heart of N. born of N. after N. born of N. in (37) these hours to-day.' Seven times. You do it on the fourteenth of the lunar month. Very excellent.

## Col. XXVI.

(1) Another invocation again of this cup of wine: (2) 'Birakethat, (3) Samara, (4) Pilpioun, (5) Iahout, (6) Sabaouth, (7, 8) Saipounithas.'

(9) Another invocation belonging to it again, in another book: (10) 'I am Biraka-that, (11) Lathat, (12) Sasmira, (13) Plipron, (14) Takou, (15) Sabakhot, (16) Sasoupounitha, (17) send the heart of N. after (18) Sasoupounithas.'

## Col. XXVII.

(1) Another vessel-divination, (to be done) alone, for seeing the bark of Phre. The invocation which you recite: 'Open to me O (?) heaven, mother of the gods! (2) Let me see the bark of Phre going up and going

l. 34. ⲥⲁⲥⲙⲣⲓⲁⲗ: note ⲗ transcribing *mr.*

l. 35. Notice the transcription of the group for 'ass,' here ⲓⲱ, in 26/14 ⲓⲁ-.

Col. XXVI.

l. 8. A gloss to l. 7.

Col. XXVII.

Lines 1–12 are a repetition of 10/22–34; see notes there.

3. e-tbe mt·t ʾr še n t·t ʾy ḥkne·t wr·t nb qnḥ·t tʾ rʿ(?)-št-rd (?) a·wn n-y t nb ʾyḫ·w

4. a·wn n-y t p·t ḥyt·t my wšte-y n n wpt·w z ʾnk Gb ʾrpe ntr·w ʾy p VII stn ʾy p VII

5. Mnt k syt nb šfe·t sḥz t by nn(?) hy rw(?) mʾ rw(?) nn(?) k kke

6. hy ḫnt-ybty·w nwn wr ḫʾw hy by srʾw by ʾmnty·w hy by by·w

7. k kke k k·w sʾ nw·t a·wn n-y ank wbʾ t ʾr pyr n Gb hy ʾnk

8. y·y·y e·e·e· he·he·he h-ʿo h-ʿo h-ʿo ank ʿnep-ʿo myry·p-ʿo-rʿ mʿ·t(?) ʾb thyby

9. ʿo ʾrw·wy wʾw yʿh-ʿo p swḥ-ʾyḫ snfe n smnw snf n qqwpt snf n ʾmwlz

10. ʿnḫ-ʾm·w snw-p·t ʿo-ʾMn qs(?)-ʿnḫ ḫstb n mʿ·t ḫl p-tgs-ʾS·t nt ʾrw m bnn·t nte-k smt

11. yr·t-k nʾm-f ḥr rym·t n by-ʿo-n-p·t n wʿ ḫ n hr n ʾny nge hbyn nte-k mr-k a pe-k qte

12. n wʿ·t pke·t n šn-bn·t ḥwt

13. p ky n ʾr p šn-hne n p ḫbs e·ʾr-k ʾny wʿ ḫbs e-f wʿb e-f wbḫ n wš n t prš mw n qme ar-f e pe-f šʿl n š-stn nte-k mḥ-f n nḥe

14. n mʿ·t nge nḥe n yt·t nte-k mr-f n ʿy IV·t n ʿyw e bnp-w st·t-w nte-k ʿyḫ·t-f a wʿ·t zʿy·t n pr·ybt

15. wʿ·t šmwe·t n ḫ n tphn nte-k t ʿḫ p ḫm-ḫl n pe-f mt a bl e-f wʿb e b·ʾr te-f še erme s-ḥm·t nte-k ḥbs yr·t-f n t·t-k

16. nte-k θ-r p ḫbs nte-k ʿš a ḫry ḫn te-f ʿpe·t šʿ sp VII nte-k t ʾr-f wn yr·t-f nte-k šn·t-f z ʾḫ n-e·nw-k a·ʾr-w

---

l. 8. Note the hieroglyphic transliterations of demotic.

l. 10. *snw-p·t*, possibly *σίναπι*, 'mustard'; it occurs in Louvre dem. mag. iii. 27 with gloss . . . *ροχλου* (?).

l. 14. *st·t-w*, or perhaps *ps·t-w*, which have not been boiled.

l. 15. *tphn*, probably *δάφνη*, Diosc. i. 106.

A good instance of ⲙⲡⲉϥⲙⲧⲟ ⲉⲃⲟⲗ.

down in it; for I am Geb, heir of the gods; prayer is what I make before Phre my father (3) on account of a thing that hath proceeded from me. O Heknet, great one, lady of the shrine, the Rishtret open to me, mistress of spirits, (4) open to me primal heaven; let me worship the angels! for I am Geb, heir of the gods. Hail! ye seven kings; ho! ye seven (5) Mônts, bull that engendereth, lord of strength, that enlighteneth the earth, soul of the abyss (?). Ho! lion as lion of (?) the abyss (?), bull of the night; (6) hail! thou that rulest the people of the East, Noun, great one, lofty one; hail! soul of a ram, soul of the people of the West; hail! soul of souls, (7) bull of the night, bull (?) of (two?) bulls, son of Nut. Open to me, I am the Piercer of earth, he that came forth from Geb; hail! I am (8) I, I, I, E, E, E, He, He, He, Ho, Ho, Ho; I am Anepo, Miri-po-re, Maat (?) Ib, Thibai (9) great, Aroui, Ouoou, Iaho. The spirit-gathering: blood of a *smune*-goose, blood of a hoopoe, blood of a night jar, (10) *ankh-amu* plant, *senepe* plant, Great-of-Amen-plant, *qes-ankh* stone, genuine lapis-lazuli, myrrh, 'foot-print (?)-of-Isis' plant, pound and make into a ball, and paint (11) your eyes with it upon (?) a goat's tear, with a 'pleasure-wood' of *ani* or ebony; you tie yourself at your side (12) with a strip (?) of male-palm fibre. (13) The way of making the vessel-inquiry of the lamp. You take a clean bright lamp without putting minium (or) gum-water into it, its wick being of fine linen; you fill it with genuine oil (14) or oil of dew; you tie it with four threads of linen which have not been cooked (?); you hang it on an East wall (on) (15) a peg of bay-wood; you make the boy stand before it, he being pure and not having gone with a woman; you cover his eyes with your hand; (16) you light the lamp and you recite down into his head, unto seven times; you make him open

17. e-f z ḥr e-y nw a n ntr·w e-w n p qte n p ḫbs ḫr z-w n-f wḥ a p nt e-w a šn·t-w ar-f e-f ḫp e·ʾr-k wḫ a ʾr-f n t·t-k wʿ·t-k

18. e·ʾr-k mḥ yr·t-k n p kys nt ḥry e·ʾr-k ʿḥ a rt-k wbe p ḫbs e-f mḥ nte-k ʿš ar-f n sp VII e yr·t-k ḫtm e·ʾr-k wḥ e·ʾr-k wn

19. yr·t-k ḫr nw-k a n ntr·w n pe-k pḫ nte-k sze wbe-w ḫr p nt e·ʾr-k wḫ-f e·ḫr ʾr-k-f n wʿ mʿ n kke p ʿš nt e·ʾr-k ʿš-f

20. z-mt·t ank mʿneby ghthethwny ⲭⲁⲃⲁⲭⲉⲗ my wšte-y·t-k p šr n ʾrpythnʾ-

21. pyrʿ pyle·ʾsʾ gnwryph·ʾrysʿ tny-yryssʾ psy psy yrys·sʾ

22. gymythwrw·phws·sʾ ʿo-qmʾtsysʾ **ⲟⲣⲉⲟⲃⲁⲍⲁⲅⲣⲁ** pertʾ-ʿo-mekh

23. perʾg-ʿo-mekh sʿkmeph ʾm n-y a ḫn nte-k šn n-y ḫr p šn nte-y šn ḫrr-f n mt·t mʿ·t n wš

24. n mt·t n ʿze pe-f swḥ-ʾyḫ p kys nt e·ʾr-k ty-f a yr·t-k e·ʾr-k ʾn·nʿ a ʾr . . . . nb n p ḫbs

25. ḫr ʾny-k hyn·w ḥrre n bel n ***ⲉⲃⲱⲕ*** ḫr gm-k-sw n p mʿ n p s-trmws e·ʾr-k ʾny·t-w e-w gnn

26. nte-k ty-sw a wʿ lq n yl e·ʾr-k ʿm r-f m šs sp-sn šʿ hw XX n wʿ mʿ e-f hep e-f n kke bn-s

27. hw XX e·ʾr-k ʾny·t-f a ḥry e·ʾr-k wn ar-f ḫr gm-k hyn·w ḫryw erme wʿ mʾz ḫn-f e·ʾr-k ḫʿ-f šʿ hw XL nte-k ʾny·t-f

28. a ḥry nte-k wn ar-f ḫr gm-k-f e·ḥr-f ʾr snf a·ʾre ḫr ʾr-k ty-f a wʿ nk n yl nte-k t p nk n yl a ḫn wʿ nk n blz

29. n mʿ e-f hep n nw nb e·ʾr-k wḫ a ʾr . . . . n p ḫbs

---

l. 19. *n pe-k bl* or *pḫ* (?): cf. l. 30.

ll. 24–29 are a repetition of 5/24–30; see notes there.

l. 24. *wḫe* (?). *šn* stands in the parallel. It seems that *wḫe* (?) is used of *μαντεία αὐτοπτική* (cf. note to 10/22), and *šn-hne*, when opposed to it (l. 34), means divination with a medium.

his eyes; you ask him, saying, 'What are the things which you have seen?' (17) If he says, 'I have seen the gods about the lamp,' then they tell him answer concerning that which they will be asked. If you wish to do it by yourself alone, (18) you fill your eyes with the ointment aforesaid; you stand up opposite the lamp when alight; you recite to it seven times with your eyes shut; when you have finished, you open (19) your eyes; then you see the gods behind (?) you; you speak with them concerning that which you desire; you ought to do it in a dark place. The invocation which you recite, (20) formula: 'I am Manebai, Ghethethoni, Khabakhel, let me worship thee, the child of Arpithnapira, (21) Pileasa, Gnuriph-arisa, Teni-irissa, Psi, Psi, Irissa, (22) Gimituru-phus-sa, Okmatsisa, Oreobazagra, Pertaomekh, (23) Peragomekh, Sakmeph, come in to me, and inquire for me about the inquiry which I am inquiring about, truthfully without (24) falsehood.' Its spirit-gathering: the ointment which you put on your eyes, when you are about to make any divination by the lamp. (25) You take some flowers of the Greek bean; you find them in the place of the lupin-seller; you take them fresh, (26) and put them into a *lok* of glass; you close its mouth very carefully for twenty days in a hidden dark place; after (27) twenty days you take it forth, you open it; then you find a pair (?) of testicles and a phallus inside it; you leave it for forty days; and you take it (28) forth; you open it; then you find that it has become bloody; you must put it into some thing of glass, and you put the glass thing into a pottery (thing) (29) in a place hidden at all times. When you wish to make a divination (?) by the lamp with it, you

l. 29. *n nw nb*: the parallel 5/29, where this is repeated with the next sentence, shows that it cannot mean 'from all sight.'

n'm-f e·ʾr-k mḥ yr·t-k n py snf nt ḥry e·ʾr-k ʾn·nʿ a n·q(te)t·k

30. nge e·ʾr-k ʿḥ wbe p ḫbs e·ʾr-k ʿš n py ʿš nt ḥry ḫr nw-k a p ntr n pe-k pḥ(?)e·ʾr-k ʿḥ nge e·ʾr-k str nfr nfr ʾp

31. ḫr sḫ-k py rn a t tys·t n p šʿl n p ḫbs n rʾw ḫl ⲃⲁⲭⲩⲭⲥⲓⲭⲩⲭ p-e·z ke zm ⲕⲓⲙⲉⲓⲑⲱⲣⲱ ⲫⲱⲥⲥⲉ

32. py ky nt sḫ ḥry p ky n p . . . . n mʿneby pe e-f ḫp e·ʾr-k wḫ a ʾr-f

33. n šn n p ḫbs py smte ʿn pe ḫr ʾr-f ʾr šw ʿn a . . . . n mwryby e-f ḫp e·ʾr-k ʾr-f

34. n šn-hne n p ḫbs e·ʾr-k mḥ p ḫbs nt ḥry ḥr wʿ·t tbe·t nmy nte-k t ʿḥ p ḫm-ḫl a rt-f

35. n p mte n p ḫbs e-f ḥbs a pe-f ḥr nte-k ʿš a te-f(?) ʿpe·t e·ʾr-k ʿḥ ḥr ʾt-f n py ʿš n mt·t wʿyʿny e·ʾr-k wḥ e·ʾr-k klp

36. ḥr-f ḫr ʾr-f z n-k wḥ n mt-t mʿ·t

## Col. XXVIII.

1. ke ky n šn-hne wʿe·t z-mt·t ʾnk p nb by ʿo-rytsym-by s-ʿo-nʿtsyr epysghes emmyme

2. th-ʿo-g-ʿo-m·phrwr phyrym·phwny rn-yk mymy by-byw sp-sn gtheth-ʿo-ny ank Wbst·t pth-ʿo

3. bʿlkhʿm a·ms bynwy sphe phas ank bʿpth-ʿo gʿm·-my·sʿtra rn-yk my·me-ʿo

4. yʾnwme pe-f swḥ-ʾyḫ ḫr š-k a wʿ mʿ e-f wʿb nte-k ʾny wʿ z n ḥmt nte-k yʿ-f n mw n ḥsm nte-k t wʿ lq

5. n nḥe ar-f nte-k wḥ-f ḥr p ʾytn nte-k θ-r wʿ·t lʿmps n ḥmt nte-k θ-s a p ʾytn ḫr t·t p z n ḥmt

6. nte-k ḥbs-k n wʿ·t šnto·t e-s wʿb nte-k erme p hne nte-k ʿš a ḫn p hne e yr·t-k ḫtm šʿ sp VII e·ʾr-k wn yr·t-k

---

l. 32. Manebai is the leading word in the invocation, l. 20.

l. 33. Muribai is a leading word in the invocation in the parallel 5/10 to which this evidently refers.

fill your eyes with this blood aforesaid, you proceed to lie down, (30) or you stand opposite the lamp; you recite this invocation aforesaid; then you see the god behind (?) you, while you are standing up or lying down. Excellent (*bis*) and tried (?). (31) You write this name on the strip of the wick of the lamp in myrrh ink, 'Bakhukhsikhukh,' or, as says another book, 'Kimeithoro Phosse'; (32) this method which is written above is the method of the divination of Manebai. If you wish to do it (33) by inquiry of the lamp, this also is the form, it is also profitable for (?) the divination of Muribai. If you do it (34) by vessel-inquiry of the lamp, you fill the lamp aforesaid on a new brick; you make the boy stand upright (35) before the lamp, he having his face covered; you recite to his head, standing over him, this Greek invocation; when you have finished, you uncover (36) his face, then he answers you truthfully.

## Col. XXVIII.

(1) Another mode of vessel-inquiry, alone. Formula: 'I am the lord of Spirits, Oridimbai, Sonadir, Episghes, Emmime, (2) Tho-gom-phrur, Phirim-phuni is thy name; Mimi, Bibiu (*bis*), Gthethọni, I am Ubaste, Ptho, (3) Balkham born of Binui, Sphe, Phas, I am Baptho, Gam-mi-satra is thy name, Mi-meo, (4) Ianume.' Its spirit-gathering: you go to a clean place, you take a vessel of bronze, you wash it with water of natron, you put a *lok*-measure (5) of oil to it; you place it on the ground; you light a bronze lamp; you put it on the ground by the bronze vessel; (6) you cover yourself with a clean

---

Col. XXVIII.

l. 1. *epysghes emmyme*: Max Müller, Rec. trav., viii. 178, reads here *episkhes epimme*, and regards it as a transcription of *ἐπίσχες ἐπί με*, 'come to me.' The reading is probably *emymme*, but it may still be a corruption of the Greek phrase he has suggested.

l. 5. *θ-s*, ϫoc.

7. e·ʾr-k šn·t-f a p nt e·ʾr-k wḫ-f e·ʾr-k wḥ a t ʾre n ntr·w n p hne sze wbe-k n r-w wbe r-k e·ʾr-k ʿš yʾh-ʿo

8. yph e-ʿo-e gynntethwr nephʿr ʾph-ʿo-e ḫr ʾr-w n-k wḥ a mt·t nb nt e·ʾr-k a šn·t-f a·ʾr-w ʿn a·ʾr-w tm z n-k wḥ e·ʾr-k ʿš

9. py ke rn ng-ʿo-ngethygs mʿntwn-ʿo-b-ʿo-e g-ʿo-kšyrhr-ʿo-nt-ʿo-r nt-ʿo-ntr-ʿo-mʿ leph-ʿo-ger

10. gephʿer·s-ʿo-re e·ʾr-k ʿš ny ḫr ʾr-w šn n-k n mt·t mʿ·t

11. ke šn-hne e·ḫr ʾr-k t·t nḥe n sym ar-f e·ḫr ʾr-k-f a ḫ p nt ḥry z-mt·t sze wbe-y sp-sn hʿmst p ntr n n ntr·w n p kk

12. ʾyḫ nb ḫyb·t nb nt ḫn ʾmnt e·ʾr-s p-e·ʾr mw nhse n-y sp-sn py by n ʿnḫ py by n snsn my pry

13. pe hne pe swt ty n p-hw e-tb p hne n ʾS·t wr·t e-s šn m-s py-s hy e-s qte m-s py-s sn ḥwt mnʿš sp-sn

14. mnʿnf sp-sn a·zy-s z mnʿš sp-sn mnʿnf sp-sn ph-ʿo-ny sp-sn n hh n sp nte-k z·t-s n p ḫm-ḫl ze a·zy-s

15. z my š n-k p kke ʾm n-y p wyn nte-k wn yr·t-k ty hte·t ḫr ʾw n ntr·w a ḫn nte-w z n-k wḥ n mt·t nb

## Col. XXIX.

1. tey-s ky n šn n p rʿ e-w z nʾm-f z e-f znt m šs sp-sn pe-f swḥ-ʾyḫ ḫr ʾny-k wʿ ḫm-ḫl e-f wʿb nte-k ʾr . . . .

2. ʾyḫ nt sḫ ar-f nte-k ʾny·t-f n p mt n p rʿ nte-k t ʿḥ-f a rt-f ḥr wʿ·t tbe·t nmy n p nw nt e·ʾre

3. p rʿ ne ḫʿ nʾm-f nte-f ʾy a ḥry tre-f m tre p ʾtn nte-k t ʾw wʿ·t qbe·t n ʿyw nmy n pe-f pḥ (?) nte-k

---

l. 11. *p ntr n n ntr·w*: cf. φνουθι νινθηρ, Pap. Bib. Nat. 1643, and πνουτε νινϐηρ τηρου, B. M. XLVI. 8.

l. 12. *pr-ʾmnt*, the det. of *ḫn* being the same sign as *pr* that should have followed, one has been omitted.

*e·ʾr-s p-e·ʾr mw*: their meaning is obscure.

Col. XXIX.

l. 1. The end of the line is quite uncertain after *ʾr t* (?).

l. 3. *qbe·t*: Boh. κοϐι, in the Vienna ritual means a mat (?); in l. 23 we have a parallel passage with *šnt·t*.

linen robe, you and the vessel; you recite into the vessel, your eyes being shut, for seven times; you open your eyes; (7) you ask it concerning that which you wish; if you wish to make the gods of the vessel speak with you with their mouths to your mouth, you cry: 'Iaho, (8) Iph, Eoe, Kintathour, Nephar, Aphoe.' Then they make answer to you concerning everything concerning which you will ask of it again. If they do not tell you answer, you recite (9) this other name: 'Gogethix, Mantounoboe, Kokhir-rhodor, Dondroma, Lephoker, (10) Kephaersore.' If you recite these, then they inquire for you truthfully.

(11) Another vessel-inquiry: you put vegetable oil into it; you must proceed as above. Formula: 'Speak unto me (*bis*), Hamset, god of the gods of darkness, (12) every demon, every shade that is in the West and the East, he that hath died hath done it (?), rise up to me (*bis*), O thou living soul, O thou breathing soul, may (13) my vessel go forth, my knot (?) here to-day, for the sake of the vessel of Isis the Great, who inquireth for her husband, who seeketh for her brother; Menash (*bis*), (14) Menanf (*bis*).' Say, 'Menash (*bis*), Menanf (*bis*), Phoni (*bis*),' a multitude of times; and you say to the boy, 'Say, (15) "Depart, O darkness; come to me O light," and open your eyes at once.' Then the gods come in and tell thee answer to everything.

## COL. XXIX.

(1) Behold a form of inquiry of the sun, of which they say it is well tested. Its spirit-gathering: you take a young boy who is pure, you make the spirit-formula (?) (2) which is written for it; you take him before the sun; you make him stand on a new brick at the moment at which (3) the sun shall rise, and it comes up entirely with the entire (?) disk; you put a new mat (?) of linen

4. t ʾr-f ḫtm yr·t-f nte-k ʿḥ a rt-k ḥr ʾ·t-f e·ʾr-k ʿš a ḫry ḫn zz-f e·ʾr-k qlhe a ḫry ḫn

5. zz-f n pe-k tbʿ n p rʿ n te-k·t t·t n wnm bn-s mḥ yr·t-f n p smt a·ʾr-k n ḥ·t

6. nʿsyrʿ ʿo-ʿpkys šfyw(?) sp-sn bybyw sp-sn rn-yk n mʿ·t sp-sn srpt a·wn n-y t p·t n py-s

7. ⟨n py-s⟩ wsḫ py-s mt a·ʾny n-y p wyn nt wʿb my ʾw n-y p ntr nte p wḥ-sḥne n t·t-f nte-f z n-y

8. wḥ a ıınt·t nb nte ἰw-y šn ḫr-ʾr-w ty n p-hw n mt·t mʿ·t e mn mt·t ʿze ḫn(?)-w ʿrkhnwtsy etʿle tʿl

9. nʿsyrʿ yʿrmekh nʿserʿ ʿmpthw ḫ-ʿo ʿmʿmʾrkʿr tel yʿʾ-ʿo

10. nʿsyrʿ hʿkyʾ srpt ḫzysyphth ʿh-ʿo ʿ-t-ne y·y·e(?)·w bʿlbel my

11. ʾw n-y p wyn e-f wʿb my pḫre p ʿlw my z-f n-y wḥ my ʾw n-y p ntr nte p wḥ-sḥne n t·t-f nte-f z

12. n-y wḥ a mt·t nb nt e-y šn ḫr-ʾr-w n mt·t mʿ·t e mn mt·t n ʿze ḫn-w bn-m-s-s e·ʾr-k ʿš pe-f ḥtr

13. n ke sp VII e yr·t-f ḫtm z-mt·t sy·sy·py·tsyrypy s·ʿ·ʾ·ʿo·nkhʿb

14. hrʿbʿ-ʿo-t phʿkthy-ʿo-p ʿnʿsʿn krʿʿnʿ krʿtrys tmʾ

15. ptʿrʿphne ʿrʿphnw ʾm n p ʿlw my ʾw n-f p ntr nte p wḥ-sḥne n t·t-f nte-f z n-y wḥ a mt·t nb

16. nt e-y šn ḫr-ʾr-w ty n p-hw a·ʾre p wyn ʿsqe a ʾy a ḫn e·ʾr-k z ke ke sʾls-ʿo-ʿthʿ yppel

17. syrbʿ n sp VII e·ʾr-k t *ⲁⲗⲃⲟⲩⲛⲟⲩⲧ* a p ʿḫ e·ʾr-k z py rn ʿo m-s ny tre-w e·ʾr-k ʿš-f

18. n ḥ·t-f a pḥ·t-f θs-pḫr n sp IV ʿueb-ʿo-th·yʿbʿthʿ-bʿyth-ʿo-beuʿ

19. e·ʾr-k z my mʾ p ʿlw p wyn my ʾw p ntr nte p wḥ-sḥne n t·t-f nte-f z n-y wḥ a mt·t nb nt e-y šn

20. ḫr-ʾr-w ty n p-hw n mt·t mʿ·t e mn mt·t n ʿze ḫn-w tey-s ke ky nʾm-f(?) ʿn e·ʾr-k θy p ʿlw a wʿ

---

l. 5. *tbʿ n p rʿ*: possibly the 'Apollo-finger' of modern chiromancy, i. e. the third (ring-) finger. The operation described in 3/12, 16, is the *προκωδωνισας παιδα* of Pap. Bibl. Nat. l. 89.

behind (?) ḥim; you (4) make him shut his eyes; you stand upright over him; you recite down into his head; you strike down on (5) his head with your Ra-finger of your right hand, after filling his eye with the paint which you made before: (6) 'Nasira, Oapkis, Shfe (*bis*), Bibiou (*bis*) is thy true name (*bis*), Lotus, open to me heaven (7) in its breadth and height, bring to me the light which is pure; let the god come to me, who has the command, and let him say to me (8) answer to everything which I am asking here to-day, in truth without falsehood therein (?), Arkhnoutsi, Etale, Tal, (9) Nasira, Yarmekh, Nasera, Amptho, Kho, Amamarkar, Tel, Yaeo, (10) Nasira, Hakia, Lotus, Khzisiph, Aho, Atone, I. I. E. O, Balbel, (11) let the pure light come to me; let the boy be (?) enchanted; let answer be given me; let the god who has the command come to me and tell (12) me answer to everything about which I shall ask, in truth without falsehood therein.' Thereafter you recite his compulsion another (13) seven times, his eyes being shut. Formula: 'Si. si. pi. thiripi S. A. E. O. Nkhab (14) Hrabaot, Phakthiop, Anasan, Kraana, Kratris, Ima-(15) ptaraphne, Araphnu, come to the boy; let the god who has the command come to him, let him tell me answer to everything (16) which I shall ask here to-day.' If the light is slow to come within, you say, 'Ke, Ke, Salsoatha, Ippel, (17) Sirba,' seven times; you put frankincense (?) on the brazier, you utter this great name after all those, you utter it (18) from beginning to end, and vice versa, four times, Auebothiabathabaithobeua; (19) you say: 'Let the boy see the light, let the god who has the command come in; let him tell me answer to everything about which I shall ask (20) here to-day, in truth without falsehood therein.'

---

l. 8. *ḥn-w*: this seems to be the reading, cf. l. 12.

21. mᶜ ḥry e-f ḗse e·ʾr-k t ᶜḥ-f a rt-f n wᶜ mᶜ e wn wᶜ ššt ᶜo n pe-f mt e r-f wn a pr-ybt e ẖr [ʾre (?)] p rᶜ wbne

22. a ẖn n ẖe·t-f nte-k smt yr·t-f n p ᶜlw n p smt nt sẖ ar-f nte-k ᶜš ar-f n . . . sp ke-z VII e·ʾr-k ᶜḥ ḥr ʾ·t-f nte-k t ʾr-f

23. kšp a ḥr p rᶜ e-f mḥ wz·t e-f ᶜḥ a rt-f ḥr wᶜ·t tbe·t nmy e wn wᶜ·t šnto·t n ᶜyw nmy n pe-f pḥ(?) e yr·t-f ẖtm

24. e·ʾr-ḳ ᶜš a ẖry ẖn zz-f e·ʾr-k qlh a zz-f n pe-k tbᶜ nt sẖ ḥry ᶜn e·ʾr-k t *ⲁⲗⲃⲟⲩⲛⲟⲩⲧ* a ḥry ne-ḥr-f e·ʾr-k wḥ e·ʾr-k t ʾr-f wn yr·t-f

25. ẖr nw-f a n ntr·w n pe-f pḥ(?) e-w sze wbe-f nt ẖr ʾr-k ty-f a yr·t-f n p ᶜlw e-f ʾn·nᶜ a šn-hne nb n p rᶜ

26. ḥr ʾny-k *ⲓⲗⲟ (?)* II n p yᶜr e-w ᶜnḫ n p II nte-k wš p wᶜ nʾm-w n ẖ n elle n p mt n p rᶜ nte-k t p snf n p ke a ḥr-f

27. nte-k t nᶜ-f erme-f ẖr ẖl nte-k ʾr-w n bnn·t e-w ẖy n tbᶜ wᶜ(?) e·ʾr-k šᶜše(?) t a yr·t-f e·ʾr-k ʾny wᶜ ʾb n lyl(?) erme wᶜ ẖ n

28. hr n ll ᶜn nte-k ẖy ty pḥre ḥr(?) wᶜ ẖm n st n t(?)-nḥs ḥr mw n elle n Kmy nte-k mḥ yr·t-k nʾm-f e·ʾr-k

29. mḥ yr·t-k n ty pḥre nte-k q(?)šp a ḥr p rᶜ e-f mḥ wz·t e yr·t-k wn a ḥr-f ẖr ʾr-f wnḥ-f ar-k nte-f z(?) n-k(?) wḥ(?)

30. a mt·t nb te-f mt·t ᶜo·t(?) wᶜb ẖr ʾr-f ʾr šw a ẖm-ẖl nte-f ʾr šw n-k ḥ-k n rm wᶜ·t

---

l. 21. *e ẖr p rᶜ* should be *e ẖr ʾre p rᶜ*; the condition of the MS. is very unsatisfactory in this part of the column.

l. 23. *mḥ wz·t*, i.e. at the summer solstice, Br., Thes., 296.

l. 26. For the use of vine-twigs as fuel for magic purposes, cf. Hyvern., Actes, p. 311; Brit. Mus. Gr. Pap. CXXI. l. 544, &c.

Behold, another form of it again. You take the boy to an upper lofty (21) place, you make him stand in a place where there is a large window before him, its opening looking to the East where the sun shines (22) in rising into it; you paint the boy's eye with the paint which is prescribed for it, you recite to him ..... times or seven times; you stand over him; you make him (23) gaze before the sun when it fills the *uzat*, he standing upright on a new brick, there being a new linen robe behind him (?), and his eyes being closed; (24) you recite down into his head; you strike on his head with your finger described above; you offer frankincense (?) before him; when you have finished, you make him open his eyes, (25) then he sees the gods behind him (?) speaking with him.

[The ointment] which you put in the boy's eyes when he goes to any vessel-inquiry of the sun (26). You take two .... of the river both alive, you burn one of them with vine-wood before the sun, you put the blood of the other to (?) it, (27) you pound it with it with myrrh, you make them into a pill, they measuring one finger (in length); you .... put into his eyes; you take a kohl-pot (?) of ...... and a kohl-stick (?) of (28) *lel* (?). You pound this drug with a little *set*-stone (?) of Ethiopia and with Egyptian vine-water; you fill your eyes with it, you (29) fill your eyes with this drug, you look towards the sun when it fills the *uzat*, your eyes being open towards it; then he appears to you, he gives you answer (?) (30) to everything. Its chief point is purity; it is profitable for the boy, and it is profitable to you yourself as a person (acting) alone.

---

l. 27. *šʿše* or *šʿme*? The reading is uncertain.
l. 29. *qšp* or *kšp*? The latter is the correct form of the word.
l. 30. *mt·t ʿo·t wʿb*: cf. 17/26.

# VERSO

## Verso Col. I.

1. ʾnḥ n rʿ οφρυς ηλιου
2. ʾnḥ n ʿḥ οφρυς (σεληνης)
3. hyn·w sym·w ne
4. ηλιογονον
5. σεληνογονον
6. hyn·w sym·w ne
7. θιθυμαλος
8. nte py sym ḫm nt ḥ̮r n km·w pe
9. nt ḥ̮r ʾre t ʾw ʾrte a bl
10. e·ʾr·k t pe-f ʾrt a ḥ̮ʿr n rm
11. ḥ̮r ʾr-f blbl

## Verso Col. II.

1. χαμεμελον thw-wʿb rn-f
2. λευκανθεμον šq-ḥtr rn-f
3. κριναθεμον mn p nfr a ḥr-y rn-f
4. χρυσανθεμον nfr ḥr rn-f ke-z a t ḥrr·t nb

---

### Col. I.

l. 1. ὀφρὺς ἡλίου is a synonym of the σχοῖνος ἐλεία in Diosc. iv. 52.

l. 4. ηλιογονον: cf. ελιογωνον as synonym of ϭⲟⲧⲥ in Peyr. Lex. 422 along with κνίκος (carthamus tinctorius, Diosc. iv. 187), ἀτρακτυλίς (ib. iii. 97), &c.; so apparently a sort of thistle.

l. 5. σεληνογονον: the name given by προφῆται to the παιονία (the modern paeonia) according to the synonyms in Diosc. iii. 147. The plant-names ascribed to the προφῆται are naturally connected with deities, heavenly bodies and the like. Sprengel (Praefat., p. xvi) identifies the προφῆται with those of Egypt, but this is perhaps too precise.

l. 9. The grammatical construction seems confused: one would expect ⲉϥϣⲁϥ or ⲉⲧⲉϥϣⲁϥ, St., §§ 426, 427. The writer has given the form of the relative ⲉⲧϥⲥⲱⲧⲉⲙ, but has inserted *ḥ̮r*, which seems to be an anomaly.

l. 10. Galen, de Simpl. medic., viii. 19/7, makes the same remark about the juice of the τιθύμαλλος (Diosc. iv. 162), viz. that if dropped on the skin it burns it.

# VERSO

## VERSO COL. I.

(1) Eyebrow of Ra: *ὀφρὺς ἡλίου.* (2) Eyebrow of the moon. *ὀφρὺς σελήνης.* (3) These are some herbs.

(4) *Heliogonon.* (5) *Selenogonon.* (6) These are some herbs.

(7) Spurge, (8) which is that small herb that is in the gardens (9) and which exudes milk. (10) If you put its milk on a man's skin, (11) it causes a blister.

## VERSO COL. II.

(1) *Chamaemelon.* 'Clean-straw' is its name.

(2) *Leucanthemon.* 'Prick-horse' (?) is its name.

(3) *Crinanthemon.* 'None is better than I' is its name.

(4) *Chrysanthemon.* 'Fine-face' is its name, otherwise

---

COL. II.

l. 1. *χαμαίμηλον*, chamomile (synonym of *ἀνθεμίς* in DIOSC. iii. 144, of *παρθένιον*, ib. 145).

*thw-wʿb* = ⲧⲟϩ + ⲟⲩⲏⲃ (?), 'clean hay,' probably on account of the scent. According to Apul. c. 24 *thaboris* (MS. var. *tuoris*) was the Egyptian name of the plant *χαμαίμηλον* (WIEDEMANN, Altaeg. Wörter v. Klass. Aut. umschr., p. 22).

l. 2. *λευκανθεμον*: synonym of *ἀνθυλλίς*, *ἀνθεμίς*, *παρθένιον*, DIOSC. iii. 143–145, but none of these plants seem to suit the Egyptian name *šq ḥtr*, 'prick(?)-horse.' Cf. ϣⲱⲕ, fodere, and Ar. شاك, 'prick.'

l. 3. *κρινάνθεμον* is said to be the houseleek; perhaps its occurrence in DIOSC. iii. 127, as synonym of *ἡμεροκαλλίς*, gives a better explanation.

l. 4. *χρυσάνθεμον*, DIOSC. iv. 58 = Chrysanthemum coronarium. The name also occurs as a synonym for *ἀρτεμισία* (ib. iii. 117) *χρυσοκόμη*, *ἑλίχρυσον*, and *ἀείζωον τὸ μέγα* (ib. iv. 55, 57, 88).

*t ḥrr·t nb*: cf. LEMM, Cypr. v. Ant., 12 a, 13, and p. 64, ⲡⲉϩⲣⲏⲣⲉ (*sic*) ⲙⲡⲛⲟⲩⲃ. The Hawara wreaths contained specimens, PETRIE, Hawara, p. 53.

5. n p s-qlm te-f gbe·t nẖt pe-f ẖ ʿkf
6. te-f ḥrre·t n nb te-f gbe·t m qty grynʿthemwn
7. p mʿknesyʿ
8. *μανεσια*
9. wʿ ʾny n ty e-f km m qty
10. stem e·ʾr-k nt-f e-f km
11. *μαγνης* p mʿknes nt ʿnẖ ẖr ʾn-w-f
12. *μακνης* e·ʾr-k ẖyt-f e-f km
13. p mʿnes n rm ẖr ʾn-w-f
14. n t ʿn-tsyke e·ʾr-k ẖyt-f
15. ẖr ʾr-f t ʾw snf a bl
16. a t . . . . . pe-k zz
17. wʿ·t *ⲉⲡϣⲉ* nte-k wš[-s (?)] n *ⲛⲉⲛⲉⲉⲃ(?)*
18. nte-k nt-s erme qt I·t n *ϫⲡⲱϩ*
19. erme wʿ·t *ⲃ(?)ⲉϩⲱⲗ* nte-k . . .
20. nte-k t wʿ·t . . . . .

## VERSO COL. III.

1. pẖre[·t a . . . . sẖy n fy]
2. pr·w zpẖ n(?) pr(?)-ʾmnt sym(?) n *ⲕⲗⲟ*
3. nt-w n wʿ sp ʾr m bnn t a p ʾrp(?)
4. *φηκλης*
5. wʿ ʾny e-f wbẖ pe e-f m qty
6. gʿrbʾnʿ wn ke wʿ e·ẖr ʾr-w ʾr-f

---

l. 7. *mʿknesyʿ* is magnetic iron ore: cf. Diosc. v. 147; Plin., H. N., 36. 25.

l. 10. *e-f km*: here *km* is probably pseudo-participle, but in l. 12 infinitive.

l. 11. *mʿknes nt ʿnẖ* = *μάγνης ζῶν*, frequently referred to by Alexander Trallianus (ap. Fabricius, Bibl. gr. Hamburg, 1724, t. xii), e.g. p. 640 in prescriptions.

*ẖr ʾn-w-f*: cf. l. 13, it is probably an imperfect sentence, unless it means 'it is imported.'

l. 13. *mʿnes n rm*: perhaps 'human magnes,' on account of the blood. Cf. Plin., H. N., 36. 25, where the haematites magnes of Zimiris in Aethiopia is described as sanguinem reddens si teratur. He also said 'the gold flower' (5) of the wreath-seller; its leaf is strong, its stem is cold (?), (6) its flower is golden; its leaf is like *crinanthemon.*

(7) Magnesia, (8) *manesia.* (9) A stone of . . . . black like (10) stibium; when you grind it, it is black.

(11) *Magnes.* Magnesia viva; it is brought (i.e. imported ?).

(12) *Maknes.* When you scrape it, it is black.

(13) *Maknes* of man. It is brought (14) from India (?); when you scrape it (15) it exudes blood.

(16) To drug (?) your enemy; (17) an *apshe*-beetle (?); you burn it with styrax (?), (18) you pound it together with one drachma of apple (19) and a . . . . and you . . . . (20) and you put a . . . . . . .

## Verso Col. III.

(1) Medicament [for a catalepsy (?). Gall of ceras]tes, (2) pips (?) of western apples, herb of *klo.* (3) Grind them together, make into a ball, put it into wine (?), and drink (?).

(4) Lees of wine. (5) It is a white stone like (6) gal-

---

speaks of magnes mas and femina, the former being strongly magnetic and of reddish colour; and W. Max Müller has suggested to us that *n rm* may here be for ἀνδρεῖος.

l. 14. *ʿn-tsyke* = Ἰνδική (Max Müller). For Coptic forms of the name cf. Lemm., Kl. Kopt. Stud. ii. (Bull. de l'Acad. St. Petersbourg, x. 405).

l. 16. Probably the word is that in 23/1.

l. 17. ⲉⲛϣⲉ: cf. the beetle *ʿpšʾy*·t of ch. xxxvi of the Book of the Dead.

ll. 19–20. Reuvens' tracing and the facsimile show many scraps in the last lines, but they are too vague to be legible.

### Col. III.

l. 1. Restored from 24/27.

l. 4. φέκλη, 'lees of wine,' 'salt of tartar' (Reuvens, Lettres, i. p. 51, who gives references).

l. 6. *gʿrbʾnʿ*: probably χαλβάνη, galbanum, the resinous sap of Bubo galbanum L., a plant of the fennel tribe used in medicine: see Diosc. iii. 87. Cf. also ϫⲁⲣⲃⲁⲛⲓ, Costum dulce, قسط حلو, Kircher, 186.

7. n sgewe p ky n rḫ·s
8. ar-f z nte-f n mʿ·t pe e·ʾr·k nt wʿ ḫm
9. ḥr mw nte-k ths·f a p ḫʿr
10. n wʿ rm n wʿ·t hte ḫm ḫr ʾr-f
11. ḫt(?) p ḫʿr
12. pe-f rn n mt·t wynn(?) *αφροσεληνον*
13. zʾḫ n ʿḥ wʿ ʾny pe e-f wbḫ
14. pḫr·t a ty ʾre s-ḥm·t mr ḥwt *θθ*·t n šnt·t
15. nt ḥr ʾby ths ḥnt-f (*sic*) nʾm-f
16. nte-k str erme t s-ḥm·t
17. zʾḫ n ʿḥ wʿ ʾny e-f wbḫ pe e-f m qty
18. yl e-f ḫyt n pke sp-sn m qty ʾrsenygwn

## VERSO COL. IV.

1. pḫre·t n msze e-f n mw
2. ḥm zf ḥr ʾrp e-f nfr
3. nte-k t ar-f bn-s šty n ḥ·t
4. nte-k ḫy(t ?) ḥm wʿ·t(?) zf(?) ḥr ʾrp
5. nte-k t ar-f a hw IV
6. *σαλαματρα*
7. wʿ·t ḥflelʿ ḫm
8. e-s n ʾwn n kʿrʿyne
9. e mn-te-s rt·t
10. tp n sr *κεφαλεκη* rn-f
11. wʿ sym e-f m qty wʿ·t bw n šmr ḥwt

---

l. 7. *sgewe.* MAX MÜLLER (Rec. tr., viii. 174) suggests that *σκευή* may have the meaning 'quick-lime,' though this sense is not found in the dictionaries.

l. 12. *wynn* (?): cf. 4/7.

*αφροσεληνον* = *ἀφροσέληνος*, DIOSC. v. 158, another name for *σεληνίτης λίθος*, selenite or foliated sulphate of lime (REUVENS, Lettres, i. p. 51, with reffs.).

ll. 14–16. These lines are repeated in V. 13/10–11.

l. 18. *ʾrsenygwn* = *ἀρσενικόν*, yellow orpiment, i. e. sulphide of arsenic: cf. DIOSC. v. 120. ALEX. TRALL., u. s., p. 632, mentions it in a prescription for gout.

banum. There is another sort which is made (7) into lime (?). The way to know it (8) that it is genuine is this. You grind a little (9) with water; you rub it on the skin (10) of a man for a short time; then it (11) removes the skin. (12) Its name in Greek (?) ἀφροσέληνον, (13) 'foam of the moon.' It is a white stone.

(14) A medicament for making a woman love a man: fruit (?) of acacia; (15) grind with honey, anoint his phallus with it, (16) you (*sic*) lie with the woman.

(17) 'Foam of the moon'; this is a white stone like (18) glass, (when ?) it is rubbed into fragments like orpiment.

## VERSO COL. IV.

(1) Medicament for an ear that is watery. (2) Salt, heat with good wine; (3) you apply to it after cleansing (?) it first. (4) You scrape salt, heat with wine; (5) you apply to it for four days.

(6) σαλαμάνδρα, (7) a small lizard (8) which is of the colour of chrysolite. (9) It has no feet.

(10) 'Ram's horn,' κεφαλική is its name, (11) a herb which is like a wild fennel bush; (12) its leaf and its stem

---

COL. IV.

l. 1. The cross × at the beginning of sections in this and the next column seems intended to catch the eye in the crowded writing on the original—see the facsimile.

Flux from the ears: cf. Pap. Eb. 91/3.

l. 7. *wᶜ·t* (?). The sign in the original is like *ḥmt*, 'bronze,' and scarcely like *wᶜ·t*.

l. 8. *kᶜrᶜyne* = καλαΐνη, chrysolite, greenish-yellow: cf. GOODWIN, Cambridge Essays, 1852, p. 44 (B. M. Gr. Pap. XLVI. 197), and KRALL, Pap. Rain. Mitth., iv. 141.

l. 9. The σαλαμάνδρα of DIOSC. ii. 67 has feet.

l. 10. *tp n sr*: probably κριός DIOSC. ii. 126 = Cicer arietinum, PLINY, Nat. Hist. xviii. 32. See SPRENGEL, ad loc.

l. 11. *šmr ḥwt* = ϣⲁⲙⲁⲣϩⲟⲟⲩⲧ, شمار برى, TATTAM, Lex. from MS. Par. 44, p. 340. The Semitic word is interesting.

12. te-f gbe·t pe-f ẖ zqᶜ m qty
13. p mr-rm e·ʾr-k nt-f e-f šwy nte-k sᶜl-f(?)
14. nte-k ʾr-f n kser-ᶜo-n nte-k ty-f a sẖ nb
15. ẖr lk-f *ταμονιακη*
16. ẖr rt-s m qty slom(?)
17. n te-f gbe·t ne-f pr·w t-qty·t
18. m qty tp n sr e-f *θ*
19. swre·t ẖm n pe-f pḥ(?)

## VERSO COL. V.

1. pẖre·t a(?) ᶜrz snf mw n ḥᶜp(?)-ᶜo
2. ḥr ḥnqe nte-k t swr-s t s-ḥm·t nʾm-f n twe
3. e b-ʾr te-s wm ẖr ᶜḥ-f
4. p ky a rẖ-s n s-ḥm·t z e-s ʾwr·t e·ʾr-k t ʾre
5. t s-ḥm·t ty-s mʾ a ḥr py sym nt ḥry ᶜn
6. ḥr rhwe a·ʾre twe ẖp nte-k gm p sym
7. e-f šhlᶜlt bn e-s a ʾwr·t e·ʾr-k gm·t-f
8. e-f wtwt e-s a ʾwr·t
9. pẖre·t a ẖt(?) snfe gbe·t n šyšᶜ
10. gbe·t n ẖmt-ᶜf e-f knn nt t
11. ar-k e·ʾr-k str erme t s-ḥm·t k·t ẖl
12. ẖzn sẖy n *ⲥϩⲁⲥ* nt ḥr
13. ʾrp ʾs n sty t ar-k e·ʾr-k str erme-s
14. *ασφοδελος*
15. ke-z a mzwl hwt

---

l. 13. *p mr rm*: cf. *φιλάνθρωπος*, synonym of *ἀπαρίνη*, Diosc. iii. 94, a bedstraw 'cleavers' (*προσέχεται δὲ καὶ ἱματίοις*, Diosc. ib.).

*šl-f* (?): cf. ϣⲗϣⲉⲗ, cribrare (?).

l. 14. *kseron* = *ξηρόν*, as suggested by Max Müller, Rec. tr., viii. 173.

l. 15. *ἀμμωνιακή*: cf. Diod. iii. 88, and above.

l. 16. *slom*: perhaps = ϣⲗⲱⲙ, *μολόχη*, a mallow.

### Col. V.

l. 1. *ḥᶜp*(?)*-ᶜo*, 'great Nile,' as name of some perhaps very juicy plant: cf. V. 33/5 for the reading.

ll. 4–8. A similar prescription in the nineteenth dynasty, Br., Rec., ii. pl. 107: cf. Renouf, A. Z., 1873, 123, for recent parallels.

are incised like (13) the 'love-man' plant; you pound it when it is dry, you gather (?) it, (14) you make it into a dry powder; you apply it to any wound; then it is cured.

Styrax, (16) it grows like *slom* (?) (17) as to its leaf; its seed is twisted (18) like the 'ram's horn' plant, it bearing (19) a small spine at its end.

## VERSO COL. V.

(1) A medicament to stop blood: juice of 'Great Nile (?)' plant (2) together with beer; you make the woman drink it in the morning (3) before she has eaten; then it stops.

(4) The way to know it of a woman whether she is enceinte: you make the woman (5) pass her water on this herb as above again (6) in the evening; when the morning comes and if you find the plant (7) scorched (?), she will not conceive; if you find it (8) flourishing, she will conceive.

(9) A medicament to stop blood: leaf of *sheisha*, (10) leaf of 'fly-bronze,' fresh; pound, put (it) (11) on you, you lie with the woman. Another: myrrh, (12) garlic, gall of a gazelle; pound with (13) old scented wine; put (it) on you, you lie with her.

(14) Asphodelos, (15) otherwise called 'wild onion.'

---

l. 4. *rḫ-s . . . ꜣ*: a characteristic construction in demotic: cf. II Kham. vi. 21. 27.

l. 9. *ḫt* (?). This seems a curious use of the word.

l. 10. *ḥmt-ꜥf*. This looks like the literal translation of some foreign name. It is clearly a plant-name; but χαλκόμυια, which it suggests, is found only as the name of a kind of fly: cf. our 'corn-bluebottle.'

l. 13. *ꜥrp ꜥs*, 'old wine,' frequently prescribed in ALEX. TRALL.: cf. Corp. Pap. Rain. II. 183.

*n sty* = οἶνος εὐώδης, Pap. Bibl. Nat. l. 1837.

l. 14. ἀσφοδελός, φύλλα ἔχων πράσῳ μεγάλῳ ὅμοια, DIOSC. ii. 199.

l. 15. χελκεβε: evidently some bulbous plant like the last; called βοτανην χελκβει in Brit. Mus. Gr. Pap. XLVI. 70. Cf. perhaps γέλγις.

16. χελκεβε
17. ke-z ḥzn hwt

## Verso Col. VI.

1. pḫre·t a t ʿlk mw ḫr s-ḥm·t t ḥyt·t n pḫre·t ḥm ḥr nḥe nt . . . n-s(?) hw(?) II
2. bn-s p hw II pḫr n mḥ II·t psymytsy nte-k nt-f erme wʿ ḫm n ʾnzyr n s-nḥe
3. m šs sp-sn nte-k t nḥe n mʿ·t ar-f e-f nfr erme wʿ·t swḥ·t nte-k nt-w nte-k ʾny wʿ ʿʾl(?)
4. n ḥbs(?) n ʿyw e-f šmʿt nte-k sp-f n ty pḫre·t nte-s zqm n t s·t-eywe·t nte-s
5. yʿ n ʾrp e-f ⟨ne-⟩nfr nte-k t p ʾ-ʿo-l n pḫre·t a ḥry nʾm-s nte-k sʿ-ʾy nʾm-f n ḥn
6. a bl ḫn ty-s ʿte·t n wʿ·t hte·t ḫm n p smt n p mz n p ḥwt šʿ nte t pḫre·t
7. ḫlḫl nte-k ʾny·t-f a bl nte-k ḥʿ-s šʿ rhwe a·ʾre rhwe ḫp e·ʾr-k sp wʿ·t qlme·t n ʾby
8. n mʿ·t nte-k ty-f a ḥry nʾm-s šʿ twe šʿ hw III ke-z IV

## Verso Col. VII.

1. k·t m-s-s mw n šwbe e-f lḫm znf wʿ mw n msz n qle·t znf wʿ a ḫ p znf
2. n wʿ z nte-k t wʿ wth n ʾrp e-f ⟨ne-⟩nfr a ḫe t·w nte-s swr-f n mre·t e bnp-s
3. wm nt nb n p t bn-s zqm n t s·t-eywe·t a·ʾr-s t ḥ·t a·ʾre rhwe ḫp e·ʾr-k t p ʾl n
4. ʾbye a ḥry nʾm-s a ḫ p nt ḥry šʿ hw VII k·t m-s-s e·ʾr-k ʾny wʿ·t lwps nmy e·ʾr-k t

---

Col. VI.

l. 1. The last signs must be *hw II*, 'two days': cf. l. 2. The group before this is unusual. The first sign may be ϒ, the uterus, reading *k·t* or *ḥm·t*(?) (Kah. Pap. V. 2 note), and the last two might stand for *n-s*, 'to her,' or for *n mn*, 'daily.'

(16) Khelkebe, (17) otherwise called 'wild garlic.'

## Verso Col. VI.

(1) A remedy to cure water in a woman. The first remedy: salt and oil; pound; apply to the vulva (?) daily (?) two days.

(2) After the two days, the second remedy: white lead, you pound it with a little pigment from an oil-dealer (3) very carefully; you put true oil of fine quality to it, together with an egg and pound them; you take a strip (4) of linen cloth which is fine-spun (?); you dip it in this medicament. She must bathe in the bath, she must (5) wash in good wine; you put the medicated strip on her; you draw (?) it in (and) (6) out of her vulva for a short time, like the phallus of a man, until the medicament (7) spreads (?); you remove it, you leave her till evening; when evening comes, you dip a bandage (?) in genuine honey, (8) you put it on her until morning, for three, otherwise said four, days.

## Verso Col. VII.

(1) Another to follow it: juice of a cucumber which has been rubbed down, one ladleful (?), water of the ears of a *kle*-animal, one ladleful (?) like the ladle (2) of a (wine-) cup; you add a *uteh*-measure of good wine to them; and she drinks it at midday, before she has (3) eaten anything whatever, after bathing in the bath, which she has done before; when evening comes, you put the rag (?) (4) with honey on her as above for seven days.

---

l. 2. *psymytsy*, as Revillout pointed out, is ψιμύθιον, 'white lead': cf. Zoega, 626; Diosc. v. 103.

5. X n wth n ʾrp ʾs e-f hlk ar-s e·ʾr-k t wʿ·t ½qt·t n bšwš e-f knn a ḫ·t-f n *θ*

6. n twe šʿ mre·t nte-s zqm n t s·t-eywe nte-s ʾy a bl nte-s swr-f a·ʾre rhwe

7. ḫp e·ʾr-k t ʾbye a ḥry nʾm-s a ḫ p nt ḥry ʿn šʿ hw VII

## Verso Col. VIII.

1. *ποδακραν*
2. e·ʾr-k t ḥms p rm nte-k t š sʿn ḫr rt-f n p rm
3. nte-k t š . . . m-s-f a rt-f ḥr ʾ·t-f e·ʾr-k šn
4. p rm z ḥr-f stm šʿ hw III m-s-s e·ʾr-k ʾny qpqp
5. e·ʾr-k psy·t-f ḥr nḥe n qwpre e·ʾr-k ths rt-f
6. nʾm-f e·ʾr-k wḥ e·ʾr-k ʾny qntʾe Rʿqt ḥr ell šw
7. ḫr sym n gyz e·ʾr-k nt-w ḥr ʾrp e·ʾr-k slk-f n p bl
8. ny nte-k nyf m-s-f n r-k

## Verso Col. IX.

1. k·t
2. *ευφορβιου* I·t qt·t
3. *πεπτερεως* ½ qt·t
4. *περηθου* sttr·t(?) I·t
5. *αυταρχες* sttr·t ?) I·t
6. sttr·t(?) I·t *διοναπερον*
7. mn ʾrp sttr·t(?) VI

---

### Col. VIII.

l. 5. *nḥe n qwpre* = *ἔλαιον κύπρινον*, Diosc. i. 65; Plin., H. N., 12. 51; 13. 1, 2; 23. 46, made from the seeds or leaves of *ἡ κύπρος*, ϫⲟⲩⲡⲉⲣ, Kircher, p. 179, Lawsonia inermis, the henna of the Arabs. The red dye made from the leaves is now the commonest cosmetic in the East, but was perhaps little known anciently. The oil frequently occurs in prescriptions in Alex. Trall.

l. 7. *sym n gyz*: lit. 'hand-plant,' with gloss ⲡⲡⲧⲁⲕⲧⲁⲗⲟⲥ, which no doubt stands for *πεντεδάκτυλος*, Diosc. iv. 42 = *πεντάφυλλον* (potentilla). According to Lenz, p. 702, it is still called in Greece by both names. Cf. Parthey, Zauberpap., ii. 34. 40; Pap. bibl. nat. 287.

ll. 7–8. *n p bl ny*: a curious construction, if correct.

### Col. IX.

l. 3. *πεπτερεως* for *πεπέρεως*, 'pepper' (Reuvens, Lettres, i. p. 50), cf.

Another to follow: you take a new dish; you put (5) ten *uteh*-measures of old sweet wine on it; you put a half *kite* of fresh rue on it from (6) dawn till midday; let her bathe in the bath, and come out and drink it. When it is evening (7) you put honey on her as above again for seven days.

## VERSO COL. VIII.

(1) Gout. (2) You make the man sit down; you place clay under the feet of the man; (3) you put .... to it (?), his feet resting on it; you ask (4) the man, saying, 'Has it hearkened?' for three days. Thereafter you take an ant (?), (5) you cook it in oil of henna; you anoint his feet (6) with it. When you have finished, you take Alexandrian figs and dried grapes (7) and potentilla; you pound them with wine; you anoint him besides (?) (8) these; and you blow on him with your mouth.

## VERSO COL. IX.

(1) Another: (2) 1 *kite* of Euphorbia, (3) $\frac{1}{2}$ *kite* of pepper, (4) 1 stater (?) of pyrethrum (?), (5) 1 stater (?) of adarces, (6) native sulphur, 1 stater (?), (7) any wine 6

---

Diosc. ii. 188; and for its use as a magico-medical ingredient, Wessely, N. Gr. Zauberpap., p. 25; and below V. 14/3; Sigismund, Aromata, p. 41.

l. 4. περηθου = πυρέθρου, apparently an umbellifer hot to the taste: cf. Diosc. iii. 78.

l. 5. αυταρχες = ἀδάρκης, Diosc. v. 136, a salt efflorescence on marsh plants. It is noteworthy that these four ingredients, spurge, pepper, πύρεθρον, and ἀδάρκης, are all found with many others in a prescription for gout given by Alex. Trall., lib. xi. p. 628.

l. 6. διονιπερον = θεῖον ἄπυρον (Reuvens, Lettres, i. p. 50), native sulphur. For its use cf. Brit. Mus. Gr. Pap. CXXI. l. 168; Zoega, 626 ⲑⲏⲛ ⲡ̄ⲁⲧⲱϣⲙ. The ⲟⲛⲁⲡⲉⲣⲟⲛ of Kir. 203 = sulphur rubrum, is doubtless a corruption of the above.

8. nḥe n mʿ·t . . . ntek nt-w
9. nte-k ʾr-w n wʿ·t splelyn t a p mʿ
10. nt šn n p rm

## Verso Col. X.

1. ke s a(?) rt-f n p-etʾgrwn
2. e·ʾr-k sḫ ny rn-w a wʿ pq
3. n ḥt nge tren e·ʾr-k ty-f
4. a wʿ ḫʿr n ʾywr nte-k mr-f a rt-f
5. n p rm n rn-f *δερμα ελαφιον* n t rt·t II·t
6. **ⲑⲉⲙⲃⲁⲣⲁⲑⲉⲙ**
7. **ⲟⲩⲣⲉⲙⲃⲣⲉⲛⲟⲩⲧⲓⲡⲉ**
8. **ⲁⲓⲟ·ⲭⲑⲟⲩ**
9. **ⲥⲉⲙⲙⲁⲣⲁⲑⲉⲙⲙⲟⲩ**
10. **ⲛⲁⲓⲟⲟⲩ** my lk mn a·ms mn
11. n šn nb nt ḫn ne-f pt·w te-f rt·w II·t
12. ḫr ʾ -k-f e ʿḥ my

## Verso Col. XI.

1. pḫre·t n rt(?) . . .
2. ḫzn ʾlbwnt
3. . . . . ʾs
4. nḥe n mʿ·t nt ths-f
5. nʾm-f e-f šwy e·ʾr-k yʿ-f
6. n mw qbe ḫr lk-f
7. pḫre·t n rt·t e-f sk m šs sp-sn nfr sp-sn
8. e·ʾr-k yʿ rt-f n mw n šwbe·t
9. nte-k ḫyt-f m šs sp-sn ḥr rt-f
10. k·t ʾlqw n . . . *θθ* n šnt·t
11. šew nt t ar-f

---

l. 9. *splelyn*: cf. Zoega, 630 **ⲥⲡⲉⲗⲉⲗⲓⲛ**, apparently a 'plaster' or 'poultice,' probably = *σπλήν*, *σπληνίον*.

staters(?); (8) genuine oil . . . . you pound them, (9) you make them into a poultice; apply to the part (10) which is painful of the man.

## Verso Col. X.

(1) Another talisman for the foot of the gouty man: (2) you write these names on a strip (3) of silver or tin; you put it (4) on a deer-skin; you bind it to the foot (5) of the man named, *δέρμα ἐλάφιον*, with the two feet. (6) '*θεμβαραθεμ* (7) *ουρεμβρενουτιπε* (8) *αιοχθου* (9) *σεμμαραθεμμου* (10) *ναιοου*. Let N. son of N. recover (11) from every pain which is in his feet and two legs.' (12) You do it when the moon is in the constellation of Leo.

## Verso Col. XI.

(1) Remedy for a . . . . foot(?): (2) garlic, frankincense, (3) old . . . . (4) genuine oil; pound (together); anoint him (5) with it. When it is dry, you wash it (6) with cold water; then he recovers.

(7) Remedy for a foot which is much sprained(?); very excellent. (8) You wash his foot with juice of cucumber; (9) you rub it well on his foot.

(10) Another: sycomore figs(?) of . . .; fruit(?) of acacia, (11) persea fruit(?); pound (together); apply (it) to him.

---

Col. X.

l. 1. *p-ei'grwn* = *ποδαγρῶν*.

l. 2. Cf. Alex. Trall, lib. xi. p. 656, for a similar method of dealing with gout. Such charms are as common in ancient times as in modern.

l. 3. Tin is frequently used for similar purposes: cf. Wessely, N. Gr. Zauberpap., p. 11.

l. 5. *n t rt·t II·t*, that is with the two feet of the skin.

l. 12. 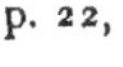 the knife is the sign of the Zodiac for Leo (Brugsch, Nouv. Rech., p. 22, Stobart tables, &c.): cf. 5/11 and note 1/12.

Col. XI.

l. 10. *twne* is perhaps the reading of the imperfect group.

## Verso Col. XII.

1. ke-z wr šer'y(?)

2. 'nk pe wr š'(?)-'y nt 'r ḥyq a t rpy·t 'o·t nb qwow(?)

3. ll mw ll p mw n sn-t(?) p nt n r-y p 't n Ḥ·t-ḥr·t šw mr

4. p nt n ḥt-y ḥt-y pz pe ḥt mr p(?) wḫe e·ḫr 're 'm·t

5. 'y-f a 'm-mw wḫe e·ḫr 're wnš·t 'y a wnš wḫe e·ḫr 're wḥr·t 'y·t-f

6. a wḥr p wḥ nt a p ntr šr spd(?) 'y-y·t-f a mw-s·t-s e-f 'n·n' a t sbt·t n nyn're-t-s

7. a wḥ mw n [p]e-f ntr pe-f ḥry pe-f y'h-'o s'b'h-'o pe-f glemwr' mwse plerwbe s my

8. 'br's'ks senkl'y my 're mn a·ms mn 'y-f a mn a·ms mn

9. my 'r-s w' pz w' mr w' lyb 'o . . . . . e-s qte m-s-f a m' nb p ḫyt

10. n y'h-'o s'b'hw ḥ-'o-ry-'o-n(?) p'n-t-rg'-t-r 'n-t-rg'-t-r 'rb'

11. nth'l' th'l-'o th'l'ks z te-y ḥwy ḫyt a·'r-tn

## Verso Col. XIII.

1. n n ntr·w 'y·w n Kmy mḥ t·t-tn n st·t sḥt·t ⟨bk-f⟩ ḥwy·t-f a p ḥt n mn a·ms mn

2. hbq n'm-s nge 'yḫ θ n ty-s qt·t mge rm 'mnt my 're p 'y

---

Col. XII.

l. 1. A gloss on l. 2.

l. 2. *qwow* (the first *w* may be a determinative ꜥ). Brugsch, Dict. Geog., 819, identifies this with the modern Qau (Antaeopolis). But Qau is derived from Copt. ⲧⲕⲱⲟⲩ, which in its turn is perhaps from the hierogl. *dw-qꜣ*.

l. 3. *p 'l*: obesity is a mark of beauty in the East.

l. 5. *'y-f*: cf. note 21/35. *'y* in this line must be an error for *'y-f*. *'y·t-f* at the end of the line must be the same word: cf. Boh. ⲁⲓϥ and ⲁⲓⲧⲟⲩ, and *ḫsy-k* 20/20, beside *ḫsy·t-k* 20/19.

## VERSO COL. XII.

(1, 2) 'I am the great Shaay (otherwise said, the great Sheray ?), who makes magic for the great Triphis, the lady of Koou (?) (3) Lol Milol, the water of thy brother (?) is that which is in my mouth, the fat of Hathor, worthy of love, is (4) that which is in my heart; my heart yearns, my heart loves. The (?) longing such as a she-cat (5) feels for a male cat, a longing such as a she-wolf feels for a he-wolf, a longing such as a bitch feels for (6) a dog, the longing which the god, the son of Sopd (?), felt for Moses going to the hill of Ninaretos (7) to offer water unto his god, his lord, his Yaho, Sabaho, his Glemura-muse, Plerube . . S Mi (8) Abrasax, Senklai—let N. daughter of N. feel it for N. son of N.; (9) let her feel a yearning, a love, a madness great . . . . . ., she seeking for him (going) to every place. The fury (10) of Yaho, Sabaho, Horyo . . Pantokrator, Antorgator, (11) Arbanthala, Thalo, Thalax: for I cast fury upon you

## VERSO COL. XIII.

(1) 'of the great gods of Egypt: fill your hands with flames and fire; employ it, cast it on the heart of N. daughter of N. (2) Waste her away, thou (?) demon; take her sleep, thou (?) man of Amenti; may the house

---

l. 6. Cf. Μωσῆς ὁ μέγας φίλος ὑψίστοιο, quoted from the Orac. Sibyll. 2. 247 by PARTHEY, 2 Gr. Zauberpap., p. 58. *s·t* is *ⲥⲏ, 'seat.'

l. 7. *wḥ mw*: very common as a title equivalent to χοαχύτης.

*[p]e-f*: this correction of the text seems almost certain.

*plerwbe* perhaps = πλήρωμα.

COL. XIII.

l. 2. *nge* . . . *mge* must be ⲛϭⲓ : ⲛϫⲉ before the subject, though here before the imperative, which is not allowed in Coptic (W. MAX MÜLLER, Rec. tr., xiii. 151).

3. n py-s yt ty-s mw·t n ny-s mʿ nte e-s n ẖe·t-w . . . ʿš e h-ʿo-h n st·t

4. ar-s e-s z ze n-ny e-s ⟨ʿḥ⟩ qrmrm n bl z ne-ʾy z ʾnk wʿ·t ryt·t n Gb

5. Ḥr r(?)-ʿo-n p rʿ rn-yt prq rn-s a bl n Kmy šʿ hw XL ʾbt XXXIII CLXXV n hw p zq-r n VI n ʾbt

6. gyre thee(?) pysytw ek-ʿo(?)-ymy ʾtʿm sp VII hs n *ⲙⲁⲥⲉϩ* wʿ ẖm n mw·t n ʿo·t

7. ḥnʿ sʾsmrym(?) ʾp·t VII·t n hs n *ϭϩⲉⲥ* sẖy n *ⲃⲉⲉⲙⲡⲉ* n ḥwt ḥ·t n yp·t n nẖe

8. nte-k st·t-w n glm n mḥ nte-k ʿš ar-f n sp VII n hw VII nte-k ths ḥn·t-k

9. nʾm-f nte-k str erme t s-ḥm·t nte-k ths ḥt-s n t s-ḥm·t ʿn

10. a t ʾre s-ḥm·t mr py (*sic*) hy θθ·t n šnt·t nt ḥr ʾbye nte-k ths ḥn·t-k nʾm-f

11. nte-k str erme t s-ḥm·t a t ʾre s-ḥm·t mr nq-s hbete n r-f n wʿ ḥtr ḥwt nte-k ths

12. ḥn·t-k nʾm-f nte-k str erme t s-ḥm·t

## Verso Col. XIV.

1. a t . . . . . .
2. ʾbn (δραχμη) I
3. *ⲡⲓⲡⲓⲣ* (δραχμη) I
4. mḥ n knwt(?) e-f šwy (δραχμη) IV
5. sʾterw (δραχμη) IV
6. nt n pẖre šwy a·ʾry yp·t nʾm-f
7. a ẖ p nt e·ʾr-k swne nʾm-f erme s-ḥm·t nb

---

l. 3. *n ẖe·t-w.* Note this Coptic form ⲛϩⲏⲧⲟⲩ instead of the usual demotic *ẖn-w* lost in Coptic. In this particular phrase, however, *nʾm-w*, not *ẖn-w*, is usual.

l. 4. *n-ny . . . ne-ʾy.* It is suggested that, in spite of the strange orthography, ⲛⲁⲓ misereri is here intended.

l. 5. It is difficult to see what is intended by the numbers.

l. 6. The first words of this line have been read by Pleyte (P. S. B. A.,

(3) of her father and her mother (and) the places where she is . . . . . ; call out "There is flame of fire (4) to her," while she speaks, saying, "Have mercy (?)," she standing outside and murmuring "Have mercy (?)." For I am an agent (?) of Geb, (5) Horus Ron Phre is my name, tear her name out of Egypt for forty days, thirty-three months, 175 days, the complement of six months, (6) Gyre, Thee, Pysytu, Ekoimi, Atam.' Seven times. Dung of crocodile, a little placenta (?) of a she-ass, (7) together with sisymbrium, seven *oipi* of antelope's dung, the gall of a male goat, and first-fruits of oil; (8) you heat them with stalks of flax. You recite to it seven times for seven days; you anoint your phallus (9) with it, you lie with the woman; you anoint the breast (?) of the woman also.

(10) To cause a woman to love her husband: pods of acacia, pound with honey, anoint your phallus with it (11) and lie with the woman.

To make a woman *amare coitum suum.* Foam of a stallion's mouth. Anoint your phallus with it and lie with the woman.

## VERSO COL. XIV.

(1) To make . . . . . . (2) alum, 1 drachm, (3) pepper, 1 drachm, (4) *mhnknwt*, dried, 4 drachms, (5) satyrium, 4 drachms. (6) Pound together into a dry medicament; do your business with it (7) like that which you know with any woman.

---

v. 152) as κύριε θεῖε πιστὲ ἐξίημι 'Αδάμ, 'O divine faithful Lord, I cast out Adam.'

l. 10. *py*: error for *py-s*.

COL. XIV.

l. 5. *s'terw* = σατυρίου, MAX MÜLLER, Rec. tr., viii. 176–177. For the plant (which is not identified) see DIOSC. iii. 133. It is a venereal stimulant.

## Verso Col. XV.

1. n rn·w n n ntr·w nt ẖr wẖe-k-s e·ʾr-k ʾn·nʿ(?) a ʾny ʿze a ẖn swr(?)

2. mʿskelly mʿskell-ʿo phnwgentʿbʾ-ʿo

3. hreks(?)sygth-ʿo perygthe-ʿo-n perypegʿneks

4. ʿre-ʿo-bʿsʿgrʿ ke-zm ʿo-bʾsʿgrʿ

5. py rn ẖr z-k-f ḥr t ḥ·t n zy e-f n·nʿ a byk e-tbe n rn·w

6. n **ⲇⲓⲟⲥⲕⲟⲣⲟⲥ** nt n ẖn nte-f wzy e·ʾr-k ʿš-w a p z(?) n **ⲁⲇⲱⲛⲁⲓ** nt sẖ

7. n bl e-f a ʾr wʿ·t bkʿy·.(?) ʿo·t e-f ʾny ʿze a ẖn

## Verso Col. XVI.

1. ʾrmy-ʿo-wt (ke-zm **ⲁⲣⲙⲓⲟⲩⲑ**) sythʿny wthʿny

2. ʾryʾmwsy s-ʿo-br-tt byrbʾt my[s]yrythʿt

3. a·ms-thʿrmythʿt a·wy mn a·ms mn a bl ẖn ny-s ʿy·w

4. nt e-s nʾm-w a ʿy nb nte mn a·ms mn nʾm-w e-s mr[·t]-f e-s lby m-s-f

5. e-s ʾr n p šp n ḥt-f n nw nb e·ʾr-k sẖ ny n rʾw ẖl a wʿ·t tys·t

6. n š-stn e-s wʿb nte-k ty-s a wʿ ẖbs nmy e-f wʿb e-f mḥ n nẖe n mʿ·t n ⟨p⟩

7. pe-k ʿy n *θ* n rhwe a twe e·ʾr-k gm p fʿe n t s-ḥm·t a ty-f a ẖn p sʿl nfr-f (*sic*)

---

### Col. XV.

l. 1. Groff has written an elaborate study on this column in Mém. de l'Inst. Égypt. iii. 377; many of his readings are wrong, but it remains very difficult to read and interpret.

*wẖe-k* (?): the second sign is imperfect; *wšte-k* (?).

*ʾn-nʿ* (?): cf. l. 5, *n-nʿ* (?).

*ʿze*: cf. 3/29.

*swr* (?). Can this be really a trace of *hn*, to be restored *n šn hn*, 'by vase-questioning.'

l. 2. For a similar list of names see Pap. Gr. Lugd., Pap. V., col. 9, l. 10.

l. 5. Can ⲉⲧⲃⲉ have the meaning 'instead of'?

l. 6. The Dioscuri were the patron gods of sailors.

## VERSO COL. XV.

(1) The names of the gods whom you want (?) when you are about (?) to bring in a criminal [by vase-questioning?] (2) Maskelli, Maskello, Phnoukentabao, (3) Hreksyktho, Perykthon, Perypeganex, (4) Areobasagra, otherwise Obasagra.

(5) This name you utter it before a ship that is about (?) to founder on account of the names (6) of Dioscoros, which are within, and it is safe.

You recite them to the bowl (?) of Adonai, which is written (7) outside. It will do a mighty work (?) bringing in a criminal.

## VERSO COL. XVI.

(A row of figures, viz. 3 scarabs, 3 hawks, and 3 goats.)

(1) 'Armioout (otherwise Armiouth), Sithani, Outhani, (2) Aryamnoi, Sobrtat, Birbat, Misirythat, (3) Amsietharmithat: bring N. daughter of N. out of her abodes (4) in which she is, to any house and any place which N. son of N. is in; she loving him and craving for him, (5) she making the gift of his desire (?) at every moment.' You write this in myrrh ink on a strip (6) of clean fine linen, and you put it in a clean new lamp, which is filled with genuine oil, (7) in your house from evening till morning. If you find a hair of the woman to put in the wick, it is excellent.

---

Bowl (?) of Adonai. Perhaps reference may be made to the familiar story of Nectanebus and the magic bowl in Pseudo-Callisthenes.

l. 7. *n bl*: see note on 18/6.

COL. XVI.

l. 7. For the use of hair in Egyptian magic, cf. the actual specimen mentioned by CHABAS, Pap. Mag. Harris, p. 184.

*nfr-f* or *nfr pe*: cf. 23/8.

## VERSO COL. XVII.

1. wʿ r a ʾny [s-ḥm·t?] n ḥwt a hb rswe·t ke-z a pre rswe·t ʿn

2. . . . . . . . . . . .

3. e·ʾr-k sẖ ny a wʿ·t gbe·t n ʾqyr nte-k ẖʿ ẖr zz-k e·ʾr-k n·q⟨te⟩·t·k ẖr

4. ʾr-f rswe·t nte-f hb rswe·t e-f ẖp e·ʾr-k a ʾr-f a hb rswe·t e·ʾr-k ty-s a r-f n wʿ qs

5. ẖr ʾr-f ʾny s-ḥm·t ʿn e·ʾr-k sẖ py rn a t kbe·t n ʿqyr n snf n *ⲏⲁ* nge *ⲕⲟⲩⲕⲟⲩⲉⲓ* (*sic*)

6. nte-k t p fʿe n t s-ḥm·t a ẖn t gbe·t nte-k ty-s a r-f n p qs nte-k sẖ n p ʾytn n py rn z a·wy

7. mn t šr·t n mn a p ʿy n p mʿ n str nte mn p šr n t mn nʾm-f

8. *εστι δε και αγωγιμων*

## VERSO COL. XVIII.

1. **ⲏⲣⲟⲩⲃⲓⲑⲟⲩ**

2. **ⲉⲕⲧⲟⲩⲗⲁ**

3. **ⲏⲣⲣⲉⲫⲉⲁⲓ**

4. wnḥ-k aʾr-y t mn p ntr

5. nte-k sze erme-y ẖr p nt e-y šn·t-k

6. ẖrr-f n mt·t mʿ·t e bnp-k z n-y

7. mt·t n ʿze *ⲕⲣⲟⲕⲟⲥ* . . . II

8. *ⲥⲧⲏⲙⲛⲕⲃⲧ* . . . II

9. nt ḥr snf n *ϩ(?)[ⲁ]ⲛⲧⲟⲩⲥ*

10. ʾr m bnn·t nte-k ḥyt-f ḥr ʾrte

11. n ms-ḥwt t a yr·t-f n wnm nte-k ʿš(?) ar-f(?)

12. a ḥr ⟨p⟩ ẖbs nb nge p ẖpš n rhwe

## VERSO COL. XIX.

1. wʿ r n ʾny s-ḥm·t(?) a bl n py-s ʿy ḥr ʾny-k wʿ *. . . . ⲥⲉ*

---

COL. XVII.

l. 8. *αγωγιμων* = *ἀγώγιμον*. Cf. REUVENS, Lettres, i. p. 50 and refs. there; also Brit. Mus. Gk. Pap. CXXI. 295, 300, and p. 115.

## VERSO COL. XVII.

(1) A spell to bring [a woman] to a man (and ?) to send dreams, otherwise said, to dream dreams, also.

(2) (A line of symbols or secret signs.)

(3) You write this on a rush-leaf and you place (it) under your head; you go to sleep; then (4) it makes dreams and it sends dreams. If you will do it to send dreams, you put it (the leaf) on the mouth of a mummy. (5) It brings a woman also; you write this name on the rush-leaf with the blood of a .... or a hoopoe (?); (6) and you put the hair of the woman in the leaf, and put it on the mouth of the mummy; and you write on the earth with this name, saying: 'Bring (7) N. daughter of N. to the house in the sleeping-place in which is N. son of N.' (8) Now it is also an *αγωγιμον*.

## VERSO COL. XVIII.

(1) '**ⲏⲣⲟⲩⲃⲓⲑⲟⲟⲩ** (2) **ⲉⲕⲧⲟⲩⲗⲁ** (3) **ⲏⲣⲣⲉϥⲫⲉⲇⲓ**.

(4) 'Reveal thyself to me, god N., (5) and speak to me concerning that which I shall ask thee, (6) truthfully, without telling me (7) falsehood.' Saffron, 2 (measures), (8) stibium of Koptos, 2 (measures), (9) pound together with blood of a lizard, (10) make into a ball, and rub it with milk (11) of one who has born a male child. Put (it) in his right eye; you make invocation (?) to him (?) (12) before any lamp or the 'Shoulder' constellation in the evening.

## VERSO COL. XIX.

(1) A spell for bringing a woman out of her house.

---

COL. XVIII.

l. 8. ***ⲥⲧⲏⲙⲙⲛⲕⲃⲧ*** = *στιμμὶ κοπτικόν*. Cf. Brit. Mus. Gk. Pap. XLVI. 67, CXXI. 336; Pap. Bibl. Nat. l. 1071.

l. 10. *rte n ms-ḥwt*: common in Old Egyptian prescriptions. Cf. *γάλα ἀρρενοτόκου γυναικός*, Diosc. v. 99, likewise in connexion with *στιμμί*.

2. n ʾm·t (*sic*) n ḥwt nte-k t šwy-f nte-k ʾny wʿ qbḥ(?) . . . .

3. n ḥsy nte-k mnqe wʿ kswr e ẖ·t-f šfe n nb . . . .

4. n my e(?) r-w wn e ḥr-f n wn a wn nʾm-w e·ʾr-k t n(?) nk . . . . ḥr(?)-f

5. e·ʾr-k wẖ a ʾny s-ḥm·t n-k n nw nb e·ʾr-k wḥ p kswr n p ḥrw n wʿ ḥbs

6. e-f mḥ e·ʾr-k z ar-f(?) z a·wy mn t šr mn a py mʿ

7. nt e-y nʾm-f n tkr ẖn ny wne·t·w n p-hw ẖr ʾw-s ty hte·t

## VERSO COL. XX.

1. a ty lk yr·t-bn(?) n rm . . . . ʾMn py ḥwt ẖy py ḥwt ʾkš ʾr ʾy a ẖry

2. n mrwe a Kmy gm Ḥr pe šr e-f fy·t-f a hn rt-f a·e-f škʿ-f

3. a zz-f n III r n mt·t ʾkš e-f gm mn a·ms mn a·e-f fy·t-f a hn

4. rt-f a·e-f škʿ-f a zz-f n III r n mt·t ʾkš g(?)ntyny·-tnty

5. nʾ qwqwby . . . khe ʾkhʾ

6. a wʿ ẖm n nḥe nte-k t ḥm ẖlyn ar-f nte-k ths p rm nt ẖr yr·t-bn(?) nʾm-f

7. nte-k sẖ ny ʿn a wʿ zm nmy nte-k ʾr-f n mze a ẖe·t-f nte-k py byl n t p·t n n sẖ . . . .

---

COL. XIX.

l. 2. *qbḥ*: the reading of the first sign is doubtful. The determinative would lead one to expect *ʾbḥ*, 'tooth,' but it is difficult to read so. *qbḥ* would perhaps be ⲕⲟⲃϩ, 'tendo,' or it may be the name of some animal which is to be drowned.

COL. XX.

l. 1. *yr·t* (?), followed by det. or word-sign for evil, 'bad eye,' which might be either ophthalmia or 'evil-eye,' ⲉⲓⲉⲣⲃⲟⲟⲛⲉ. The prescription perhaps favours the former.

l. 2. Amon was the god of Meroe: cf. II Kham. iv. 15.

You take a . . . . (2) of a wild she-cat; you dry it; you take a heel-tendon (?) [of a (?) . . . . which has been (?)] (3) drowned; you fashion a ring, the body (? bezel) of which is variegated (?) with gold [in the form of two (?)] (4) lions, their mouths being open, the face of each being turned to the other; you put some . . . . its face (?). (5) If you wish to bring a woman to you at any time, you place the ring on the upper part of a lamp, (6) which is lighted; you say, 'Bring N. daughter of N. to this place (7) in which I am, quickly in these moments of to-day.' Then she comes at once.

## VERSO COL. XX.

(1) To heal ophthalmia (?) in a man. '[Ho ?] Amon, this lofty male, this male of Ethiopia, who came down (2) from Meroe to Egypt, he finds my son Horus betaking himself as fast as his feet move (?), and he injured (?) him (3) in his head with three spells in Ethiopian language, and he finds N. son of N. and carries him as fast as his feet move (?), (4) and injures his head with three spells in Ethiopian language: Gentini, Tentina, (5) Kwkwby, [Ak]khe, Akha.' (6) (Say it) to a little oil: add salt and nasturtium seed to it, you anoint the man who has ophthalmia (?) with it. (7) You also write this on a new papyrus; you make it into a written amulet on his body:—'Thou art this eye of heaven' in the writings (followed by an eye with rays, as drawn in the papyrus).

---

The spell seems very corrupt, but some sense may be made of it by supplying *e-f* before *gm*.

l. 3. *a hn rt-f*, 'according to the movement (?) of his feet.'

l. 6. *ḫlyn*, ϣλⲁⲉιⲛ, Sah. in Peyron = *κερδαμων* (*κάρδαμον*, Diosc. ii. 184) *κερδαμωμο* (*καρδάμωμον*, ib. i. 5).

l. 7. *mze*: cf. II Kham. ii. 26; P. S. B. A., 1899, p. 269; perhaps connected with *μαγία*.

## VERSO COL. XXI.

1. . . . . . . . .
2. . . . . .
3. . . . . .
4. . . . . t-nḥs(?) ʿnḫ-ʾm
5. nt ʾr(?) . . . . . . n p yʿr
6. . . . . . . . smt yr·t-k nʾm-f

## VERSO COL. XXII.

1. . . . . . [e-f] znt
2. tey-s [p kys nt ḫr ʾr-k(?)] ty-f a yr·t-k e·ʾr-k ʾn-
3. nʿ a p hn n šn wʿe·t-k wyt
4. ms-tme qs(?)-ʿnḫ s(?) . . . ḥrrw n šr-ʿo·t(?)
5. km nte *ερεκο(?)c* pe snf n qwqwpt
6. nt . . . m bnn nte-k smt yr·t-k nʾm-f ḥr mw
7. n elle n(?) Kmy(?) ḥr st n t(?)-nḥs ḫr
8. nw-k a t ḥyb·t n ntr nb ntr·t nb
9. . . . . -f te-y ʿš n-tn n ntr-w ʿy nt ḫʿ-w erme p rʿ t(?)semwks
10. ʾmp(?) . . . . p-yʿm·enpʿyʿ yb-ʿo-th yʿe sʿbʿ-ʿo-th
11. a·[wn] n-y sp-sn n ntr·w ʿy nt ḫʿ-w erme p rʿ my wn yr·t a p
12. [wy]n nte-y mʾ p ntr nt šn n p-hw ys sp-sn ze p s . . . . . . ʾblʿ
13. n[ʿth]ʿnʿlbʿ p ntr wr mʿrʿrʿ ʿn-t-ne ʾbyʾth
14. n . . . . snn(?) . . ʿe n-t-sʿtrʿperqmʿe Wsr ly
15. l[?]m rn-f a·wn n-y sp-sn n ntr·w ʿy my wn yr·t a p wyn
16. nt[e-y] mʾ p ntr nt šn n p-hw a·wn n-y sp-sn te-y ḥwy ḫyt a·ʾr-tn n p ntr ʿo sp-sn
17. . . . nte(?) ne-ʿy(?) te-f pḥt·t nt ʿnḫ šʿ z·t my pḥt·w sp-sn n p rnn

---

COL. XXII.

l. 4. *šr-ʿo·t km·t* = the edible seed *šr·t km·t*, E. E. F. Paheri, Pl. III. top ine; BRUGSCH, Wtb., 1405: cf. the white *šr·t ḥz·t* from which beer was

## Verso Col. XXI.

(1–3) (Fragments) (4) . . . . . of Ethiopia (?), ***ankh-amu*** flowers, (5) pound, make (?) . . . . . . . of the river, (6) . . . . . . . paint your eye with it.

## Verso Col. XXII.

(1) . . . . . . . . . . tested. (2) Behold [the ointment which you] put on your eye when you (3) approach the vessel of inquiry alone: green eye-paint, (4) stibium, *qes-ankh* (?), amulet of . . . ., flowers of black *sher-o* (?) (5) which are beans (?), blood of hoopoe, (6) pound, [make] into a ball, and paint your eye with it, together with juice (7) of Egyptian (?) grapes, and *set*-stone (?) of Ethiopia; then (8) you see the shadow of every god and every goddess.

(9) Its . . . . . . 'I invoke you (plur.), ye great gods who shine with the sun, Themouks (10) Amp . . . Piam, Enpaia, Eiboth, Eiae, Sabaoth, (11) open (?) to me (*bis*), ye great gods who shine with the sun, let my eyes be opened to the (12) light, and let me see the god who inquires to-day, hasten (*bis*); for the protection . . . . (13) Ablanathanalba, the mighty god, Marara, Atone, Abeiath, (14) N . . . . Senen (?), [Psh]oi, Zatraperkemei, Osiris, (15) Lilam is his name. Open to me (*bis*), ye great gods, let my eyes be opened to the light, (16) and let me see the god who inquires to-day. Open to me (*bis*). I cast the fury on you (plur.) of the great (*bis*) god, (17) . . . . whose might is great (?),

---

prepared, ib., Suppl., 1200. Here the former is made equivalent to *ερεκοc*, presumably *ἄρακος* (= Vicia cracca L., common vetch according to Lenz, Bot. d. alten Griechen u. Römer, p. 726), which was a common cultivated plant in Egypt. Cf. Oxyrhynchus Pap. II. cclxxx. 16, Tebtunis Pap. pass.; in Coptic Corp. Pap. Rain. II. p. 176 (**αρακι**), Crum Copt. MSS. Fay. p. 78 verso, l. 35 (**αρακα**).

l. 7. *elle n*(?) *Kmy*(?): cf. **ελελκημε**, 'black grapes,' but see 29/28, which is practically a parallel.

18. . . . . . . . . . . . sp-sn p rn n p [ntr ?] . . . . a·wn n·y sp-sn

19. [n ntr·w] ʿy nt ḫʿ-w erme p rʿ my wn [yr·t a p wyn nt]e-y

20. [mʾ p ntr] nt šn n p-hw ys sp-sn . . . sp . . .

## Verso Col. XXIII.

1. . . . . . . .
2. nt . . . . .
3. ḫr(?) . . . . .
4. ke . . . . .
5. . . . ⲛⲁϩ . . . .
6. ʾny . . . . .
7. pr·w . . . .
8. . . . . . . . .
9. ke . . . . . ʿn
10. hs . . . . . šwy e-f wš . . . II
11. nt [ḫr nḥe(?) n q]wpr ḥr ʾby
12. ths [ḥn·t-k(?)] nʾm-f nte-k str erme-s

## Verso Col. XXIV.

1. . . . . . . . . . . . . . . . .
2. . . . . . ar-f nte-k . . . .
3. . . . . . n š-stn ar-f e py(?) rnn III sḫ ar-f
4. . . . . ḫr ḫl nte-k *θ*-r-f nte-k wḥ-f
5. . . . . . zz-k nte-k ʿš-w ar-f ʿn n sp IX
6. . . . . . ḫbs ḫr ʾr-k-f n p nw n p *θ* III n rhwe
7. . . . . . ·t-k z-mt·t y-ʿo-bʾsʾwmpth-ʿo
8. [ghr-ʿo-me lw]ghʿr my wn yr·t a bl
9. [n mt·t] mʿ·t ḫr t mn t mt·t nt e-y šll ḫrr-s ty
10. [n p-hw n] mt·t mʿ·t n wš n z n-k mt·t n ʿze
11. ⲓⲱⲃⲁⲥⲁⲟⲩⲙⲡⲧⲑⲱⲭⲣⲱⲙⲉⲗⲟⲩⲭⲁⲣ
12. my wn yr·t a bl n mt·t mʿ·t ḫr t mn t mt·t nt e-y šll
13. ḫrr-s ty n p-hw

who lives for ever, give power to the name (?) (18) . . . . . . . . the name of the god (?) . . . . . . . . open to me (*bis*), (19) ye great [gods] who shine with the sun, let [my eyes] be opened [to the light, and let] me (20) [see the god] who answers to-day, hasten (*bis*) . . . times . . .'

## VERSO COL. XXIII.

(Lines 1–9 fragments.) (10) dung . . . . . dried and burnt, 2 (measures), (11) pound (with oil of) henna and honey, (12) anoint [your phallus] therewith, and lie with her.

## VERSO COL. XXIV.

(1) . . . . (2) . . . . on it, and you . . . . . . (3) . . . . . . of fine linen on it (? him); these three names being written on it, (4) . . . . . . . with myrrh; you light it and place it (5) . . . . . . . . . . your head; you recite them to it again nine times. (6) . . . . . . . . the lamp; you do it at the time of the third hour (?) of evening (7) [and you] lie down (?). Formula: 'Iobasaoumptho (8) [Khrome(?) Lou]khar; let my eyes be opened (9) in truth concerning any given matter which I am praying for here (10) [to-day, in] truth without telling thee (*sic*) falsehood.'

(11) 'Iobasaoumptthokhromeloukhar, (12) let my eyes be opened in truth concerning any given thing which I am praying (13) for here to-day.'

---

COL. XXIII.

l. 1. Probably some five or six short lines have completely disappeared before the beginning of the existing fragments of this column.

COL. XXIV.

Following this on LEYDEN, Pl. XIV., there are several scraps of Greek, &c., numbered 1–7. They are written on pieces of papyrus used for patching worn places, and have no necessary connexion with the text.

## Verso Col. XXV.

1\. . . . . . . .

2\. hs n bk ḥm ʾsy

3\. bel nt n wʿ sp ths

4\. ḥn·t-k nʾm-f nte-k str erme

5\. t s-ḥm·t e-f ḥp nte-f šwy e·ʾr-k

6\. nt wʿ ẖm nʾm-f ḥr *ⲉⲣⲡ* nte-k

7\. ths ḥn·t-k nʾm-f

8\. nte-k str erme t s-ḥm·t nfr sp-sn

## Verso Col. XXVI.

1\. e·ʾr-k [wẖ a t ʾre n] ntr·w n p hne(?) sze wbe-k

2\. a·ʾre n ntr·w ʾy a ẖn e·ʾr-k z py rn [a·ʾr-w] sp IX

3\. yʾ-ʿo yph e-ʿo-e gynntʾthwr nephʿr

4\. ʾph-ʿo-e ẖr ʾr-f wḥ-sḥne n-k a p nt e·ʾr-k a šn·t-f ar-f a·ʾr θ-ḥr

5\. ḥp a tm z n-k wḥ e·ʾr-k z py ke rn a·ʾr-w n sp IX šʿ

6\. nte-w šn n-k n mt·t mʿ·t ng-ʿo-ngetsyks mʿntw

7\. n-ʿo-b-ʿo-e g-ʿc-ghyr hr-ʿo-n-t-r nt-ʿo-ntr-ʿo-mʿ

8\. leph-ʿo-ger gephʿers-ʿo-re sp VII

9\. **ⲓⲁⲧⲱ · ⲉⲓⲫⲏ · ⲱⲛ · ⲕⲓⲛⲗⲁⲑⲟⲩⲣ · ⲛⲉⲫⲁⲣ · ⲁⲫⲟⲉ**

## Verso Col. XXVII.

1\. a ẖ p nt ḥry ẖn z ank pe syt-tʾ-k stm rn-yt

2\. stm pe pe rn n mt ank gʾnthʿ gyn-tw gyry-tw

3\. ḥry-ntr ʾrynwte lʿbtʾthʿ lʾptwthʿ

4\. lʿksʿnthʿ sʿrysʿ mʿrkhʿrʿhwt-tw

5\. ʾrsyngʿ·ghlʿ k-zm ʾrsy·ngʿlʿbel b-ʿo-l-b-ʿo-el

6\. b-ʿo-el sp-sn l-ʿo-tery gl-ʿo·gʾsʿntrʿ yʿh-ʿo

7\. rn-yt yʿh-ʿo pe pe rn n mt bʾlkhʿm p šft n t p·t

---

Col. XXVI.

l. 1. This column is a reproduction of 28/7–10 with slight variations.

l. 4. *θ-ḥr* = Boh. ϭⲓϩⲟ, ‘delay.’ This phrase is omitted in the parallel.

## Verso Col. XXV.

(1) . . . . . . (2) hawk's dung, salt, *asi* plant, (3) *bel*, pound together, anoint (4) your phallus with it and lie with (5) the woman. If it is dry, you (6) pound a little of it with wine, and you (7) anoint your phallus with it (8) and you lie with the woman. Excellent (*bis*).

## Verso Col. XXVI.

(1) If you wish [to make] the gods of the vessel (?) speak with you, (2) when the gods come in, you say this name to them nine times: (3) 'Iaho, Iphe, Eoe, Kintathour, Nephar, (4) Aphoe.' Then he makes command to you as to that which you shall ask him about. If delay (5) occur, so that answer is not given you, you recite this other name to them nine times until (6) they inquire for you truthfully: 'Gogethix, Mantou, (7) Noboe, Khokhir, Hrodor, Dondroma, (8) Lephoker, Kephaersore.' Seven times. (9) Iaho . Eiphe . On . Kindathour . Nephar . Aphoe.

## Verso Col. XXVII.

(1) According to that which is above within, saying, 'I am this Sit-ta-ko, Setem is my name, (2) Setem is my correct name. I am Gantha, Ginteu, Giriteu, (3) Hrinoute, Arinoute, Labtatha, Laptutha, (4) Laksantha, Sarisa, Markharahuteu, (5) Arsinga-khla; another volume (says) Arsinga-label, Bolboel, (6) Boel (*bis*), Loteri, Klogasantra, Iaho, (7) is my name, Iaho is my correct name,

---

l. 9. Repeats the invocation names in ll. 2–3.

Col. XXVII.

l. 1. This column is parallel to 1/13–16.

*nt ḥry* (*n*?) *ẖn*: *ẖn* must refer to the recto. Cf. *n bl* = 'verso,' 18/6, V. 15/7.

8. ʾblʿnʿthʿnʿlbʿ srrf n t qnḥ·t n p ntr nt ʿḥ n p·hw(?)

## Verso Col. XXVIII.

1. e·ʾr-k ne t š(?) syw(?) . . m(?) a ẖry(?) . . .
2. e ʿḥ zl·t(?)

## Verso Col. XXIX.

1. . . . ty lb rm nb nge s-ḥm·t nb
2. e·ʾr-k *θ* p fʿe n p rm nt e·ʾr·k wẖ-f erme p fʿe
3. n wʿ rm e-f ***ⲙⲁⲟⲩⲧ*** nte-k mr-w erme ne-w ʾre-w
4. nte-k mr-w a ẖe·t-f n wʿ ***ⲃⲉϭ*** nte-k wrḥ-f
5. e-f ʿnẖ e-f ẖp e·ʾr-k wẖ a ʾr-f n hyn·w hw·w
6. e·ʾr-k ẖʿ p ***ⲃⲉϭ*** n wʿ mʿ e·ʾr-k s·ʿnẖ nʾm-f n pe-k ʿy

## Verso Col. XXX.

1. e·ʾr-k . . . . . . hs n ***ⲥⲙⲟⲩⲛⲉ***
2. ẖr hy ẖe·[t]-s
3. k·t e·ʾr-k ths ḥn·t-k n hs n
4. ***ⲕⲉⲗ*** nte-k str erme s-ḥm·t ḥr ʾr-s mr·t-k
5. e·ʾr-k nt hs n ***ⲥⲓϣ(?)ⲁⲥ*** ḥr ʾby
6. nte-k ths ḥn·t-k nʾm-f a ḥ p nt ḥry ʿn
7. ke hs n ***ϩⲁⲓⲧⲉ*** ḥr sknn n
8. wrt a ẖ p nt ḥry ʿn
9. ke e·ʾr-k qp s-ḥm·t n hs n ***ϩⲁⲧⲟⲩⲗ***
10. e p snf ẖrr-s ẖr lk-s
11. hs n ***ⲉⲟ*** ʿn py smte

---

Col. XXVIII.

l. 1. This short column appears to be the only part of the papyrus written in a different hand from the rest. It is very obscure, and the words seem much abbreviated. The group elsewhere reading *nk* (ⲛⲕⲁ) is conspicuous, but is without the determinative, and perhaps has another meaning here.

l. 2. Cf. V. 10/12. The zodiacal sign ♏ ★ stands for Scorpio (Brugsch, Nouv. Rech., p. 22). For the reading *zl·t* (?), cf. O. L. Z., 1902, V. col. 6, 223.

Balkham, the mighty (?) one of heaven, (8) Ablanathanalba, gryphon of the shrine of the god which stands to-day (?).'

## Verso Col. XXVIII.

(1) You shall cause a star (?) to go . . . place (?) under the earth (?) (2) when the moon is in the constellation of Scorpio.

## Verso Col. XXIX.

(1) [Spell to] make mad any man or any woman.

(2) You take the hair of the man whom you wish, together with the hair (3) of a dead (murdered ?) man; and you tie them to each other, (4) and tie them to the body of a hawk, and you release (?) it (5) alive. If you wish to do it for some days, (6) you put the hawk in a place and you feed it in your house.

## Verso Col. XXX.

(1) If you . . . . . . . . . dung of a *smoune*-goose, (2) then her body falls.

(3) Another: you anoint your phallus with dung of (4) a *kel*, and you lie with (the) woman, then she feels thy love (i.e. for thee). (5) You pound dung of . . . . . . with honey, (6) and you anoint your phallus with it as above again.

(7) Another: dung of hyaena (?) with ointment of (8) roses as above again.

(9) Another: you fumigate a woman with ichneumon's dung (10) when the menstruation is on her; then she is cured.

(11) Ass's dung also—this method (of treatment).

---

Col. XXIX.

l. 5. *n hyn·w hw·w.* Does this mean 'for several days' or 'after several days'?

Col. XXX.

l. 2. *hy ẖe·t-s*: perhaps of abortion, ϩⲟⲩϩⲉ : ⲟⲩϫⲉ.

## Verso Col. XXXI.

1. ϲιϲιϯωοϯϯ
2. ke-z ⲁⲣⲙⲓⲱϯⲉ
3. p ntr nt ʿwḫ p ḥbs nt θ-
4. r-yt ʾm a ḫn
5. ḫr zz-y nte-k z n-y wḥ
6. ḫr p nt e-y šn ḫrr-f ty n p-hw

## Verso Col. XXXII.

1. a t ʾre . . . . . *ⲗⲓⲃⲉ*(?) m-s ḥwt
2. e·ʾr-k ʾny wʿ *ⲉⲙⲓⲙ* e-f ʿnḫ
3. nte-k ʾny pe-f *ⲥⲉ[ϩ]ⲉ* a bl nte-k ḫʿ-f n wʿ mʿ
4. nte-k ʾny pe-f *ϩⲉ[ⲧ]* nte-k ḫʿ-f n ke mʿ e·ʾr-k
5. fy pe-f swmʿ tre-f e·ʾr-k nt-f m šs sp-sn
6. e·ʾr e-f šwy nte-k fy wʿ ḫm n p nt nt·yt erme wʿ
7. ḫm n snf n pe-k tbʿ n mḥ II n p sʿlʿpyn
8. n te-k t·t n gbyr nte-k ty-f a wʿ z n ʾrp
9. nte-k t swr-s t ḥm·t ḫr ʾr-s *ⲗⲓⲃⲉ* m-s-k
10. e·ʾr-k t pe-f *ⲥⲉϩⲉ* a wʿ z n ʾrp ḫr *ⲙⲧⲉⲥ*
11. ty hte·t nge ty-f a ef nge nk n wm
12. e·ʾr-k t pe-f *ϩⲉⲧ* a wʿ ḫtm n nb nte-k ty-f
13. a t·t-k ḫr ty-f n-k ḥs·t ʿo·t mr·t šfe·t

## Verso Col. XXXIII.

1. a Ḥr . . . . . . . . . [e-]f mšʿ a ḥry ḥr tw n mre·t n ʾḫ e-f t ʿlʿyt a wʿ ḥtr ḥt . . . . . . a wʿ ḥtr km

2. e n zm . . . [ḥr ʾ·]t-f na p wr-ty ḫn qne-f a·e-f gm n n ntr·w tre-w e-w ḥms·t a ḥry a t s·t wype·t

3. e-w wm [n p rt] n ḥʿp pe wr ḫr-w Ḥr ʾm n e·ʾr-k wm Ḥr ʾm n e·ʾr-k ne wm ḫr-f ʿl·wt-tn a ḥr-y

---

Col. XXXII.

l. 1. This column is a paraphrase of 13/17–21.

l. 6. *e·ʾr e-f*: possibly for ⲉⲁϥ. The parallel has *e-f šwy*.

Col. XXXIII.

l. 1. *a Ḥr*. *a* in this papyrus appears as the auxiliary of the past ⲁ-, but not of the present ⲉ-.

## VERSO COL. XXXI.

(1) 'Sisihoout (2) otherwise Armiouth, (3) the god who liveth, the lamp which is (4) lighted, come within (5) before me, and give me answer (6) concerning that which I ask about here (7) to-day.'

## VERSO COL. XXXII.

(1) To make . . . . . . . . rave for a man. (2) You take a live shrew-mouse (?), (3) and take out its gall and put it in one place, (4) and take its heart and put it in another place. You (5) take its whole body, you pound it very much; (6) when it is dry, you take a little of the pounded stuff with a (7) little blood of your second finger, (that) of the heart, (8) of your left hand, and put it in a cup of wine (9) and you make the woman drink it. Then she has a passion for you.

(10) You put its gall into a cup of wine, then she dies (11) instantly; or put it in meat or some food.

(12) You put its heart in a ring of gold and put it (13) on your hand; then it gives you great praise, love, and respect.

## VERSO COL. XXXIII.

(1) Horus . . . . . . . . he was going up a hill at midday in the verdure season, mounted on a white horse . . . . . . . on a black horse, (2) the papyrus rolls [of . . .] being on (?) him, those of the Great of Five in his bosom. He found all the gods seated at the place of judgement (3) eating [of the produce ?] of the Nile (?), my (?) Chief,

---

[*e*?-] *f m*ḳ'*, &c.: cf. O. C. in A. Z., 1883, 100; 1900, 90 ⲡⲉⲧⲛⲏⲟⲩ ⲛ̄ⲛⲧⲟⲟⲩ ⲛ̄ⲙⲉⲣⲉ ⲛ̄ϭⲱⲙ.

For Horus on horseback, cf. PLUT., de Is. et Osir., c. 19.

l. 2. *ḥms·t*: probably as Ach. ϩⲙⲁⲥⲧ (as used for infinitive in l. 6) rather than ϩⲉⲙⲥⲛⲟⲩⲧ.

l. 3. *ḥ'p* (?): cf. l. 6 and V. 5/1. A feminine word similarly spelt is found in connexion with embalming in BRUGSCH, Thes., 893, 895.

4. mn [ky?] n'm-y n wm te-y šn zz-y te-y šn ḫe·t a wʿ gʿwmʿ θy·t a wʿ tw rs ty ʿh-y

5. ne ʾS·t [lk]-s e-s šte ne Nb-ḥt lk-s e-s s·wze ne p XVI n Ne-tbew·w ne pe(?) wʿ n nḫt

6. n ntr n[e p? 3?]65 n ntr ḥms·t a ḫry a wm n p rt n t sḫ·t n ḥʿp pe wr šʿ nte-w šte n p gʿwmʿ

7. n zz[-f n p] šr n ʾS·t n zz-f n mn a·ms mn n n gʿwmʿ n grḥ n n gʿwmʿ n mre·t p šn zz py srrf

8. py ḫmm [n n gʿ]wmʿ·w n ne ʾr . . . . n rt-f šte a bl n zz-f n mn a·ms mn ʾh nḥe n mʿ·t

9. n sp VII [nte-k th]s t·t-f ḫe·t-f rt-f nte-k mt·t ar-f

---

Probably the word here, with divine determinative, is different, and may well represent *Ḥʿp*, 'the Nile.' The same group occurs in Pap. Insinger 16/21.

*pe wr* is difficult, 'belonging to the Great,' or 'son of the Great,' or 'my Great one.'

ⲁⲣⲁⲉⲓ: cf. note 1/20.

l. 5. *ne*: probably fut. neg. ⲛⲛⲉ.

*XVI n Ne-tbew·w*: cf. 2/9 note; perhaps *οι δεκαεξ γιγαντες* of Berl. Pap. (Parthey), II. 102. There were also the 16 cubits of the Nile, and according to one account the body of Osiris was torn into sixteen pieces, Rec. tr., iii. p. 56, v. p. 86; other texts give fourteen parts (Plutarch) or seventeen (Rhind. bil. i. p. 3).

l. 6. [3]65 gods, i. e. one for each day of the year. Cf. the 365

Said they, 'Horus, come, art thou eating? Horus, come, wilt thou eat?' He said, 'Take yourselves from me; (4) there is no [desire?] in me for eating. I am ill in my head; I am ill in my body; a fever hath taken hold of me, a South wind hath seized me. (5) Doth Isis [cease] to make magic? Doth Nephthys cease to give health? Are the sixteen Netbeou, is the one Power (6) of God, are [? the 3]65 gods seated to eat the produce of the fields of the Nile (?), my (?) Chief, until they remove the fever (7) from the head of the son of Isis (and) from the head of N. born of N., the fevers by night, the fevers by day, the headache, this burning, (8) this heat of the fevers of . . . . . . of his feet, remove from the head of N. born of N.' (Say it) over genuine oil (9) seven times, and anoint his hand, his body, his feet, and pronounce the words to him.

---

names of the great god in Leyd. Pap. Gr. V. 4, 32, and the 365 gods, ib. W. 3, 13.

*n t sẖ·t*: erased in original.

l. 7. *srrf*: probably for *srf*.

l. 8. *ne ʾr*  (?).

*šte*: a participle resuming the idea of *šte* in l. 6 after the long parenthesis.

# CORRESPONDENCE OF COLUMNS

*Recto.*

| | Old No. | | New No. |
|---|---|---|---|
| London | I | = | I |
| „ | II | = | II |
| „ | III | = | III |
| „ | IV | = | IV |
| „ | V | = | V |
| „ | VI | = | VI |
| „ | VII | = | VII |
| „ | VIII | = | VIII |
| „ | IX | = | IX |
| „ | X } | = | X |
| Leiden | I } | | |
| „ | II–III | = | XI |
| „ | IV–V | = | XII |
| „ | VI | = | XIII |
| „ | VII | = | XIV |
| „ | VIII | = | XV |
| „ | IX | = | XVI |
| „ | X | = | XVII |
| „ | XI | = | XVIII |
| „ | XII | = | XIX |
| „ | XIII | = | XX |
| „ | XIV | = | XXI |
| „ | XV | = | XXII |
| „ | XVI | = | XXIII |
| „ | XVII | = | XXIV |
| „ | XVIII | = | XXV |
| „ | XIX | = | XXVI |
| „ | XX | = | XXVII |
| „ | XXI | = | XXVIII |
| „ | XXII | = | XXIX |

*Verso.*

| | Old No. | | New No. |
|---|---|---|---|
| Leiden | I | = | I |
| „ | II | = | II |
| „ | III | = | III |
| „ | IV | = | IV |
| „ | V | = | V |
| „ | VI | = | VI |
| „ | VII | = | VII |
| „ | VIII | = | VIII |
| „ | IX | = | IX |
| „ | X | = | X |
| „ | XI | = | XI |
| „ | XII | = | XII |
| „ | XIII | = | XIII |
| „ | XIV | = | XIV |
| „ | XV | = | XV |
| „ | XVI–XVII | = | XVI |
| „ | XVIII | = | XVII |
| „ | XIX | = | XVIII |
| „ | XX | = | XIX |
| „ | XXI | = | XX |
| „ | XXIII | = | XXI |
| „ | XXII, XXIV | = | XXII |
| „ | XXV, XXVI | = | XXIII |
| „ | XXVII | = | XXIV |
| London | I | = | XXV |
| „ | II | = | XXVI |
| „ | III | = | XXVII |
| „ | IV | = | XXVIII |
| „ | V | = | XXIX |
| „ | VI | = | XXX |
| „ | VII | = | XXXI |
| „ | VIII | = | XXXII |
| „ | IX | = | XXXIII |

It has been found necessary to make some changes in the numbering of the lines in Leid. I–V, XVII, and Verso Leid. III, VIII, XXII–XXVI.

Coming soon in this series:

*Gypsy Magic Spells and Incantations Not to Try at Home*

Also available from Plus Ultra Books:

*In Search of the Origin of Pyramids and the Lost Gods of Giza*
by Dr Charles R. Kos

Made in the USA
Monee, IL
11 July 2021

73365491R10275